Intellectuals, Socialism, and Dissent

Contradictions of Modernity

Edited by Craig Calhoun
University of North Carolina at Chapel Hill

The modern era has been uniquely productive of theory. Some theory claimed uniformity despite human differences or unilinear progress in the face of catastrophic changes. Other theory was informed more deeply by the complexities of history and recognition of cultural specificity. This series seeks to further the latter approach by publishing books that explore the problems of theorizing the modern in its manifold and sometimes contradictory forms and that examine the specific locations of theory within the modern.

Intellectuals, Socialism, and Dissent

The East German Opposition and
Its Legacy

John C. Torpey

Contradictions of Modernity, Volume 4

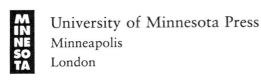
University of Minnesota Press
Minneapolis
London

Chapter 6 originally appeared as "The Abortive Revolution Continues: East German Civil Rights Activists since Unification," *Theory and Society* 24, no. 1 (February 1995).

"The Solution" and "The Office for Literature" are reprinted from John Willett and Ralph Manheim (eds.), *Bertolt Brecht Poems 1913–1956* (London: Eyre Methuen; New York: Routledge, 1976), by permission of the publishers and the Brecht Estate.

Published by the University of Minnesota Press
111 Third Avenue South, Suite 290
Minneapolis, MN 55401–2520

Printed in the United States of America on acid-free paper

Library of Congress Cataloging-in-Publication Data

Torpey, John C.
    Intellectuals, socialism, and dissent : the East German opposition and its legacy / John C. Torpey.
        p.   cm. — (Contradictions of modernity ; v. 4)
    Includes bibliographical references and index.
    ISBN 0-8166-2566-2. — ISBN 0-8166-2567-0 (pbk.)
    1. Intellectuals—Germany (East)—Political activity. 2. Germany (East)—Cultural policy. 3. Germany (East)—Intellectual life. 4. Opposition (Political science)—Germany (East). 5. Germany (East)—Politics and government—1989–1990.   I. Title.   II. Series.
DD289.T67 1995
320.9431'09'045–dc20   95–9218

To my parents,
for their love and support —
even when they knew not why

Contents

Preface and Acknowledgments

An earthquake shook the Communist-ruled states of East Central Europe in 1989, resulting in the Communists' surrender, with little significant violence, of their "leading role" in society. Tremors from that earthquake reached around the globe, giving renewed impetus to democratic forces from South Africa to Taiwan and Brazil. Despite aftershocks that include a cascading descent into barbarism inspired by the national idea, the significant fact about 1989 remains that a form of domination theretofore widely viewed as immutable and insurmountable unraveled with only token resistance.

Though hardly the only relevant actors in this extraordinary process, intellectuals throughout East Central Europe played a highly visible role among those who prepared the ground for the break with Communist rule. The intelligentsia figured especially prominently among the forces that brought down the one-party dominance of the Socialist Unity Party (Sozialistische Einheitspartei Deutschlands, or SED) in the German Democratic Republic (GDR) in the fall of 1989. Yet the political views of the East German intellectuals who spearheaded the challenge to the party diverged in important respects from those of their counterparts elsewhere in the Soviet bloc. Instead of calling for the system's replacement by some variant of liberal democratic capitalism as typically occurred in the other East Central European Communist countries, they loudly proclaimed their desire for a "true," "democratic," "reformed" socialism. Most visibly among opposition movements in the region during this period, East Germany's reformist intellectuals sought to pursue the vision of a "third way" between capitalism and Soviet-style socialism that had inspired political intellectuals in Central Europe for at least a half-century.[1]

Yet events quickly demonstrated that, for all their prominence, the GDR's dissident intellectuals spoke primarily for themselves when they announced their allegiance to a noncapitalist "third way." To be sure, the slick professional politicians from West Germany moved quickly to exploit the political opportunities then opening up in the crumbling East. But it is naive to claim, as many did at the time, that this was the main reason for the rapid waning of popular support for the political groups the dissidents created. Rather, the great majority of the GDR's citizens abandoned the dissident intellectuals because they did not share the political goals articulated by the dissidents. To the prospect of building a newer, better socialism, they preferred the prosperity and democracy of West Germany, which they thought could be had easily enough via unification with the Federal Republic. Exploiting the guarantees enshrined in West German constitutional and citizenship law, the majority of East Germans turned reasonably enough to the Federal Republic for the solution of the myriad problems their society had accumulated during forty years of dictatorial rule.

Why was the allegiance between the intelligentsia and the rest of the population so short-lived in the GDR? Why did the views of the dissident intellectuals prove representative primarily of their own narrow circles? More broadly, why did they hold the views that they did? And what does this portend for their role in the political landscape of united Germany?

The study that follows is an effort to understand why East German intellectuals, especially those disenchanted with the rule of the SED, held the political views they did at the time of the collapse of the party's rule in 1989–90. Having had its beginnings in the observation of an anomaly with respect to the other East Central European Communist countries as party rule collapsed, the investigation focused initially on that dramatic denouement. As the study proceeded, however, I became increasingly convinced that the views advanced by intellectuals in that period of profound upheaval could be understood only against the background of East German socialism's origins in the defeat and postwar division of Nazi Germany.

To be sure, the legacy of the Stalinized, pre-1945 German Communist Party decisively shaped (and deformed) the order created in the Soviet Occupation Zone (Sowjetische Besatzungszone, or SBZ) and, later, the GDR. Yet the GDR always had a special status in the East bloc, uniquely the antifascist phoenix that rose from the ashes of the Nazi inferno. At the same time, the GDR — "East Germany" — was always both the western flank of the Soviet external empire and the eastern quarter of a more or less homogeneous cultural and linguistic area known historically as "Germany." By retracing some of the more critical steps along the path of the intellectuals' relations with the ruling SED, I hope to show that the GDR's historical origins as well as its complex geo- and ethnopolitical environment profoundly and enduringly shaped the attitudes of East Germany's intellectuals, especially the most prominent and influential among them. The story of their politics offers, in its very anomalousness, an opportunity to examine some of the broader features of the politics of intellectuals.

Chapter 1 examines the East German regime's efforts to create a new "socialist" intelligentsia during the early post–World War II period and how these policies shaped the intellectuals' responses to the first major revolt against Soviet-style rule in East Central Europe, the East German workers' rebellion of 1953. Chapter 2 discusses the crushing of the "revisionist" challenge among East German intellectuals in 1956–57 and the subsequent alternation of repression and restraint in the party's policy toward the intelligentsia. Despite the attacks visited upon many intellectuals by the East German regime, the intellectuals generally stuck to the conviction that, regardless of its current deformations, the GDR represented the "better German state." This view was sustained even through the 1970s, after the bloody suppression of the Prague Spring in Czechoslovakia had disabused many Soviet bloc intellectuals of the idea that socialism could be reformed and made "humane."[2]

In the 1980s, however, as the legitimating power of the Communists' antifascist past began to wane, younger, less established intellectuals in particular began to register serious disillusionment with the GDR's "really existing socialism." The less established intellectuals, spared a direct encounter with Nazism, had grown increasingly impatient about the party's repeated delays in fulfilling promises of a coming democratization. Their impatience intensified as their counterparts elsewhere in Eastern Europe began to take an active role in the effort to achieve reforms with the legal backing of such international agreements as the Helsinki Final Act. Chapter 3 describes the tortuous path to the emergence of a more self-consciously oppositional intelligentsia during the 1980s. That development could not occur until a tiny group of intellectuals went beyond the GDR's official antifascist, anti-imperialist, and antiwar nostrums to demand basic civil and human rights denied by the regime. Still, they remained committed to a noncapitalist alternative to the Federal Republic, a feature of their thinking that helped keep them from developing broader links with the East German population.

The next two chapters discuss the role of the intelligentsia in the final collapse of the East German Communist regime. Chapter 4 seeks to uncover the reasons underlying the dissident intellectuals' inability to forge ties with wider segments of East German society. I analyze the background to the split between the reform-socialist intellectuals and the broader East German population that would emerge after the opening of the Berlin Wall. The source of this fissure lay in the continued tensions between those who had decided to leave the GDR and the dissidents who preferred to stay and oppose the regime — the representatives of "exit" and "voice," to use Albert Hirschman's terms. I also attempt to sketch the social background to "exit" and "voice" in the GDR in 1989 and suggest that these divergent responses to the regime's crisis of legitimacy pointed the way toward future developments.

Chapter 5 examines the reform intellectuals' response to the popular embrace of the project of unification with the Federal Republic that quickly followed the emergence of widespread opposition to the regime. In particular, I analyze the former dissident intellectuals' efforts to influence the terms under which the GDR would unify with the Federal Republic and their attempts to stimulate a debate over constitutional reform in the new, united Germany. In chapter 6, I examine the activities of the East German dissident intellectuals in the period since unification in late 1990, focusing especially on their efforts to reconstruct the new "all-German" civil society through constitutional reform and their attempt to appropriate the GDR's past in the interest of a more democratic Germany.

Most observers of these events have been preoccupied with the question of why these regimes collapsed. Yet one might ask not why things in the GDR fell apart but rather: How could a social formation with no electorally demonstrated popular support, and with so many self-imposed structural obstacles to the sort of adaptive change widely thought to be vital to modern societies, have persisted for as long as it did? Aside from the ultimate guarantor of Communist power, the Red Army, what held the GDR together for four decades?

These questions direct our attention away from the sources of collapse and toward those of stability in Communist regimes, a shift of focus that may seem idiosyncratic in view of these regimes' spectacular departure from the world stage. It is of the utmost importance to recall, however, that no prominent observer of the East bloc foresaw with any precision the coming collapse of Soviet domination in Eastern Europe. Moreover, virtually everyone in East Germany in the early fall of 1989 (not to mention West German chancellor Helmut Kohl) acted as though they believed that the GDR would continue to exist for some years to come. Unless we are simply to dismiss the East German intellectuals as naive and misguided for their attachment to a "third way" or their failure to protest more loudly against the regime's injustices, we must understand how the socialist project in the GDR succeeded both in eliciting their support and in provoking their criticisms over a period of some four decades.

A scholar incurs a considerable number of debts in the course of carrying out a project involving interviews with people in a far-off country. I would first like to thank the numerous citizens of the former GDR who readily assented to my requests for interviews and who gave generously of their time when we talked. I gratefully acknowledge the German Academic Exchange Service and the International Research and Exchanges Board, each of which provided financial support allowing me a year-long stay in Berlin in 1990–91 during which most of this research was conducted. Professor Heiner Legewie, Erika Dechert-Knarse, and their associates at the ATLAS project of Berlin's Technical University warmly provided material, intellectual, and moral support while I was in Berlin.

Back in Berkeley, I have enjoyed the unstinting guidance and support of Professor Jerome Karabel, who chaired my dissertation committee. In addition, Professor Robert Bellah offered encouragement and criticism throughout the process of writing the dissertation; Professor Martin Jay, who has shared with me over the past few years a bit of his enormous knowledge of German intellectual life, gave useful suggestions and saved me from some senseless mistakes; and Jeff Manza, a colleague without peer, read and offered helpful criticisms on a draft of the entire manuscript. We should all have such wise and generous advisers and colleagues as I have had during my graduate studies.

My intellectual and professional debts accumulated further during a stimulating year as a Conant Post-Doctoral Fellow of the Program for the Study of Germany and Europe at Harvard's Center for European Studies. For valuable criticism, advice, and encouragement while I was in Cambridge, I wish to thank Sarah Farmer, John Connelly, Grzegorz Ekiert, Catherine Epstein, Charlie Maier, and, last but not least, Andy Markovits, who helped smooth my move from Berkeley to Boston. A young scholar could hardly find a more engaging and pleasant environment in which to work — a fact that is due in considerable measure to the efforts of Associate Director Abby Collins and the center's cordial and efficient staff.

Finally, I would like to thank Craig Calhoun and Lisa Freeman of the University of Minnesota Press for their enthusiasm about the project. Each provided valuable suggestions for improvement of the manuscript. I hope the final product matches their expectations.

I would also like to take this opportunity to thank Steve Aron, Scott Busby, Gerd Busse, Jan Carter, Abby Ginzberg, Fred Hunter, Matt Kramer, and Jay Pulliam for their support during the long years of graduate school at Berkeley. These dear friends are responsible for my completion of this book in ways that they will never know and that I cannot repay.

I gratefully acknowledge the following journals, in which previous versions of some of the material in this book have appeared: "Two Movements, Not a Revolution: Exodus and Opposition in the East German Transformation, 1989–90," *German Politics and Society* 26 (summer 1992): 21–42; "The Post-unification Left and the Appropriation of History," *German Politics and Society* 30 (fall 1993): 7–20; "Coming to Terms with the Communist Past: East Germany in Comparative Perspective," *German Politics* (December 1993): 415–35; "The Abortive Revolution Continues: East German Civil Rights Activists since Unification," *Theory and Society* 24, no. 1 (February 1995).

Some unwritten but assiduously observed law obliges all scholarly authors to declare that the above-named individuals are absolved of blame for any blunders I have made, despite their unflagging efforts to see them expunged. Although I see no reason why anyone should impute to them the guilt for my sins, may they be herewith so exculpated.

List of Abbreviations

ABF	Arbeiter- und Bauernfakultäten (Worker and Peasant Faculties)
BDKD	Bund demokratischer Kommunisten Deutschlands (League of Democratic Communists of Germany)
BEK	Bund Evangelischer Kirchen (Federation of Evangelical Churches)
CDU	Christlich Demokratische Union (Christian Democratic Union)
CPSU	Communist Party of the Soviet Union
CSCE	Conference on Security and Cooperation in Europe
CSSR	Czechoslovak Socialist Republic
CSU	Christlich Soziale Union (Christian Social Union)
DBD	Demokratische Bauernpartei Deutschlands (Democratic Peasant Party of Germany)
DSU	Deutsche Soziale Union (German Social Union)
FDGB	Freier Deutscher Gewerkschaftsbund (Free German Trade Union Federation)
FDJ	Freie Deutsche Jugend (Free German Youth, the SED's youth organization)
FDP	Freie Demokratische Partei (Free Democratic Party)

FRG	Federal Republic of Germany
GDR	German Democratic Republic
IFM	Initiative Frieden und Menschenrechte (Initiative for Peace and Human Rights)
KPD	Kommunistische Partei Deutschlands (German Communist Party)
LDPD	Liberal-Demokratische Partei Deutschlands (Liberal Democratic Party of Germany)
NDPD	Nationaldemokratische Partei Deutschlands (National Democratic Party of Germany)
NÖSPL	Neues ökonomisches System der Planung und Leitung (New Economic System of Planning and Management)
NSDAP	Nationalsozialistische deutsche Arbeiter Partei (National Socialist German Workers' [Nazi] Party)
PDS	Partei des demokratischen Sozialismus (Party of Democratic Socialism)
PUWP	Polish United Workers' Party
RIAS	Radio in the American Sector
SBZ	Sowjetische Besatzungszone (Soviet Occupation Zone)
SDP	Sozialdemokratische Partei (Social Democratic Party) (*Note:* shortly after its founding in late 1989, the East German Social Democratic Party [SDP] fused with the West German Social Democratic Party [SPD])
SED	Sozialistische Einheitspartei Deutschlands (Socialist Unity [Communist] Party)
SMAD	Soviet Military Administration for Germany
SPD	Sozialdemokratische Partei Deutschlands (Social Democratic Party of Germany)
UB	Umweltbibliothek (Environmental Library)
UFV	Unabhängiger Frauenverband (Independent Women's Association)

Introduction

Intellectuals and Politics

Who are the intellectuals, and what is their role in politics? In particular, what is the relationship of intellectuals to the dominant and subordinate classes? These questions assumed great importance with the spread of mass education and the development of a socialist movement distinguished by its commitment to "theory" — and hence to theorists — during the past century and a half. Under these conditions, how adequate is the traditional conception of intellectuals as "men of letters" (Tocqueville) or as defenders of a purist vision of the life of the mind (Benda)? Are intellectuals the sycophants and apologists of the bourgeoisie (Marx), or are they antagonists of the status quo by their very definition (Schumpeter)?

The Italian socialist thinker Antonio Gramsci once suggested that all people are "intellectuals," in the sense that they have a conception of the world on the basis of which they act. Still, Gramsci noted, this hardly makes them intellectuals in the modern sense, just as we do not regard as a chef anyone who can cook a meal. While all people may be potential "intellectuals," therefore, in societies with an advanced division of labor the term must be reserved for specific occupations rooted in specialized training. Gramsci quite presciently foresaw that this growing stratum in the more industrialized societies would come to play an increasingly decisive role in modern political life. Moreover, he argued that the development of capitalist industry would generate increasing numbers of intellectuals whose ties to the dominant classes would be weaker than those of their predecessors. These groups could function, in Gramsci's view, as the "organic intellectuals" of the subordinate classes. In the struggle for ideological "hegemony" over the "civil society" of Western parliamentary democracies, the organic intellectuals of the dominated classes would do battle with those of the dominant in the contest for the hearts and minds of the masses (see Gramsci 1971, 5–23).

Gramsci's approach broadened considerably the scope of the definition of intellectuals in comparison to anything that had gone before. Yet he was relatively vague about exactly which groups would fall under this category. In keeping with Gramsci's insistence on the importance of occupations and training in defining the stratum of intellectuals, Seymour Martin Lipset has added sociological precision to this discussion by including among this group

> all those who create, distribute, and apply *culture,* that is, the symbolic world of man, including art, science, and religion. Within this group there are two main levels: the hard core or creators of culture — scholars, artists, philosophers, authors, some editors, and some journalists; and the distributors — performers in the various arts, most teachers, most reporters. A peripheral group is composed of those who apply culture as part of their jobs — professionals like physicians and lawyers. When Europeans speak of the *intelligentsia,* they mean all three categories. (Lipset 1981, 333)

A definition of intellectuals based on this "concentric circles" imagery is useful because it points to distinctions in the degree of intellectuality involved in a person's occupational activity, which Lipset has elsewhere shown to have a powerful influence on a person's political orientation (Ladd and Lipset 1972, 1094).

In a more recent attempt to specify the meaning of the term "intellectuals," Katherine Verdery rejects this functional approach, proposing instead to include "anyone whose social practice invokes claims to knowledge or to the creation and maintenance of cultural values and whose claim is at least partly acknowledged by others." While her stress on the significance of knowledge and value claims may at first seem to move us in the direction of the specification upon which Gramsci insisted, it actually returns us to his point of departure. For who does not make, and receive some acknowledgment of, "claims to knowledge" in their "social practice"? It is difficult to see how this approach escapes her own criticism that functional approaches to defining the category of intellectuals are "part of an

exercise whereby the persons offering them draw a boundary between themselves and everyone else."[1] Either Verdery is saying that
everyone is an intellectual (which she obviously does not intend), or
she is restricting that appellation to those who raise knowledge and
value claims of a kind more exalted than those routinely advanced by
virtually everyone in their everyday lives.

More promising is Verdery's proposal to treat intellectuals as
"sometime occupants of a site that is privileged in forming and trans-
mitting discourses, in constituting thereby the means through which
society is 'thought' by its members, and in forming human subjec-
tivities" (Verdery 1991, 17). This structural definition has the virtue
of focusing on intellectual *activity* over the social attributes of the
persons who carry it out. It deemphasizes the particular social characteristics of intellectuals, which are notoriously difficult to determine.
Especially in the case of Soviet bloc intellectuals, this approach is
valuable because many of the figures we routinely regard as intellectuals were unable to complete the programs of study to which they had
wished to devote themselves or to work in the intellectual field for
which they were trained. Interestingly, this phenomenon forces us to
take account of various autodidacts, a species generally thought to be
faced with extinction as a result of the forward march of bureaucra-
tized mass education. Verdery's definition includes such figures, even
though they might not have fulfilled the requirements of a functional
definition of intellectuals.

Yet even Verdery's structural approach smuggles in, through the
back door provided by the passive voice, a functional definition
of intellectuals as a social group: *By whom* is this special activity
"privileged"? The answer, of course, must include at least other intellectuals, but it may or may not go beyond them. Certainly not
all people regard the activities of the mind with the same enthusiasm as do intellectuals themselves. Clearly, a role-specific definition
of intellectuals is difficult to avoid altogether.

It thus seems useful to employ a compromise definition lying between the functional and the structural. In this book, therefore, I
combine the more traditional approach to defining intellectuals in
terms of occupation and training with the more recent emphasis on a
"space" of activities that clearly entail forays into the symbolic realm
of ideas and values, even in the absence of the relevant "role" characteristics. Without reverting to Gramsci's capacious understanding of
all people as "potential" intellectuals, this approach allows accom-

modation of many important figures in the East European dissident scene whom most of us would be more inclined to regard as "intellectuals" than we would many doctors, even though the latter have had far more specialized training (and may even fancy themselves "intellectuals"). In my approach, then, both the untutored party hack and the well-pedigreed artist working as a clerk should be regarded as intellectuals, even if their *politics* may be very different for a variety of reasons. It is these reasons that must be explored.

Above all, we cannot assume, as is too often done, that intellectuals are necessarily critics of the status quo. Joseph Schumpeter expressed this view when he asserted that the intellectual stratum "lives on criticism, and its whole position depends on criticism that stings" (Schumpeter 1942, 150). This is certainly true of important segments of the intelligentsia. Although Schumpeter (like his neoconservative heirs) was thinking mainly about intellectuals in *capitalist* society, proponents of the totalitarian model of state socialist societies argued similarly that intellectuals would, almost by definition, find themselves in opposition to their regimes. The totalitarian states' striving for complete social mastery, these writers suggested, would lead unavoidably to conflict with intellectuals, who would find the requirements of their work undermined or destroyed by the party-state's strictures on intellectual freedom (see Friedrich and Brzezinski 1965, 316).

Yet, as Ralf Dahrendorf once wrote, the assumption that all intellectuals are "left-wing" (in the sense of "critical") betrays an observer whose social perspective has "slipped altogether" (Dahrendorf 1967, 269). This point may be especially obvious to Germans, whose intellectuals have been closely allied to the powers-that-be perhaps more frequently than elsewhere; Luther and Goethe leap immediately to mind as prominent intellectuals who served the dominant powers of their day, but they are only the beginning of a very long list. Simply put, the presumption that all intellectuals are at odds with the order in which they live cannot cope with the wide range of views and behavior that may be encountered among this group.

After all, intellectuals have at times been every bit as much involved in advocating restrictions on freedom of expression as were the party cadres from factory and field. Stalin's culture czar Andrei Zhdanov may be the paradigm case here, but Ronald Reagan's cultural high priest, William Bennett, also comes to mind in this connection. Likewise, although some may regard pacifism as almost instinctive among intellectuals, representatives of this group can often be found among the more enthusiastic advocates of the virtues of war.[2] And while it is true that intellectuals typically predominated among the dissident and opposition groups that challenged the Communist Party's control in the East bloc, it can hardly be said that *all* intellectuals opposed the party. In short, intellectuals may be conformist, apologetic, or merely apathetic, *just like anybody else.* Rather than assuming anything in advance about the politics of intellectuals, therefore, we must examine the *conditions* under which intellectuals may move toward accommodation or opposition to their social order.

In an article entitled "The Problem of the Intelligentsia," which was written to clarify the position he developed in *Ideology and Utopia* and to emphasize its sociological aspects, Karl Mannheim outlined a number of factors involved in studying the politics of intellectuals (Mannheim 1956, 158). Three of the considerations he advances are particularly useful in analyzing the case at hand, the politics of the East German intellectuals. The first concerns the generational context in which a person acts: How does the shared historical experience of an age cohort shape its responses to political developments? Generational experience is of special importance in understanding the politics of those East Germans who participated in but never consciously chose to support the Nazi war effort. Born in the 1920s and 1930s, representatives of this group were frequently inclined to support the GDR's "antifascist anticapitalism" in order to atone for their complicity, whether real or imagined, in Nazi crimes. This group also had had some lived experience of a united Germany. While some of them regarded the division of Germany as just punishment for the catastrophe of Nazism, others remained loyal to the vision of a "reunified" Germany. By contrast, a later generation, born and raised (almost) entirely in the GDR, came of age in a routinized, "really existing socialism" about which they had fewer illusions, even if they saw little reason to reject much of the state's preachings about peace, equality, and antifascism. This age cohort would dominate the ranks of the dissident intellectuals who sought a reformed socialism in the fall of 1989.

The second factor Mannheim emphasizes for analyzing the politics of intellectuals is the nature of their organizational ties, especially including their sources of income. Do they work for the state, the church, or as "freelancers"? If they are academics, do they work at a

university or in a research institute, where greater freedom of opinion frequently prevailed in socialist countries because party bosses
were less concerned that unorthodox views would be purveyed to
students? Or have they been entirely separated, involuntarily or by
their own choice, from the means of intellectual production? Are
they integrated into relevant professional organizations such as the
Writers' Union, or have they been professionally marginalized and
ghettoized? And how much autonomy do those professional organizations have: Are they instruments primarily of the professionals they
represent or of the party-state? In East Germany, for example, occasional outbursts of obstreperousness notwithstanding, the Writers'
Union remained, on the whole, under the control of the Socialist
Unity Party. Its Czechoslovakian counterpart, by contrast, offered
critics of orthodoxy a leading platform during the watershed 1968
experiment in reform Communism, the Prague Spring.

Finally, Mannheim attaches special significance to the question of
individual and group social mobility and to the politics of intellectuals who confront barriers to their career advancement. The matter
of social ascent and decline plays a prominent role in understanding
the political views of intellectuals in Communist societies, where at
least initially the lower classes experienced enormous opportunities
for social advance. Their upward movement was facilitated by educational policies favoring the previously disadvantaged and by the
creation of new party and state institutions in which workers and
peasants received preferential treatment in hiring. People from these
social strata enjoyed vast improvements in their access to higher education and white-collar work. While the new order at first smiled
broadly upon the formerly dispossessed, those from more exalted
backgrounds perceived a diminution in their life chances and those
of their children.

It was not only social background that mattered here; party membership came to play an increasingly decisive part in determining
career chances. Accordingly, Pierre Bourdieu's notion of "political
capital," understood as analogous to economic capital, suggests itself as a way of distinguishing among the social situations, and
hence the possible political trajectories, of intellectuals in a Communist order. Differences in political capital, particularly in the form
of party membership, were crucial in determining income, employ-
ment opportunities, access to scarce goods, housing, and the like.
In a shortage economy, many citizens of Communist societies re-

garded "Vitamin C" (for "connections") as more important than cash-on-hand, and party membership was generally a sine qua non for patronage, promotion opportunities, permission to travel, and so on. Those with the requisite political capital benefitted from what Bourdieu has called the "patrimonialization of collective resources" by Communist regimes (Bourdieu 1991, 37).

Mannheim's stress on the structural factors internally dividing the intellectual stratum and on the generally individualistic nature of intellectual work led him to conclude that the intelligentsia would be incapable of making common political cause in defense of shared interests. Consistent with this assumption, Thomas Baylis was unable to find any signs of an oppositional alliance "between the technicians and leading members of the cultural intelligentsia" in a study of the politics of the East German intelligentsia conducted during the late 1960s (Baylis 1974, 271).

Kicking sand in the face of the massive evidence of political disharmony among intellectuals, Alvin Gouldner argued that the highly educated share interests in the control over and remuneration for their "cultural capital," an asset that finds expression in a common "culture of critical discourse." This shared interest would, according to Gouldner, bring the highly educated, conceived as a rising "New Class," into contention with the "old classes" in socialist (and capitalist) societies. The part of the "old class" in this drama was to be played by the Communist political bureaucracy. In contrast to the Marxist scenario, however, the antagonists of the old class would not be the revolutionary working class. Rather, Gouldner wrote, "The New Class contest [with the 'old class'] sometimes has the character of *a civil war within the upper classes*. It is the differentiation of the old class into contentious fractions" (Gouldner 1979, 18). In short, Gouldner's New Class often appeared as descended from the dominant class, a sociological Trojan horse both tied to the old class in myriad ways and at odds with it. As we shall see, this approach is particularly helpful in understanding the intellectuals' role in the unraveling of the East German Communist order beginning in the fall of 1989, even if, on the whole, Gouldner was overly optimistic about the emancipatory role of the "New Class."[3]

Useful though Mannheim's and Gouldner's suggestions are, however, they cannot adequately account for the political attitudes of East Germany's intellectuals. One of the more striking features of the upheaval of late 1989 in the GDR was the salience of the national question and of the Nazi cataclysm in the East German intellectuals' rhetoric. It has been argued, correctly in my view, that the Germans in the GDR nurtured a deeper historical consciousness than their compatriots in the Federal Republic. The reason for this was that their state owed its very existence to, and the ruling party strongly drew its everyday self-understanding from, the catastrophic events unleashed by German fascism (see Gaus 1986, 23). East Germany's intellectuals always played a special role in sustaining the memory of the "wrong way of [the German] nation"[4] that so profoundly informed the widespread early support for a noncapitalist order in postwar Germany.[5] Their persistent preoccupation with the genocidal consequences of virulent nationalism drove them toward a "postnational" ideology that remains an important element in their thinking and activism.

To understand this group, therefore, it is essential to consider Germany's *national* situation in the postwar period, for this had profound consequences upon the politics of the GDR's intellectuals, as it did on the country as a whole. Of special importance was West Germany's steadfast refusal to recognize a separate East German citizenship; all East Germans had an automatic right to West German citizenship, as well as to funds to facilitate their integration into West German society. These constitutional and legal arrangements sharply distinguished the East Germans' political situation from that in other East bloc countries. Residents of the GDR were always *virtual* citizens of the Federal Republic, a state with whose inhabitants they shared a language and, at least until 1945, history and traditions. Accordingly, exile in West Germany (and those who left the GDR normally went to the Federal Republic rather than to some other German-speaking country) was simply not the same as exile from other East Central European countries. Familial, regional, and other affective ties helped sustain elements of communal feeling. By the time of the upheaval of 1989, it is noteworthy that some two-thirds of East Germans had relatives in the West, although only one-third of West Germans had relatives in the East (Niethammer 1990a, 277).

Unlike other ruling Communist parties, furthermore, the SED had at its disposal a means of disciplining its population that permitted the party to avoid the difficulties associated with open repression: its control over the "safety valve" of emigration to the Federal Republic. The immediate adjacency of the "other" German state greatly facilitated the East German regime's relatively restrained treatment of at least the better-known intellectuals. When the party-state considered it expedient to rid itself of those it found unpleasant or to disrupt the development of opposition activity without causing a furor, it always had the option (especially after the building of the Berlin Wall in 1961) of simply dumping undesirables in West Germany or of granting their requests to emigrate. Throwing "troublemakers" into jail creates an embarrassing situation for any government, but justifying this sort of behavior had grown considerably more difficult in the period since the Helsinki Final Act (1975) and the emergence of nongovernmental human rights organizations such as Amnesty International. For their part, those who chose to leave the GDR rather than suffer the travails of the struggle for a better society naturally reduced the direct pressures on the regime to change and, perhaps equally significant, demoralized those who wished to stay and fight that battle. Accordingly, the alternatives termed "exit" and "voice" by Albert O. Hirschman occupy a central place in my discussion of the political attitudes of East Germany's intellectuals.

These considerations raise the difficult issue of the meaning of terms such as "opposition" and "dissent" in the East German context. While they may have nurtured a certain sense of alternative possibilities, the older, more established intellectuals rarely underwent the rigors of isolation and incarceration so characteristic of the dissident "type" elsewhere in the East bloc (e.g., Andrei Sakharov, Václav Havel, and Adam Michnik). Yet even the younger, more radical critics of the East German regime did not necessarily understand themselves as involved in "opposition" activities. One of the most striking findings of my interviews was the insistence among many longtime independent political activists that they were not involved in "opposition" at all: indeed, that this was a label pinned on them by the "bourgeois" media of the West.[6]

Retrospectively, at least, it nonetheless seems clear that even many who eschewed the Western characterization of themselves as "oppositionists" were "objectively" acting against the interest of the system, which decisively depended on monolithic party control of organized political life. Dissent, to be sure, is intrinsically difficult to define, encompassing almost anyone who diverged from the "party line" on some issue. This definition, of course, would include everyone at some point, for it was in the very nature of the "party line" that it shifted, sometimes quite abruptly, for any number of reasons. It may thus be necessary to disregard the self-understanding of the actors in order to arrive at a cogent definition of "opposition." On this basis, one might argue that "opposition" consisted in "unwelcome pressure for significant political change" (Woods 1986, 20–21). This approach has the important virtue of taking into account the ruling party's view of what it considered a challenge to its rule, which offers a reasonably useful guide to grasping how the party understood the conditions of the perpetuation of its dominance.

This definition runs into problems in the fall of 1989, however, when many of the independent grassroots leaders declared themselves, initially at least, in favor of a reformed socialism. The mass emigration that created the political breach into which the grassroots groups stepped, by contrast, was signaling a truly fundamental opposition to the GDR: that is, indifference or hostility to the state's continued existence. Because much of the intellectual opposition remained anticapitalist in outlook, their rejection of the system that frequently oppressed them was often more muted than that of the majority of the GDR's citizenry, who dismissed "socialism" (if not all of the values they associated with it) out of hand. The younger dissident generation often opposed a notion of "grassroots democracy" *(Basisdemokratie)* to what they sometimes described, very much in keeping with the terminology of the Communist regime, as "bourgeois democracy" *(bürgerliche Demokratie).*

These kinds of remarks suggest that East Germany's rather unrevolutionary "revolutionaries of the first hour" might better have been described as "dissidents" than as "oppositionists," a suggestion supported also by their defense of the East German state's continued independent existence and their reluctance to seize power as it lay on the streets of the GDR in the fall of 1989. They could perhaps be described, inelegantly, as "a dissident opposition." Like many of their counterparts elsewhere in Eastern Europe, East Germany's dissident intellectuals were "nonutopian" in the sense that they were not committed to a *specific* program for a future society. (Jürgen Habermas had these characteristics of the East European revolutions in mind when he termed them "catching-up revolutions" almost bereft of "innovative, future-oriented ideas.")[7] But the East German intellectuals generally remained more sympathetic to the term "socialism" than did the political opposition elsewhere in the Soviet bloc. The difficulty associated with a straightforward definition of the terms "dissent" and "opposition" is itself an indication of the peculiar political complexion of the dissident intellectuals in the Communist quarter of divided Germany.

These features of the national context of the East German socialist project would come to have substantial political consequences.
Once the reform-socialist hopes of the dissident intellectuals ebbed
with the coming of unification, moreover, the political relevance
and the historiographical interpretation of German national history
would themselves become a central arena of intellectual politics. As
the East German dissidents' influence faded after their brief moment of political prominence, the public understanding of their role
in bringing down the old regime became decisive in determining
whether their efforts would be enshrined in or expunged from postunification German self-understanding. The odyssey of the GDR's
reform-socialist intellectuals would eventually culminate in the fusion of their vehicle for electoral politics, the Bündnis '90 (Alliance
'90), with West Germany's Green Party. Yet the process of unifying
these two organizations was considerably more protracted than that
of uniting the two German states had been, largely because of the
East Germans' jealous regard for their independence and their mistrust of the Greens' tendency to accommodate Communism as "the
enemy of their enemy" before 1989. After unification, the East German intellectuals' opposition to Communism became a potentially
positive touchstone of a new German understanding of citizenship.
But this effect could not be achieved without a wrenching discussion
of the interpretation of that past that may only have consolidated
the broader population's belief that the intellectuals' concerns were
not their own. In any case, the inheritance of the East German opposition contributed to the extended and often stormy courtship that
preceded the merger of two political groupings whose sociological
and ideological similarities otherwise appeared so striking. For all
their similarities, the merger of the East German intellectuals' political
groupings with the intellectually dominated Greens revealed that their
respective origins in dramatically divergent social systems could not
be overlooked. The difficulties associated with this political marriage
might be seen as a microcosm of the problems involved in bringing
the two Germanys under the roof of a single state.

Gramsci's discussion of the problem of intellectuals is best known
for his attention to the matter of their relations to other classes. Yet
Gramsci also sketched the broad outlines of an analysis of the specific
trajectories taken by the intellectuals of different countries, suggesting that such analyses would be essential to any adequate grasp of
the historical role of intellectuals in politics (see Gramsci 1971, 17–

23). This book had its beginnings in the observation of an anomaly in the larger process of the collapse of Communist societies of East and Central Europe: namely, that the East German intellectuals were much more enthusiastic than their East European dissident counterparts about the idea of "socialism" — and at precisely the time when any order bearing that label seemed so totally discredited. I went on to ask whether there was some connection between these attitudes and the apparently rapid loss of popular support suffered by the GDR's intellectual "revolutionaries of the first hour" in the course of the demise of Communist rule. What follows is an attempt to analyze these issues and thus to contribute to the project called for by Gramsci in his seminal writings on intellectuals: to comprehend historically the ways that intellectual groups in various countries relate to the groups above and beneath them in the social structure.

As a corollary, this book may also add something to the perennial debate about the "peculiarities of German history." Yet it must always be recalled that, to the extent that these special features of the German experience exist at all, they are the product of history and circumstance rather than of the vagaries of the gene pool. Accordingly, we must begin by examining the historical conditions under which the East German intelligentsia came into being.

One

The Making of an East German Intelligentsia

The defeat and collapse of the Third Reich left Germany under the control of Allied occupying forces. Much of the German population viewed the "Russians" in the SBZ with considerable mistrust as a result of direct or indirect knowledge of their pillaging and cruelty toward war's end or out of simple anti-Communism. In contrast, those who had been associated with the left before Hitler's ascendancy typically viewed the arrival of Soviet armed forces as a liberation from tyranny; for some, indeed, the Red Army quite literally freed them from Nazi jails. Amid the general devastation and misery in Germany after the defeat of the Third Reich, Social Democrats and Communists were eager to overcome the animosities that had divided the working-class movement during Weimar — divisions, it was widely believed, that had made possible Hitler's rise to power. Even beyond the ranks of the politically organized working class, broad elements of the population across the German political spectrum shared a desire to create a social order that would ensure peace and facilitate reconstruction after the Nazi catastrophe.

When Stalin's German minions returned from emigration in Moscow in early 1945 to undertake an "antifascist democratic transformation," they entered this political constellation. At the time, the Communists enjoyed considerable authority as a consequence of their persecution by the Nazis and their important role in antifascist resistance activities (see Merson 1985). The democratic component of their program was a matter of greater uncertainty, however. The KPD (German Communist Party) had existed for only a few years during the Weimar Republic and had been substantially "Bolshevized" and "Stalinized" during that period. The party's experience with and commitment to the unwieldy processes of "bourgeois" constitutional government could only be speculated about after it was forced into the underground or into exile during the Third Reich. Doubts on this score were especially pronounced when it came to the KPD leadership cadres that returned to Germany from Moscow near war's end. The initial signs were not promising. Shortly after his arrival on German soil, Walter Ulbricht, the soon-to-be leader of the SED, set a disturbing tone when he instructed his lieutenants in the rebuilding of local administration in the SBZ: "It has to look democratic, but we have to have everything in our hands."[1]

Still, many left-wing intellectuals soft-pedaled the deficit of democracy in the Stalinized KPD and subsequently in the SED, emphasizing instead the KPD's antifascist and socialist aspects. In a feature of their thinking that would become prominent as time wore on, German intellectuals beholden to the promise of a socialist and hence supposedly peaceful future tended to overlook the lack of democracy in the SBZ/GDR. Under the non-Communist Allies, meanwhile, the capitalist "restoration" proceeded apace in western Germany — eventually also including the restoration of high Nazi Party functionaries to positions of power and influence. In a speech at the West Berlin Academy of Arts on the occasion of the fiftieth anniversary of the Nazi attack on Poland, the highly regarded East German author Christa Wolf recalled the importance of these experiences for her generation of East Germans:

> In the years before and after the founding of the GDR, the confrontation with German fascism was carried out thoroughly and uncompromisingly in our part of Germany, and precisely this phase of postwar development became the basis among us then-young people for a gradual identification with the later GDR and with those revolutionary traditions in German history to which it appealed, and which were negated or opposed in the Federal Republic under Adenauer.[2]

The Communist and hence putatively antifascist credentials of the German leadership in the SBZ and the relative laxity of denazification in the western zones of Allied occupation (see Vollnhals 1991, 9–42) thus helped strengthen the perception that the SBZ/GDR laid legitimate claim to the title of being "the better German state," the heir of the traditions of the "other," antifascist Germany. Wolf's remarks, made in the very twilight of the GDR's existence, suggest the surprising durability of the antifascist legitimation of East German Communism for many intellectuals, particularly among the older generation. Bärbel Bohley, a cofounder of the independent group New Forum in the fall of 1989, noted in an interview at some remove from the upheavals of that time that she, too, had believed for far too long in the claims of East Germany's leaders that the GDR was an antifascist bastion.[3]

The vigorous initial efforts of the Soviets and their German allies to create a more egalitarian social structure lent further credence among many to the notion that the SBZ/GDR embodied the "better Germany." In addition to being consistent with traditional Communist social goals, these efforts were regarded as vital to the longer-term aim of ensuring that the social basis for a fascist resurgence — in a word, capitalism — would be destroyed. The profound shake-up of the social structure undertaken by East German socialists and Communists (after early 1946 as the SED) during the Soviet occupation was thus not confined simply to the elimination of private ownership of productive resources and the legal structures connected with such ownership. Land reform, the nationalization of industry, and the abolition of a professional civil service were only the principal elements of a policy intended to smash the power of the bourgeoisie in German society — those strata deemed in the reigning Marxist theory to have been the principal props of National Socialist power. In order to complete this design, a thoroughgoing overhaul of the educational system and the pillars of the bourgeois order among the intellectual professions was considered necessary as well.

One crucial element of this project of social reorganization was the SED's plan to create a postfascist, "socialist intelligentsia." This extraordinary task of social engineering presented the rulers of the new socialist regime with a profound dilemma, however. The development of an industrialized nation that could satisfy the needs of its population and compete with the western part of divided Germany, which had been blessed by the Western Allies in 1948 with the economic support of the Marshall Plan, was impossible without highly trained experts capable of organizing and designing the infrastructure of the economy. Yet most such experts were beholden in greater or lesser degree to the old order. Moreover, the SED's attempt to achieve an exclusive role in guiding the direction of social development left little room for independent centers of intellectual activity. In short, as one West German analysis put it, the party had to solve two important problems at once: "the creation of a 'new intelligentsia' outfitted with an unconditional claim to validity yet at all times under its social control, on the one hand, and the integration of an 'old intelligentsia' committed only in existential terms to the system, on the other" (Lange, Richert, and Stammer 1953, 199). To complicate this situation, as long as the intra-German border remained permeable, the old intelligentsia's merely "existential" commitment to the emerging socialist regime could always be terminated by departure for the West.

The Communist forces that took control of the SBZ under the aegis of the Soviet occupation set about the dual tasks of creating the new and integrating the old intelligentsia from the ground up. Like the changes in ownership and property relations, the first school reform of 1945 was motivated to a considerable degree by the desire to strip power from former Nazi Party members and their sympathizers. Carried out, as it was, under the auspices of the Soviet Military Administration for Germany (SMAD), it also foresaw an educational system closely modeled on that of the Soviet Union. The reform package thus called for the denazification of intellectual and cultural life, an end to the educational advantages of children from the upper classes, targeted "counterprivileging" of the children of workers and peasants, and the development of a new intelligentsia (Belitz-Demiriz and Voigt 1990, 159). Such policies and, in time, the growing politicization and Sovietization of higher education encouraged many among the better-educated groups surviving from the Nazi era to make their way to western Germany. By 1948, the administrative process of denazification in the SBZ had largely been completed, resulting in the removal of more than one-half million persons from the educational, justice, economic, and administrative sectors (Staritz 1985, 55). In the process, considerable opportunities were created for those whose political views were more congenial to the new regime to step forward and assume positions in these areas. Even if many of them were initially untutored, the government sought rapidly to make such opportunities available to those who had previously enjoyed few such chances.

During the years before 1960, the SED did much to advantage the previously disadvantaged in gaining access to higher education, an increasingly important route to upward social mobility in a society where the privileges of property were being gradually but dramatically diminished. In order to appreciate the extent of the transformation of the university student population effected during the GDR's early years, one must keep in mind that, at war's end, the children of workers had constituted a mere 3 percent of the undergraduate population in German universities (Lange, Richert, and Stammer 1953, 212). During the academic year coinciding with the first full year of the GDR's existence (1949–50), this figure had already risen more than tenfold. The increasing absorption into the student population of matriculants drawn from among the "counterprivileged" groups reached its apogee of nearly 58 percent toward the end of the 1950s, after which it began what would prove to be an irreversible decline. From the 1958 peak, when nearly three out of every five university students were said to have been of working-class and peasant origins, that group's share had fallen by 1966 to 31.1 percent — a level not seen since pre-GDR days. By that year, the proportion among the student population of those from such backgrounds barely exceeded that of the offspring of the intelligentsia, whose resurgence among the student body could no longer be overlooked (Belitz-Demiriz and Voigt 1990, 57, table 7).

Yet despite this development, the census of 1964 found that 80 percent of the East German intelligentsia (including graduates of the technical institutes *[Fachschulen]*) had completed their tertiary training after 1951 (Wienke 1989, 45). By 1965, in fact, 91.2 percent of all East German university graduates proper had received their higher education in the "socialist university" (Belitz-Demiriz and Voigt 1990, 94). A major objective of the socialist regime had thus been achieved in a remarkably short time. Along with the completion of the "transition from capitalism to socialism," whose basic elements were the elimination of most private economic activity and the large-scale collectivization of agriculture during the 1950s, the SED had succeeded to an extraordinary degree in creating a new intelligentsia "in terms of its social composition and, at least in part, of its mentality" (Erbe 1982, 90). Within a generation, the East German regime had replaced one of the principal pillars of bourgeois and National Socialist society with an intelligentsia largely of its own making and hence to a considerable degree indebted to the regime for the opportunities it enjoyed.

The circumstances under which the SED molded this new socialist intelligentsia had been particularly auspicious for this dramatic attempt at social engineering. These conditions included a considerable sympathy within the population for doing away with the social structures upon which National Socialism had arisen, the new regime's need to cultivate loyalty among its subjects, and the expansion of the party and governmental infrastructure required to administer a surveillance state and a strongly centralized economy. Even under the presuppositions of "extensive development," moreover, the intelligentsia occupied a central position in the quickening economic competition with West Germany — a contest that, as long as the borders remained open, the GDR could not afford to lose.

Between Exit and Loyalty: Intelligentsia Policy in the SBZ/GDR, 1945–53

Despite the Soviet-dominated government's "counterprivileging" policies and its efforts to create a "new intelligentsia" during the early postwar years, it hardly treated the "old intelligentsia" from the pre-1945 period exclusively with contempt. For two simple reasons, such a policy would have been quite foolish. First, the new order depended greatly on the contributions to economic reconstruction of the only people available with experience in running a complex economy. Next, despite the rapid strides that were made in the direction of the development of a new "socialist" intelligentsia, achievement of this goal would take time. From the very beginning, therefore, when short rations were the order of the day for the majority of the population, the Soviet authorities sought to persuade members of the intelligentsia to stay in the SBZ with extra rations of food and hard-to-obtain goods (Staritz 1985, 44).

While those with technical expertise often had to be enticed with material privileges to remain and serve the socialist order,[4] many of the humanistic intellectuals who had been driven into exile by the Nazis returned enthusiastically to a German state with which they felt a substantial sympathy. Within the Communist/SED leadership itself, however, there was a split between those who had spent the Nazi years in the Soviet Union and those who had spent them elsewhere.[5] Many of the leftist intellectuals who had passed the years 1933–45 (to a greater or lesser extent) in Soviet emigration, and who were active in such organizations as the League of Proletarian-Revolutionary Writers, later assumed positions of prominence in East Germany's cultural institutions.[6] Among those outside the Soviet Union during this period, a further distinction might be made between those who fought against Franco in the Spanish Civil War or participated in other armed antifascist resistance activities in Germany or the Nazi-occupied countries, and those who escaped to safer areas not directly involved in warfare, such as the United States.[7] In contrast to the rank-and-file membership of the working-class parties, relatively few prominent cultural figures from the Weimar period remained in Hitler's Germany. In a phenomenon that would largely be repeated in the GDR during the course of its existence, the most sophisticated and politically astute representatives of the "better Germany" fled the country, leaving behind them a relatively less distinguished group that was more closely tied to the National Socialist regime or neutralized *(gleichgeschaltet)* by it.

Many of Germany's best-known Weimar-era cultural and intellectual figures who chose to return to their home country in the early postwar period chose to go to East Germany, however.[8] The regime certainly encouraged this cultural window dressing as an important prop to its legitimacy. Largely of proletarian origins itself and with no pronounced sympathies for artistic activity, however, the Stalinist leadership around Walter Ulbricht imposed considerable constraints on freedom of thought and expression, a fact that quickly soured relations between the intellectuals and the regime. The conflict between the Stalinists and the more democratically inclined socialists among the intellectuals became increasingly intense after the extension of the doctrine of "socialist realism" to the GDR in the early 1950s.[9] One observer close to these events, Gustav Just, retroactively described the party's 1951 resolution condemning formalism as "power's first declaration of war on the life of the mind. That which, during the Weimar period, had been considered progressive — and, indeed, Communist-sympathizing — art was now excoriated as cosmopolitanism and formalism."[10]

The honeymoon of the Communist and fellow-traveling intellectuals with their socialist masters was essentially over already by this time. Yet the artistic intellectuals, in particular, showed little inclination to press for an annulment. As one analyst put it, "Given the resentments and antipathies of the older intellectuals [toward the bourgeois West], there [was] simply no alternative to which the Ulbricht regime has not seemed 'the lesser evil' " (Croan 1962, 244). On the whole, intellectuals sympathetic to the socialist cause simply felt they had no place else to go; to leave for the West, many felt, would have meant an abandonment of deeply held beliefs and sympathies. In the late 1950s, the prominent literary critic Alfred Kantorowicz described in striking terms the German Communists' reluctance to part ways with the Communist cause "in this bifurcated world that no longer suffered in-between positions":

> As long as the open rejection of communist domination *(Zwangs-herrschaft)* was tantamount to abetting fascist or even just reactionary, militaristic, imperialistic tendencies, many preferred to be condemned to eternal silence and ruin over there rather than to incur the odium associated with the apparent betrayal of their convictions.[11]

But this view was by no means held by all members of the cultural and scientific elite in the fledgling GDR, who did not necessarily share these ideological reservations about leaving for the West or who simply overcame them if they did hold these beliefs.

Indeed, the SED soon had to confront the fact that the intelligentsia's relative privilege was proving insufficient to keep the highly qualified from seeking their fortunes elsewhere. The intensification of the drive to "build socialism," announced at the second party conference of July 1952, led to a considerable exodus of professionally and technically trained personnel during the large exodus of 1952–53.[12] Figures on the exact proportion of the intelligentsia represented among that group are not available. In the period from 1949 to 1961, however, at least 5,000 members of the intelligentsia left the GDR annually (Erbe 1982, 89). Moreover, between 1954 and 1961, 47,016 practitioners of professional and intellectual occupations departed the GDR for the West. Among these highly trained emigrants were 3,371 doctors, 1,329 dentists, 960 pharmacists, 6,798 lawyers, 752 university teachers, 16,724 school teachers, and 17,082 engineers. The total figure (47,016) is equivalent to nearly one-fifth of the entire intelligentsia identified in the last previous census in 1946; among engineers, the proportion approached one-third of that total (Wienke 1989, 154). By the end of the 1950s, many of the more energetic among the better-educated residents of the GDR with antipathies toward the regime — whether out of ideological conviction or for more mundane, "material" reasons — had left for the West.[13]

The continued permeability of the "intra-German" border and the considerable inclination of the East German intelligentsia (and, of course, other groups as well) to cross it permanently thus made some further accommodation with them an unavoidable fact of life for the young socialist regime. In order to stanch the outflow of these especially valuable workers, political criteria favoring the lower classes had to take a back-seat to pragmatic considerations of expertise — despite the uproar this policy appears to have caused among the party rank and file.[14] Beginning in 1949, therefore, the government afforded certain elements of the intelligentsia numerous privileges and perks beyond the ration supplements that had been distributed to them in the early days of the SBZ. These preferments were granted particularly to the technically schooled and skilled, although they were also accorded to educators, administrators, and artists whose cooperation in building socialism the SED considered indispensable. Especially for those highly qualified experts with whom the government concluded "individual contracts" *(Einzelverträge),* these privileges included better vacation opportunities, more generous health insurance policies, additional old-age compensation known as the "intelligentsia pension" *(Intelligenz-Rente),* and similar perquisites. Despite the myriad policies intended to enhance lower-class access to advanced education, the preferential treatment accorded the children of the intelligentsia in obtaining access to higher education contributed to its persistently high rate of social self-recruitment. Nor were the advantages afforded the highly qualified limited exclusively to nonwage compensation. The salary packages included in the "individual contracts" granted monthly wages of from four thousand on up to fifteen thousand marks per month, as well as performance bonuses, at a time when the average monthly income in the GDR was around three hundred marks.[15]

Still, the demands of the economic plan and the continuing brain drain to the West led the party to intensify its efforts to curry favor with the old intelligentsia. In May 1951, not long after the SED had promulgated its first Five-Year Plan (1951–55), the Central Committee issued a statement insisting on the need for "comradely cooperation between the working class and the intelligentsia" in order to achieve the ideal of a socialist order. In an appeal that was unlikely to promote such cooperation, however, the Central Committee also called for further privileges for the old intelligentsia and the "cultivation of the youthful, progressive forces of a new intelligentsia." The plan thus foresaw an increase of 53,500 technicians and engineers during the coming five-year period.[16]

Immediately prior to the party's decision in 1952 to begin the project of "building socialism," the East German government offered its highly educated personnel another round of material advantages. An executive order from 28 June 1952 raised the incomes of scientists, engineers, and technicians vis-à-vis skilled workers to 2.6 to 1. With this increase of nearly 50 percent over the previous ratio of 1.75 to 1, the regime acknowledged anew that the old intelligentsia was indispensable to the realization of the goals of the economic plan (see Lange, Richert, and Stammer 1953, 197).

The East German government's policies toward the intelligentsia indicated its conviction that the demands of economic growth, so crucial to its legitimacy, required a more conciliatory position toward the intelligentsia than had been characteristic of the early years of its rule. Yet soon enough, the SED again shifted course regarding the special place of the intelligentsia in the GDR's socialist development. First Secretary Walter Ulbricht gave the signal for the shift at the historically crucial second party conference of the SED held from 9 to 12 July 1952.[17] On that occasion, Ulbricht announced that East Germany had completed the phase of the "antifascist-democratic transformation" and that the building of socialism had become the "fundamental task in the German Democratic Republic."[18]

This proposed intensification of socialist development would expose wide segments of the intelligentsia — and, indeed, of East German society generally — to greater political and economic pressures from the SED than they had theretofore known. Under these circumstances, a social explosion matured that would constitute the most radical challenge to Stalinist rule in Soviet-dominated East Central Europe until that time. The gulf dividing much of the intelligentsia from the economic and political concerns of the broader population in the GDR was glaringly revealed in June 1953, when East German workers mounted the first large-scale rebellion against Soviet-style rule in Eastern Europe.

The Intelligentsia and the Workers' Rebellion of 1953

According to Stalinist doctrine, the evolutionary phase of "building socialism" was to be devoted primarily to the large-scale development of heavy industry. The Stalinist orthodoxy also held that resistance from the bourgeoisie could be expected to grow during this stage of social development, which would thus be characterized by an "intensification of the class struggle." That heightened social conflict actually emerged from the party's plans to "build socialism" in the GDR can hardly be surprising in view of its failure to explain how it intended to finance the immense industrial expansion proposed at the second party conference. The SED leadership resolved simply that "measures directed toward an increase in labor productivity...and the introduction of a strict austerity regime in all branches of the economy and in all layers of the economic and state administration must play a major role in the struggle to fulfill and exceed the Five-Year Plan."[19] Already squeezed by short rations and the general rigors of postwar reconstruction, East Germany's citizens were now being asked to draw their belts even tighter in the service of a socialist order they had never chosen in the first place.

When implemented, this new "austerity regime" had a profound impact on all levels of East German society. Taxes were raised, wage increases above those fixed by the plan were forbidden, insurance premiums were increased for those engaged in private enterprise, and the food ration cards of entrepreneurs and free professionals working in West Berlin were eliminated. The intelligentsia was to make its special contribution to freeing up the economic means required for the expansion of heavy industry by forfeiting, beginning on 1 May 1953, its privileged and discounted access to consumer goods (Staritz 1985, 79).

Disenchantment with these policies grew quickly and dramatically. Perhaps the most obvious indication of disgruntlement, as well as the one most costly to the party's economic program, was a rapid swelling of emigration to the West. In the second half of 1952, 110,000 out of a total population of some 18,000,000 East Germans had turned their backs on the GDR, an increase of more than 50 percent over the first six months of the year before the second party conference. This figure more than doubled, to 225,000, in the first half of 1953. At the end of April, the Central Statistical Office of the GDR was forced to concede that the economic targets for 1953, which were already burdened with considerable unfulfilled plan targets from the previous year, had not been met during the first quarter — undoubtedly due in part to the ballooning emigration figures (Baring 1966, 35).

The intelligentsia was likely to have been considerably overrepresented among these emigrants, hard-hit as they were by the terms of the new austerity program. There is good reason to suspect that the intelligentsia was especially sensitive to the stepped-up ideological campaigns associated with the effort to "build socialism." Particularly to the extent that the "intensification of the class struggle" entailed at least the perception of heightened discrimination against "bourgeois" elements, the well educated would likely have regarded their prospects in the GDR as less than rosy, especially in comparison to those opening up in West Germany. For example, with all the energy and rhetoric being devoted to improving the access to educational opportunities of the offspring of workers and peasants, the children of the intelligentsia were widely thought to have been disadvantaged in this respect.[20] Between 1954 and 1961, in any case, practitioners of intelligentsia occupations constituted approximately 4 percent of the overall emigrant population, whereas the 1946 census had found that this group made up only 1.4 percent of the total population of the "central German" territories occupied by Soviet troops.[21]

The increasingly critical loss in early 1953 of some of the country's best-trained citizens stimulated considerable debate within the party hierarchy regarding its attitude toward the intelligentsia. On 5 May, the party organ *Neues Deutschland* published an article entitled "More Respect to the Members of the Intelligentsia!" which argued that the party must not destroy that important group's belief that they are "seriously" viewed as "an essential factor in social life." The following day, the paper aired an official statement of Central Committee policy toward the intelligentsia in which the party's leaders conceded that the state had to "win the cooperation of broad elements of the old bourgeois intelligentsia for governmental, economic, and cultural development." On 7 June, just two days before the Politburo's decision to embark on a "New Course" — a strategic retreat from the economic program promulgated at the second party conference of a year before — *Neues Deutschland* informed its readers that the party leadership considered it impossible to "build a new social order" without "the broadest integration of the old intelligentsia." Accordingly, those currents in the party "antagonistic to the intelligentsia" should henceforth be stifled.[22] The propagation of such ideas as official party doctrine must have been a bitter pill to those in the party reared in the anti-intellectual traditions of the KPD.[23]

Faced with a situation that anticipated in remarkable ways the crisis of 1989, the party leadership had to do something to stanch the alarming flow of emigration to the West. In a notably self-critical

Politburo resolution adopting the "New Course," the SED elite conceded that the policies associated with the "building of socialism"
had caused substantial problems in the GDR's economy. The resolution particularly noted the loss of population to the Federal Republic,
admitting that those policies had neglected "the interests of certain
segments of the population — such as small farmers, retail merchants,
skilled tradesmen, and the intelligentsia. . . . As a result, numerous persons have left the republic."[24] In keeping with the New Course's
overall tone, the resolution regretted the excessive demands that had
been imposed on these groups but said little about the flight of or
disenchantment among workers. The party leaders' failure to recognize working-class grievances would soon prove to have been a nearly
fatal miscalculation.

The "New Course" charted by the party leadership on 9 June and
made public on 11 June was too little and too late to forestall the upwelling of dissatisfaction that came to a head a week later. The June
uprising, indeed, offers an excellent illustration of the Tocquevillean
maxim that "the most perilous moment for a bad government is one
when it seeks to mend its ways."[25] Under strong pressure from the
post-Stalin Soviet leadership around Molotov, Beria, and Malenkov
to pursue a more restrained approach, the party reversed virtually
all of the measures it had introduced at the second party conference
of a year earlier. The emphasis on heavy industrialization at the expense of consumer goods was moderated, the tax increases intended
to underwrite that economic program were eliminated, pressure on
private entrepreneurs was to be reduced, farmers who had fled the
country were to be enticed to return with offers of land and credits,
and ration cards were once again to be made available to all groups.
Responding to a widespread complaint among intellectuals, the freedom of scientists and artists to participate in professional activities
in West Germany was to be restored. The SED leaders' promises to
raise the standard of living of the East German population across
the board could not be fulfilled exclusively with goodwill, however.
Alone among the measures that had been introduced to speed the
pace of socialist development, therefore, the production norm increases for workers that had been announced in late May 1953 were
to remain in force (see Baring 1966, 42–47).

The party leadership's insistence on pursuing an acceleration of
labor productivity ultimately catalyzed the strikes of 15–16 June in
Berlin that spread to include well over three hundred thousand par-

ticipants throughout the country on the seventeenth of the month (Ewers and Quest 1988, 33). The norm increases were, however, by no means the only or even the principal cause of the workers' disenchantment. More important were the intensified administrative pressures associated with the party's proposed acceleration of socialist development, and more generally the perception that the government's behavior flew in the face of its own insistence that it was merely the executor of the workers' interests. In short, the regime — which based its legitimacy in substantial degree on the notion that it was a government "of, by, and for" the workers — was being called to account for violating its own ideological premises.[26]

Historians not subject to party discipline generally agree that the strike movement was carried principally by workers who initially raised only economic demands ("Down with the norms!" "More bread and meat!").[27] The protests took on more political overtones, however, as events developed, the social composition of the rebellion broadened, and the workers lost decisive control of the movement. The list of demands then expanded to include the release of political prisoners, Ulbricht's resignation, and free elections leading to the reunification of Germany.

Widespread consensus exists, moreover, concerning the conclusion that — with isolated exceptions among technical experts in larger factories — the intelligentsia, and the middle classes more broadly, stood for the most part on the sidelines of the 1953 rebellion. An analysis of records from the Ministry of State Security made available since the fall of the SED in 1989 revises these findings in detail but not in substance. The secret police records do indicate, however, that the solidarity of white-collar and technical workers in the central German industrial plants around Halle and Merseburg was "one of the most important causes" for the persistence in those areas of organized worker opposition to the SED after Soviet tanks had moved in to crush the uprising on 17 June (Mitter 1991, 38). Despite this cross-class cohesion, the regime responded to the rebellion with a harsh wave of repression. The number of those killed during the rebellion has been (inconclusively) estimated at as few as twenty-five and as many as three hundred (see H. Weber 1985, 243). State retribution included the arrest of some eight thousand to ten thousand persons, at least four of whom were sentenced to life imprisonment, while at least six were condemned to death (see Mitter 1991, 34; and Baring 1966, 114).

For its part, the fourteenth plenum of the SED's Central Committee, meeting in the immediate aftermath of these events, attributed the East German workers' uprising to the machinations of Western agents, particularly those of West Germany and the United States. While it is certainly true that workers from West Berlin joined the protests and that the broadcasts of RIAS (Radio in the American Sector) helped spread news of the events, convincing evidence of significant participation by Western secret services — the chief culprit in the view of the Central Committee — has yet to be produced. According to the party leadership, these agents sought to "erect a fascist order in the German Democratic Republic." The Central Committee's analysis is striking for its repeated invocation of the ethos of conspiratorial underground opposition to fascist treachery. The document is typical of the regime's manipulation of the alleged threat of a resurgent fascism as a justification for its own dictatorial measures. In fact, the party's leaders recalled the Comintern's official 1935 definition of fascism as "the open, terroristic dictatorship of the most reactionary, most chauvinist, and most imperialist elements of finance capital" (cited in Merson 1985, 307) by insisting that those workers who had been "deceived" into supporting the rebellion needed to be made aware of the fact that they had thus unintentionally "fallen under the influence of their sworn enemies, the monopoly capitalists and fascists." Despite the party's vigorous denunciations of the role of Western agitation, however, the resolution also conceded that "the enemy exploited the disenchantment of some segments of the population in getting its provocation underway."[28] Assessment of the internal and external causes of the workers' rebellion of 1953 would play a central role in the discussions among East German intellectuals regarding the legitimacy of the workers' demands, and thus concerning their own attitudes toward the uprising as well.

As noted above, non-Communist scholars generally agree that the intelligentsia played an extremely limited role in the 1953 rebellion in East Germany. Less scholarly agreement prevails, however, as to why the intelligentsia in general, and the technical intelligentsia in particular, failed to take a significant part in the rebellion of June 1953. Three factors appear to have been crucial. First, certain elements of the intelligentsia had less material cause to rebel. This was especially true of those professionals (engineers, scientists, etc.) who benefited from the high salaries and perks dispensed through the "individual contracts" and from related policies designed to encourage loyalty to the regime among the intelligentsia. The measures so recently promulgated in the "New Course" and official statements appearing in *Neues Deutschland* suggested, moreover, that the government had adopted a more conciliatory attitude toward the intelligentsia than had prevailed during the recent past.

Next, workers and intellectuals possessed unequal capacities for opposition. Despite the party's vigorous campaigns against Social Democrats and against "social-democratism" after the merger of the KPD and the SPD that created the SED, and despite the imposition of a trade union organization, the Free German Trade Union Federation (FDGB), that acted as a "transmission belt" for party directives rather than as an independent representative of labor's interests, the workers still had recourse to traditions of labor struggle inherited from the Communist and socialist labor movements. These traditions played some role — how great is unclear — in stimulating protest and organization in the principal bastions of working-class mobilization during the June rebellion.

The capacity for resistance among the intelligentsia, in contrast, had been greatly weakened by political pressures. This was especially true of its unorganized and nonparty elements. More importantly, however, the ranks of the intelligentsia had been considerably thinned by emigration to the West. As a result of this complex of factors, those representatives of the East German intelligentsia who might have been inclined toward active opposition to the regime were therefore "atomized, resigned, and to a great extent prepared — on the basis of a wrongheaded and fundamentally futile striving for security — to accommodate themselves to the regime in order to hold on to what remained of their means of existence."[29]

Finally, members of the "new" intelligentsia, numerically insignificant in any case, showed little proclivity to oppose the order to which they owed their opportunities for social advancement. This attitude also characterized the response to the rebellion among university students, who for the most part kept their distance from the workers' demands. In short, the intelligentsia was relatively privileged materially and neutralized politically, if not positively beholden to the regime.

While the intelligentsia remained largely on the sidelines during the rebellion, this is not to say that it had no impact on them politically or that they refrained from commenting on it. This was especially true of those involved in the "core" intellectual occupations, such as writers, poets, and philosophers. In contrast to the technical intelligentsia, which had a closer familiarity with the workers' experience and at least sporadically supported their efforts, the most prominent representatives of the intelligentsia — committed as so many of them were to the GDR as an antifascist socialist experiment — tended to side with the party-state while accepting that the workers were airing legitimate grievances. At least the published responses to the workers' challenge of leading East German intellectuals, who were themselves tied more or less strongly to the party and were frequently the beneficiaries of its vigorously antifascist cultural policy,[30] typically ranged from unreserved endorsement of the SED's hegemony to a critical solidarity that mixed calls for reform with endorsement of the party's leadership in the creation of a socialist society.

The reaction of Stefan Heym, a young leftist writer who would in time become one of the GDR's best-known novelists, offers one noteworthy example of the intelligentsia's critical solidarity with the regime during this tumultuous period. Recently returned to the GDR from the United States, with whose forces he had fought against Nazi Germany during World War II, Heym had been asked by the editor of the Soviet-controlled newspaper *Tägliche Rundschau* to write an account of his impressions during the June days. Echoing Tocqueville's aforementioned remarks on the perils of reform, Heym identified what he considered to be the central problem involved in the SED's sudden about-face embodied in the New Course: "The demonstrative public admission of errors by a government to which wide segments of the populace are opposed, *and which rules in only one part of a country,*" he wrote in his report, "is a very questionable tactic." Heym was pointedly critical of the pervasive application of Stalinist "administrative" methods in the GDR, which he claimed had been the underlying cause of the workers' rebellion. At the same time, however, Heym inclined toward the SED's official interpretation that the June events had been instigated by "agents from the West," noting that these operatives were able to till "fertile soil" due to the real frustrations among the population.[31] Heym concluded his reflections with the following assessment of the situation in the Soviet Zone: "The fundamental fact in Germany is that the German workers have *not* made a revolution and, though the majority of them were fed up with the war in 1945, they did not therefore wish for any new social order."[32] Here Heym pointed to a central feature of the antifascist socialist experiment on German soil about which he himself was so enthusiastic.

In contrast to Heym's recognition of worker grievances, tones considerably more critical of the workers could be heard emanating from party and fellow-traveling intellectuals. For example, Kuba (Kurt Bartel), the secretary of the Writers' Union, published a short verse about the uprising entitled "Wie ich mich schäme" (How ashamed I am) in the party organ *Neues Deutschland* on 20 June 1953. There Kuba castigated "masons, housepainters, [and] carpenters" for their participation in the rebellion, "for which you have no cause." Asking his readers whether "you are not ashamed as I am," he concluded the poem with a note of arrogance that could not have been lost on any nonintellectual who read it: "You will have to lay a great deal of brick and very well, and will in the future have to act very smartly, before you will be forgotten this disgrace."[33] The chasm separating the socialist intelligentsia from the workers during the June rebellion could hardly have found more explicit expression.

Perhaps the best-known figure on the East German cultural scene, Bertolt Brecht, found it impossible to let Kuba's sentiments go unremarked. Brecht penned the well-known poem "The Solution" as an ironic commentary on "How Ashamed I Am":

> After the uprising of the 17th June
> The Secretary of the Writers' Union
> Had leaflets distributed in the Stalinallee
> Stating that the people
> Had forfeited the confidence of the government
> And could win it back only
> by redoubled efforts. Would it not be easier
> In that case for the government
> To dissolve the people
> And elect another?[34]

It would be wrong, however, to conclude too much about Brecht's response to the workers' rebellion from the cryptically sympathetic character of these remarks. First, it must be noted that, like most of his poems about contemporary political events, Brecht chose not to publish "The Solution" at that time, circulating it instead only privately among friends. Next, returning to Berlin from his country idyll on the morning of 17 June, Brecht felt compelled to send SED general secretary Walter Ulbricht a personal letter avowing his loyalty to the party — of which he was not even a member! Only the last line of the letter, which contains a rather servile profession of "solidarity" *(Verbundenheit)* with the party, was reproduced in *Neues Deutschland.* Because Brecht did not publish "The Solution," the party daily's tendentious omission left the lasting public impression that he simply opposed the workers' insurrection and endorsed the party's response carte blanche.[35]

Yet Brecht's numerous other statements regarding the June uprising indicate that he joined in the opinion that the workers' frustrations were justified. At the same time, he argued in the pages of *Neues Deutschland* that the demonstrations to which these frustrations had given rise had been "misused for bellicose purposes" by "provocateurs," whom he hoped had been "isolated and their networks destroyed." Still, Brecht cautiously pleaded against equating the workers with these "provocateurs," for this interpretation would, he believed, vitiate "the great discussion of the mistakes made on all sides before it even began."[36] Brecht's remarks here and elsewhere indicate that he was more sympathetic to the interpretation of the June uprising that traced the workers' rebellion to the "mistakes of the past" than to that advanced by the group around Ulbricht, indicated in the aforementioned Central Committee resolution of 21 June, which attributed the rising to the work of "fascist agents."[37]

From a different perspective, however, Brecht's position — as well as that of many other East German intellectuals — may be seen as characteristic of the dilemma of a revisionist "third way" in East Germany: the ultimate loyalty expressed was to the GDR and to "socialism" because, irrespective of all justifiable criticism, the socialist project in Germany was on shaky ground without the GDR. The intimate, indeed symbiotic, connection between the two had the effect of muting criticism of the party, even when such criticism was considered appropriate and necessary. Moreover, the legitimating power of the antifascist credo and the persistence of the hope for a socialist society continued to lead many intellectuals to overlook the party's shortcomings and to concentrate on "the big picture" *(die grosse Sache).*

The East German intellectuals thus tended to evaluate the socialist ideal in terms of the reigning interpretation of fascism as a degenerate but always potential form of capitalism and of the GDR as a bulwark against its resurgence. Naturally, this attitude influenced their responses to the workers' rebellion of mid-1953. In this connection, West German sociologist Sigrid Meuschel has written: "The

SED was able to push through its interpretation of the 17th of June because the antifascist consensus between the intellectuals and the party, and the intelligentsia's reservations vis-à-vis society and democracy, gave rise to an unholy syndrome that put narrow boundaries on the critique of Stalinism" (Meuschel 1992, 168). Meuschel's remarks capture well the limits imposed upon the East German intellectuals' criticisms of the SED regime as a consequence of their fundamental endorsement of its antifascist, anticapitalist aims in post-Nazi Germany.

The 17th of June of the Intellectuals

Even when the intellectuals were not hostile to the workers' aims during the June rebellion, the intelligentsia, which had been one of the principal beneficiaries of the policies constituting the "New Course," had by and large stayed out of the rebellion. Yet, seizing the opportunity presented by the weakness and division in the party leadership in the early summer of 1953, the core intellectuals — writers, artists, dramatists, and so on — initiated vigorous efforts to loosen the bonds of censorship and to get the party to relax its control over intellectual activity. Indeed, so outspoken were they in these efforts that the conflicts between the party and the "creators of culture" *(Kulturschaffenden)* during the period after the workers' uprising came to be known, at least in the Western media, as "the 17th of June of the intelligentsia" (Rühle 1988, 185). Since Stalin's death on 5 March 1953, strong winds of change had begun blowing from Moscow, and these the intellectuals sought to exploit in an effort to gain improvements in their lot. In a constellation that would repeat itself more than once during the GDR's history, reform-oriented elements of the intelligentsia would take advantage of revisionist impulses emanating from the Soviet Union and divisions within the GDR's party elite to advance their own political agenda.

In this case, the East Germans could point in support of their own position to the process of cultural reform then underway in the Soviet Union, where Soviet culture boss Andrei Zhdanov's proletarian-cultural orthodoxies had recently come under attack. In a speech at the nineteenth congress of the CPSU in the fall of 1952, Georgi Malenkov had vigorously criticized the primitive state of artistic life in the Soviet Union, without actually naming Zhdanov himself as the person responsible for this state of affairs. Soon thereafter, both

Zhdanov and Stalin passed from the historical stage.[38] From the point of view of the would-be East German cultural reformers, there were clear signs of movement at the Communist center that promised changes in the stifling ideological control under which they toiled on its western periphery.

In this situation, it was not long before intellectuals formed such organizations as the Academy of Arts and the Cultural Federation for the Democratic Renewal of Germany (known simply as the Kulturbund) and struck up their own campaign for liberalization of the GDR's confining cultural policies. Already in meetings in the spring of 1953, members of the Kulturbund throughout the GDR had begun to discuss their frustrations with the regime's cultural bureaucracy, without yet advancing concrete proposals to the government concerning possible reforms. Immediately following the events of 17 June, however, the organization's leadership adopted a resolution outlining a number of "suggestions" designed to enhance the autonomy of intellectual activity.[39] The resolution began by noting that "the majority of the intelligentsia demonstrated on 17 June its loyalty to the government of the German Democratic Republic and its solidarity with the task of democratic reconstruction" — a declaration that may have been merely a tactical ploy intended to curry favor with the resolution's addressees in the party leadership. Even so, the statement accurately reflected the response of important segments of the cultural and literary intelligentsia to the workers' rebellion.

The authors of the petition clearly felt that the loyalty of the intelligentsia in the party's hour of need entitled them to demand substantial changes in cultural policy. The catalog of "suggestions" ran the gamut of those freedoms typically asserted by intellectuals to be crucial to their work: freedom of opinion; freedom of writers, publishers, and artists from interference by the state; freedom of scientific research and teaching; and, finally, freedom and accuracy of the press. The resolution noted laconically, however, that "the precondition for all of these demands is legal security on the basis of the inviolable constitution of our republic," a precondition that would have required considerably more far-reaching changes in party dominance than those actually enunciated in the resolution. These demands nonetheless constituted a frontal attack on the SED's cultural policy, which had come to be characterized by the regular intrusion of party bureaucrats into the freedom of intellectual activity.

The Kulturbund resolution thus amounted to an effort to put

an end to the Stalinist-Zhdanovist approach to cultural policy in the GDR, a process that had by no means been completed in East Germany despite the party's general endorsement of "socialist realism" and its attacks on "formalism" in the arts. According to one analyst, in fact, the demands contained in the document had "virtually the character of an opposition program"; they were, according to this observer, "without parallel in the entire East bloc at that time" (Jänicke 1964, 54). Still, the resolution stopped well short of calling into question the "leading role" of the SED in East German political life. To the contrary, its authors were at pains to emphasize their loyalty to the Communist regime.

The Kulturbund resolution was also noteworthy for its preoccupation with the national question. Despite its emphatic avowals of loyalty to the GDR, the organization's presidium stated firmly that it would evaluate all measures of the GDR's government concerning cultural matters in terms of whether or not they "promote the unity of Germany." Indeed, the resolution concluded by affirming the Kulturbund's commitment to the two larger objectives that the authors of the resolution considered the individual "suggestions" to serve: "democratic renewal and the reunification of our German fatherland in peace." The Kulturbund's leadership thus pronounced their endorsement of two goals whose interdependence was not yet widely recognized or conceded among East Germany's prominent intellectuals. There need not have been any contradiction, then, when the organization's leaders simultaneously protested their fealty to the East German regime and their devotion to the cause of German unity. Clearly, loyalty to the fledgling socialist regime was not viewed as precluding what in those days was still unhesitatingly referred to as "the reunification of Germany."

The Kulturbund resolution had been preceded four days earlier by a substantially similar manifesto from the prestigious Academy of Arts. So stinging was the indictment of previous policies contained in that document, and so remarkable its demands, that *Neues Deutschland* initially refused to publish the text of the academy's resolution. The prohibition apparently issued from Ulbricht loyalist Hermann Axen, secretary for agitation in the Central Committee. When what Alfred Kantorowicz later called the "good half" of the academy, under Brecht's "resolute and courageous" leadership, threatened to resign their membership in the organization in protest, East German premier Otto Grotewohl intervened to clear the document for publication (Kantorowicz 1961, 401). It first appeared in the more independent-minded *Berliner Zeitung,* which played an important role as a platform for unorthodox views among the intelligentsia around the time of the workers' rebellion.

Both resolutions were, in considerable part, the product of a "rare unanimity" (Rühle 1988, 185) between Bertolt Brecht and Johannes R. Becher, a longtime Communist poet who had become one of the GDR's most important cultural functionaries. Unlike Brecht a member of the SED, Becher was from 1945 until his death in 1958 president of the Kulturbund and, from 1952 to 1956, president of the Academy of Arts. (Not favorably disposed, Kantorowicz described him in a 1953 diary entry as a "publicity agent of the powerful, a traitor to the intellect.")[40] The resolutions passed by these two organizations would quite simply have been impossible without Becher's powerful backing.

Despite Becher's critical statements during the June crisis and his support for cultural reforms, he, too, was an enthusiastic supporter of the socialist cause in East Germany. Indeed, as Becher had written three years before, the contradiction between knowledge and power was "on the way to being resolved" there. Never before, he asserted, had "art and cultivation *[Bildung]*" been so "integrated *[verbunden]* with power" as in the GDR.[41] These were doubtless heady prospects for any intellectual. Becher thus appears to have concluded that the Kulturbund, created immediately after the end of World War II, had achieved the aim he envisioned for that organization at its inception. In his remarks at the Kulturbund's founding ceremonies on 4 July 1945, Becher spoke of the "rich humanistic legacy" bequeathed by the German classics to those intent on rebuilding a democratic Germany from the rubble left behind by the Nazis. At the same time, he bemoaned the fact that a "classical politics" had never been built upon the classical cultural inheritance. "We must escape from this disastrous contradiction between the intellect *[Geist]* and power, which has become the most ominous fate in our history and ultimately has destroyed all free intellectual creation" (cited in Jäger 1982, 2). The Kulturbund should, in Becher's view, help to resolve this rift. Be that as it may, one might argue just the opposite: it has been precisely the myriad connections between intellectuals and power that had doomed Germany to a history without a successful, democratic revolution.

Despite Becher's optimism about the prospects for the life of the mind under the emergent socialist order in the GDR, he was not unaware that relations between the intellectuals and the powers were experiencing considerable strain by the time of the June crisis. Writing in early 1953 in *Sinn und Form,* the prominent journal of the Academy of Arts, Becher himself had attacked the narrow-minded philistinism of the party's cultural apparatchiks: the "bureaucratic snoopers" who "examine all literary works...to determine whether or not they conform to Marxism-Leninism" nonetheless lack the courage of their convictions, which would otherwise lead them "to declare either the abolition of the comparison or the uselessness of poetry as such."[42] Yet Becher shared the conviction, widespread among German intellectuals at the time, that "fascist and war-mongering" views did not deserve to have access to cultural outlets in the GDR. And as an SED member, he was perhaps even more strongly inclined to support the party's leading role in defining cultural policy. Becher was thus in an awkward and ambiguous position with respect to the censorship and party control that he decried in this attack.

For his part, Brecht had published a poem in the *Berliner Zeitung* attacking the GDR's principal censor only two days before the explosion of 17 June. The satirical piece poked fun at the simple-minded criteria guiding the censorship practices carried out by the much-hated "Office for Literature":

> The Office for Literature is known to allot
> Paper to the republic's publishing houses, so many hundred-weight
> Of this precious substance for such works as are welcome.
> Welcome
> Are works with ideas
> Familiar to the Office for Literature from the newspapers.
> This custom
> Given the sort of newspapers we've got
> Should lead to great savings in paper, so long as
> The Office for Literature confines itself to licensing one book
> For each idea in the newspapers. Unfortunately
> It allows virtually all those books to be printed which take an idea
> From the newspapers and doctor it.
> Hence
> For the works of various masters
> There is no paper.[43]

Brecht voiced the discontent of many would-be literary "masters" who felt their works were not being published because of the East German censors' dogmatic philistinism.

Shortly before the fifteenth plenum of the SED's Central Committee, Wolfgang Harich, a professor of philosophy at Berlin's renowned Humboldt University and the editor of the highly respected *Deutsche Zeitschrift für Philosophie,* likewise weighed in with a withering broadside against the practices of the State Arts Commission and against those critics who supported its policies.[44] The commission was, according to Harich, "hated by the majority of fine artists" for inducing "creative crises of a psychotic character" even — indeed, especially — among artists who "stood politically without vacillation on the ground of our republic." He lambasted the functionaries of the State Arts Commission as tasteless dilettantes whose low aesthetic standards had led many artists to depart from the GDR or to refuse to collaborate with official cultural institutions. Typical of the advocates of a "third way," however, Harich offered his critique of contemporary policies very much in the spirit of socialism. He argued that only the elimination of these "grave circumstances" would make it possible "to satisfy the intellectual needs of the population and to convince broad strata of our nation of the rightness of our republic." Given Harich's ringing indictment of the party-state's arts policies and his simultaneous endorsement of socialism, it was perhaps no coincidence that he would be at the center of the GDR's most significant intraparty controversy over "revisionism" just three years later.

The party's leaders, internally divided and weakened by the June rebellion, apparently felt they needed to make at least some concessions to the intellectuals. They probably also believed that it would be less risky to offer such carrots to intellectuals than to workers, numerically and economically a vastly more significant group. Moreover, given the insistence even of the party's critics on their loyalty to the "republic," the SED leaders might reasonably have calculated that concessions to the intellectuals would have the effect of binding them more strongly to the East German state and its Communist regime. After all, this pacifying approach had clearly been the thrust of the party leaders' motivation in embarking upon the "New Course." The workers, in contrast, had demanded reforms such as free elections, resignation of the government, and reunification, all of which constituted life-threatening assaults on the party's dominance.

As the Kulturbund resolution had asserted, the most prominent intellectuals, especially those organized in such bodies as the Kulturbund and the Academy of Arts, had, on the whole, supported the regime when the workers took to the streets in mid-June, a fact that party leader Ulbricht noted warmly in his speech at the Central Committee session of 24–26 July 1953. In part as a reward for their support at that time, the SED general secretary agreed that the reform proposals adumbrated by the Kulturbund's presidium should now be carried out. Even if "some of these proposals must be taken under serious consideration [i.e., cannot be granted immediately], the greatest part admit of being realized. The proposals of the Academy of Arts likewise deserve the most serious consideration and speedy realization."[45] The most significant concrete result of the SED's concessions was the regime's promise to abolish the despised State Arts Commission. That little-loved institution was to be replaced by a new Ministry of Culture under the direction of Johannes R. Becher, a useful compromise figure who was both a friend of Ulbricht's and — as noted above — a sometime advocate of a more liberal line in the party's cultural policy. In order not to appear to be giving in directly to the intellectuals' demands, however, this part of the plan was not to be effected until 1954. Within two years the widely detested Office of Literature was likewise to be eliminated.

Thus despite the rejection by prominent intellectuals of the workers' aims during the June crisis, their success in toppling the State Arts Commission and the Office of Literature made the intellectuals, who had "raised their demands in the shadow of the rebellion," winners after the fact (Spittmann 1988, 131). At the fifteenth plenum of the Central Committee, Walter Ulbricht nonetheless insisted that much of the intensification in the regime's economic approach announced in the summer of 1952 would remain because the "general line concerning 'the building of socialism' " had been correct all along. In fact, while the intellectuals succeeded in wringing concessions from the party apparatus, a massive wave of arrests was taking place in the factories, where worker unrest had not yet been entirely squelched (see Mitter 1991, 32ff.). Meanwhile, the purge of party cadres proceeded with considerable vigor.

The "core" intellectuals — or at least those who remained in the GDR after the 17th of June — had won themselves some greater latitude in publishing and ideas, at least temporarily. Yet this thaw in cultural policy, which would last until around 1956–57, was to a substantial degree the product of the workers' ultimately futile exertions concerning relatively mundane matters far from the realm of culture that moved the intellectuals. The irony was that the workers' objective of overthrowing General Secretary Walter Ulbricht ultimately led to the consolidation of his control over party and state.

Thus while the 17th of June in the GDR is generally described as a "workers' rebellion," there had actually been something like two "17ths of June" — one for the workers and another for the intelligentsia — with dramatically different results. While large numbers of workers, farmers, small merchants, professionals, and technical intelligentsia left the country under the pressure of the intensified "building of socialism," the workers mounted a sharp challenge to the burgeoning East German party-state. Prominent representatives of the intelligentsia, however, broadly sympathetic to the putatively antifascist socialist project in the GDR, were reluctant to take up the workers' cause in this conflict. Yet they exploited the opening it created to advance their own freedoms. At the same time, bitter controversies were being carried out within the SED elite between an insurgent intellectual faction grouped loosely around Rudolf Herrnstadt and the "proletarian" faction headed by Ulbricht. The lack of an alliance between the working class and the intelligentsia against the party, rooted to a substantial degree in the intelligentsia's endorsement of the party's claim to legitimacy as an antifascist force, would in subsequent years become a familiar feature of political opposition to the SED.

The workers' rebellion of 1953 was the last overt, widely supported working-class challenge to the regime. Thereafter, the social basis of public opposition to the regime in East Germany migrated to the ranks of the intelligentsia, particularly those of its elements within the party. In the process, however, the opposition lost all connection to a mass base. On the whole, the evidence points to the conclusion that the party's ambivalent, zig-zagging course vis-à-vis the East German intelligentsia succeeded in large measure in consolidating the party's grip on political power.

Two

Intellectuals, the State, and Opposition, 1956–80

The period of liberalization inaugurated by the "New Course" and the intellectuals' own moderately successful campaigns in the aftermath of the workers' rebellion would ultimately prove a Pyrrhic victory for the East German intelligentsia. Co-opted by its own allegiance to the GDR's antifascist socialist experiment, the intelligentsia was reluctant to challenge the fundamental foundation of the party's power: namely, its "leading role" in political affairs as a Leninist "party of a new type." The intelligentsia thus remained beholden to the SED as the supposed protagonist of socialism in the "German workers' and peasants' state."

In part as a result of this constellation, Stalin's death in 1953 did not necessarily signal domestic liberalization in the GDR to the same degree as in the other Soviet-dominated countries of East Central Europe. For this loosening of control was intrinsically related to the resurgence of the notion of "national roads" to Communism — an option that, as the intraparty struggles concerning the "Herrnstadt faction" had made clear, had become anathema to the East German party leadership despite the early support for a "specifically German road to socialism." Because the very uniqueness of the GDR's experiment lay in its attempt to develop "socialism in a quarter of a country," the SED was not free to invoke the ideological imagery of a *national* Communism as an alternative to Soviet tutelage. After all, the SED's failure to win a majority in the only relatively free elections in the SBZ in the Berlin elections of 1946 — and the CDU's dominance in West German politics since that time — had made abundantly clear that the SED could hardly claim to represent the entire German nation. The continued widespread enthusiasm among both the intelligentsia and the party rank and file for a reunited Germany therefore constituted a mortal danger to the rule of an increasingly isolated party elite whose relations with Moscow were at least intermittently marked by considerable strain in the post-Stalin period. Still, the Soviet Union had granted the GDR full sovereignty in 1954, a step that further cemented the division of Germany and anticipated East Germany's entry into the Warsaw Pact military alliance. Even as the Soviet bloc countries were liberated from the bloodier features of Stalinist rule, the division of Europe into hostile camps grew increasingly consolidated during the mid-1950s.

The Twentieth Party Congress of the CPSU and Its Consequences in the GDR

It was in this context that Khrushchev rocked the Soviet bloc with his speech detailing Stalin's crimes at the twentieth congress of the CPSU in March 1956. These revelations could hardly have been calculated to reassure the East German leadership of its hegemony. In his address to the Soviet party, Khrushchev criticized not only the enormous human toll exacted by the Soviet collectivization drive and the purges of the 1930s but the un-Marxist "cult of personality" with which Stalin had allowed himself to be flattered as well.

The Stalinists in the East German leadership appeared to have been caught quite off guard by Khrushchev's speech and the change of course it heralded in the Soviet bloc. Soon after the twentieth party congress, the East German leadership — which had for so long praised the "great teacher" Stalin — was forced to reverse rudder abruptly. To the befuddled astonishment of the party faithful, Walter Ulbricht brazenly contradicted all of his previous pronouncements concerning the Soviet leader, declaring in the pages of *Neues Deutschland* that "Stalin cannot be considered a classic thinker of Marxism."[1] To be sure, Ulbricht could not be accused of having staged elaborate show trials in the GDR on the scale of those involving Laszlo Rajk in Hungary or Rudolph Slansky in Czechoslovakia. Yet he was quite vulnerable to the charge of having promoted a "cult of personality" around himself. The SED leader thus had a strong interest in downplaying the implications of Khrushchev's revelations for future developments in East Germany.

Of greater importance to Ulbricht in his efforts to maintain power, however, was Khrushchev's reassertion of the concept of divergent national roads to socialism. Similarly, the notion of "peaceful coexistence" between East and West posed a considerable challenge to the party's control over East Germany and hence to the state's continued existence. As in Stalin's 1952 offer to the Allies to exchange the reunification of Germany for its neutrality,[2] Soviet policy considerations once again sharply confronted the East German regime with the limits and conditions of its power in divided Germany.

The closing of the window of liberalization that had briefly opened in the GDR in the mid-1950s was thus quite directly connected with the intractability of the national problem for the country's Communist regime. Indeed, Ulbricht is reported to have said during a conversation in the halls during the fourth congress of the Writers' Union in January 1956: "The New Course is over. The task here is no longer that of bringing East and West together. The task now is that of consolidating socialism."[3] In his formal address to the gathering, Ulbricht strongly emphasized the development of a specifically East German literature, which should be characterized by its contributions to peace and to the "patriotic education of the people."[4] Liberalization at the center of the Soviet empire had paradoxical consequences on its western periphery, where socialism was being built in a quarter of a country: a crackdown on all tendencies toward an ethnically defined national project, on the one hand, and a heightened attention to the inculcation of a "socialist national consciousness," on the other. Minister of Culture Johannes R. Becher spoke in a similarly GDR-nationalistic vein of the "greatness of *our* literature." In fact, according to Gustav Just, at that time an editor of the well-respected cultural-political weekly *Sonntag,* that "greatness was derived more from his speech than from the works themselves."[5] Indeed, only days before the Hungarian uprising in October, Just would write in the pages of *Sonntag* that "little that is genuinely innovative in the arts has been produced in the socialist camp during the last twenty years," mainly due, he said, to ideological constraints on experimentation (cited in Kersten 1957, 154).

The spirit of criticism, called forth not least by the party's own insistence on a more vigorous "conflict of opinions,"[6] was very much in the air in the aftermath of the twentieth Soviet party congress. At

a conference on literary criticism in May–June 1956, nonparty literary critic Hans Mayer spoke for many on the East German cultural
scene when he challenged Ulbricht's approach to literature as being
implicitly based on the Stalinist-Zhdanovist notion of the writer as
an "engineer of the human soul." To the contrary, Mayer responded,
"the human soul is not something that one should let an engineer get
at. The application of the analogy of technology [Technik] and natural science to the work of the writer must lead to an impoverishment
of the latter."[7]

The liberal views that Mayer expressed at the conference and
a few months later in a lecture entitled "The Contemporary Situation of Our Literature" (the planned radio broadcasting of which
had been canceled for political reasons) were greeted with considerable enthusiasm among the GDR's cultural figures. In the lecture,
Mayer criticized the inadequate appropriation of modernist trends
in East German literature. The tendency was, rather, to create literature in tune with such uplifting characteristics as "realistic, typical,
positive, optimistic, and the like." This "sectarian" trend contrasted
noticeably, according to Mayer, with the highly experimental 1920s,
during which an "imposing variety" of quality literary works had
been produced.[8] In a revealing remark, one contemporary observer
of the "revolt of the intellectuals" against the party's philistinism described the controversy pitting the group of cultural "liberals" against
the "supporters of Ulbricht's orthodox course" as that of a confrontation between "intellectuals" and "proletarians." This remark was,
perhaps, more a reference to the prolet-cultural artistic preferences
of the latter group than to the two factions' actual social origins, but
the characterization is telling nonetheless (Kersten 1957, 165).

The leaders of the East German party — itself certainly dominated by "proletarians" in cultural matters — took these issues quite
seriously. Indeed, their concern with the political ramifications of
cultural activities found dramatic expression when Mayer's remarks
became the focus of an intense debate that reached into the upper levels of the party apparatus. In July 1957, more than six months after
the appearance of Mayer's latest broadside, the thirty-second plenum
of the SED's Central Committee made his criticisms of GDR culture
the object of sharp controversy. Central Committee Secretary for Science and Culture Kurt Hager, Leipzig SED secretary Paul Fröhlich,
and the writer Alexander Abusch, soon to become minister of culture after Johannes Becher's death in 1958, all took Mayer to task in

their remarks to the assemblage.[9] These and other attacks eventually hounded Mayer into departing for the Federal Republic. He later reflected that "the period of the genuine cultural thaw in the GDR" had been the span from early summer 1955 until late summer 1956 — the period during which he had made his own critical contributions to the debate. Yet as subsequent events would demonstrate, Mayer went on, this period of relative cultural relaxation had in fact proven to be "a thaw that was not one" (Mayer 1977, 441, 446).

Unrest in Eastern Europe:
The Resurgent Challenge of "National Communism"

Indeed, the anxiety unleashed among the Stalinist core of the East German party leadership by the twentieth congress of the CPSU was only heightened by the eruption of a workers' rebellion in June 1956 in Poznan, not far from the Oder-Neisse border that divided East Germany from Poland. The specter of a repetition of "the 17th of June" unquestionably haunted the SED apparatchiks in such situations, as it would continue to do for as long as the GDR survived. Yet the same memory was still alive among the working class. The legacy of the 1953 defeat — along with repressive controls on the job and recent policy changes intended to improve the general standard of living of the East German population (see H. Weber 1985, 283) — helped keep the workers relatively passive in the face of unrest among their eastern neighbors. In addition, the continued easy availability of the "exit" option to West Germany once again played its role as a safety valve at a time of substantial political strain for the SED. Despite a temporary reversal in emigration trends after the mid-1953 announcement of the New Course, the party elite's piecemeal abandonment of that liberalization policy had helped fuel a renewed jump in departures for the Federal Republic.[10] After abating somewhat in the aftermath of the workers' rebellion of 1953, emigration from the GDR to West Germany rose in 1955 to over a quarter of a million, climbed further to 279,189 in 1956, and declined only slightly (to 261,622) in 1957. Potential popular pressure for change was thus correspondingly reduced.

The emigration safety valve did not altogether spare the party of public manifestations of discontent, however. Still, while newly released records of the Ministry of State Security indicate that working-class protest in East Germany during the fall of 1956 was more widespread than has generally been understood (see Wolle 1991, 42–51), such unrest was the exception rather than the rule. More dangerous than workers' protests, the SED leadership seems therefore to have believed, was the restoration of Wladislaw Gomulka to the Central Committee of the Polish United Workers' Party (PUWP) in mid-October. Known as a protagonist of "national Communism," Gomulka was, according to then–GDR Minister of State Security Ernst Wollweber, "a red flag" for Walter Ulbricht.[11] This could hardly be surprising in the political circumstances prevailing in the Soviet bloc in late 1956. Indeed, one of the figures arrested for his involvement in the revisionist opposition in the GDR phrased the concerns of that opposition in the form of the question: "Who could replace Ulbricht, who is the German Gomulka?"[12] As indicated earlier, "national Communism" was not an option for the East German Communist leadership, which felt deeply threatened by the spread of what it regarded as "the Polish disease" elsewhere in the Soviet bloc.

The distress of the SED leadership thus rose further with the outbreak of what it termed a "counterrevolutionary putsch" in Hungary. That uprising, inspired in no small part by the intellectuals grouped around the so-called Petöfi Circle of Budapest intellectuals, briefly installed the reform-Communist Imre Nagy into power. The Hungarian opposition, which drew considerable support from among intellectuals and students as well as workers, bore parallels to that in the GDR, a fact that the East German leadership regarded as quite troubling. For, in addition to the ferment among older East German intellectuals — suggested, among other things, by the controversy surrounding Hans Mayer — considerable unrest had developed among the country's university students as well. According to one observer, in fact, students were at that time "probably the largest oppositional group in the GDR" (Kersten 1957, 166). This was perhaps especially true among students drawn from more comfortable social origins, such as the medical and veterinary students.[13] Minister of State Security Wollweber himself noted the presence of "a certain unrest among the students at the Humboldt University, especially among the veterinary medicine students."[14]

Despite an apparent overrepresentation of students from higher status backgrounds among those involved in protest against the regime, however, it was by no means the case that discontent was confined exclusively among such students. Indeed, it was widely complained in university party organizations that even the students from worker and peasant families, whose loyalty to the regime was thought to be beyond question, "had separated themselves from the working class" (Kersten 1957, 166). Apparently even the new "socialist intelligentsia" — upon whom the SED had spent so much effort to cultivate a proper class consciousness — was vulnerable to the blandishments of the imperialist enemy.

Under these domestic circumstances, developments in Hungary caused intense distress among the Ulbricht leadership. This concern was especially great in view of the party's findings concerning the social and political background of the Hungarian rising: "Certain voices, particularly among [Hungary's] writers and students, . . . no longer saw individual mistakes, but instead attacked the very foundations of the socialist movement."[15] The East German party apparatus was intent upon forestalling any repetition of the Hungarian unrest among its own intelligentsia and moved quickly to ensure the continued visible support of its backers among the "creators of culture."

One of the first signs of a closing of the ranks behind the regime on the part of the cultural elite was the resolution passed by the presidium of the Writers' Union condemning the "counterrevolution" in Hungary. The document was signed by Johannes Becher, Kuba, and Stephan Hermlin, among others. Alfred Kantorowicz's refusal to sign the Writers' Union resolution was, for him, a sort of Rubicon; he emigrated to the Federal Republic less than a year later. Never one to shrink from drawing what he considered to be parallels between the practices of the Nazis and of the Stalinist functionaries in the GDR, Kantorowicz noted laconically in his diary: "Hungary was for Ulbricht what the Reichstag fire had been for Hitler" (Kantorowicz 1961, 682, 701, and passim). But Kantorowicz's response to the Hungarian uprising was not echoed widely among the GDR's prominent intellectuals.

Revisionism and Its Suppression in the GDR

Suppression of the less malleable representatives of the East German intelligentsia began in earnest soon after Soviet tanks rolled into Budapest in October 1956. The most spectacular case of repression against dissident intellectuals involved several academics, journalists, and editors dissatisfied above all with the party leadership's halfhearted de-Stalinization efforts, the dogmatism of East

German cultural policy, and the hardening of opposition to German reunification among the SED leadership. The "revisionist" opposition[16] was focused around Wolfgang Harich, at that time a highly regarded young professor of philosophy at Berlin's prestigious Humboldt University. In addition to his post at the Humboldt, Harich was a founding editor of the prestigious *Deutsche Zeitschrift für Philosophie* (German journal of philosophy) and an editor at Aufbau Verlag (a publishing house), both of which were bastions of reform sentiment.

This intraparty Communist opposition was centered above all in three cultural institutions — all of them notable for their essential endorsement of socialism in the GDR. First, the *Deutsche Zeitschrift für Philosophie,* edited by Harich and Ernst Bloch, could perhaps be described as the intellectual headquarters of the group. Its managing editor, Manfred Hertwig, was arrested in late November and tried along with Harich, as was Bernhard Steinberger, a young economist at the Academy of Sciences who had only recently returned from six years in a Siberian gulag after having been sentenced as a "Titoist" in 1949.

Despite the fact that Bloch had just been awarded an East German National Prize and was widely celebrated for his philosophical achievements in 1955, Attorney General Ernst Melsheimer had had a warrant issued for his arrest. SED leader Ulbricht intervened personally, however, to quash the execution of that order (Mayer 1977, 442). A student of Bloch's at the Institute of Philosophy in Leipzig, Günter Lehmann, recalled in an interview that despite Bloch's renown in international Marxist circles, "the political leadership always let it be known that they did not consider him a *genuine* Marxist. . . . He was window dressing for the regime." Moreover, despite his erudition, Bloch was widely understood to have had a "naive," "fantastic" relationship to mundane political matters, such that it was possible for him to praise Stalin on occasion, and making him easy prey for political intrigues.[17] In short, Ulbricht seems to have considered Bloch sufficiently ineffective politically — or simply too famous — to arrest. In a feature of East German political justice that would grow in importance over time, fame, and particularly notoriety in the West, often acted to protect its possessor from imprisonment or other repression to which less prominent individuals were exposed.[18] Instead of going to jail, Bloch was forced into retirement and effectively forbidden to publish in the GDR.

In view of the fact that the Harich group claimed intellectual patrimony from Bloch, Georg Lukács, and the Polish philosopher Leszek Kolakowski,[19] Bloch's assessment of the significance of the twentieth congress of the CPSU is noteworthy as an indication of the group's concerns. Bloch addresses himself specifically to four themes that would be central to the political platform of the revisionist opposition: democratization, the elimination of the cult of personality, the struggle against dogmatism, and the matter of individual national roads to socialism (Bloch 1977, 424–29). This last issue would occupy a decisive place in the political platform discussed by the group around Harich and subsequently drafted by him. As we have seen, this conception had long been associated in German Communist politics with a more "liberal" approach to socialist development, taking account of the peculiarities of Germany's historical development. It had, likewise, been combated by the SED's Stalinist leadership for some time precisely because such an approach threatened to erode the distinction between the two German states and hence to undermine the power of that elite.

Another center of the group's activities was Aufbau Verlag, whose best-known author, the German-speaking Hungarian Marxist philosopher Georg Lukács, had substantial influence in dissident East German intellectual circles at that time. Aufbau's director, Spanish Civil War veteran Walter Janka, was the focus of a second wave of arrests. He and Gustav Just, formerly general secretary of the Writers' Union and by 1956 an editor at the weekly Sonntag, were regarded by the party as the principal figures in the affair after Harich. The connections of both of these institutions to intellectual circles in other Soviet bloc countries, and particularly to Lukács, led the authorities to detect "extensive parallels" between the "Harich group" and the Petöfi Circle in Budapest, the principal center of the Hungarian intellectual opposition in 1956.[20]

Moreover, both the Aufbau house and Sonntag were, in organizational terms, subsidiaries of the Kulturbund, the institution that had played a leading part in supporting the liberalization of cultural policy around the time of the 1953 workers' rebellion. Its president, the contradictory Johannes R. Becher, was considered something of a "loose cannon" among the more narrow-minded apparatchiks and as unduly sympathetic to the cultural liberals. Yet his signature on the Writers' Union resolution condemning the Hungarian uprising indicated that, by this time at least, he was unwilling or unable to protect critical intellectuals who attacked the cultural verities of East German orthodoxy. Moreover, the death of Bertolt Brecht on 14 August 1956 had robbed the liberal-minded intellectuals of their most distinguished and influential figure. Indeed, one participant in these events has argued that while the Ulbricht group's repression of the cultural opposition would probably have been carried out in one form or another, the trials against Harich, Janka, and others would not have been possible during Brecht's lifetime: "Brecht was at that time the only person in the GDR powerful enough to protect Harich, his fellow literary figure, and Janka, his publisher. [Had Brecht still been alive,] State Prosecutor Melsheimer would have had to think up another group to fill the defendants' places on the bench" (Mayer 1977, 443–44). Despite the signs of political liberalization elsewhere in the Soviet bloc, the balance of forces was clearly tilting away from the more "revisionist" Communist and liberal intellectuals in East Germany.

For a time, however, these forces challenged the Ulbricht group's dogmatic views on artistic matters openly and with substantial support from the GDR's cultural community. In this campaign, the weekly *Sonntag,* edited by Heinz Zöger and Gustav Just, played a vital role. The journal took a major part in sustaining an alternative public sphere for the East German intelligentsia in the mid-1950s. Indeed, its role as a bearer of intellectual dissent during the period of the "thaw" was analogous to that played by the *Berliner Zeitung* in the period around the 1953 workers' rebellion. As early as January 1956, the newspaper's editorial policies had been the object of Walter Ulbricht's negative attention in his remarks to the fourth congress of the Writers' Union.[21] During 1956, *Sonntag* had printed both of Hans Mayer's above-described broadsides, numerous critical articles by other East German authors, and contributions from revisionist intellectuals elsewhere in the Soviet bloc. But after the double-blow of events in Poland and Hungary, the SED leadership apparently concluded that it could no longer tolerate such demonstrative public criticism.

Indeed, soon after Gustav Just's removal from the *Sonntag* staff in January 1957, "order" was restored in its editorial policies. Heinz Zöger, who would soon be arrested along with radio producer Richard Wolf and Just, ran the newspaper after the latter's departure "dutifully according to the official line" (Just 1990, 153). In early February, the paper ran the text of a resolution passed by the presidium of the Kulturbund remonstrating that that organization was "not a playpen for the ideologists of imperialism" and condemning "the attempt of several leading associates of Aufbau Verlag and of *Sonntag*... to use these institutions for purposes inimical to the republic."[22] Around the same time, the SED extracted a profession of loyalty to socialist realism from the Writers' Union, and several other organizations representing the producers of culture followed suit soon thereafter.[23] Harich's trial began in early March 1957, and Janka, Just, and the others were arrested directly from their seats on the witness stand. They had been tried and sentenced by late July.

There had, of course, been no conspiracy to overthrow the regime on the part of the small discussion group around Wolfgang Harich. Indeed, the group had been so naively optimistic about the possibility of a legal opposition to the Stalinists in the SED that Harich had initially informed then-Soviet ambassador Georgi Pushkin of his programmatic thinking, precisely because he had been unable to get a hearing from several highly placed SED functionaries. Shortly thereafter, the bright young philosophy professor was ordered to appear before Ulbricht, who interrogated him about his draft platform. That audience must surely have confirmed Ulbricht's suspicions regarding the aims of Harich and his discussion partners. Still, Harich's eagerness to discuss with the SED elite the reform proposals hammered out by a number of the party's most prominent intellectuals made the conspiracy charge especially ludicrous. Gustav Just told me in an interview that he had, in fact, asked repeatedly during the trial: "What kind of a conspiracy against Ulbricht is it that goes and tells Ulbricht its plans?"[24]

Yet the group had certainly begun to formulate the outlines of a program that, had it found wider support, would have led to the disappearance of the GDR as a separate German state. In his written version of the group's aims, Harich is especially preoccupied with the German question. The group sought a reform of the SED from within and a reconciliation with the SPD in West Germany. Because the Communists had lost all influence in the Federal Republic, the document asserted, the division of Germany could only be overcome through cooperation between a reformed SED and the SPD. Harich believed that reunification could be brought about as a result of free all-German elections, in which he optimistically assumed the SPD would win a majority. This assessment of the constellation of political forces was only one of the illusions under which the Harich group labored. More notable, perhaps, in the face of the burgeoning West German "economic miracle" and the widening material gap between East and West was the notion that, assuming that economic improvements over the "Stalinist era" were achieved, "then we have the right to impose conditions on West Germany" regarding the terms of reunification. In particular, this meant that this process "cannot come to a capitalist restoration in a reunified Germany."[25] Gustav Just, who claimed he never saw the "platform" drafted by Harich at the time, developed his own plan for a German confederation based on the reconstitution of the states *(Länder)* that had been dissolved by the SED soon after it took power (Just 1990, 150). Once Ulbricht felt strong enough to move against them, these "all-German" aspects of the revisionist intellectual opposition's thinking would be cause for a dramatic response.

The point of the trials and the lengthy jail sentences meted out to the Communist renegades of the Harich group was to make an example of them and thus to discourage other intellectuals from any repetition of the developments in Poland and Hungary. The Ulbricht faction was, it must be said, substantially successful in realizing these aims. Indeed, as Walter Janka complained in a radio interview shortly after the opening of the Berlin Wall, his early release from prison in 1960 resulted "not from the help of writers in the GDR, but from the persistent efforts and professions of solidarity of well-known people outside the GDR."[26] The cultural luminaries who had been invited to attend the trial as observers, including the occasionally critical Willi Bredel, Brecht's widow Helene Weigel, and the prominent novelist and chairwoman of the Writers' Union Anna Seghers, indicated their sympathy but failed to protest the falsehoods presented by the prosecution against the accused during the trial. Janka was especially disturbed by the silence of Seghers, who had spearheaded an effort to persuade him to go to Budapest to rescue the endangered Lukács during the quelling of the Hungarian rising — a fact later used by the state to bolster the charge of connections to the Petöfi Circle.[27] Gustav Just, however, believes that it was foolish to have expected any broad solidarity. The general public knew little of these events and could thus hardly have been expected to take any risks. The representatives of the cultural elite, meanwhile, "had made their peace with the system."[28]

Virtually nothing was known of these activities of the intraparty opposition outside small circles of intellectuals and party members at the very top. Indeed, this revisionist intellectual opposition, of which the Harich group was the most visible manifestation, remained a matter of virtually no broader political consequence, although considerable support for their reformist approach existed among the party rank and file and among certain elements of the leadership. Nor did the group have any connection to the challenge to Ulbricht mounted around this time by Central Committee Secretary for Party Cadres Karl Schirdewan and Security Minister Wollweber. These figures and others around them in the SED leadership were relative moderates who advocated a less coercive course than that pressed by Ulbricht. But that hardly made them supporters of Harich or of the inflammatory developments on East Germany's socialist flank. Indeed, in a recently published statement originally written in early 1958 to clarify his position and to respond to the charges then being leveled against him, Schirdewan explicitly condemned both the "treasonous Harich group" and the "counterrevolutionary putsch in Hungary."[29]

In the aftermath of the Hungarian crisis, when Ulbricht went over to the counteroffensive against his critics in the party, Schirdewan and Wollweber were driven out of the leadership. The once highly placed Berlin SED functionary Heinz Brandt reported, however, that Khrushchev had initially supported plans to replace the unpopular Ulbricht with Schirdewan, in whom the Soviet leader — like many of the revisionist elements in the party — saw "the German Gomulka" (Brandt 1967, 328). But developments in Poland and Hungary threatened to spiral out of control, and Khrushchev felt compelled to withdraw his backing for the change of leadership in the SED. Ironically, just as had occurred during the workers' rebellion of 1953, Ulbricht's hand had been strengthened by forces that had been intended to loosen the grip of post-Stalinist rule in East Central Europe. And, once again, initial support for such a move within the Soviet leadership gave way to caution in the face of crisis in its sphere of domination.

Moreover, the power struggles that arose in the imperial center as a result of the crises in the subordinate states came directly to bear on the repression of the East German intellectual dissidents. Manfred Hertwig recounts in his description of his pretrial interrogation that the state's attorney, Ernst Melsheimer, cynically told him: "You bet on Khrushchev, and realized too late that Molotov is the man of the future" (Hertwig 1977, 483). Events would ultimately prove Melsheimer himself wrong, of course. But the remark indicates how unsettled the power relationships in Moscow were at the time and how difficult life had been made for the East German leadership by Khrushchev's de-Stalinization.

The year 1956 was thus a watershed for intellectuals in the GDR as for those elsewhere in the Soviet bloc. It was "an uneasy, disquieting year," according to Helmut Warmbier, then a young party member who would later become a professor of Marxism-Leninism in Leipzig. "That affected me deeply, the way Ulbricht stood there and said, 'Stalin is no longer a classic thinker of Marxism,' as if nothing had happened."[30] Similarly, while Robert Havemann had begun to have doubts about the dictatorial order that had developed in the GDR by the time of the workers' rebellion of 1953, "the events of the 17th of June were not enough to 'open my eyes' about the Stalinist system. That only happened after the twentieth congress of the CPSU in 1956" (Havemann 1978, 76).

The point from which Havemann dates his conversion to being a critic of the system is significant, for he would go on to play the role of intellectual godfather of the East German leftist opposition during the 1960s and 1970s. Thirty years later, members of an East German human rights group that played a prominent role in the GDR's dissident scene signed, along with numerous other supporters from Poland, Hungary, and Czechoslovakia, a declaration commemorating the thirtieth anniversary of the Hungarian uprising of 1956. The East German regime responded by orchestrating a campaign of verbal vitriol against the signatories in the pages of a state-dominated church publication, attacking them as "fascists."[31] Despite the state's agitated reaction to the statement, the point is that no similar appreciation of the 1953 workers' rebellion by the East German dissident movement ever received such prominence. Indeed, as one participant in the circle around Ernst Bloch put it in retrospect: "Hungary was much more important for us than the 17th of June, and 1968 in Czechoslovakia was more important as well."[32] To be sure, the events in Hungary in 1956, and in Czechoslovakia in 1968, had had considerably more far-reaching consequences than those in the GDR in 1953. In social and ideological terms, however, it is notable that at least the intellectual elements involved in the Hungarian and Czechoslovak rebellions had aimed primarily at a reformed socialism,[33] whereas the 1953 East German uprising, carried out almost exclusively by workers, had called that system sharply into question and would in fact have led to its dissolution. In short, because the 1953 rebellion had been led by workers and would have entailed the abandonment of the socialist project in the GDR, whereas the Hungarian and Czechoslovak movements were essentially reform-socialist undertakings led by intellectuals, the latter were "more important" to East Germany's intellectuals than the first anti-Stalinist uprising in Soviet-dominated Eastern Europe ever was.

The Reconstruction of Orthodoxy

The clampdown in the GDR that followed the crushing of the Hungarian rising inaugurated a renewal of SED orthodoxy in cultural matters. In his report to the thirty-fifth plenum of the Central Committee in February 1958, future East German party chief Erich Honecker proclaimed that the party-directed conference on culture held the previous October had "put an end to the ideological and political vacillation demonstrated by individual comrade writers and artists during the last year."[34] The cultural thaw in East Germany that had been spurred so much by Khrushchev's speech to the twentieth congress of the CPSU was definitively over.

Despite the dashing of emancipatory longings among wide segments of the East German intelligentsia that resulted, however, at least certain elements of that stratum remained optimistic about the socialist project in the GDR. Indeed, significant segments among the producers of culture joined with the party in calling for a redoubled emphasis on a "socialist realist" aesthetic. In particular, writers, artists, and other cultural producers were to take more seriously the everyday experiences of the traditionally dispossessed, especially their experiences on the job. This trend in East German cultural life received its most important expression at the so-called Bitterfeld conferences organized by the SED beginning in the spring of 1959. The first of these meetings — which sought to promote the emergence of "worker-writers" as well as to discipline the professional authors — was held under the motto "Grab the Pen, Mate!" In his speech to the assembled in April 1959, party leader Walter Ulbricht emphasized the conference's importance for "the further development of socialist national literature,"[35] a theme that continued to grow in importance as the party's legitimacy among the East German population remained uncertain. Nearly ten years later, Ulbricht would emphasize in a speech to the Central Committee that "the essence of the Bitterfeld conference [had been] the development of socialist national culture."[36]

Probably the most successful literary product of this period, termed the "Bitterfeld Way," was Christa Wolf's *Der geteilte Himmel* (The divided heaven, 1963). Wolf was a committed socialist in consequence of her revulsion at the experience of German fascism, which had actually come to an end by the time she was only sixteen. The novel deals with a young woman who, after an affair in West Berlin with an émigré East German who has left the GDR out of disillusionment, returns to the East intent upon contributing to socialist development. Consistent with the party's urging that writers not lose contact with the lives of ordinary workers, Wolf had taken up contacts with the railway-car factory in Halle, and this interaction influenced the novel considerably. The book won for its author the GDR's Heinrich Heine Prize for Literature in 1963. In the same year, Wolf was elected a candidate member of the SED's Central Committee (see Childs 1988, 211–12).

Two years previously, of course, the German heavens had been definitively divided by the construction of the Berlin Wall on 13 August 1961. Justified by the party leadership as an "antifascist protective wall," the fortification had been deemed necessary by the SED elite as the only way to stem a resurgent outflow of the East German citizenry in the late 1950s and early 1960s. In part, the population was responding to the renewed intensification of political and economic pressures, not the least of them being a stepped-up drive to collectivize agriculture (see H. Weber 1985, 314–18). To many people, the construction of the wall seemed to prove, if proof was still necessary, the inhumanity of the SED regime and its inability to bind its citizens to the socialist project voluntarily. The political elite's desperate attempt to stabilize the country's economy by halting the exodus of many of the GDR's most productive citizens was justified as an essential condition for pursuing the socialist project without outside interference.[37]

Many of the "core" intellectuals shared the party's belief that the country could settle down to solving its serious problems once that of emigration was taken care of. These intellectuals took for granted that the process of building socialism would entail sacrifice and hardship and thus generally looked askance at the decision to leave the GDR for the West. Of course, the construction of the wall provoked a variety of responses among East Germany's remaining intellectuals, ranging from reluctant acceptance of the rigors imposed upon the socialist project by the capitalist class enemy to enthusiastic endorsement of the party's solution to the emigration problem. One might expect that intellectuals would view the fortification of the border as an obvious threat to their freedoms and that they would reject the wall as such. But this was hardly the case. Christa Wolf responded positively to the wall as the basis for getting on with the development of a socialist society freed of the problem of the constant drain of its citizens to the West.[38] This response may seem unsurprising from someone such as Wolf, who felt deeply committed to the GDR's antifascist anticapitalism. Yet later dissident activist Bärbel Bohley, only a teenager at the time, by and large shared this view of the wall when it was first built.[39] Manfred Lötsch, a sociologist at the SED's Academy of Social Sciences, suggested that this view was, in fact, widespread among the intelligentsia in 1961.[40]

Those intellectuals who supported the wall's construction assumed that, once relieved of the pressures generated by the immediate proximity of the capitalist West, the SED would grow more "self-confident and tolerant in its dealings with its citizens."[41] Interestingly, the intellectuals thus anticipated the main outlines of the Social Democrat–inspired *Ostpolitik* (eastern policy) of the late 1960s, which sought to achieve improvements in the everyday lives of the East German citizenry by seeking to persuade the beleaguered party elite that it was not under constant siege from the other German state. Yet for the advocates of *Ostpolitik,* the policy was a response to the growing stability of the East German regime that had been achieved as a result of the wall's construction, not a matter of supporting or rejecting the decision to build the Cold War's most poignant and palpable symbol.

Despite an initial period of heightened repression and restriction of domestic freedoms in the aftermath of the border closing, a relative relaxation began in the party's attitudes toward cultural affairs. Perhaps more important, the SED soon thereafter initiated an era of reformist experimentation in economic matters. Among the broader East German population, a certain resignation and even limited acceptance of the socialist order seem to have been the result of the dramatic caesura of 1961, if only because the earlier availability of the "exit" option had now been eliminated by the wall (see Staritz 1985, 151).

Experimentation behind the Berlin Wall

Economic reform in the GDR found expression in the New Economic System of Planning and Management (Neues Ökonomisches System der Planung und Leitung, or NÖSPL) announced in mid-1963. The New Economic System was, like its counterparts elsewhere in Eastern Europe, primarily an attempt to decentralize control of the economy and to restore the sundered relationship between prices and costs of production. The SED also sought to enhance work motivation and performance by instituting a system of wage incentives for workers.[42] In keeping with the drive for heightened production, the regime also undertook to revise the priorities among the criteria used to select the future members of the socialist intelligentsia: the earlier emphasis on social origins receded into the background, while achievement moved to the fore. The status of the technical intelligentsia, at least, was notably enhanced by the increasing importance accorded to science as a force of production (see Geißler 1983, 762–64). The intelligentsia's star seemed to be very much on the rise in the GDR.

Adoption of these ideas by the East German leadership amounted to a belated tribute to the revisionist economists whose ideas the party had scorned during the hothouse days of 1956–57. Grouped around such figures as Fritz Behrens, Arne Benary, and Günther Kohlmey and based in the GDR's premier economic research institutes, the revisionists had generally escaped severe punishment during the reprisals against reformers in the GDR following the crushing of the Hungarian revolution. When the Soviet Union took up plans for economic reform based on the proposals of Yevsei Liberman, the ideas of the East German revisionists were "silently rehabilitated," as one observer put it. These modifications to socialist planning, in turn, would later help to stimulate the calls for decentralizing reforms during the Prague Spring.[43]

In the cultural sphere, the reform movement in the Czechoslovak Socialist Republic (CSSR) was preceded by the now-familiar zigzagging policy toward intellectuals adopted by the East German party apparatus. The Kafka conference in Liblice, Czechoslovakia, in 1963, organized by Prague's Academy of Arts, the Writers' Union, and the Charles University, brought together Marxists and literary scholars from both Eastern and Western Europe. Although Communist critics had for years vilified Kafka's nightmarish vision of the modern world as a product of "bourgeois decadence," its relevance to socialist society now occupied a central place in the discussion. After the authorities had refused to allow critic Hans Mayer to participate in the gathering, the East German participants were prominent among those who sought to prop up the prevailing party wisdom that such alienation was peculiar to capitalist societies. But the stakes here were much greater than the interpretation of Kafka's literary legacy. Ultimately, the debate over Kafka amounted to the "metaphorical cloak for a political struggle against dogmatism" (Jäger 1982, 109). Very much aware of the political significance of the discussion surrounding the interpretation of Kafka's works, the SED's Politburo reported to the Central Committee's fifth plenum in February 1964 that it would not silently accept the "theory of the 'new springtime of culture, of mind, of thought, of searching' " that had arisen in the wake of the Kafka conference. In a striking anticipation of later developments, the report continued, "We are extremely mistrustful of people who represent a 'new' Marxism."[44] The East German Politburo might very well have used these same words four years later in response to developments in Prague, where reformist intellectuals captured control of the Communist Party and embarked upon a potentially far-reaching exploration of the limits of Soviet-style socialism's reformability.

One indication of the party elite's seriousness regarding its monopoly on determining the one and true Marxism was its recent treatment of the old Communist professor of physics Robert Havemann. After Havemann delivered a series of lectures concerning the "natural scientific aspects of philosophical problems" during 1963, the same fifth plenum of the Central Committee sharply attacked his heterodox socialist views. Soon thereafter, Havemann was thrown out of the SED, dismissed from his position on the Humboldt University faculty, and fired as director of the Institute for Physical Chemistry. For a time, however, he was permitted to retain his job with the Academy of Sciences. Yet after the publication of an article in the West German newsweekly *Der Spiegel* calling for the creation of a new Communist Party in the Federal Republic, Havemann finally had to go. Despite the failure of a resolution at the Academy of Sciences demanding his ouster from its ranks, that body's presidium soon found a way to expel him, presumably on orders from above (Havemann 1978, 16–22). This by no means kept Havemann from acting the part of the "Nestor" of the critical socialist intelligentsia in East Germany, however. Havemann's views on developments in Prague in 1968 were symptomatic of the reaction of many of the GDR's intellectuals during that dramatic episode in the saga of Soviet-style socialism.

Yet before that upwelling of reform sentiment, a new frostiness developed in relations between the GDR's cultural producers and its political leaders. Delegated to render the report of the Politburo to a meeting of the Central Committee in 1965, Free German Youth (FDJ) chief and later party leader Erich Honecker vigorously attacked a variety of recent cultural developments in the GDR, specifically including works by singer-songwriter Wolf Biermann and novelist Stefan Heym. Honecker began his diatribe by asserting that "our GDR is a clean state" and went on to insist that there was no place there for a "life-denying, petit-bourgeois skepticism" among the producers of culture. The future SED leader then proceeded to play off the workers against the intelligentsia in remarkable fashion. He accused Stefan Heym, for example, of maintaining that it is "not the workers, but rather the writers and scholars alone who are called to lead the new society." Honecker saved his most vicious attacks for Biermann, however. The critical young singer's "cynical verses," he claimed, amounted to treason against "the state that made it possible for him to receive an excellent education." Because all paternalistic institutions seek to undermine criticism in this facile manner, Biermann could probably have lived with this charge. Yet Honecker went on to assert that Biermann's lyrics also constituted a denigration of "the life and death of his father, who died at the hands of the fascists."[45] To be sure, Honecker — who spent a decade in a Nazi prison for his antifascist resistance activities — was on firmer ground with such a remark than his comrades in the SED leadership who had spent the years of the Third Reich in Moscow. But the attempt to co-opt criticism by reference to the antifascist legacy was surely out of step with the heritage of those who had paid dearly for their opposition to Nazism. Nor are such remarks likely to have reassured those distressed by the contradiction between the GDR's putative antifascist commitments and its de facto support of anti-Zionism and the Palestinian cause. The mood of cultural narrow-mindedness suggested by these official comments prevailed, with occasional breaks, until the flowering of the Prague Spring in 1968.

The East German Intellectuals and the Prague Spring

The Czechoslovak reform movement of 1968 generated considerable enthusiasm among East Germany's intellectuals. Robert Havemann's response to the developments in Czechoslovakia in 1968 are representative of those of a great many East German producers of culture during those heady days. In a May 1968 article that appeared in the prestigious West German weekly *Die Zeit,* Havemann noted the "warm sympathy and great hopes" with which socialists and Communists around the world were following political developments in Prague at that time. These developments were of worldwide significance, he argued, because

> here, for the first time, the attempt is being undertaken to recon-
> cile socialism and democracy. To be sure, there have been various
> efforts in the socialist countries to explode the vicious circle of Stal-
> inism with a sort of creeping democratization. But the lead-weight
> of the party bureaucracy has always paralyzed the few hopeful be-
> ginnings and brought them to a standstill.... Should this attempt
> go well, the success will be of a historical significance comparable
> only to that of the Russian October Revolution.[46]

In contrast even to the initially tolerant Soviet leaders (see Roth-schild 1989, 170), the SED leadership expressed its disapproval of the trend of events in Prague early on. As the Warsaw Pact allies began to conclude that things in Czechoslovakia were getting out of hand, however, the East German party leaders joined with those of the Soviet Union, Poland, Hungary, and Bulgaria to condemn developments in Prague in a mid-July "joint letter" addressed to the Central Committee of the Czech Communist Party.[47]

Yet the SED leaders' distress over the Prague Spring by no means squelched the sympathetic response among wide segments of East Germany's intelligentsia to the Czechoslovak reform experiment. Wolf Biermann penned a song in 1968 entitled "In Prag ist Pariser Kommune" (The Paris Commune is in Prague), in which he celebrates the assistance of "Marx himself and Lenin and Rosa and Trotsky" in the unfolding process of the revolution "liberating itself." Robert Havemann recalled later that the song was mimeographed and passed out as a flyer by protesting East German youths after the August invasion of Czechoslovakia by Warsaw Pact forces.[48]

The younger East German intelligentsia, in particular, enthusiastically embraced the model advanced by reform intellectuals of a "multiparty parliamentary state with socialist objectives." In April 1968, handbills demanding liberalization and democratization were reported to have been found at the Weimar School of Architecture (Burens 1981, 70). Little attention appears to have been paid, however, to the ambiguities between the model advanced by reform intellectuals and the Czechoslovak party leaders' vision of a "constitutional one-party order" (Burens 1981, 34). Indeed, Robert Havemann explicitly recognized that the Czechoslovak undertaking was a "revolution from above," but this by no means diminished his celebration of the reformers' cause.

Striking a note less prominent among the GDR's younger reform enthusiasts, Havemann's optimism concerning the Prague Spring went beyond support for democratization to include what he hoped would be the reform movement's positive contribution to a "democratic and socialist solution to the German question." He believed that such a solution would be "almost unimaginably facilitated if the path now being taken by the CSSR were to be trod here [in the GDR] as well" (Havemann 1990, 154), for it was, in Havemann's view, precisely the Stalinist deformations of socialism that made it so unattractive to its potential supporters in the West. Havemann belonged to that generation of East Germans that still had a living memory of a united but prefascist Germany and for whom the German question remained a vital element of their thinking in the larger political calculus of opposition to the SED regime.

As the GDR approached the twentieth anniversary of its founding in 1949, however, this cohort was beginning to give way to a population that no longer shared the *lived* experience of fascism that had done so much to undergird the legitimacy of the "socialist state on German soil." The younger intellectuals may have been raised to espouse the socialist ideals for which the GDR stood, and especially those from more humble social backgrounds would have had good reason to be loyal to their government. But the fact that at least some of the GDR's leaders had paid a heavy price for their contribution to the antifascist struggle had begun to count for less around this time, even if meritorious service to that cause never entirely lost its veneer of near-martyrdom. For this younger segment of the East German intelligentsia, the reform experiment in Czechoslovakia would be judged largely in terms of the degree to which it realized the high standards of democracy articulated in socialist ideology itself.

This was true, for example, of Jürgen Fuchs, a young writer and psychologist. Fuchs was a young man of seventeen with a self-described "antimilitarist and antifascist" attitude — developed in part, he told me, through his reading of such pacifist works as Wolfgang Borchert's *Draußen vor der Tür* (Outside the door) and those of other German and Russian antiwar writers — when Warsaw Pact tanks swept into Prague to crush the Czechoslovak reform movement. He recounted that Soviet and allied troops (including those of East Germany's Nationale Volksarmee) marched directly through his part of the country near the Czech and West German borders on their way toward the CSSR. This was for him a crucial experience in terms of his judgment of the GDR. Up till then, he had thought, "OK, the GDR might not be as democratic as the West, but at least the socialist countries did not go around invading other countries."[49] This belief was shattered by his experience of the Soviet bloc armies' invasion of Czechoslovakia to ice the Prague Spring.

Analysts have traditionally agreed that the East German army joined with forces from the Soviet Union, Poland, Bulgaria, and Hungary in squelching the Czechoslovak reform movement (see Burens 1981, 34). Indeed, the SED's official statement informing the GDR population of the military invasion names these five "fraternal socialist states" as those responding to the Czechoslovak Communist Party's request for assistance in responding to what they said had become an "acute political crisis."[50] Yet the participation of the GDR's armed forces in the Warsaw Pact action has been called into question by a number of high-ranking SED officials. One of them, Werner Eberlein, then the SED's chief Russian interpreter, was present at all discussions of these matters among the Soviet bloc's leaders; another, Wolfgang Herger, had been highly placed in the party's security apparatus. In my interviews with each of these party functionaries, they volunteered the information that the leaders of the Warsaw Pact's Communist parties had concluded that East German participation in the invasion would be unwise. Despite the alliance's desire to present a united front in opposing the Czechoslovak reforms, it was decided at the highest levels that it would be politically unacceptable to risk reawakening the memory of the Nazi occupation of Czechoslovakia in 1938.[51]

Whether the GDR's armed forces took part in the invasion or not, that action caused profound disillusionment among many East German intellectuals who had followed hopefully the developments in Prague. Indeed, recalled Günter Lehmann, a professor of cultural sciences at the Karl Marx University in Leipzig:

> All intellectuals strongly sympathized with the movement in the CSSR, because they were trying to create a socialism like the one that we envisioned in our ideals.... When the Prague Spring was crushed, that had a really enduring impact.... A gap opened up between our image of socialism and its empirical reality. The Czech events led to a certain reflectiveness.[52]

Yet however great a blow the invasion may have been to most, it did not necessarily shake the East German intellectuals' *fundamental* conviction that a "socialism with a human face" was possible. Moreover, political developments in Prague were not alone among the developments that captured the attention of critical intellectual circles in 1968. Helmut Warmbier, then a professor of Marxism-Leninism in Leipzig, recalled that the regime insisted in that same year on demolishing the city's old University Church "as a demonstrative act of power against the Church." The event provoked citizen protests against the government's construction plans, events that are said to be known to this day as the "Leipzig Rebellion." Moreover, the "student revolution against state monopoly capitalism" in the West attracted considerable notice as well. These movements, part of a wave of anticapitalist sentiment sweeping the industrialized world at the time, helped sustain the notion that socialism remained a viable and desirable alternative to Western capitalism. Yet the disenchantment with Soviet-style socialism deepened among many intellectuals with socialist commitments after the suppression of the reformist undertaking in Prague. "We did not see our alternative in the West at all," according to Warmbier. "We saw it here, in Prague. And then they marched in with the tanks. The distance from the party leadership grew increasingly greater."[53] Indeed, at least one prominent East German writer, Reiner Kunze, turned in his party card in response to the invasion; his next volume of poetry after that time bore the inscription, "To the Czech people, to the Slovakian people" (see Burens 1981, 70–71). In an indication of the remarkable staying power of the Czechoslovak experiment for East Germany's dissident intellectuals, nearly twenty years later an underground journal devoted to issues of peace and human rights ran a serial history of the Prague Spring. Because the series addressed a relatively younger audience, it is likely that some of its readers would have been unfamiliar with the events. As the series suggested, the ideas of the Prague Spring remained important touchstones for those small circles of intellectuals actively engaged in dissident politics.[54]

While disappointment over the Warsaw Pact invasion may have been widespread among the GDR's socialist intelligentsia, open protests remained confined among relatively small groups, especially of youths. In Eisenach, where the East German "Wartburg" automobile was manufactured, some three thousand to four thousand young people demonstrated for approximately two and one-half hours against the military intervention. Workers and soldiers indicated their lack of enthusiasm for the action in a variety of ways. Some one thousand signatures were gathered for a statement of solidarity with the Czechoslovak people at the CSSR embassy in East Berlin — and this despite the presence of East Germany security personnel. The church called for the withdrawal of all invading troops. There was also some evidence that SED members and functionaries were unhappy with the intervention (Burens 1981, 72–74). Flyers believed to have been written by students at the Humboldt University in East Berlin read: "Citizens! Comrades! Foreign tanks in the CSSR serve only the class enemy. Reflect on socialism's reputation in the world. Demand truthful information. No one is so stupid he can't think for himself."[55] Despite these indications of popular disapproval, such opposition appears to have been isolated and ineffectual.

For the critical intelligentsia in the GDR as well as that in the CSSR, the Prague Spring was destined to go down as a watershed defeat for the cause of a more humane socialism. Yet unlike the period of "normalization" in Czechoslovakia, the suppression of the intelligentsia's emancipatory strivings did not lead among the more prominent to the abandonment of the socialist ideal. To the contrary, the setback in some ways led to a redoubling of efforts to build a more attractive and democratic model of socialism.

After the Deluge: Repression, Liberalization, Reaction

For the GDR's critical socialist intelligentsia, the most important political development arising out of the bloody end to the Czechoslovak experiment was the formation of underground discussion circles. These circles of students and intellectuals, which were most likely to be found in East German university towns such as Berlin, Halle, Leipzig, Jena, and Dresden, focused on the discussion of the GDR's

Stalinist past. Eventually, however, some of them sought to go beyond mere discussion and became the breeding ground for Trotskyist, Maoist, or anarchist groups. Others took their activities into the "houses of culture" *(Häuser der Kultur)*, officially sponsored institutions that served surreptitiously as vehicles for carrying private political discussions to a somewhat larger audience. The first of these was the "Worker and Student Club of Berlin." Less obvious were the attempts of the underground circles to influence existing state-permitted student organizations. All of these activities served as the basis for the development of a nascent counterpublic sphere in the GDR concerned with the search for an "antiauthoritarian socialism that, in the spirit of individual and social emancipation, strives for human independence and self-governance." These small groups became the organizational foundations for a new "cultural opposition" that would last until the 1976 expatriation of Wolf Biermann inaugurated a new "ice age" (Jordan n.d., 2–5) in cultural politics (see below). This cultural opposition consisted almost exclusively of leftist dissidents concerned with the reform and renewal of socialism. Indeed, even the author of these lines, anti-Stalinist and ecological activist Carlo Jordan, told me in an interview that the participants would generally have shunned the characterization "imposed upon them by the Western media" of having been an "antisystem opposition."[56]

The new "cultural opposition" in the GDR initially received impetus from the replacement of aging party leader Walter Ulbricht by Erich Honecker in mid-1971. To be sure, Honecker quickly proclaimed an end to Ulbricht's utopian visions of a "socialist community of man" *(sozialistische Menschengemeinschaft)*. In place of the hopeful transformation of human nature envisaged during the early years of socialist development, a chastened "really existing socialism" would seek to raise the standard of living of the East German citizenry in exchange for their loyalty — or at least their passivity — toward the socialist system and its principal force, the SED. As in other socialist countries of the East bloc during this period, the attempt was simply to buy off political quiescence.[57] In Honecker's GDR, this new approach to securing legitimacy was embodied in the notion of "the unity of economic and social policy" — the notion that heightened production would redound to the benefit of consumers rather than contributing to the development of heavy industrial capacity.

Despite Honecker's tendency to retreat from the vision of a utopian order, liberal hopes in the cultural realm were nourished by the new party chief's remarks closing the fourth plenum of the SED's Central Committee in December 1971: "If one proceeds from a firmly socialist position, there can, in my opinion, be no taboos in the sphere of art and literature."[58] Upon hearing these encouraging words, many intellectuals believed that a renewed thaw was underway after the cold spell that had set in with the crushing of the Prague Spring by Warsaw Pact forces. Around this time, a marked tendency developed to retreat to a "new subjectivity" and to avoid direct engagement with social or socialist themes, giving expression instead to a diffuse disenchantment with "really existing socialism." The signal event in this emerging trend was the publication, shortly after Honecker's "no taboos" speech in late 1971, of Ulrich Plenzdorf's novel *Die neuen Leiden des jungen W.* (The new sorrows of Young W.), an appropriation of Goethe's romantic classic *The Sorrows of Young Werther* for decidedly unromantic purposes.[59] The brief window of cultural opportunity that was thought to have been opened by Honecker's remarks would be closed soon enough, however.

The Biermann Affair

Particularly in the case of singer-songwriter Wolf Biermann, however, seasoned observers of East German affairs would have had good reason to doubt Honecker's apparent transformation into a magnanimous patron of cultural experimentation. The son of Communist parents from Hamburg, Biermann had moved to the GDR in early 1953 at the age of seventeen. His father died in Auschwitz in 1943 when he was a young boy, but Biermann himself had had no mature experience of Nazism. Still, though his devotion to the "socialist state on German soil" had a great deal to do with his Jewish and Communist family background, his commitment to the GDR was clearly influenced substantially by its antifascist legitimation.[60] Yet after the infamous eleventh plenum of the Central Committee in 1965 — which Biermann later described as "the cultural plenum against culture"[61] — he was denied the right to work *(Berufsverbot)* and refused further permission to appear or publish in the GDR. These restrictions did not necessarily prevent him from publishing in the West, however, which he continued to do until he suddenly and unexpectedly became a resident of the Federal Republic against his will. When the party agreed, in 1976, to allow Biermann to make a series of concert appearances in Cologne, West Germany, under the sponsorship of the West German metalworkers union, political sympathizers and friends fretted about whether he should go, whether the risk of his being denied permission to return was not too great. Biermann's decision to accept the invitation resulted in the most spectacular instance of the SED's political manipulation of the intra-German border in the history of postwar divided Germany.

The SED leaders' decision to strip Biermann of his East German citizenship and to bar him from reentering the GDR — punishment, according to *Neues Deutschland,* for his "gross violation of civic duty"[62] — caused popular reaction of considerable proportions. Protest rallies and petition drives were reported among factory workers and students in East Berlin and Jena, as well as in West Germany. The very same day that Biermann's expatriation was reported in the East German press, a dozen of the GDR's most prominent cultural figures signed a statement protesting the measure. Within days, approximately one hundred others had followed their example in endorsing the document. Unable to find an East German outlet for the statement, the leaders of the group released it to the West German media almost immediately after the news of Biermann's fate appeared. The well-known West German literary critic Marcel Reich-Ranicki wrote that the SED's "stupid" move had created for the party a situation that is "as embarrassing as it is risky: a solidaristic front among the writers."[63] The Biermann affair, one interviewee told me, "was especially decisive for the artistic intelligentsia as a whole."[64] The fallout from the affair was, indeed, profound: the case led to waves of protest and disillusionment, on the one hand, and of departures among the GDR's artistic community, on the other.

The statement issued by the East German cultural elite on the occasion of Biermann's expulsion sheds considerable light on the dilemma of a leftist opposition in the socialist quarter of divided Germany in the mid-1970s. It begins by noting approvingly that, like the best artists everywhere, "Wolf Biermann was and is an uncomfortable poet." The limitations imposed by the GDR's unique national situation on criticisms of the East German regime by those supportive of "socialism" become obvious, however, when the petitioners continue by adding, "We do not identify with every word and every deed of Biermann's and we wish to distance ourselves from attempts to misuse the events surrounding the Biermann case to make the

GDR look bad. *Biermann himself never left any doubt — not even in Cologne — about which of the two German states he supports despite all criticism.*"[65]

In a similar vein, Robert Havemann appealed directly to Erich Honecker to reverse the decision, insisting that "for Wolf Biermann, the GDR is the better German state, the great hope for socialism in all Germany, precisely because capitalist ownership has been abolished here." Writing from the West several years after his own reluctant departure from the GDR, however, Havemann's old friend Heinz Brandt rejected Havemann's and Biermann's naive view of the GDR as the "better German state." "Wolf Biermann errs if he sees in the GDR 'the better German state,'" Brandt wrote. "We radical democrats, we libertarian socialists in the Federal Republic have one decisive advantage over those in the GDR: democratic freedoms. Here they are to be protected; there, they must first be achieved. The struggle for economic liberation requires the precondition of political liberation from bureaucratic despotism."[66] Brandt could scarcely have identified more clearly the essential weakness in the fundamental belief that drove so many of the GDR's sympathetic socialist intellectuals: the notion that the GDR had to be the "better German state" simply in consequence of its having abolished (most) private ownership of the means of production, irrespective of the utter lack of "bourgeois" freedoms routinely guaranteed in nonsocialist democracies. The failure to grasp this point, rooted in the antifascist anticapitalism that had originally given birth to the GDR, was the most important ideological factor delaying the emergence in East Germany of a truly oppositional movement for "bourgeois" civil rights comparable to Czechoslovakia's Charter 77 and similar organizations in the other Soviet bloc countries.[67]

In addition, however, the Biermann affair provoked a renewed preoccupation with the choice that contributed significantly to inhibiting the emergence of a strong opposition movement: namely, whether to stay in the GDR or to emigrate. Perceiving correctly that relations between the regime and the intelligentsia had sunk to a low point, large numbers of cultural figures applied to emigrate, and the authorities dealt with those applications on the whole both expeditiously and affirmatively.[68] Of those who preferred to stay and fight it out with the regime, several were later expelled from the Writers' Union in a rigged proceeding in Berlin in the summer of 1979. Most prominent among them was the longtime sympathetic critic of socialism, novelist Stefan Heym. The proximate cause of the punishment meted out to the others, several of whom had signed the petition criticizing the Biermann expatriation, was their protest against a decision to punish Heym for publishing his recent novel *Collin* in the West without the permission of the GDR's censors.

At the same time, the regime sought to send a message to its less docile writers and their sympathizers by adding "treasonous slander" *(staatsfeindliche Hetze)* and "public defamation" *(öffentliche Herabwürdigung)* to the index of actionable offenses. In addition, the paragraph concerning "illegal contacts" was expanded to include the criminalization of anyone "who, in contravention of legal codes, transmits or allows to be transmitted to organizations, institutions, or persons abroad any writings, manuscripts, or other material that may damage the interests of the GDR."[69] Clearly, the East German regime was intent on closing off access to the ersatz public sphere of the Federal Republic, which had come to play such a vital role in disseminating the views of dissident intellectuals in the GDR.

Indeed, during the intense debate over the Biermann case in the GDR, the failure to keep the discussion a purely GDR domestic affair would prove one of the most serious grounds for criticism of the document's signers by the party and its minions in the cultural apparatuses. This element of the protest against Biermann's expatriation played a central role, for instance, in the official censure meted out by the party organization of the Berlin chapter of the Writers' Union to nine of its members for their public opposition to the SED's action. The party loyalists condemned the protest's signers for "turning to imperialist news organizations and thus objectively serving the anti-Communist slander of our opponents."[70] Indeed, only a week after helping to initiate the protest statement, playwright and Brecht-epigone Volker Braun concluded that "Western commentators" were misusing the statement with the aim of "driving a wedge between us and our party." Braun went on to "decisively reject these efforts."[71]

Braun's behavior in this situation says much about the degree to which some of East Germany's most respected cultural figures agreed with the party elite on the defense of the "socialist" GDR against attacks by the "capitalist" West, even when they believed the government deserved criticism for sullying socialism's good name. These intellectuals appear to have believed that, just as the Berlin Wall might "solve" the problem of unwanted emigration, strict avoidance of the "capitalist" Western media would ensure that these controversies would remain squabbles all in the socialist family. Needless to say, this was a rather naive view of the nature of modern communications media; only a dozen years later, during the Tienanmen Square demonstrations, Chinese opponents of the Communist Party faxed their statements to Western media organizations to ensure their dissemination *in China*. It was, in all events, a curiously truncated view of intellectual liberty, a political freedom the untrammeled achievement of which is routinely assumed to be at the top of intellectuals' wish lists. This situationally created impulse toward "mental isolation" from the West always helped lend a certain provincialism to the activities of East Germany's intellectuals and contributed to their anomalousness among the Communist countries of the Soviet bloc.

At the same time, the circumvention of East German censorship via the ersatz public sphere of the Federal Republic had grown increasingly vital as a means for intellectual dissidents to convey their views to both the party leadership and the population of the GDR. The attempt to exploit a Western media market characterized by a panoply of political orientations was not without risks for the GDR's left-wing dissidents, however, as they well understood. Specifically, the dissidents' would-be sympathetic socialist criticism of the GDR might well be — and, indeed, was — put to political uses more conservative than those its authors had intended.

Yet there is an intrinsic contradiction involved in condemning wholesale a political order that affords the legal guarantees necessary to effect changes in one's own system. Committed to a "socialist" order that was said to exist at once de facto and only embryonically, East Germany's critical intellectuals had difficulty recognizing or accepting that theirs was not an order that granted its citizens greater civil rights and freedoms than the "capitalist" Federal Republic.

The Resurgent Problem of "Exit" versus "Voice"

The expatriation of Wolf Biermann raised another issue of critical significance to the reform hopes of East German intellectuals: namely, their attitude toward those who left the country, for whatever reason. In Biermann's case, to be sure, the matter is clear: he had no choice about staying or leaving and would have preferred to stay where he was. But the authorities apparently deemed his continued presence politically unacceptable and were thus merely exporting a troublemaker. (Less prominent troublemakers generally suffered more, frequently being shipped off to jail with little prospect of out-side help unless the Federal Republic bought them their freedom.) In those instances in which the departure had been voluntary, however, dissidents typically reacted less sympathetically. Indeed, three years before the Biermann affair, Robert Havemann had written that the disappointment that would be caused by his leaving made it impos-sible for him to go. But the disappointment was not the worst of it; "worse would be the fact that I would stimulate [sympathizers'] doubts about our righteous cause.... [Thus] it is really betrayal if one simply takes off from here in the absence of great distress."[72] However unintentional this convergence of views may have been, the overlap between Havemann's view of leaving the GDR as a kind of "betrayal" and the party's interest in retaining its population was noteworthy. Needless to say, Havemann's views regarding the deci-sion to leave the GDR were by no means universally shared among East Germans.

In the first half of the 1970s, the GDR had acceded to a num-ber of international protocols on human rights that had signaled crucial support for human rights activists throughout the East bloc, affording them an international legal basis for their claims to civil and political rights. Of particular importance in this context were the Universal Declaration of Human Rights and the Helsinki Final Act. The regime's violation of these agreements, still a common if un-predictable practice, would undermine the SED leadership's efforts to gain international respectability during the early years of West German chancellor Willy Brandt's recently initiated *Ostpolitik*. The GDR's acquiescence in these agreements thus came to constitute a sort of "soft underbelly" for a regime that, like its counterparts else-where in the Soviet sphere, routinely violated its citizens' human and civil rights. Whereas these agreements provided other East European dissidents with a basis for criticizing the human rights abuses of their governments in the broadest way, however, their impact in the GDR energized a specific challenge to the socialist order rooted in the peculiar geopolitical circumstances of a divided nation: would-be em-igrants saw in them a buttress to their efforts to gain "release from GDR citizenship" *(Entlassung aus der DDR-Staatsbürgerschaft)*. The SED regime's endorsement of these human rights accords made espe-cially awkward its systematic denial — or, more precisely, its arbitrary approval — of its citizens' freedom to live where they wished.

Exploiting the regime's vulnerability on this point, a number of organized groups of would-be emigrants *(Ausreisewillige* or *Ausreiser)* soon emerged. Such an initiative arose, for instance, in 1976 in the Saxon industrial city of Riesa, where thirty-three people submitted to the authorities a "Petition to Secure Full Human Rights" explicitly demanding the rights to freedom of domicile guaranteed in the Universal Declaration and the Helsinki Final Act.[73] Then, in the university town of Jena in 1983, another group of emigration applicants began silent vigils each Saturday over a period of some eight weeks, by which time the initial circle of thirty protesters had swollen to nearly two hundred. It is notable that these first organized efforts to obtain approval of applications for emigration took place in the East German provinces, far from the headier world of the intellectual dissidents headquartered in East Berlin. Not long after the vigils in Jena, however, a small group of would-be absconders from the GDR stole into the American embassy in East Berlin and released to the Western press a request, directed to President Ronald Reagan, for political asylum in the United States.[74] They thus made a trial run of the occupations of West German embassies in Prague, Budapest, and Warsaw that captured headlines throughout the world in the summer and early fall of 1989. The efforts of these would-be emigrants began to focus attention on the inability of the East German regime to afford its citizens the widely recognized human right of emigration without jeopardizing its precarious attempt to consolidate a socialist conception of nationhood. For those not preoccupied with the question whether the GDR was or could be reformed into a "truly" socialist order, the freedom to emigrate was often the alpha and omega of the human rights question in the GDR. Indeed, a late 1970s essay entitled "Human Rights in the SED State" — written, admittedly, by a West German observer — revolved *exclusively* around the matter of freedom of movement and of emigration (Bilke 1980).

Yet for many dissident intellectuals, the emigration issue represented an extremely thorny problem, one that contributed decisively to delaying the emergence of human rights issues as central to the agenda of dissident activity in the GDR. For those who had decided to stay and work for change in the GDR, emigration posed a profound — and profoundly human — dilemma. In an interview, Wolfgang Templin, a cofounder in early 1986 of the Initiative for Peace and Human Rights, the first group from the GDR's leftist dissident milieu to be devoted explicitly to human rights matters, described the powerful effect of the emigration issue on dissident politics as follows:

> One very direct or almost practical reason [that human rights issues emerged relatively late as a focus of activity among East German dissidents] was that the first human rights efforts ten years earlier had had to do with the most difficult issue, namely, that of emigration. After the first international and European agreements that the GDR also signed, that must have been around '76 or '77, there were several initiatives in the East German provinces, in various towns. I recall one in Riesa, a town in Saxony, where a letter became public in which twenty or thirty people came together and said, "We demand our right to freedom of movement." And that put everybody in the GDR with a critical or oppositional attitude in a difficult position psychologically.... The experiences that drove one to say, "I cannot or do not want to stay in this country any longer, I want out," that was one side. But somebody else who might have had just as many critical experiences, that led him to say, "I'm staying here in this country, but things have to change." So, once you've reached this alternative decision — it was hard enough to say, "I don't just want to complain, I don't want to just accept things as they are, I want to do something" — then someone else's decision, the decision of a friend, who had had just as many critical experiences, and then says, "There's no point in staying, you can't change anything here," that was very difficult.[75]

In assessing Templin's remarks, it is important to bear in mind that emigration — defined by the regime as "flight from the republic" and frowned upon accordingly — typically entailed permanent separation from friends and family.

Another reason why those committed to remaining and working for change in the GDR were at best weakly sympathetic to the emigration issue was that, once applicants for emigration had achieved their objective, they were as a rule lost for opposition activity. The truth of this proposition is perhaps most apparent in those exceptional cases where "troublemakers" were forced to leave the country against their will. After Biermann, the most prominent examples included such figures as Jürgen Fuchs, Roland Jahn, and Ralf Hirsch. Despite their unceremonious expulsion from the GDR, the latter two figures, in particular, were frequently mentioned in Stasi reports on opposition activities after their forcible expatriation in 1983 and 1988, respectively. Fuchs's mother-in-law appears to have been hounded into suicide by the Stasi, but this did not keep him from supporting dissident forces in the GDR after his unwilling departure.[76] But these were exceptions; the average emigrant was presumably preoccupied with the vagaries of starting a new life in the West and was in any case less likely to have had deep attachments to — or, depending on one's perspective, illusions about — reforming the socialist order in the GDR.

As Templin's remarks suggest, tensions between dissidents and emigrants went back a long way. Indeed, such frictions can be documented at least as far back as 1976. In the widely publicized case of the Dresden writer Siegmar Faust, for instance, the contradictory attitude toward human rights revealed in the dissidents' reluctance to support the right of emigration became manifest. After applying to leave the GDR in 1973, Faust was subjected to the usual harassment, loss of work, and eventually imprisonment. His case gave rise, in the provincial Saxon city of Pirna (near Dresden), to what is believed to have been the first citizens' initiative against the restrictions on emigration (see Fricke 1984, 163–64). This solidarity failed to produce the desired results, however.

In mid-March 1976, longtime regime critic Robert Havemann intervened personally with SED general secretary Erich Honecker on Faust's behalf. Reminding the SED leader of the hardships they both had endured during their imprisonment in a Brandenburg jail under the Nazis, Havemann pleaded for clemency for Faust, whom Havemann insisted was "one of those who criticize our conditions sharply precisely because they are passionate socialists." Faust was released from jail unexpectedly less than a week later and submitted another application to emigrate soon thereafter. In September, he and his family were finally granted their request and left for the Federal Republic. Writing about his experiences later, however, Faust claimed that Havemann and Wolf Biermann considered him "finished" when, after his period of incarceration had led him to a conclusive rejection of socialism, he renewed his efforts to leave the GDR.[77] Ironically, only weeks later Biermann would himself experience the profound ramifications of the regime's arbitrary control over the right to choose one's place of residence, and Havemann would be placed under house arrest for his involvement in the attendant protests.

The difficulty inherent in the position of those dissidents who were unsympathetic to the would-be emigrants (even if their reasons for this attitude were comprehensible enough), however, was that they came to echo the regime's arguments as to why it was wrong to leave the "socialist fatherland." The SED leadership had introduced the policy of "demarcation" *(Abgrenzung)* in the early 1970s as a defensive response to the opening toward West Germany entailed in the Basic Agreement *(Grundlagenvertrag)* between the Federal Republic and the GDR, the crowning achievement of *Ostpolitik*.[78] Egon Bahr, Brandt's deputy and the chief architect of the Social Democrats' "eastern policy," had characterized the West German approach as "change through getting closer" *(Wandel durch Annäherung)*. For all its potential economic and political advantages, however, the prospect of "getting closer" to the Federal Republic was a source of considerable unease for the East German leadership. "Getting closer" to West Germany always threatened to blur the distinction between the two German states — a distinction the Berlin Wall had been built to consolidate.

Of course, the motives of dissidents for opposing the emigration option were fundamentally different from those of the government. The regime was concerned most with the potential loss of labor power and with the general damage to its credibility (and, as the emigration of 1989 would demonstrate, to its very existence) were East Germans permitted to leave the country unobstructed. In contrast, those who opted to stay in the GDR and work for reforms — those who would "rather fight than switch," so to speak — were more concerned about the injurious impact of emigration on the vitality of opposition activity. These differences in underlying motives notwithstanding, however, the dissidents' commitment to "actively staying put" frequently issued in a rather condescending attitude toward would-be emigrants.

Dissidents typically insisted that "leaving doesn't change anything" or that those who "just wanted to leave" had been "seduced by the higher Western standard of living." Applicants for emigration were commonly dismissed as "apolitical," interested only in gaining the fruits of West German–style freedom and prosperity without submitting to the travails of reforming the government under which they lived. Nor were these criticisms entirely without foundation. Many — perhaps most — of the would-be emigrants lacked the passionate devotion to politics expected in the dissident milieu.[79] As later events would reveal, however, the dissidents erred in their evaluation of the political explosiveness of the emigration issue.

Moreover, the dissidents' *own* behavior tended to diverge from what they said about emigration matters. Helmut Warmbier, who sat out a two-year jail term in the mid-1970s, found that visions of the freedom and prosperity available in West Germany were not unfamiliar even to those who insisted they wished to stay to exercise the "voice" option. During his conversations with fellow political prisoners, Warmbier found that "initially they went on about their political motives. But after one had sat with them for a couple of weeks, one could notice that their talk was heavily saturated with the expectation of a decent life in consumer society. Vera Wollenberger [a dissident activist who later became a prominent figure in the East German Green Party] was offered the chance to go study in England [instead of serving a threatened lengthy jail sentence], and she accepted immediately, didn't she?"[80] This apparently hypocritical stance on the part of the dissident intellectuals would be cause for some of the skepticism toward them as opposition toward the SED regime spread during the 1980s.

The Stirrings of Intellectual Opposition during the Late 1970s

As the end of the decade approached, however, two episodes, in particular, helped fuel speculation about an apparent upsurge of opposition among East Germany's intellectuals. First, the publication of Rudolf Bahro's extensive critical analysis of "really existing socialism," *The Alternative,* sent shock waves through the left-wing intellectual scene in both East and West Germany. A relatively unknown figure until the spectacular interview on West German television and radio in which he promulgated the ideas outlined in the book, Bahro had broken with the party over the squelching of the 1968 reform experiment in Prague: "In the first hours and days after the intervention," he would later say, "something within me changed forever."[81] The publicity tactics with which the formerly unknown engineer sought to disseminate his ideas — in particular, his use of the Western media — helped ensure that Bahro would be punished harshly. Sentenced in June 1978 to eight years in prison, Bahro was released after only ten months in jail and allowed to go to the Federal Republic. Prominent intellectuals from around the globe had raised their voices in protest against Bahro's incarceration. Due primarily to Bahro's previous obscurity, however, solidarity actions remained relatively rare.[82] His book nonetheless became an important theoretical touchstone for many of East Germany's intellectual dissidents.

It is worth noting that, in view of its importance among certain circles of East Germany's critical intelligentsia, Bahro's alternative to "really existing socialism" in the East bloc did not necessarily entail the institutionalization of political pluralism. In an approach so typical of the contrast between the East German dissident movement and its East European neighbors, Bahro's proposed transformation of the system depended not so much on constitutional guarantees of political competition but rather on the creation of a "genuine" Communist Party, a new "League of Communists": "Whether this league will be formed as a new party alongside the old, or will take the shape of a renovated old party, we cannot prescribe to history."[83] The question of competition *among* parties, by contrast, does not play a prominent role in Bahro's considerations.

Shortly after the Bahro affair, hopes for the realization of Bahro's reform-Communist vision were stoked when the West German newsweekly *Der Spiegel* published a "manifesto" from a group calling itself the League of Democratic Communists of Germany (Bund demokratischer Kommunisten Deutschlands, or BDKD). Despite an inability to establish with certainty who stood behind the document, experts on East Germany such as Wolfgang Leonhard and Heinz Brandt concluded that it was genuine. The judgment that the manifesto was authentic stemmed in part from its rejuvenation of the traditional reform-Communist concern with a "German national road to socialism" and with the reunification of Germany, preferably on the basis of military neutrality.[84] In a situation reminiscent of Bahro's long refusal to make his views known in order to be able to complete work on his critical broadside, the authors of the manifesto were believed to be dissident SED functionaries unsure of their appeal outside their own ranks. Yet no one ever came forward to represent the BDKD publicly, nor was the group ever heard from again. Despite *Der Spiegel*'s insistence as late as 1991 that the "manifesto" was genuine, against this background it is difficult to reject the conclusion that the document was in fact a falsification.[85] Irrespective of the document's authenticity or of any significant social backing for the BDKD, the manifesto's vigorous attack on conditions in the GDR was nonetheless thought by expert commentators to reflect "a very broad mood of dissatisfaction in the population and in wide segments of the SED."[86]

Thus as the 1970s came to a close, the stirrings of a serious intellectual opposition had begun to be heard in East Germany. Yet the party had moved vigorously to keep such stirrings from taking any firm organized shape. Moreover, dissident forces themselves were constrained to a considerable degree by the complexities of the German question from developing into a truly fundamental opposition to the rule of the SED. Surprisingly, Bahro appears to have been quite unaware of the relevance to himself and his East German intellectual comrades-in-arms when he wrote critically of the "progressive Communist forces" in the East bloc because, "at bottom, they still stood on the same political and theoretical basis as their opponents, and could be ideologically blackmailed by them via their common interest in the noncapitalist road" (Bahro 1978, 311).

The persistent lack of attention to the achievement of political pluralism cannot be attributed to some genetic deficiency among German intellectuals. Rather, it derived mainly from the prior commitment of the GDR's dissident intellectuals to socialism, which they understood had dim prospects without the vehicle of the GDR. To embrace the institutions of parliamentary democracy was tantamount to a flirtation with the abandonment of the GDR and to absorption into the thriving Federal Republic. The vagaries of the GDR's geopolitical circumstances thus helped forestall a concern among the dissident community for the kinds of fundamental political changes being called for around this time by their counterparts in Poland and Czechoslovakia. Although the focus of intellectual dissent would shift during the 1980s, this basic problem continued to plague the GDR's intellectual critics as the new decade began.

Three

The Intelligentsia and the Development of Opposition in the GDR during the 1980s

By the 1980s, the older, established critical intelligentsia, for whom the antifascist component of the GDR's anticapitalist project was paramount, began to recede into the background of the East German dissident milieu. The death of Robert Havemann in April 1982 was perhaps the most important symbolic indication of this passage. To be sure, writers such as Stefan Heym and Christa Wolf sustained a vision of a more libertarian, "true" socialism, but they undertook no overt efforts to mount any broader opposition to the SED's dictatorial rule.[1] Although such figures were by no means uncritical of the East German status quo, they were constrained by their ideological commitments to the "socialist state on German soil" as well as by their curious position as both officially honored exemplars of socialist art and popularly revered tribunes of dissent. Meanwhile, although figures such as Harich, Biermann, and Bahro remained in the German-speaking world, their exile from the GDR diminished their impact there correspondingly. At the same time, as was noted earlier, a substantial number of critical younger authors, not persuaded that staying in East Germany was really worth the effort, had left the GDR in the aftermath of the Biermann affair.[2]

These developments left the East German intelligentsia rent by an important generational divide. On the one hand, there was a small group of high-profile older artists and intellectuals with deep sentimental ties to the antifascist socialist project in the GDR; on the other, a younger generation of less established intellectuals with no lived experience of or strong attachment to the notion of a "unified" Germany. This latter group thus developed different political preoccupations than its elders among the intelligentsia. In particular, these intellectuals grew increasingly preoccupied with the threat to Germans East and West caused by the post-Yalta division of Europe into antagonistic military blocs and with the putatively socialist GDR's failure to offer its citizens the fundamental rights guaranteed in "bourgeois" constitutions. One critic, reviewing a volume of stories by a group of younger authors in the early 1980s, addressed head-on the political implications of the new literary generation's experiences:

> Not merely are the war and fascism history for them, but the development of the GDR as well. *They have no direct experience of the complexity of the postwar years nor of the sharp conflict entailed in laying the foundations of socialism.* ... One must presume that this gives rise to many of the difficulties they have in understanding the dialectic in socialism.[3]

One may further presume that the author of these lines regarded the party as the exclusive interpreter of the "dialectic in socialism," and it was to precisely this hubris that growing numbers of younger intellectuals were to object in the coming years.

Before the new generation of dissident activists could focus attention on the lack of human rights in the GDR, however, it had to disentangle that theme from the overriding predominance of the peace issue — a concern with obvious power for a population on the very front line of the Cold War. One essential precondition for the shift of focus away from antimilitarist concerns and toward human rights was that East Germany's dissidents needed to step out of the long institutional shadow of the Lutheran Church. The church, to be sure, had come to play a crucial role as a "free space" within which dissidents could meet, discuss their concerns, and organize political activity. Yet the church's bargain with the East German state, and its historically rooted dogmatic tendency to place a higher priority on peace than on freedom, led it to favor antiwar activism over that concerned with challenges to the regime's violations of human rights. Tensions between dissident activists and church leaders thus became a persistent feature of dissident politics in the GDR as opposition to the party's policies grew more pronounced during the 1980s.

Ironically, the development of a more decisive opposition to the Communist government in East Germany received a powerful boost from a social movement in one of its neighboring Soviet bloc countries that frequently mobilized religious symbolism and personnel on its behalf: Poland's Solidarity trade union.

The Impact of the Polish Insurgency

The 1980s burst onto the East European scene with a series of events in Poland that would rivet international attention on that part of the world. The Polish workers' attempt to build an independent trade union struck at the heart of the party-state's claim to monopolistic control over political organization. In addition, however much it may have had the backing of prominent Warsaw-based intellectuals, "Solidarność" was demonstrably a working-class affair.[4] Solidarność upset the order of things in the Soviet bloc precisely by mounting a proletarian challenge to what was said by its power-holders to be working-class rule.

While critical East German intellectuals may have considered Solidarity's demands legitimate enough, the strongly working-class origins and character of the struggle may nonetheless have left the intelligentsia feeling somewhat at a loss as to how to respond to the insurgent trade union. Especially among those on the left, the intellectuals' relative social distance from the movement was surely compounded by Solidarność's religious overtones. Still, Wolf Biermann wrote scathingly from West German exile of the "high-minded reserve of so many leftist intellectuals," which "reveals itself at second glance as brutal intervention on the side of the counterrevolution" of Polish party leader General Wojciech Jaruzelski.[5] Though Biermann aimed his ire primarily at the left-wing intelligentsia in the Federal Republic, the disorientation caused by the emergence of a working-class movement that appropriated religious symbolism in its opposition to a socialist regime made for considerable bewilderment and skepticism among leftists in East Germany (and elsewhere as well).

Despite Solidarność's enormous potential for transforming the ossified political structures of the East bloc, the Polish workers' movement met with relatively little sympathy in the GDR. Perhaps most significant for understanding the reaction of the East German citizenry to the earthquake rumbling through Poland during the second half of 1980 was the SED's blatant exploitation of traditional German anti-Polish feeling. In describing the East Germans' reaction to Solidarność, one interviewee noted that "this rather difficult [German-Polish] relationship played an important role. People say the Poles don't know how to work.... The party succeeded in developing a social psychology that was anti-Polish."[6] Wittenberg pastor Friedrich Schorlemmer, who in the fall of 1989 would go on to help found the ill-fated citizens' initiative Democratic Awakening, raised the matter of the regime's exploitation of older *ressentiments* toward the Poles. This tactic had become especially apparent in the rejuvenation of "Polish jokes," some of which reminded listeners of the spread of such jokes under the Nazis.[7]

In addition, the economic consequences of the Polish strikes and disruptions were a matter of no small consequence to East Germans. For they were not wrong to think that the GDR would have borne the lion's share of the responsibility for keeping up the flow of goods that had become so essential to political stability in Poland (see Pravda 1982). The GDR already supplied its Polish neighbors with foodstuffs, clothing, small household appliances, and the like. Seeking to shake such enthusiasm as the East Germans had developed for the Polish workers, a September 1981 article in the official *Neues Deutschland* focused directly on these economic fears and on anti-Polish (and pro-German) stereotypes when it asserted:

> When citizens of the GDR hear time and again about strikes in Poland organized by "Solidarność," and about the decline of production, they begin to ask themselves whether the [economic] help for our neighbors is not being dumped into a bottomless pit. We in the GDR have achieved what we have through hard work. One can only consume what one has produced. No people can live without work.[8]

Clearly, the SED leaders' desire to maintain their grip on power superseded any reluctance about breaking with the canons of socialist internationalism and fanning the flames of national enmities.

Indeed, to a considerable extent, the SED led the charge of the Warsaw Pact allies in criticizing the inability of the Polish United Workers' Party (PUWP) to keep order in its own house and in advocating a hard line toward the illegal trade union (see Winters 1981b, 686–89). To be sure, the SED displayed considerable enthusiasm for crushing the Polish "counterrevolution" and the threat it represented to untrammeled party control over political life. Yet, in view of the

SED's special requirements for maintaining its dominance in a quarter of divided Germany, even more significant may have been the SED's attempt to transform developments in neighboring Poland into an "imperialist" conspiracy of "revanchist" elements in the Federal Republic. Before readers of the party daily had ever seen the names Lech Walesa or "Solidarity" in its pages, they had been informed about the "anti-Polish conspiracy of the FRG's Bundesnachrichtendienst [the West German version of the FBI] and the [conservative] Springer [publishing] firm" in tones reminiscent of those used at the time of the 1953 East German workers' rebellion.[9] One subtle indication of the way in which the SED perceived the renewed virulence of the "Polish disease" as a threat to its *national* existence could be found in the SED propagandists' rendering of a PUWP Central Committee appeal to the Polish populace in December 1980. Where the official version in *Neues Deutschland* spoke exclusively of the Polish *Volk* (people or nation), that of the West German Deutsche Presse Agentur consistently employed the term *Nation*.[10]

By no means confident that ideological salvos undercutting the Polish workers' cause would spare them the spread of the "Polish disease" to the GDR, however, East German authorities moved to curtail all unofficial contacts between Poles and citizens of the GDR. As of 30 October 1980, the regime essentially eliminated visa- and passport-free travel for East Germans traveling to or Poles traveling from Poland — a freedom that had existed since 1972. Henceforth, requests for such travel would have to be cleared by East German police officials, who approved such requests only grudgingly. Those lucky enough to travel between Poland and the GDR at the time, however, reported border controls more stringent even than those at the German-German frontier. East Germans at first responded positively to the travel restrictions, however, because they helped eliminate the Poles' widely decried habit of emptying East German shops of goods unavailable in Polish stores (see Winters 1981a, 1009, 1011; Winters 1983).

The SED could perhaps count on traditional anti-Polish sentiment to help immunize the East German citizenry against the Polish disease. Yet the GDR's established critical intellectuals, who railed against the nationalistic bias that had informed National Socialism, likewise demonstrated little open sympathy toward the Polish upheaval. Just as the Polish crisis was coming to a head, a conference of prominent intellectuals from both Germanys gathered at the invitation of East German author Stephan Hermlin to discuss their concerns about maintaining the peace in Europe. Dubbed the "Berlin Meeting for the Promotion of Peace," the gathering clearly had the approval of the SED and, indeed, had been sponsored by East Berlin's prestigious Academy of Arts. The meeting was part of a larger effort, provoked by the NATO "double-track decision" to station Pershing and Cruise missiles in the Federal Republic, to portray the Western allies as the principal threat to peace and the Soviet-led Warsaw Pact countries as its principal guarantor. The conclave followed directly on the heels of a "Peace Appeal of European Writers" signed by some 150 authors from either side of the Iron Curtain. The appeal had been initiated by the West German Communist historian and Writers' Union chairman, Bernt Engelmann, and by one of the SED's most enthusiastic devotees among East Germany's authors, Hermann Kant, who had been president of the East German Writers' Union since Anna Seghers's retirement in 1978.[11] Kant played a high-profile role at the conference as a defender of Soviet bloc military policy. For example, while Günter Grass insisted that the danger of nuclear war came from both sides, Kant, former atomic spy Klaus Fuchs, and Academy of Arts president Konrad Wolf (brother of the GDR's top spy, Markus Wolf) strenuously maintained that the intentions of the Soviet Union and its allies were peaceful.[12]

Yet the gathering was by no means entirely a propaganda success for the government. Author Jurek Becker, who had resigned from the Writers' Union and moved to West Berlin in the aftermath of the Biermann affair, wondered aloud why no peace demonstrations took place in the GDR. Answering his own question, Becker asserted quite simply that the reason was that such demonstrations were forbidden by the government. Moreover, Stefan Heym openly advocated that the assembled cultural figures join forces to promote independent, all-German peace initiatives. Indeed, insisting that he was serious, Heym proposed near the end of the symposium to lead a demonstration of the German-German participants on the fabled Alexanderplatz with SED leader Erich Honecker at the head, "because our government says it's for peace."[13]

As fate would have it, the two-day forum on questions of peace coincided with two dramatic events in the history of postwar Central Europe. First, Helmut Schmidt, in his first official trip to the GDR as chancellor of the Federal Republic, traveled to Lake Werbellin to discuss with General Secretary Honecker various improvements in "intra-German" relations and to press for a reversal of the Soviet bloc's decision to station new missiles on East German soil.[14] This important gesture toward détente was quickly upstaged, however, by developments elsewhere in the East bloc. For on the very day that the intellectuals' conclave began, the Polish authorities under General Jaruzelski declared martial law in an effort to squelch Solidarność.

Astonishingly, however, the Polish regime's repression of Solidarność's independent organizing activity had little impact on the recorded remarks, at least, of the assembled representatives of the all-German cultural elite. Indeed, on the second day of the conference, Stefan Heym was moved to comment:

> When I listen to our discussion here...I sometimes have the feeling that I'm dreaming.... We are talking here about the maintenance of peace in this nuclear weapon-filled region, and completely ignoring the fact that, a few kilometers away from us the fuse is already burning.... A world war has been started over Poland already once before.[15]

Heym had, indeed, put his finger on an eerie abstractness that pervaded the discussions at this meeting of prominent intellectuals from both sides of the intra-German border. A month later, Heym disseminated one of the very few public statements concerning Solidarność to be issued from the GDR's dissident intellectual community. This response to Polish developments, however, revealed none of the ambivalence toward the workers' aims that characterized Heym's response to the East German rebellion of June 1953: "What kind of socialism is it," the novelist asked, "in which the army and other security forces are deployed gun in hand against the working class?"[16]

The only other figure of international renown to raise the matter of the Polish workers' activity at the Berlin meeting had been notable West German author Günter Grass, who spoke more concretely of the "imperialistic implications" of Soviet domination in the East and specifically in Poland. Longtime SED cultural functionary Alexander Abusch immediately countered Grass's remarks by suggesting that the Polish leadership had moved to put down an organized attempt "violently to overthrow the legitimate government. How would any government behave?"[17] Abusch's response to the Polish upheaval suggests the degree to which well-regarded artistic figures felt committed to, or had been co-opted into, supporting the Communist regime. Perhaps even more indicative of many intellectuals' devotion to SED rule than the overt reaction enunciated by Abusch, however, was the near absence of the Polish martial law declaration from the meeting's public discussions. For, as sociological discussions concerning the concept of "power" have pointed out, a resounding silence about certain issues may have a more profound impact on the course of events than the decision to pursue one course over another (Giddens 1987, 8–9).

For the more politically engaged and less socially established East German dissident intellectuals, however, the regime's studied silence about and its virtual quarantine around Poland — both elements of a prophylactic strategy designed to prevent infection with the "Polish disease" — meant protection from an illness they dearly wanted the GDR to catch. Yet such enthusiasts were few. Certainly one of the most important figures among this group was Wolfgang Templin, a figure of particular interest for understanding the evolution of the East German intellectual dissident outlook and milieu. First, his personal background was only partially German. His mother, originally from a German area of Poland, had been expelled into what became the GDR after World War II. His father was a doctor and officer in the Red Army who had violated strict rules of the Soviet occupying authorities against fraternization with the German population by siring a child with an East German woman; the man had to leave the country after his tour of duty was over, and Templin grew up fatherless. To this background he himself ascribes his relatively liberal stance on the issue of working with would-be emigrants (see below).

He and his mother barely managed on her income as an unskilled worker, but Templin nonetheless developed an early passion for reading. Although he also knew about manual work firsthand, he trained to become a librarian. He was also active in the Communist youth organization FDJ and in the late 1960s was offered a chance to study at Berlin's Humboldt University. Committed to the East German socialist project as a way to improve the lives of the lower classes, Templin at that time condemned the Prague Spring as the route to forfeiting the possibility of achieving the socialist society. He joined the SED around this time, but — anxious for a more vigorous pursuit of utopia at a time when Erich Honecker was announcing East Germany's version of socialist consumerism — he soon enough grew disenchanted with its course.

A party representative in student organizations, Templin also became involved at the Humboldt University in a small Trotskyist discussion circle. Around the same time, he was approached by representatives of the Ministry for State Security, who asked him for his cooperation. Templin agreed. After approximately four years of collaboration with the Stasi, when he realized that he was more caught up in the secret police's web than he had initially (and naively) believed, he told the Stasi he wished to discontinue his conversations with them and made known his Stasi contacts to his fellow Trotskyists. Thinking this was all there was to the matter, he continued his conspiratorial discussions with his fellow Trotskyists. Little did he know that another member of the group was also an informer; the Stasi knew all about the group's activities despite Templin's refusal to cooperate further. In time, Templin would become one of the Stasi's most harassed targets.

At the time of Solidarity's emergence, Templin was still an enthusiastic young Marxist, intent on realizing a better socialist society. After completing his degree in philosophy at the Humboldt University, Templin went to Poland on a one-year fellowship to pursue his scholarly interest in phenomenology. Once he arrived in Warsaw, however, he almost completely ignored his academic studies because he discovered a situation that was "totally different from ours":

> Here [in the GDR], the critical people were in the minority and had to hide, while there the party people were in the minority [laughs], and they couldn't afford to be too obvious. And almost everybody was critical, and a whole lot of them were directly involved in opposition activity. . . . When I asked people why they did everything so openly, they said they needn't have bothered to study if they weren't going to draw any consequences from what they learned. That was exactly the opposite of our little secret society [i.e., the Trotskyist discussion group]. We had agreed among ourselves that we would stay in the party, that we would outwardly remain good party members, and that we would prepare the revolution in the living room. First we had to write the theory of the revolution.[18]

In view of his self-described "rigorism," this heavily intellectualized approach to social change was a stance with which Templin was bound to grow impatient.

The tendency to remain passive and to be absorbed by theoretical activity rather than grappling concretely with social and political affairs is, of course, an old stereotype about German intellectuals. As is so often the case with the failings of that group, however, it is a criticism frequently made *by* German intellectuals themselves. In contrast to the widespread negative images concerning Poles among many Germans, the more politically involved (especially on the left) often saw their eastern neighbors as models to be emulated rather than pariahs to be denigrated. The doctor and microbiologist Jens Reich, later a cofounder of the citizens' initiative New Forum, complained in an interview in 1989 that "we had the good diagnoses and the clear critiques and theories, but we just didn't get active. We were talkers.... Through all these years, Poland very much upset us and made us feel ashamed. All the countries that made this breakthrough made us ashamed, because we never managed to muster up the same kind of civic courage *[Zivilcourage]* in this country."[19]

As a representative of the scientific-technical intelligentsia, Reich represents a different sort of intellectual than does a "humanistically" trained figure such as Wolfgang Templin. Indeed, Reich's experience helps flesh out sociologist Alvin Gouldner's reflections on the limits to the frequently observable lack of overt political mobilization among the technical intelligentsia:

> Given the chance [Gouldner wrote], they will support those who support their "habit." Their compulsive-obsessive involvement in the technical may make them apolitical, but there is a limit to this apoliticism. They can ignore politics only so long as they can indulge their narcotizing technical obsessions. Once blocked in this, they, too, enter into contention with their bureaucratic superiors. (Gouldner 1979, 66)

Perhaps it would be more accurate to say that, like all groups, the technical intelligentsia *may* "enter into contention" with those they perceive as constraining their activities. Still, Gouldner describes well the process of politicization during Reich's own slow drift into the dissident milieu around this time. In explaining his gradual conversion to activism, he told me that he had come to the conclusion "that it was pointless to continue working in one's discipline unless the entire system changed. It was a crisis for me personally.... I couldn't maintain international contacts, the equipment was outdated, that sort of thing.... *There was simply no possibility of doing good work under these conditions.*"[20]

Interestingly, however, there was a peculiarly German twist to Reich's explanation of the limits of his ability simply to accept the political order and to continue doing his scientific work irrespective of the political context. He had "a bit of a bad conscience," he related, because his father, a doctor during the Nazi period, had been one of the many who had "kept his mouth shut and done his duty." Particularly after the rise of Solidarność, the persistent rebelliousness of the Polish people acted as a nagging spur to active opposition against the SED among some elements of East Germany's critical intellectuals, even if the Polish workers' movement had not generated much open support among the intelligentsia at the time.

Indeed, Wolfgang Templin's interest in and connections with the Polish opposition, especially the group Peace and Freedom (frequently referred to by its Polish initials, WiP), would decisively influence the outlook of the later Initiative for Peace and Human Rights.[21] Templin's enthusiasm for the vigorous opposition to Communist rule that he encountered in Poland profoundly affected his attitudes toward church-based opposition of the kind then increasingly taking shape under the aegis of the East German Protestant churches. Quite simply, Templin said, unlike his fellow dissident activists — most of whom came from a more or less agnostic and leftist political milieu — he no longer felt like a stranger when he was among church people. Similarly, in his recollections of this period, East German Green activist Carlo Jordan has written that "the surprising connection for us between political opposition and the church in Poland" played an exemplary role in drawing the earlier participants in the intellectual discussion circles of the "cultural opposition" into the activities developing on the fringes of the church (Jordan n.d. [1991], 6). At the same time, however, just as the church played an increasingly important role in sustaining independent political activism, its powerful institutional penumbra and its dogmatic proclivity toward issues of peace rather than those of freedom contributed in their own ways to the delay in putting the pursuit of human rights and democratic freedoms squarely onto the dissident agenda in the GDR.

The Changing of the Guard: The Transformation of Dissident Activity in the 1980s

The East German dissident scene in the early 1980s increasingly came to be dominated by issues of peace and environmentalism. Attention to matters of war and militarism in the GDR grew considerably with the government's announcement in 1978 that it intended to introduce compulsory military education *(Wehrkundeunterricht)* into ninth and tenth grade classes in the schools. The NATO "double-track decision" to install Pershing and Cruise missiles in West Germany in response to the Warsaw Pact's stationing of Soviet SS-20s in the East had given rise to a tremendous outpouring of pacifist sentiment on both sides of the German-German border. The Lutheran Church played a substantial role in making this resurgent antimilitarist feeling the focus of public concern in the GDR. The church added its voice to the wave of public protest against the militarization of the East German education system.[22] Beyond this support for antimilitarist activity, however, the church hierarchy had recently come to an accommodation with the SED regime under the terms of which it would henceforth understand itself as a church "not against, not next to, but within socialism."[23] In the wake of this rapprochement between the clerisy and the Communist regime, the church increasingly provided an institutional umbrella for the emerging grassroots groups addressing such issues as the environment, women's concerns, militarism, and the problems of Third World underdevelopment.

A preoccupation with peace issues was consistent both with the anticapitalist, antifascist heritage underlying much left-wing critique of East German socialism and with the traditional understanding of Protestant dogma. Undoubtedly the most widely publicized expression of this shared concern was the "Berlin Appeal" for disarmament promulgated by Robert Havemann and East Berlin pastor Rainer Eppelmann during early 1982. In addition to a generalized call for weapons reductions by the two military blocs, the document specifically demands the removal of "occupation troops" from both parts of Germany. These concerns echoed those advanced by Havemann in his "Open Letter to Leonid Brezhnev" of late 1981, in which the tireless old Communist called for the demilitarization and neutralization of Germany.[24]

In a joint interview with Eppelmann shortly after publication of the letter to Brezhnev, Havemann reiterated the traditional vision of the anti-Stalinist German Communists by invoking the prospect of German reunification on the basis of reforms in *both* parts of the divided nation, not just the dictatorial GDR. That is, however desirable it may have been as a goal, reunification should not take the form of the Federal Republic's absorption of East Germany — which Havemann continued to understand as the "better German state." "But," Havemann continued in a realistic vein, "in the interest of reunification I am prepared to accept that it might not go entirely according to my wishes." In a striking example of the generational change taking place among dissident East German intellectuals concerning the

aims of political reform, however, Eppelmann — many years Havemann's junior — responded to the latter's lengthy excursus about
reunification with the terse comment, "I don't think that's the decisive problem, as long as people can get along with each other across
borders."[25] These remarks notwithstanding, Eppelmann would prove
to be one of the most enthusiastic advocates of unification when that
option presented itself as a real possibility in 1989.

In a similarly generationally determined shift of focus, the preoccupation with ecological problems and the associated critique of
industrial society *tout court* signaled a departure from inherited
Marxist and socialist analysis.[26] The GDR, too, thus experienced the
emergence of "new social movements" with strong parallels to the
West German Greens, including a predominance of supporters from
among the younger, the better-educated, and those employed in the
tertiary sector of the economy.[27] While the environmentalist "turn"
may have been rather alien to many raised in the theoretical tradition
that gave top priority to the class struggle, the church had relatively
little difficulty assimilating those distressed by the degradation of the
natural surroundings. For such concerns could easily be subsumed
under the Christian churches' theological obligation to protect all life.
One example of this set of concerns was the church's later organization of the so-called Ecumenical Assembly for Justice, Peace, and the
Preservation of Life.[28]

Offering the only social spaces relatively free from the reach of
state control, the East German churches assumed during this period
an increasingly central role as meeting places for those seeking to organize activities autonomous from, if not necessarily in opposition
to, the government. At the same time, the locus of intellectual dissent shifted away from the ranks of the party, in the bosom of which
most public opposition had developed until the late 1970s. As a result of this shift, the church grew more pivotal as the institution
within which — or, on occasion, against which — grassroots groups
mobilized. The church itself thus took on a more decisive role in
the institutional environment that shaped the character of opposition
and dissent in the GDR. This was especially true of human rights activism, which, paradoxically, may have received a decisive boost from
the church's *retraction* of support for such activism (see below). One
Leipzig activist, Edgar Dusdal, of the Solidaristic Church, a grassroots
group critical of what its members regarded as the official church's
obsequiousness toward the regime, has suggested one reason why the

church's institutional backing of the peace movement might have delayed the emergence of a direct concern with human rights in the GDR's dissident milieu: "The preoccupation with human rights is not so central to the theological outlook. The matter of peace is more central."[29] Indeed, the human rights problematic had to extricate itself, so to speak, from the overarching predominance of the peace issue in the church-based dissident groups and in the church itself.

Above and beyond its immediate sources, the antimilitarist impulse in East Germany derived in decisive ways from the legacy of the German past. The indisputable enormity of the catastrophe of *German* militarism fueled the belief in a special *German* responsibility to prevent the recurrence of war. East German peace activism thus converged notably with the East German regime's claims to legitimacy on the basis of its putative antifascism and antimilitarism.

The resignation induced by the German peace movement's inability to forestall the implementation of the NATO "double-track decision" had been cause for widespread disillusionment among peace activists in the GDR in the early 1980s. East Germany's antimilitarist activists were dealt an additional blow around this time as well. The movement not only failed to reverse the introduction of military education in the schools; worse yet, such instruction was extended to eleventh graders in 1981. One analyst intimately familiar with the East German dissident scene attributed the "emigration wave" of early 1984 to the discouragement that set in after these major setbacks (see Kroh 1988b, 43). It is unlikely, however, that disappointed peace activists themselves — who were relatively few in number in any case — constituted a significant proportion of the exodus of some thirty-one thousand East Germans during the first six months of 1984, the largest outflow from the GDR in such a short period since the building of the Berlin Wall in 1961.[30] Once again, the dynamic of defeat and departure among the intellectual dissidents led to a renewed preoccupation with the question whether or not one ought to remain in the GDR.

The mood of confusion and disillusionment that overtook wide segments of the peace movement during this period was a watershed for dissident activists. It was clear, in any case, that the East German peace movement needed to pause and take stock of its situation. For those committed to staying and working for change in the GDR, this was thus a time of tactical and strategic searching. With the decline of the peace movement in the GDR after the stationing of

NATO and Warsaw Pact missiles in the early 1980s, dissident politics in the GDR began to take a new direction. In the aftermath of repeated disappointments and a failure to have a significant impact on the Communist regime, a handful of critical intellectuals began to insist that working for peace — or any other political goal, for that matter — was chimerical without the democratic constitutional rights necessary to control the government. Critics of the East German regime, especially younger, less established intellectuals, were slowly coming to recognize that it was futile to argue with a government that had little reason to pay attention to their complaints.

The shift in the Berlin dissident scene toward a greater concentration on human rights issues received considerable inspiration from the 1985 changing of the guard in the Kremlin, where Mikhail Gorbachev called for a loosening of opinion control in Soviet society under the rubric of "glasnost." Yet because of the precarious situation of "socialism in a quarter of a country" confronted by the GDR's party leaders, the East German regime was notably reluctant to follow the reform path of the Soviet Union — about which it had been said for so many years that "learning from the Soviet Union means learning to win" ("Von der Sowjetunion lernen heißt siegen lernen!"). As a result of the regime's lack of sympathy for reforms, it was once again, as in 1953 and 1956–57, the dissidents who wished the SED to take its cues from the Soviets. Just as with those earlier episodes, divergences in policy between the Communist center and its westernmost periphery opened opportunities that the dissidents could exploit for their own ends. Gorbachev's ascendancy thus fanned the smoldering embers of discontent in the GDR. For, despite objective economic improvements, the East German order now compared badly not only to the West in terms of democratic freedoms; even worse, it also lagged behind the socialist center in the USSR. Still, however, movement in the direction of political pluralism and "bourgeois" human rights was not without its difficulties in an intellectual dissident milieu that remained decidedly left-wing and generally sympathetic to the Communist notion of the class character of political rights.[31]

Above all, a reordering of dissident priorities was in order. Until this time, the conviction had been widespread in peace circles that human rights concerns were essentially subsidiary to the more important matter of preserving peace (see Hirsch 1988, 211). By the summer of 1985, however, a number of well-known Berlin activists had begun to conclude that the priorities entailed in this position needed reexamination. Seeking a forum in which to air their views concerning the relationship between peace and human rights, the initiators set about organizing the first independent seminar in the history of the East German opposition on what two of them later termed the "neuralgic topic of human rights." According to these participants, Wolfgang Templin and Reinhard Weißhuhn, the organizing group consisted "in large part of those subject to work prohibitions [Berufsverbote]."[32] Such people, who had typically been so punished for political reasons, would have had an obvious interest in attention to human rights questions. Indeed, in contrast to the more established critical intellectuals, this group of "blocked ascendants" constituted the core from which the most decisive opposition to the SED regime was drawn, even if they did not necessarily understand themselves as being in "opposition" or even as "dissidents." One important example of this general type was Gerd Poppe, a trained physicist and protégé of Robert Havemann who had been forced to work in manual jobs since his involvement in the protests following the Biermann case.[33] Poppe, whose political touchstone was more the Czechoslovak reform experiment of 1968 than it was the Third Reich, would soon become one of the leading spokespeople of the human rights movement in the GDR along with Wolfgang Templin.

This first human rights seminar was to have thrust the human rights issue into a more central and visible place on the East German dissident agenda. The event was scheduled to take place in the rooms of a church in the Treptow district of East Berlin on 11–12 November 1985. When the participants arrived for the meeting, however, they were informed by the hierarchy of the Berlin-Brandenburg Lutheran Church that the event could not be held due to pressure from "above." For a number of the participants, this was the straw that broke the camel's back; they no longer believed it made sense to remain beholden to what they considered the church's overly accommodating attitude toward the regime, and they said so in a blistering statement criticizing the hierarchy's action.[34]

Later critics would note, however, that despite these activists' readiness to find fault with church policies, opposition activity was ineluctably dependent on the support — or at least the forbearance — of the churches, for they offered the only "free spaces" in a totalitarian order that sought to control all public activity.[35] In contrast to the widely held belief that the East German Lutheran Church was the backbone of the GDR's opposition, however, the point remains that the more impatient dissident activists themselves often found the church far too conciliatory toward the regime and by no means always sympathetic to the activities of the grassroots groups who used them as a refuge. In this view, the formula "church in socialism" was essentially a recipe for co-optation of the church by the party-state.[36]

These activists also believed the time had come to reach beyond the relatively circumscribed limits of the church-based grassroots groups and to speak directly to the East German public. In so doing, as Templin and Weißhuhn put it, they sought to "link up with the opposition experience in neighboring Eastern European countries." As with all dissident activity that threatened to overstep the bounds of patience of the totalitarian state, this strategy was a matter of intense controversy among dissident activists. Some members of the initiating group insisted that this approach was a recipe for "political suicide" (Templin and Weißhuhn 1991, 150), obviating any advantages of this approach by leading to massive repression and the group's early demise. Despite these objections, those who advocated a more aggressive and public stance on the human rights problem in the GDR carried the day, forming the Initiative for Peace and Human Rights (Initiative Frieden und Menschenrechte, or IFM) — the first of the grassroots groups explicitly to reject church endorsement of (though not church rooms for!) their activities. In an example of what were widely perceived in the East German provinces as the *querelles berlinoises,* however, a more radical faction calling itself Gegenstimme (Countervoice) split off from the IFM almost immediately.[37] Even at the moment of its arrival in the world, human rights activism in the GDR bore the scars of a long and difficult gestation.

Unsympathetic to firm organizational structures, the IFM was a membership organization consisting simply of those involved in its work. One of its early official spokespeople, Ralf Hirsch, described the group as having been made up of "Christians and Marxists, workers and intellectuals" (Hirsch 1988, 214), and the IFM indeed bridged the persistent gulf between the secular left and religiously oriented dissidents. Yet this description appears to exaggerate the breadth of the IFM's social recruitment base. Another early IFM activist, Wolfgang Templin's wife, Lotte, recalled ruefully that the group was unable to transcend the narrow base of the younger East Berlin intellectual milieu: "We were just unable to reach beyond these circles," she told me in an interview.[38] Indeed, a list of the IFM's supporters reads like a "who's who" of the Berlin intellectual dissident scene, including Robert Havemann's widow, Katja; Wolfgang and Lotte Templin; Gerd and Ulrike Poppe; Werner Fischer; Bärbel Bohley; and a number of others who later became prominent figures in the East German transformation process beginning in the fall of 1989. The group's early membership clearly reflects origins in the long shadow cast by Robert Havemann's notions of a humane, democratized socialism, despite the IFM's openhanded approach to recruitment and a rather implausible retrospective insistence that the group was not interested in "a perfected socialism" (Templin and Weißhuhn 1991, 152). A number of the other early participants in the IFM, such as Ibrahim Böhme, have since been revealed as "informal collaborators" (inoffizielle Mitarbeiter, or spies) of the Stasi secret police. According to Ulrike Poppe, in fact, Stasi spies amounted to perhaps 40 percent of the IFM's circle of initiators.[39]

The fledgling group, which quickly developed a reputation as the intellectual elite of the East German dissident scene, first went public with a statement in January 1986. Noting that the "realization of the close connection between peace and human rights is spreading in the peace movement," the IFM announced the formation under its aegis of several subgroups addressing various human rights issues.[40] Soon thereafter, the group initiated what would become a series of petitions to the East German government raising its concerns and requesting a dialogue with the SED leadership. In its first petition, dated 24 January 1986, the IFM activists noted six areas in which they regarded the government as illegitimately restricting fundamental rights:

1. lack of freedom to travel, the restriction of which the group said it considered a sign of "the government's mistrust of its citizens";

2. political persecution based on laws prohibiting "treasonous transmission of information" (verräterische Nachrichtenübermittlung), "unconstitutional association," and so on;

3. lack of rights of democratic participation;

4. lack of freedom of association, assembly, and so on;

5. lack of an alternative to military service for conscientious objectors; and

6. the regime's refusal to enter into dialogue with "those who think otherwise" (Andersdenkenden).

The document's authors signaled their origins in and sympathies with the peace movement particularly in their endorsement of the goal of legal alternatives to military service. Notably, however, though the authors were themselves too young to have experienced National Socialism firsthand, the petition also revealed the persistence of an antifascist component in their thinking. To be excluded from the demand the IFM raised for an amnesty for political criminals were those guilty of "glorifying fascism, militarism, or racial and war hysteria" (see Hirsch 1988, 214–17).

By mid-1986, the IFM had begun publishing its underground newsletter *Grenzfall*. In an intimation of the journal's agenda, its cover depicts a wall topped with barbed wire; the word *Grenz* (border) appears in a section of the fortification that remains standing; the word *fall* (fall or case) is inscribed in a crumbling part of the wall. The periodical, produced with out-of-date technology, had a print run of eight hundred to one thousand but, according to IFM cofounder Ralf Hirsch, "had several times that number of readers."[41]

The publication of *Grenzfall* signaled a new stage in the development of intellectual opposition and dissent in the GDR. Unlike their neighbors elsewhere in the Soviet bloc, the East German dissidents had theretofore produced virtually no samizdat literature. To some degree, this dearth of independent publishing reflected the availability to the GDR's dissidents of the ersatz public sphere of the Federal Republic. Just as many of those dissatisfied with life in the GDR could seek their salvation via the "nightly emigration" to West Germany via television, those seeking an outlet for disseminating material unacceptable to the SED-controlled media could turn to their contacts in the West to have their views broadcast back to the GDR. They could, so to speak, "borrow" the Western media for their own purposes — assuming, of course, that they did not regard this as politically undesirable, a reaction among some intellectuals that we have already seen in the context of the Biermann affair.[42] The extent to which this problem underlay the advent of *Grenzfall* is unknown; it is clear enough why one might prefer to have one's own organs of communication. In any case, the creators of the journal finally sought to make possible the exchange of political communication among the GDR's independent peace, ecology, human rights, and so-called two-thirds world (*Zweidrittel-Welt*, or third-world solidarity) groups without recourse to West Germany's ersatz public sphere. In so doing, the journal offered East German dissidents the opportunity to develop the rudiments of a "civil society" of their own. Yet the absence of any extensive East German samizdat literature and the belated emergence of journals such as *Grenzfall* also reflected the relatively weak impact upon East German dissident intellectuals of the very notion of "civil society" — the idea of institutions for social and political discussion free from state control — which by this time had become of considerable importance in the discourse of dissent elsewhere in Eastern Europe. At the same time, however, the creation of *Grenzfall* helped sustain that mental "demarcation" *(Abgrenzung)* from the Federal Republic that facilitated the persistence of the anticapitalist attitudes so often articulated by the GDR's intellectuals, both orthodox and dissenting.[43]

The founding of the Initiative for Peace and Human Rights marked the opening of a new chapter in the development of dissident activity in the GDR. The group's insistence on open, public activism and on "laying claim to not-yet-guaranteed rights as if they already were so" suggested a bold new approach to opposition politics in East Germany.[44] This formulation also suggests the influence of other East European opposition movements generally, and of Charter 77 in Czechoslovakia and its most famous figure, Václav Havel, in particular. Indeed, Charter 77's influence can be seen, for instance, in the IFM's "Letter to Charter 77," written in early 1987, a decade after that organization's founding. That epistle notes that, for its signatories, "the existence of Charter 77 and of other human rights movements in Eastern Europe is a source of inspiration," and emphasizes the importance for the GDR of those groups' commitment to "absolute openness and publicity" and to "pluralism as an overarching value."[45]

To be sure, as the editors of *Grenzfall* put it, they understood themselves as part of the GDR's peace movement.[46] Yet the IFM went beyond the usual "on the one hand, on the other hand" typical of German peace activists' approach to the respective military blocs' responsibility for the nuclear menace. Instead, the group explicitly characterized the alleged military threat from the West as an opportunity for the East German government to "divert attention from domestic problems and to remain silent about their causes." Thus while the IFM certainly bore the earmarks of its origins in the peace movement, the group placed the achievement of democratization and constitutionally guaranteed rights at the center of its efforts (see Hirsch and Kopelew 1989, vii–viii).

This focus on democracy and human rights, of course, put the dissident intellectuals on a collision course with the regime. That objective fact, however, did not necessarily entail a conscious move to "system opposition" on the activists' part. Still beholden to an essentially reform-socialist vision beyond the post-Yalta bloc system, they did not understand themselves as fundamentally at odds with "really existing socialism." Instead, they sought to ensure democratic rights and freedoms within a socialist system.[47] At the same time, however, they argued that "taking action for human rights understood as inalienable necessarily entails forfeiting the possibility of measuring social development against a particular utopian vision of society."[48] Even if those active in the IFM remained fundamentally sympathetic to the notion of socialism, they had begun to judge the "really existing" version of that system exclusively in terms of its *reality,* not in terms of the *promises* of democratization allegedly intrinsic to the socialist order. In this respect, they had indeed begun — after some delay relative to the other East Central European countries — to "link up with the opposition experience" there.

The Spread of Intellectual Dissent and the Development of a "Parallel Culture"

The founding of the Initiative for Peace and Human Rights was a watershed, the breaking of a certain barrier in the evolution of dissent and opposition in the GDR. Yet in the East German capital, the tiny IFM alone worked principally on human rights matters within the broader rubric of the peace movement. Not long after its advent in early 1986, however, another group of Berlin dissident activists who until then had availed themselves of the protective cover of the churches similarly concluded that this relationship was no longer satisfactory. At the time, the grassroots church groups were gearing up for the imminent church conference *(Kirchentag)* of the Lutheran Church to be held in East Berlin in April 1987. Criticizing what they considered the church hierarchy's excessively conciliatory attitude toward the regime, the groups published a statement a month later in the underground *Fliegende Blätter* (Flying pages) announcing plans to organize an alternative "church conference from below" *(Kirchentag von unten)*. Indicating that they were activists "from environmentalist, peace, women's, and third-world groups," they attacked the church for pursuing policies out of step with the interests of its members and thus driving them away. "Years ago," they wrote, "the church lost an essential part of its membership — the workers. It is now doing its best to lose the rest of the membership" (cited in Kroh 1988b, 47). Out of this undertaking grew the so-called Church from Below *(Kirche von unten),* one of whose most prominent members was former SED member Vera Wollenberger. As the founding of the *Kirche von unten* suggested, the strains between the church and the groups to which they offered refuge were growing more open and more bitter.

The creation of the Umweltbibliothek (Environmental Library, or UB) in the rooms of East Berlin's Church of Zion in September 1986 gave further impetus to the grassroots groups in the GDR's capital city. The founders of this important underground institution included committed environmentalists such as the anarchist Wolfgang Rüddenklau and Carlo Jordan, a longtime activist on ecological issues who had once been thrown out of an academic job at the Humboldt University and who later went on to help found the East German Green Party. They sought to gather and disseminate information on the ecological situation in the GDR, as well as to build up a network of environmentalist groups throughout the country. Yet the UB was far more than a mere environmentalist organization. Indeed, it became the principal meeting place in Berlin for alternative and dissident groups of all kinds.

Despite the UB's repeated attacks on the regime's absolute control over ecological information, the independent environmentalists occasionally worked together with ecological activists of the Kulturbund on such projects as "tree-planting actions" in the GDR's graying cities. At bottom, indeed, their political attitudes were not necessarily antisocialist. As Carlo Jordan put it in an interview:

> We never characterized ourselves exactly as an opposition, because the concept of opposition that was applied to us was drawn heavily from the self-understanding of bourgeois democracy.... Speaking for myself, I never [thought of] myself as a "regime critic" or an "oppositionist" in the terms that constantly came out of the Western media.[49]

Jordan's remarks strongly suggest the persistently anti-Western — or at least anticapitalist — attitude of many of the GDR's intellectual critics.

The activists grouped around the Umweltbibliothek were soon publishing a widely circulated samizdat publication, the *Umweltblätter* (Environmental pages), which made the UB's activities known to the large circles of those in the GDR interested in environmental issues. Despite a primary focus on ecological concerns, the *Umweltblätter* — which had a print run of about one thousand — carried material on the broad range of issues addressed by the widely varied groups meeting in the rooms of the UB. The *Umweltblätter* also paid considerable attention to the progress of glasnost in the Soviet Union, an indication of the enthusiasm inspired by Gorbachev in East German dissident circles.[50]

By this time, in fact, cultural, political, and religious activists had created a plethora of samizdat literature throughout the GDR. These publications were primarily forms of political communication but also included independent literary journals produced without explicit permission from the official cultural authorities. The outlets for creative writing such as *Mikado, Ariadnefabrik,* and *Der König ist nackt* (The king is naked), in particular, were important elements in a small but burgeoning "parallel culture," which also included a variety of alternative institutions such as cafés in which were held events organized within this subcultural milieu. The literary quarters of this "second public sphere" *(zweite Öffentlichkeit)* were populated primarily by younger writers who were refused — or themselves proudly refused to seek — the imprimatur of the SED's cultural apparatchiks. Based above all in the alternative cafés of Leipzig, Dresden, and especially the Prenzlauer Berg district of East Berlin, this emerging parallel culture constituted the glue that held together the network of East Germany's younger, less established intellectuals who were disenchanted with what they regarded as the listless and repressive reality of life under socialism.[51]

Despite these growing indications of an internal challenge to — or, perhaps worse, a simple lack of interest in — the SED's policies in East German intellectual and political life, the party in late summer 1987 received a considerable boost to its legitimacy from a source on the other side of the intra-German border. The Federal Republic's Christian Democratic chancellor, Helmut Kohl, had finally consented officially to receive Erich Honecker as the leader of a separate state. In addition, only days before the trip, which in itself represented a major achievement for the East German leader, several members of the GDR's social-scientific elite joined with leading West German Social Democratic Party (SPD) figures to work out the details of a position paper titled "The Conflict of Ideologies and Mutual Security" ("Der Streit der Ideologien und die gemeinsame Sicherheit").

Pushing forward with their long-standing approach to *Ostpolitik,* the SPD's Commission on Fundamental Values (Grundwertekomission) dispatched a delegation led by longtime détente advocate Erhard Eppler to negotiate a common position on security issues with a group from the powerful Academy of Social Sciences (Akademie für Gesellschaftswissenschaften) of the SED's Central Committee. Otto Reinhold, the academy's director, played a highly visible role on the East German side.

Amid much discussion of the dangers of nuclear holocaust, the position paper stated flatly that "both sides must get used to the idea that they will exist side-by-side and will have to get along for some time to come." There was, the negotiating teams concluded, simply no alternative to the "peaceful competition of social systems."[52] Having agreed to accept each other's existence for the foreseeable future, the two sides agreed to disagree about their respective interpretations of such concepts as democracy, human rights, and freedom (though there was, tellingly, no elaboration of the Marxist-Leninist position on the matter of "freedom," but only of a more vaguely defined "progress").

Still, the position paper outlined specific conditions for this mutual coexistence that were designed to improve the day-to-day situation of the East German population. The document held out the prospect, for instance, of greater freedom for scientific, cultural, and political contacts and called for adherence to the CSCE (Conference on Security and Cooperation in Europe) guarantee of the availability of periodicals and other publications "from the other member states." These clauses were obviously directed at the GDR, since only that part of Germany forbade the introduction of periodicals from the other signatory countries of the CSCE agreements. Erfurt bishop Heino Falcke, long an ally of East German advocates of reform, greeted the paper as an indication of the government's conversion to "a policy of opening up, of reducing tensions, of building trust."[53] A West German observer of the GDR's dissident scene with close ties to its activists insisted that the SPD-SED paper was of great value to those seeking to reform the GDR from within (Rein 1990, 17). In a recent discussion of the document's significance, Jürgen Fuchs, who maintained ties to East German dissident circles despite having been driven into exile in West Berlin, recalled that he regarded the paper as "useful for demanding dialogue" between dissidents and the regime.[54]

Still, in the eyes of some, these elements of the position paper could not make up for the document's implicit suggestion that the SPD fundamentally acquiesced in SED rule and in the division of Germany. Moreover, because the SPD seemed willing to negotiate certain matters that really are not negotiable, such as the meaning of pluralism, the position paper met with an ambiguous echo among the dissident intelligentsia. The position paper was negatively received, for example, by the only author in the pages of *Grenzfall* to respond to it directly.[55]

In a commentary on the political situation in the GDR toward the end of 1987, however, IFM activist Ulrike Poppe nonetheless insisted, "All the skeptics to the contrary notwithstanding: things are starting to move.... Now is the time to take the SED at its word and to make use of the opportunity to develop broader coalitions." Poppe took particular note of some recent remarks by Rolf Reissig, a professor at the Academy of Social Sciences and a member of the SED delegation that had produced the position paper, highlighting especially his assertion that the time had come for "the promotion of genuine discussion."[56] Recalling his intentions at the time, Reissig has recently said that those from the SED who had helped draft the SED-SPD joint document "wanted to democratize, to reform, to open up the GDR, but we also wanted to hold on to the GDR as such *[aber sie als DDR erhalten]*." Reissig's words are strikingly similar to those that would be used by the intellectual opposition in East Germany in the fall of 1989. Despite this overlap in political objectives, however, Reissig understood, and was forthright enough to say, that "I was no oppositionist, but I stood in contradiction *[aber ich stand im Widerspruch]*."[57]

Reissig's comments in 1987, obviously reflecting the impact of Gorbachev's glasnost on many Soviet bloc Communists, were hardly in keeping with the sentiments toward Soviet developments of the more orthodox elements among the SED leadership. Their unsympathetic attitudes toward glasnost and perestroika were indicated most clearly when Politburo member and Central Committee secretary for science and culture Kurt Hager was asked by the West German weekly *Stern* in early 1987 about his reaction to recent domestic policy shifts in the Soviet Union. In what became a widely quoted indication of the SED leaders' hostility toward internal reform, Hager quipped, "Would you feel compelled to replace your wallpaper just because your neighbor changed his?"[58] The SED leaders' sneering dismissal of the notion that they needed to initiate any reforms could hardly have encouraged the East German populace about the prospects for improvement in what they increasingly considered their declining situation vis-à-vis other, less reform-resistant Soviet bloc countries.[59]

The competing views on reform embodied in Hager's remark and in the SPD-SED position paper indicated that a split was maturing within the SED between those who wanted to dig in to defend the system against change, on the one hand, and those who supported the kinds of reforms associated with Gorbachev's policies of liberalization, on the other. Indeed, according to another participant in the SPD-SED discussions, Academy of Social Sciences sociologist Manfred Lötsch, the position paper provoked intense controversy within the East German party's intellectual and power elites — not least because of its invocation of such anathemas as "new thinking."[60] In his sociological work in the 1980s, Lötsch himself had played a leading role in developing a critique of what he called the "dysfunctional leveling" and "dysfunctional elite-formation" characteristic of Soviet-style socialist society. He insisted that social differentiation was a structural condition of technological innovation and that the "critical potential" to be found among the intelligentsia needed to be promoted by the institution of new, anti-"leveling" policies that would restore the intelligentsia's traditional sense of status.[61]

Lötsch described the conflict raging among the party elites around this time as one between "ideologues" and "technocrats." Among the party's institutions of social analysis, he said, the former group was anchored in the Institute for Marxism-Leninism under the directorship of the very dogmatic Kurt Tiedke, while the latter was centered in the Academy of Social Sciences under Otto Reinhold.[62] It is important to note, however, that neither of these factions wished fundamentally to call into question either socialism or the leading role of the party. Those critical of the orthodox approach taken by the aging SED leaders wanted to regenerate socialism — to perfect it, not to destroy it. They were dissenters, perhaps, but hardly "dissidents," much less "oppositionists." Still, at least some parts of the intellectual opposition thought this bifurcation within the party offered an opening that could be exploited for their own reformist ends.

Clampdown on Dissent, 1987–88

What appeared to be the onset of a thaw deriving from German-German pressures around the time of Honecker's visit to the Federal Republic would be transformed into a deep chill almost immediately after his return. On the night of 24 November 1987, Stasi agents carried out an unexpected raid on the Umweltbibliothek (UB), confiscating duplicating machines, paper, and copies of the *Umweltblätter* as well as of the forthcoming issue of the IFM's journal *Grenzfall*. Seven of the UB's principal activists, including cofounder Wolfgang Rüddenklau, were briefly arrested. Despite the boost to the regime's legitimacy recently received from the other side of the German-German border, the domestic truce between the East German regime and the dissidents had clearly been interrupted, if not abandoned altogether.

Contrary to the aims of the regime, however, the Stasi action and the attendant arrests set off a chain of solidarity protests in East Berlin and elsewhere in the GDR that breathed new life into the GDR's dissident movement. Numerous vigils and protest actions sprang up spontaneously in the various churches of the East German capital, drawing recruits from well beyond the usual circles of the church-based grassroots groups. In a declaration at the vigil in the Gethsemane Church in the Prenzlauer Berg district, Uwe Kolbe, a young author and coeditor of the samizdat journal *Mikado*, denounced with scathing irony the SED's recently professed commitment to "tolerance." Kolbe noted in particular that, although "the CPSU has drawn its conclusions, the ruling party in the GDR apparently has not." He also cast doubt on the value of the recent rapprochement embodied in the SPD-SED position paper: "What good does it do for the SED and the SPD to reach an agreement about a 'culture of debate' ... when that agreement silently includes the exclusion of all those who, independent of their party affiliation, seek to make the 'culture of debate' a reality?"[63] These remarks suggest that while the dissident community may have considered "détente" generally desirable, such a policy nonetheless needed to include more concrete measures to protect the rights of East Germans than those agreed upon in the SPD-SED joint declaration.

In part as a result of differences between Wolfgang Rüddenklau and Carlo Jordan concerning the dissident groups' reaction to the state repression and to the wave of solidarity that developed in response to it, a split emerged within the leadership of the UB in the aftermath of these dramatic events. Soon thereafter, Jordan and several associates broke off and created the Green Network "Ark" (Grünes Netzwerk "Arche"), and the *Umweltblätter* was soon succeeded by the journal *Arche Nova*.[64] Clearly, the remarkable outpouring of solidarity for those jailed had done little to overcome the endemic *querelles berlinoises* among the dissident intellectuals in the East German capital.

Although the arrested individuals were primarily associated with the UB, the IFM had probably been the principal target of the Stasi's action.[65] In mid-January 1988, the group belatedly published the issue of *Grenzfall* that had been confiscated in late November. Not surprisingly, the issue included considerable commentary on and documentation of the events at the Church of Zion in late November. A few days after its appearance, according to IFM activist Lotte Templin, three Berlin professors wrote an evaluation of *Grenzfall* in which they found the publication to be "unconstitutional and inimical to the state." At the end of January, the Templins and three other members of IFM were arrested and jailed. The professorial evaluation of *Grenzfall* surfaced again at that time, and one of the activists' lawyers used the document to suggest that, should they wish political trials, they ought to prepare themselves for lengthy prison terms. It was generally believed, she noted, that the IFM had been singled out for especially harsh repression because of the potentially volatile combination of its extensive international contacts and its publishing activities. Clearly, both of these strike at the heart of a system based on the ruling party's monopoly of information and organization. "Our arrests had to do with their attempt to demoralize the IFM and to disrupt its functioning," Lotte Templin told me. "And it succeeded." Indeed, the issue of *Grenzfall* that appeared in mid-January would prove to have been the last.[66]

Moreover, the activist core of the IFM was dispersed to the Federal Republic and beyond as a result of the regime's efforts at suppression. Soon after their arrests, the group was released to West Germany—several of them with East German passports and a promise that they could return after a certain period of time. Unaware that their incarceration had provoked a renewed wave of solidarity throughout the GDR involving tens of thousands of protesters in the country's churches (Kroh 1988b, 53), the group accepted the authorities' offer to exchange temporary or permanent exile in the Federal

Republic for the lengthy prison terms with which they were being threatened. One of the IFM members involved, Ralf Hirsch, later wrote bitterly of the group's acceptance of this deal: "This compromise is not a success for the independent groups in the GDR: the solidarity was unprecedented, the arrested were too weak, they didn't withstand the pressure.... Self-critically, we must...ask ourselves: Did we not have too little trust in our friends in the independent groups?"[67] The wave of protests was, indeed, unprecedented and signaled a growing disenchantment with SED rule among the East German populace. Although the activists in the GDR's church-based grassroots groups may have mobilized the protest movement, the large numbers involved indicated that the protests had reached beyond the narrow, more intellectual boundaries of the dissident milieu to include wider segments of East German society. Yet the dissidents' decision to accept the regime's bargain reflected a continuing sense of embattled isolation from the broad mass of East German society.

Having accepted this deal with the government, the dissident intellectuals were now vulnerable to being hoist by their own petard. For all their insistence that one should stay in the GDR and fight for change there, the intellectual oppositionists failed — however understandable this failure may have been — to pay the costs endured by other East European dissidents for their political convictions. Indeed, in a forceful denunciation of the deal agreed to by the IFM arrestees that appeared in an East Berlin underground publication, Reinhard Schult, later a cofounder of New Forum, asked harshly: "How are we to explain the[ir] quick departure to the 250 East Europeans (Russians, Hungarians, Poles, Yugoslavs, Czechoslovakians) who, taken together, have spent more than one thousand years in jail, and who proclaimed their solidarity in a joint declaration?"[68] Once again, the difficulties, tensions, and distortions caused for the opponents of SED rule by the GDR's anomalous attempt to build "socialism in a quarter of a country" had come back to haunt them.

During this time, the intellectual dissidents continued to maintain their distance from those who preferred emigration to the arguably futile effort to stay in the GDR and fight to bring about reforms. This tragic aspect of dissident politics emerged anew in developments occurring simultaneous yet parallel to those surrounding the raid on the Umweltbibliothek. Not long before those events, in September 1987, a new human rights group had made its appearance on the Berlin scene: the Working Group on GDR Citizenship Rights (Arbeitsgruppe Staatsbürgerschaftsrecht der DDR). The group's principal founder, Günter Jeschonnek, was a theater director who had been unemployed since applying for permission to emigrate in January 1986.[69] Because of the general reticence on the part of the church-based grassroots groups with respect to the emigration issue, his earlier visibility in church activities was crucial, he believed, to his success in persuading these circles to support an initiative devoted to progress on the freedom to emigrate. For years, the church had called on East Germans to stay in their country while also carrying out its more traditional, pastoral role, consoling those awaiting disposition of their applications. Jeschonnek had begun to talk up the emigration issue at the aforementioned church conference in East Berlin in the spring of 1987, which he described as a "turning point" in the church's treatment of the emigration problem.[70]

Despite his efforts to stimulate discussion about the emigration question, however, the *Kirchentag* took no concrete steps to address the concerns of would-be emigrants. Jeschonnek and a handful of sympathizers therefore decided to organize a group devoted specifically to this problem, the Working Group on GDR Citizenship Rights. Harking back to earlier such attempts in the East German provinces, the group constituted the first organized attempt in the country's capital to attack head-on the regime's denial of this human right and to offer mutual aid to those waiting out the disposition of their applications to emigrate. The working group thus sought to harness the energies of those who, for whatever reasons, had decided they would prefer emigration to staying and working for reforms in the GDR.

The group of potential emigrants — estimated by (perhaps self-interested) West German observers in the mid-1980s at between 150,000 and 500,000 out of a total population of some 17 million — was always of vastly greater *numerical* significance than those committed to political reform activity. It is therefore undoubtedly correct to say that the availability of this option helped account for "the general *absence* of a large-scale civil rights movement in the GDR" (Woods 1986, 21, 32). Yet as later developments would reveal, this was true only up to a certain point: the *unlimited* availability of the right to emigrate was tantamount to a death knell for the GDR. The new grassroots group on emigration rights thus addressed the concerns of a very substantial element in East German society, and one that potentially provided the yeast for a massive movement of opposition to SED rule.

Membership in the Working Group on GDR Citizenship Rights mushroomed rapidly. Initially, according to Günter Jeschonnek, the group drew strongly but by no means exclusively from among the ranks of East Berlin's better-educated population — "university graduates, Ph.D.'s, medical doctors," he told me. "The majority were well-educated people,...smart folks."[71] Similarly, Pastor Christian Führer of St. Nicholas Church in Leipzig, the church at which the dramatic Monday demonstrations of fall 1989 would originate, noted in an interview that the would-be emigrants who congregated in and around his church, and who participated in his "Circle of Hope" for emigration applicants, "were often highly placed people in the society."[72] These assessments of the social composition of those involved in organized efforts to gain the freedom to emigrate suggest that the better-educated may have been more inclined to become politically active on the issue, or perhaps only that such people stand out by virtue of their speech or dress. The evidence remains sketchy and anecdotal concerning the social origins of those who pressed the emigration cause before late 1989 in a more than individualistic, privatized way.

At the working group's first meeting on 3 October 1987 in the rooms of the UB, in any case, some thirty people showed up from East Berlin and elsewhere in the GDR. Shortly thereafter, on 9 December, Jeschonnek was informed by Stasi agents that he and his wife had until the next morning to prepare to depart the GDR; their long-standing requests for permission to emigrate, they were curtly told, had finally been granted. In a clear instance of the regime's exportation of those it deemed troublemakers, the Jeschonneks were escorted to the border by Stasi agents the following day.

The working group went on without them, however. Interest in the group's activities clearly remained high, for about 150 people from all over the GDR showed up for a meeting on 9 January 1988. With the grounds of the Church of Zion "crawling with Stasi agents" on the day of the event, Wolfgang Rüddenklau of the UB informed the group that it could no longer use the church's meeting rooms. The Working Group on GDR Citizenship Rights had simply grown too large, he informed them, and — especially in view of the recent raid on the UB — it was decided that this expansion constituted too grave a threat to the survival of the other independent groups that met under its roof. The group survived for some time thereafter, but with Jeschonnek and several of the other initiators gone after early 1988, it lost momentum. With the arrest or emigration of the core members of both the IFM and the working group, indeed, the spark of opposition activity in the GDR jumped to Leipzig, where would-be emigrants began to play an increasingly prominent role in the church-based activist milieu.

Shortly before Jeschonnek's expulsion from the country in late 1987, however, the working group had conceived the idea of organizing a counterdemonstration to the annual party-sponsored ritual commemorating Rosa Luxemburg and Karl Liebknecht on the anniversary of their deaths, an event that would take place in mid-January 1988. Coming from a group devoted principally to securing for its members the freedom to emigrate, this suggestion met with a characteristic response from the dissident circles in the East German capital. While many in the dissident milieu greeted the idea enthusiastically, as a rule they refused to collaborate formally with those who, as they frequently said, "just wanted to emigrate."

The Rosa Luxemburg demonstration of 1988 thus brought to a head a dilemma of long standing within GDR dissident circles. Preparations for the event raised poignantly the issue of the East German dissidents' attitude toward an internationally recognized human right that simultaneously implied a decisive rejection of socialism in the GDR. Moreover, the (individual) achievement of that right did not necessarily entail the commitment to "political work" — a telling phrase — typically expected of dissident activists. Indeed, pursuit of the freedom to emigrate called into question the very rationale of such work. In contrast to those committed to working for reform, the emigrants operated on the basis of an implicitly "totalitarian" theory of the nature of Soviet-type systems, rejecting the possibility that the GDR could be reformed at all — or at least enough to persuade them of the value of remaining in the country.

Notwithstanding their significant ideological differences, there was clearly an element of competition underlying the antipathies between would-be emigrants and those who preferred to stay and work for change. Even as the ranks of the independent groups swelled during the 1980s, the number of those East Germans who would have left given the freedom to do so undoubtedly exceeded at all times the number who became actively involved in independent political activities.[73] Thus, as the would-be emigrant population came to take a more substantial role in the opposition, fears grew among the dissidents that their concerns would fade into the background if they allowed themselves to be out-muscled by the emigrants. This concern was especially apparent in the preparations for the Rosa Luxemburg counterdemonstration of early 1988. Members of the grassroots groups agreed to go along with the event only on the condition that no banners be carried that called attention to the emigration issue (Jeschonnek 1988a, 256). Carlo Jordan, cofounder of the Green Network "Ark" and a Green Party representative at the Round Table negotiations beginning in late 1989, related in an interview that his group, adopting an ecumenical approach, accepted anyone who shared its general goals. Yet the group was wary of being "misused" by would-be emigrants — a group, Jordan told me, that "grew much faster and sought to dominate certain decisions." In contrast to the broad-mindedness of the Green Network "Ark," several groups strictly refused membership to applicants for emigration; Jordan referred specifically in this context to the "Church from Below."[74]

At one level, the different independent groups were competing for adherents within the East German "political space." From a different perspective, however, the tensions between the forces of "voice" and those of "exit" might be seen as a confrontation between ordinary citizens, with their mundane concerns and episodic involvement in worldly affairs, and what Michael Walzer has called the "political entrepreneur." The analogy with Weber lies not so much in his distinction between those who live "off" and those who live "for" politics, though the latter may well apply to the figure of the political entrepreneur. Rather, it was the "systematic and sustained character" of the Calvinist intellectuals' political activity that constituted their central contribution to the origins of modern radicalism, according to Walzer (see Walzer 1965, 17 and passim). Only in the aftermath of the Calvinist saints' politicization of all life, so characteristic of the East German intellectual dissident milieu and of radical activists more generally, was the notion of "political work" even conceivable.

The would-be emigrants from the GDR were thus maligned by the advocates of "voice" fundamentally because they did not share their "systematic and sustained" attitude toward political involvement. Under the conditions prevailing in East Germany, however, those who expressed their disaffection from the system via the "exit" option were every bit as liable to encounter state-sponsored harassment and repression as those committed to the mechanisms of "voice," clearly indicating that the regime considered both groups to be its "opponents." Yet the peculiarities of the geopolitical context of opposition and dissent in East Germany fostered division between the two groups rather than promoting common cause between them.

For example, many of the advocates of "voice" insisted that, even when would-be emigrants did become involved in dissident-initiated political activities, they did so primarily to promote their own narrow cause of emigrating from the GDR. Aware that the state frequently dealt with perceived troublemakers by kicking them out of the country, it was often said, they simply "got active in order to get out."[75] To be sure, many who wished to emigrate took this gamble in their decision to participate in independent political activities, for it was true that the regime frequently disposed of disturbers of the socialist peace in this manner. Yet applicants for emigration were typically branded traitors to the socialist fatherland and harassed accordingly. Indeed, such persons were believed in the mid-1980s to comprise the majority of political prisoners in the GDR (Woods 1986, 32).

Applying to emigrate was thus by no means a decision lightly taken. The possible consequences included demotion at or dismissal from work, the attendant loss of income, difficulties in getting or keeping housing, refusal of requests for vacation accommodations, denial of travel visas, problems for oneself or one's family members in gaining access to desired educational institutions, and regular "invitations" to appear for conversations with local Stasi officials, not to mention imprisonment.[76] Moreover, applications were acted upon arbitrarily by the authorities, and final disposition could take years.

At least for younger applicants, then, the decision to emigrate required courage and the resolve to bear up under a potentially lengthy limbo involving considerable suffering. As Günter Jeschonnek put it:

> The would-be emigrants — the majority, I would say — were the ones who had the courage to say, "That's it, I'm leaving," knowing that that decision had consequences: getting thrown out of work, etc....At least they made a decision....And the majority of the East German population never made any decision. Staying in the country was not a decision, it was simply a matter of course. But the decision to leave was at least a decision.[77]

For the various reasons discussed above, however, this particular decision — even though it was punished by the state in ways quite similar to the kinds of intimidation meted out to those who directly challenged SED rule — was typically dismissed by dissident activists as a sort of apolitical selfishness.[78] Reflecting on this split among the opposition forces, IFM activist Lotte Templin remarked in retrospect: "I think that was a point on which the peace movement always abdicated [*versagt*] morally, where they imposed a demand for martyrdom on themselves and on the population that just is not appropriate for human beings."[79]

The matter of collaboration with the Working Group on GDR Citizenship Rights in organizing the 1987 Rosa Luxemburg demonstration caused considerable soul-searching among those active in the IFM.[80] Yet such cooperation appears to have been hardly a subject for debate among the other groups: at least some of them, including the "Church from Below" and Gegenstimme, were said to have had explicit policies rejecting such cooperation in principle.[81] In any case, Wolfgang and Lotte Templin's stance toward the emigration issue was rare among the GDR's dissidents. In the debates within the IFM over collaboration with Jeschonnek's group in planning the Rosa Luxemburg demonstration, in fact, only they and a couple of others supported the idea of working with an initiative devoted single-mindedly to the right to emigrate. Along with state repression, the nearly universal refusal of the dissident groups to collaborate formally with an organization devoted specifically to the cause of emigration contributed its part to the lack of a vibrant, broad-based movement of opposition to SED rule in East Berlin.

Despite its divisive background, the Rosa Luxemburg counter-demonstration organized by the Working Group on GDR Citizenship Rights nonetheless caused a major stir. In a clear reflection of the re-action of the SED leadership, Professor Dr. Heinz Kamnitzer, writer Arnold Zweig's successor as president of the East German PEN Center, articulated a quasi-official response to the action in the pages of *Neues Deutschland*. Apparently untroubled by the awkward implications of comparing socialism to a religious institution, Kamnitzer fulminated in a bombastic article entitled "The Dead Admonish" ("Die Toten mahnen") that the unauthorized demonstration was "as abominable as a blasphemy. No church could tolerate the denigration of a procession commemorating a Catholic cardinal or a Protestant bishop. Neither can anyone expect us to accept it when someone intentionally disrupts and degrades our honoring of Rosa Luxemburg and Karl Liebknecht."[82] The party could hardly have demonstrated more clearly its rejection of the Luxemburgian motto that the counterdemonstrators had written on their banners: "Freedom is always the freedom of those who think otherwise."

The considerable media attention given these events in the West German press incorrectly suggested that the church-based dissident groups that might normally have been expected to organize such an event had played a more significant role in mobilizing the demonstration than had in fact been the case. In an article tinged with an unmistakable bitterness, Günter Jeschonnek vigorously criticized the West German media's account of the Rosa Luxemburg demonstration for giving too much credit to the better-known dissidents in organizing the event. There was, he insisted, no cooperation between his group and the other dissident organizations in staging the event. On the contrary, the latter had refused to collaborate with his group, despite their agreement in principle that the counterdemonstration was a worthwhile undertaking (Jeschonnek 1988b, 850).

Slowly, however, efforts were being undertaken by certain elements of the dissident scene to overcome the antipathies between the church-based dissidents and the would-be emigrants. Perhaps the most vigorous critique from within the opposition ranks of the dissidents' tendency to shun applicants for emigration was articulated by a psychiatrist named Ludwig Drees from the provincial city of Stendal. In a remarkable passage from his remarks supporting a petition pleading for the "renunciation of the practice and principle of demarcation" *(Absage an Praxis und Prinzip der Abgrenzung)*, Drees spoke scathingly about the treatment of would-be emigrants among the church-based independent groups. After a brief review of the constraints and distortions imposed by the Berlin Wall on the GDR's citizens — and of the willingness of so many in the dissident milieu to repress those facts of life — Drees said:

> In the end, we went so far as to take over the state's ideological justification as our own and to make Christian virtue out of it by saying that the desire to leave the GDR is immoral. We went so far as to proclaim self-righteously that a Christian may not emigrate: Christians must remain in the place that God put them. To be sure, applicants for emigration have found charitable support in the churches — by being hired on as coal-stokers, for example — but they were nonetheless morally discriminated against.... It was not those who stayed who had a problem, an "illness," an "isolation syndrome"; rather, failure and an "illness" was ascribed to

those who emigrated. "They couldn't handle their problems, which they will also take with them to the West," we said. "They let themselves be seduced by the good life." Ultimately, the emigrant came to be viewed from our narrow *[verleugnenden]* perspective as a psychopath. And that is what is so horrible: that the emigrants have been driven into the position of outsiders, into a peculiar political "scene" in which they really do think otherwise than those who stayed, and in which they are forced to accept their isolated social development.[83]

Drees had touched a real sore point with these remarks. The petition upon which they are a commentary, which called for a "renunciation of the practice and principle of demarcation," had been submitted by several members of Berlin's Church of St. Bartholomew to the April 1987 synod of the Evangelical Church of Berlin-Brandenburg. The IFM's journal *Grenzfall* reported to its readers in May of that year that the Berlin-Brandenburg synod had rejected the petition.[84] It came up for discussion again at the national meeting of the Federation of Evangelical Churches (Bund Evangelischer Kirchen, or BEK) in September 1987 in Görlitz, where it once again failed to be adopted. The church leadership appears to have considered the issues raised in the petition too controversial, particularly in view of the recent SED-SPD paper and the political thaw it was initially believed to have signaled.

Despite its central preoccupation with the right of freedom of movement, it is notable that the petition raises the issue of *emigration* only obliquely. Indeed, the problem is addressed in the context of asking which measures might be undertaken to reduce the desire of the East German citizenry to depart for the West. The petitioners, a number of whom would later help found the citizens' initiative Democracy Now, noted the perception of those who left the country that it was "fatally" ill, and insisted on "a public discussion of social and political changes that would be appropriate to motivate former citizens of the GDR to return to the country." While the petition notes that "in the GDR, détente has increasingly gone hand in hand with a policy of 'demarcation' *[Abgrenzung]*," the authors are more explicitly concerned about the inaccessibility of Poland than they are about that of the Federal Republic. The petition's first demand is, in fact, for restoration of the freedom to travel to Poland, links to which remained difficult to sustain due to the continued restrictions imposed by the SED regime.[85] This aspect of the petition appears to have been driven principally by a concern that the policy of "demarcation" vis-à-vis Poland would facilitate the resurgence of those aspects of the Polish-German relationship that had led to the excesses of National Socialism and that, it will be recalled, were exploited by the SED in its efforts to immunize the GDR against the "Polish disease" during the Solidarity period of the early 1980s.[86]

Still, the petition demanding a "renunciation of the practice and principle of demarcation" was remarkable for its frontal attack on the regime's policy of demarcation. For the SED leadership had regarded such demarcation as a cornerstone of its survival virtually since the advent of *Ostpolitik* — a policy that, after all, promised "change through getting closer" *(Wandel durch Annäherung)*. At the same time, however, it was also notable for its reluctance to call openly for the right to choose one's place of residence, which in the East German context, of course, typically meant departure for West Germany.[87] Thus despite a certain sympathy for the concerns of the would-be emigrants, even these critics of the regime's failure to guarantee its citizens freedom of movement were unable to bring themselves to address head-on the freedom to emigrate: perhaps an understandable oversight, but an oversight nonetheless.

Conclusion

To be sure, the dissident intellectuals' reluctance to identify with the human right to choose one's place of residence is best understood as a response to the peculiarities of the conditions under which they operated. Still, it is probably also correct to say that the peculiar conditions of opposition and dissidence in the dictatorially ruled quarter of divided Germany were not auspicious for the development of a liberal outlook. Moreover, the continuing (though fading) vitality of the antifascist legitimation of the East German order among the intellectuals who dominated the dissident movement made them skeptical of identifications with German nationhood. As the two German states increasingly grew apart during forty years of enforced separation, such identification suffered further among younger East Germans.

These factors inhibiting the emergence of a broader liberalism give the lie to the still frequently invoked notion that German intellectuals are somehow congenitally "illiberal." Still, Ferdinand Kroh had put his finger on a central weakness of the opposition to the East German regime when he asked rhetorically, "Why should one struggle for more freedom in the GDR, when it practically seemed to fall into one's lap in the Federal Republic?" (Kroh 1988b, 11). Putting the matter this way, however, presupposed that West Germany's political, social, and economic achievements represented a satisfactory repository of one's hopes for the future. Yet it was precisely the East German dissident intellectuals' denial that this was the case that separated most of the them from the broad mass of the GDR's population. To complicate matters further, demands for "bourgeois" civil rights such as the freedom to emigrate might be met with the retort, "If that's what you want, why don't you just emigrate to the West?"[88] (The ease with which the question could be put by no means does justice, of course, to the potential difficulties confronting those who applied for emigration.) Clearly, the complexities associated with building "socialism in a quarter of a nation" were not a problem for the government alone. The peculiarities of the German division deeply affected the development of opposition among the GDR's intellectuals as well.

The discrepancy in outlook between those choosing the "exit" option and those committed to "voice" helped drive the dissidents into an unintentional but implicit alliance with the regime vis-à-vis the "other" German state. Neither could wholeheartedly embrace the Federal Republic without forfeiting their special claims to represent another, better Germany. This subterranean communion could not fail to influence the dissidents' attitudes on the emigration question. These attitudes, in turn, would have profound consequences for the course of events when the SED was faced with a massive challenge to its rule in 1989. Despite their continued distance from the most disenchanted elements of the East German population, however, those in the dissident scene — chastened by the events of late 1987 and early 1988 — had increasingly come to think of themselves as an "opposition" (see Knabe 1990b, 21). It was with a sense of growing disillusionment and alarm, though certainly without any premonition of the GDR's imminent demise, that the dissident intellectuals approached what would prove to be the denouement of socialism in the GDR.

Four

The Intelligentsia in the Socialist Denouement, 1989: Exodus and Opposition in the East German Transformation

The transformation of East German society that got underway in 1989 begins with a paradox: those who were to become the most prominent actors rode a wave of dissatisfaction that drove their fellow citizens not so much into their arms as — metaphorically speaking — into those of their West German compatriots. By comparison to their counterparts elsewhere in what used to be called the Warsaw Pact countries, the opposition to the SED was confronted with a special and unique problem in its challenge to the state in 1989. In order to control the direction of the transformation, the opposition had to develop support among a population that had two possible alternative identities: one as East German citizens and one as "Germans." Those elements of the opposition who advocated a reformed socialism in an independent GDR, in particular, faced the challenge of persuading the East German masses that their first loyalty was to socialism and the GDR and not to a "Germany" that took the concrete form of a comparatively democratic and prosperous West Germany.

The combination of exodus and opposition in the East German transformation process — unique in the Communist world in 1989 — requires a conceptual framework different from that used to analyze the break with Communist rule elsewhere in the Soviet bloc. In East Germany, the national question loomed larger for the opposition than for its East Central European neighbors, but it also loomed, so to speak, quite differently in the GDR than elsewhere. The East German intellectuals thrust into the forefront of the movement of opposition to one-party socialist rule that burst forth without warning in the fall of 1989 did not seek to link their emancipatory goals to the reconstitution of an ethnically defined nation. To the contrary, they were typically quite skeptical of anything that smacked of nationalist sentiment. As in the past, this negative (or, at least, indifferent) attitude toward German nationhood left them isolated from the mass of the citizenry and unprepared for the historic political developments they would soon face. Ironically, however, they owed their sudden prominence precisely to the persistence of constitutional and legal arrangements that gave the "Germans" in the GDR the right to claim West German citizenship simply by arriving on its territory. It was an important but then largely unrecognized harbinger of future developments that, contrary to the Tocquevillean scenario, the denouement of socialism in a quarter of the German nation was fueled by disappointment and desperation rather than by rising expectations of reform. The intimation of coming changes created by the advent of the Gorbachev era was repeatedly dashed, contributing then to a sense of despondency rather than of hope.[1] As the SED faced its final crisis of legitimacy, the dissident intellectuals sought to chart a new course for what soon proved to be a sinking ship. While they hoped to patch it up and make it seaworthy again, events showed that the leaky vessel could not withstand the riptide caused by relative material deprivation and the Federal Republic's constitutional nurturance of the notion of a "united Germany."

The Crisis Matures: The Reemergence of the "Exit"/"Voice" Dynamic

Mikhail Gorbachev's ascendancy to power at the center of the East European Communist order in March 1985 had raised hopes of domestic reform among ordinary citizens throughout the countries of the Soviet bloc. Yet, as we have already seen, the East German regime consistently dashed the population's hopes for changes along the lines of glasnost and perestroika. As in the period before the East German workers' rebellion of 1953, the SED's interest in maintaining its dominance in a quarter of divided Germany led it to resist the reform impulses emanating from Moscow. Further paralleling that earlier period, East Germany's reform-minded intellectuals would exploit the breach between Moscow and East Berlin to press their own campaign for a loosening of party controls.

At least outwardly, however, top party leaders refused to take account of political developments around them. Still, around this time the signs were multiplying that all was not sweetness and light at the highest levels of the SED. In 1987, Deputy Minister of State Security Markus Wolf, chief of the GDR's external spying activities, resigned his post. During the summer of 1988, rumors surfaced that Gerhard Schürer, director of the State Planning Commission and a member of the Politburo, had proposed to party leader Erich Honecker the dismissal of fellow Politburo member Günter Mittag, Central Committee secretary for economic affairs (Wielgohs and Schulz 1990, 17). Nothing of the kind occurred, however. Indeed, according to former Politburo member Werner Eberlein, among the indications of the paralysis that had taken hold of the leadership in the late 1980s was its failure to discuss a paper outlining Schürer's critique of Mittag's economic policies. The reason was that such a discussion would have reflected ill upon Honecker as well, and *that* sort of discussion simply did not belong to the rituals of the Politburo's weekly meetings.[2] By February 1989, Schürer was discussing plans to overthrow Honecker with Secretary for Security and Cadre Affairs Egon Krenz, in whom many had already come to see an heir apparent. A product of the party's youth and security apparatuses, Krenz seems to have been the only person the Politburo members considered seriously as Honecker's successor. The preference for Krenz began to take hold despite growing enthusiasm among the party rank and file for Hans Modrow, whom many regarded as the "German Gorbachev." But no one was prepared to assume the risks of bringing these plans out into the open until the fall of 1989, when it was already too late for the aging SED leadership to rescue itself. Indeed, in early 1989, a palace coup against Honecker was postponed in favor of the proverbial "biological solution."[3]

Despite the continuing failure of nerve among disaffected elements of top party officials, the political mood in the GDR had grown increasingly critical by that time. In November 1988, the East German government had forbidden the Soviet satire magazine *Sputnik,* a German-language publication that embodied many of the hopes of the GDR population for a liberalization along the lines of that taking place in the Soviet Union. While the magazine had been something of a thorn in the authorities' side for some time, the publication of an article critical of the German Communist Party during the 1920s apparently provoked SED General Secretary Erich Honecker personally to outlaw the publication. With its unmistakable message that the GDR would not follow the Soviet Union down the path of glasnost, the ban fell like a bombshell among the East German population. Yet *Sputnik*'s prohibition was only the peak of a wave of repression directed at independent publications in late 1988.[4] The independent *Umweltblätter* commented acerbically that "for the first time since Gorbachev's accession to power, the GDR government has let down its mask for all to see."[5]

The party leaders were, indeed, throwing down the gauntlet to those eager for changes in the government's policies on information and public life — which by this time had come to include broad segments of the GDR's population. Accordingly, the protests against the banning of *Sputnik* were by no means restricted to the usual circles of the critical intelligentsia. Indeed, numerous SED rank and filers turned in their party cards in response to the move. Strikes lasting several hours broke out in the old Saxon industrial center of Leuna, a hotbed of opposition during the workers' rebellion of 1953. In Berlin, a number of factory groups canceled their membership in the Society for German-Soviet Friendship, the official organization for cultivating East Germans' loyalty to the "great socialist brother-state." Protests even developed in the GDR's universities, where calm and conformity typically predominated as a result of the party's careful admissions and appointment policies. Actions decrying the ban were organized at the universities in Berlin, Halle, Weimar, and Jena. In the latter city, however, the protest amounted to a case of glasnost in action: the event was initiated not by East Germans, but by visiting students from the Soviet Union.[6] Still, the government's prohibition of *Sputnik* sharply undercut popular hopes that the GDR would follow the path of reform recently embarked upon by the Soviet Union and several of its satellites. The mood in the GDR came increasingly to be marked by desperation and despondency.

Soon after the controversy over *Sputnik,* dissatisfaction among the East German population peaked again in the wake of the party's fraudulent conduct of local elections on 7 May 1989. East Germans had long understood that election results were falsified, of course. This time, however, the burgeoning opposition took steps to demonstrate the hypocrisy and illegitimacy of SED rule by a sort of practical immanent critique of the system. Representatives of the group pressing for "renunciation of the practice and principle of demarcation," the IFM, the "Church from Below," and other independent groups organized a network of activists to monitor the voting results. As a result of this process, the activists were able to establish beyond any doubt that the elections had, indeed, been rigged. In an interview, New Forum cofounder Sebastian Pflugbeil described the impact of the May electoral fraud. The scandal, he said,

> embittered large segments of the population.... That was a bad situation, and one that led even some of the party members to start wondering. We were really organized that time, monitoring the vote count.... It was the first time that we could really say, "Look, these numbers are falsified." It was important that we could prove it.[7]

Indeed, it has rightly been said that the election monitoring carried out by representatives of the independent groups was the "first nationwide organized action of the emerging opposition in the GDR" (Wielgohs and Schulz 1990, 18). Especially in urban centers such as Berlin and Leipzig, and particularly among the younger, less established intelligentsia, the East German opposition was beginning to mature into a cohesive social and political force. A secret police report concerning what the Stasi characterized as "hostile, oppositional" forces, dated 1 June 1989, similarly concluded that the independent groups had achieved a "new level of cooperation" among themselves.[8]

At the same time, it was an indication of the continuing isolation and marginality of the opposition that the extent of the electoral fraud was not as great as one might have imagined. Most East Germans voted as usual on 7 May for the slate of candidates proposed by the party. According to Politburo member Günter Schabowski, the fraud was not a matter of raising the percentage "from 40 percent to 60 percent. It was an idiotic electoral fraud involving one-point-x percent here, zero-point-x percent there, carried out by the apparatuses who had always taken care of these things in order to mollify the excessive sensitivity of the leadership."[9] Schabowski appears to have downplayed the actual extent of the fraud, which the opposition monitors' figures suggest amounted to some 20 percent of the totals reported by Election Commissioner Egon Krenz (see Knabe 1989a, 14). Even if one accepts this estimate of the extent of the fraud, however, the fact remains that some 80 percent of the voting-age population of the GDR went and cast its votes as usual on election day.

Whether out of fear or out of mere conformity, the East German population that would so soon begin streaming out of the country as well as into its streets still showed considerable inclination toward docility in the face of SED control. This is by no means necessarily to say, however, that they were contented or that they considered legitimate the continued monopoly on power of the party's old guard.

The population's sense of disenchantment — and of fear — was exacerbated by the SED Politburo's enthusiastic endorsement of the Chinese government's suppression of protest demonstrations in Peking in early June. According to *Neues Deutschland,* the security forces' massacre of students at Tienanmen Square was a necessary response to "the counterrevolutionary rebellion of an extremist minority."[10] This language, familiar from the party's statements regarding Poland in the early 1980s and Czechoslovakia during the Prague Spring, could not have failed to help cool the ardor of rebellious spirits.

Despite the stirrings of indignation about these policies, therefore, the opposition remained merely an irritation to the party leaders, even if this fact was in itself an indication of the Politburo's waning grasp on political reality. According to both Günter Schabowski and Wolfgang Herger, chief of the Central Committee's Department of Security Affairs and a close associate of Egon Krenz, it was the emigration that led to the maneuvering in the Politburo to overthrow Erich Honecker, not the pressure mounted by the opposition. Indeed, Schabowski claimed that, despite the growing visibility of opposition activity especially after the fraudulent elections in May, such matters failed even once to find their way onto the agenda of the Politburo's weekly Tuesday morning meeting.[11] In mid-August 1989, the West German daily *Die Tageszeitung,* a legacy of the student movement of 1968 that was probably more sympathetic to the East German opposition than any other nationally distributed West German newspaper, wrote that the GDR's dissident groups at this time still did not amount to "an oppositional force worth taking seriously."[12] Contrary to the notion that the intellectually dominated anti-Communist dissident movement in the GDR was a powerful force in the fall of 1989, they had only begun to congeal into a serious political challenge to the East German regime.

The perfectly natural tendency to accord greater weight to those whose active and courageous opposition to the SED helped pave the way for the party's downfall — in some cases over many years and at considerable sacrifice — distorts our understanding of their actual role in the transformation process. It must be recalled that, with the exception of the tiny Initiative for Peace and Human Rights, *none* of the groups that came forward to challenge one-party rule in the autumn of 1989 existed other than on paper before late August of that year. Thus despite growing signs of the political maturation of the dissident movement, the various independent groups from which the opposition forces would soon emerge remained scattered and isolated until after the mass exodus that gathered force in the course of the summer months.

Those who left the GDR behind them suggested that the country was simply not worth saving, while many of those who stayed on to fight it out with the ruling party signaled a preference for retaining the state as an alternative to the Federal Republic. Indeed, it is by no means fanciful to speak of *two* East German movements: one facing west and, once this possibility took on greater plausibility, advocating rapid (re)unification with West Germany; and the other oriented to "dialogue" with the party over democratic reforms within a system still understood in some meaningful way as "socialist." The latter movement was dominated by the less established, younger intellectuals who had carried the tiny organized opposition to the regime in the grassroots groups in and on the periphery of the East German churches. As a result of the legitimacy crisis forced on the SED by the mass emigration, these relatively marginal figures were catapulted to the head of a mass movement of opposition to one-party rule that they had not themselves built. For a brief but important historical moment, however, the formerly marginalized intellectuals acted as conduits for and gave voice to mass discontent. The opposition forces gained adherents as the SED leadership dithered in the face of the emigration wave.

The mass emigration that began with the opening of the Hungarian border to Austria starting in May 1989 thus played a vital role in stimulating the formation of opposition organizations in the fall of that year. This central fact about the East German break with Communism is often misunderstood in analyses of the rise of regime opposition during that period. Such analyses accord *causal* significance in the collapse of socialism to the wave of protest demonstrations that gripped the country beginning in September.[13] Clearly, the demonstrations were important expressions of popular dissatisfaction with SED rule. But these massive challenges to the legitimacy of the regime were themselves a *product* of the crisis created by the mass emigration. In short, the mass flight of those voting with their feet was, as Timothy Garton Ash put it, "the final catalyst for internal change in East Germany" (Garton Ash 1989a, 16).

More exactly, the exodus was the very *condition of possibility* of the general use of the "voice" option in the GDR. Perhaps it would be most accurate to say that the mass emigration of 1989 was the *precondition for the emergence of the exit/voice dynamic itself* — that is, of a real *choice* between these two options. The mass exodus thus finally prodded the relatively marginal ranks of East Germany's dissidents into taking concrete steps to overcome the paralysis that gripped the country.

The Mass Exodus: Social and Political Aspects of the "Exit" Movement

Those East Germans who left the GDR before the opening of the Berlin Wall on 9 November 1989 thus paved the way for those who left after them as well as for those people committed to staying in the country to work for change. As a consequence of the emigrants' decision to leave the GDR behind, East Germans generally were starkly confronted with a choice many of them had never seriously faced before: Should I stay or should I go? The social characteristics of those who responded in different ways to that question tell us a good deal about the political situation in which, willy-nilly, the East German intellectual dissidents found themselves in the heady days of fall 1989. An understanding of the social composition and attitudes of the emigrant population helps make sense of the rapid decline in support for the dissident intellectuals in the citizens' movements as the break with Communist rule unfolded during late 1989 and early 1990.

The building of the Berlin Wall in 1961 had certainly helped attenuate the connections between the populations of the two German states. Yet it was significant for later developments that the desired destination of the vast majority of East Germans remained West Germany rather than other possible German-speaking countries such as Austria or Switzerland. The persistence of national feeling among the GDR-Germans derived in considerable part from the fact that refugee East Germans had a legal right to citizenship and certain forms of financial support if they went to the Federal Republic, as well as from West Germany's economic subsidies to the East German government over the years.[14] Other than those in the "valley of the clueless" around Dresden, which was unable to receive the broadcasting signal, the East Germans are generally believed to have routinely consumed West German media products. Indeed, they were said to have "emigrated each night via television." Irrespective of the causes, in any case, there remained a substantial feeling of connection to West Germany among broad segments of the GDR's population.[15]

Still, these legal and economic supports for national sentiment were not enough to counteract a decline in identification with the respective "other" German state, particularly among younger and better-educated Germans (see Brämer and Heublein 1990). This downward trend in ethnically defined national identification was natural enough, given that such forms of identification are historically determinate and not primordial. Moreover, the Social Democratic *Ostpolitik* beginning in the early 1970s, premised as it was on the reduction in West German ill will toward the GDR, had helped solidify the perception that there were, in fact, two separate German states. The SED responded to *Ostpolitik*'s potentially dangerous embrace by cultivating the "two-nation theory" as an essential ideological prop to its power. It is difficult to evaluate empirically the success of party intellectuals' efforts to disseminate the notion of a "socialist fatherland" rooted in class membership rather than ethnic identity. In view of the comparative lack of material advantages associated with this outlook in the GDR, however, such a project — though not intrinsically doomed to failure — faced serious difficulties.

In short, despite significant ruptures in identification with "Germany" brought about by forty years of separation, feelings of community among Germans East and West remained broadly anchored in popular consciousness. At least rhetorically, the goal of German unity constituted the touchstone of official West German pronouncements on "intra-German relations" *(innerdeutsche Beziehungen)* during the entire post–World War II division of the country. But the serious economic disparity between the two states would always help to keep the East German population focused on the advantages of West German–style freedoms.

The continuing preoccupation with, and attraction to, the Federal Republic is suggested in the statistics concerning emigration from the GDR to West Germany. Between 1962 and 1988, annual legal emigration from the GDR ranged between a low of 8,667 in 1973 and a high of 34,982 in 1984 (see Wendt 1991, 388). On average, these officially approved emigrants comprised some two-thirds of all those who left East Germany each year. Considering that the regime now largely controlled population outflows, the trend since the Berlin Wall was put up was, not surprisingly, toward much lower numbers of emigrants. More important even than its impact on the overall numbers of emigrants, however, the wall had dramatically transformed the age structure of the departing population, at least for a time. The regime's purpose in building the wall was primarily to hold on to the labor power of the young and vital; those approaching or already beyond retirement were regarded as expendable. Thus, in contrast to the situation before the building of the wall, most emigrants in 1965 were above the age of sixty-five, and only a small minority under twenty-five. In time, however, this pattern would be reversed. By 1974, the number of emigrants aged twenty-five to sixty-five outstripped those in the over-sixty-five group; by 1985, the under-twenty-five age group likewise dwarfed the number of emigrants over sixty-five. In 1989, the age structure of those departing the GDR legally almost reproduced that of 1955, when the under-twenty-five age group predominated, with the twenty-five to sixty-five category in the middle and the over-sixty-five group far behind (see Wendt 1991, 390–92). A West German analyst suggested in the early 1980s that — in addition to political dissatisfaction in the narrower sense — the disproportion between educational training and the actual level of qualification required for many jobs in the GDR was developing into a substantial problem of legitimacy for the regime (Kuhnert 1983; see also Kozakiewicz 1984).

Perhaps as a response to youthful discontent, the trend toward declining overall numbers of legal emigrants was dramatically reversed during 1984. Suddenly and without explanation, the number of those permitted to leave the GDR quadrupled from less than eight thousand in 1983 to almost thirty-five thousand; at the same time, the proportion of such persons among all emigrants rose to over 85 percent (see Wendt 1991, 390, table 2). Surveys of the first wave of that emigration in early 1984 found that "the largest group [of emigrants] were fitters, mechanics, administrators, engineers, health service workers, salespersons, and transport workers, and most came from the lower grades of these jobs." These emigrants named principally political reasons for leaving the GDR. Yet it is unlikely that all of them should be considered straightforward "political refugees." Indeed, one observer specifically rejected this notion, insisting instead that the available evidence suggested that "many of those who left did so because they thought their economic prospects would be better in the West" (Woods 1987–88, 159).

After 1984, the tide of officially permitted emigrants once again receded, but their numbers still remained higher than they had been before that unusual year. Between the emigration wave of 1984 and the end of 1988, well over one hundred thousand citizens of the GDR emigrated to West Germany, two-thirds to three-quarters of them with legal permission. The relative reduction in emigration resulted from the East German government's resumption of its earlier more restrictive emigration policies. In contrast, the East Germans' desire to leave the country appears to have continued unabated. Partially as a consequence of loosened travel restrictions that allowed more East Germans to visit relatives in the West, the share of total emigration made up by departures without permission between 1985 and 1988 returned to levels not seen since the mid-1970s (Schmidt n.d. [1990], 5–6). With the East German regime showing little willingness to undertake the kinds of reforms that had engendered so much hope elsewhere in the East bloc in the late 1980s, many East Germans came to view flight as their only escape from what was widely regarded, especially among the young, as the suffocating paternalism of the SED.

In the massive migration of 1989, some 340,000 people — an average of nearly 30,000 persons per month — left the GDR in an outflow that was unprecedented since the building of the Berlin Wall in 1961.[16] Although Hungarian soldiers began to cut holes in border fortifications with Austria in May 1989, it was not until August that emigrations effected by way of the occupation of West German embassies in Prague, Budapest, and Warsaw dramatically drove up the proportion of those fleeing the GDR without permission. Indeed, from January through October 1989, the percentage of those emigrating illegally (39 percent) was actually no greater than it had been in 1987, the most recent peak year. Although the absolute number of emigrants (167,204) was more than four times as great as that in 1988, and although the proportion of all emigrants who left without permission exploded in August and September 1989, the *total* percentage of emigrants to whom the authorities had granted permission to leave was, at least through September 1989, not significantly different than that prevailing in previous periods such as 1987. Still, the dramatic rise in illegal departures clearly began to spiral out of control by October, creating a situation of profound crisis for the Communist regime.

These surprising findings suggest that the SED leaders might have had at least some reason to think that they could safely continue to refuse a change of political course, or that they intentionally instructed local officials to grant more emigration applications as a means of letting off political steam. Indeed, new arrivals in the reception camps in West Germany reported that, after enduring various periods of time awaiting action on their applications for emigration, they were suddenly informed that they should prepare for immediate departure to the Federal Republic (see Schützsack 1990, 15). In any case, beginning in May — the month of the electoral fraud — the authorities became much more inclined to grant such applications than they had been since 1984. During that month, nearly twice as many applications for emigration were granted as during April. As the number of illegal emigrants swelled in the late summer months, however, what may have been a calculated release of pressure took on very different dimensions. The detachment from political realities among the top SED leaders grew increasingly apparent as the exodus swelled. It was in this increasingly critical situation that the party's official organ, *Neues Deutschland,* cynically counseled its readers that the emigrants were traitors for whom "no one should shed a tear."[17]

In a literal sense, the emigrants were indeed traitors, renouncing as they were their allegiance to their country. Yet it is precisely their radical rejection of the GDR that makes them of special interest in understanding the social dynamics of the break with Communism in East Germany, for the emigrants did not evenly reflect the East German population as a whole. In fact, the migrants' social profile diverged substantially from that of the overall population of the GDR. As images from the news media made clear at the time, young, economically active men were noticeably overrepresented among the 1989 emigrant population. In many cases, their families or relatives would later join them in the West if they did not accompany them at the time of their emigration, thus creating a "pull effect" that intensified the loss of population from the GDR.

There were also important disparities in the emigrants' geographic origins that pointed to politically relevant features of East German society at that time. One study of the emigration, based on data from 537 respondents during the period 29 August to 11 September 1989, found that emigrants with official permission to leave came disproportionately frequently from Dresden, whereas those who simply fled were drawn relatively evenly from the various administrative districts *(Bezirke)* of the GDR (Hilmer und Köhler 1989a, 1387). Generally speaking, the emigrants came disproportionately from larger cities, especially Berlin, and from the industrial centers in the south of the country (e.g., Dresden, Leipzig, Karl-Marx-Stadt [Chemnitz], and Gera). A study covering the entire year of 1989 corroborated these findings, establishing a direct correlation between population density and the relative size of out-migration losses. Emigration (as well as opposition) was concentrated in those urban areas of Saxony and Thuringia where the disastrous consequences of SED policies — such as environmental pollution, deterioration of the housing stock, and the neglect of historic town centers in favor of "extensive development" on the urban periphery — were most glaring (Grundmann n.d. [1990], 8).

Of particular interest to the present investigation, however, is the qualification structure of the emigrant population of 1989. This, too, diverged notably from that of the general population of the GDR. Two studies of emigrants registered at the central West German reception center in Giessen and at branch centers elsewhere in the Federal Republic offer insight into the educational background of those who turned their backs on the GDR in 1989. The first investigation, already noted above, was carried out between 29 August and 11 September. It found 86 percent of those questioned to have completed apprenticeships *(Lehre)*. Meanwhile, some 10 percent of the sample held academic degrees. Relative to their share of the overall population, both groups were thus overrepresented in the emigration during this especially hectic and trying period.[18]

The second inquiry is of somewhat greater value than the first because it is based on a much larger sample (4,696) representative of refugees and emigrants eighteen years of age or older and covers the period from 10 October until 14 March 1990, shortly before the GDR's first (and last) free elections on 18 March. On the basis of this study, we can compare those emigrants who left before the opening of the Berlin Wall on 9 November and those who left thereafter, when doing so became considerably less risky and difficult. Among emigrants from whom data were collected between 10 October 1989 and the opening of the border on 9 November, holders of university and technical school degrees *(Hoch- und Fachschulabsolventen)* were once again found to be overrepresented with respect to their share of the labor force. This period was characterized by a rapid and disproportionately great exodus of teachers, university-trained engineers, and medical personnel. After the announcement that East Germans no longer required visas to travel to the West, however, those with university degrees came to be *under*represented among emigrants, while the proportion of skilled workers *(Facharbeiter)* soared. In short, after 8 November 1989, the relative proportions among the emigrant population of those with higher education and of skilled workers, respectively, came to be reversed, such that the highly educated were underrepresented and skilled workers overrepresented among emigrants (Voigt, Belitz-Demiriz, and Meck 1990, 735–36).

Two studies based on official East German statistical sources help round out the picture of the educational qualifications of the 1989 emigrants. In one study, Siegfried Grundmann found that workers in the nonindustrial (and hence, in East Germany, less backward) sectors of the economy comprised a disproportionately large share of those who left the GDR in that year. Consistent with their greater absolute percentage of the overall labor force, the numerical majority of the emigrants were employed in industry. Yet such persons were underrepresented relative to their proportion among the resident population. Overrepresented were, in contrast, those employed in the nonindustrial sectors of the economy: in trade and distribution, the health sector, construction, and transportation. In general, Grundmann concluded that those with higher education were overrepresented in the overall migration of 1989 (Grundmann n.d. [1990], 11).

Due to the divergent educational profiles of workers in the GDR's industrial and nonindustrial sectors, respectively, Ines Schmidt has pointed out that overrepresentation among the emigrants of persons employed in the "nonproductive" sectors of the economy would suggest relatively greater losses of more educated workers. In the GDR in 1988, only 16.7 percent of employees in industry belonged to the broader category of the intelligentsia (i.e., graduates of a *Hoch-* or *Fachschule*), while 60.6 percent of those in the tertiary sector of the economy were counted as doing so (see Schmidt n.d. [1990], 24).

The contrasting patterns of migration among skilled workers and members of the East German intelligentsia point to important differences in their relative enthusiasm for a market economy and in their respective levels of identification with the GDR. But there were also considerable differences *within* the intelligentsia concerning the desirability of migration to the West. Indeed, Schmidt concludes in her study of migration from East Berlin that such differences in the propensity to emigrate among various segments of the intelligentsia "were greater than those between different groups of skilled workers. It may be assumed that in Berlin the frequency of emigration is particularly high among the medical, the artistic, and the technical intelligentsia in industry." For instance, graduates of higher education made up 29.9 percent of the Berlin emigrants employed in the industrial sector of the economy in 1989, whereas only 16.7 percent of employees in industry nationwide were beneficiaries of such training.[19]

Despite the overrepresentation of certain segments of the intelligentsia in the 1989 emigration as a whole, a number of forces would have contributed to their inclination to remain in the East. These factors, operative among the Berlin intelligentsia in particular, included:[20]

1. The high concentration of graduates of higher education among those in upper-level positions in the state and party apparatuses, at least outside the Politburo. In 1981, for instance, 83.6 percent of the candidates and members of the Central Committee of the SED held degrees from technical institutes or universities (Meyer 1985, 523, table 3).

2. A substantial portion of the Berlin intelligentsia, at least, had earned their degrees in the peculiarly East German Communist discipline known as "social sciences" *(Gesellschaftswissenschaften)* — a field that, due to its strongly ideological orientation, is not likely to have afforded degree-holders promising prospects in the West German labor market. Of the 83.6 percent of the candidates and members of the Central Committee with higher education in 1981, for instance, more than one-quarter of them held degrees in "social sciences."[21]

3. With a few exceptions, particularly among medical personnel, the relative technological backwardness of East German industry and research and development was likely to make more difficult a successful transition of members of the GDR's technical and natural-scientific intelligentsia into the West German labor market.

4. At least for certain groups within the intelligentsia, their standard of living — which often considerably exceeded the nationwide

average — had the effect of binding them more strongly to the GDR and thus weakened their inclination to emigrate to the West.

5. By 1989, the East German intelligentsia was almost entirely a product of the social development of the GDR, to which its members largely owed their opportunities for upward social mobility. This fact would have helped to cultivate at least some loyalty to the regime, even if the beneficiaries of these policies had criticisms of the system.

A variety of structural determinants — over and above the simple desire to stay put — thus generated a stronger loyalty to the GDR among much of the intelligentsia, even among those elements who may have been dissatisfied with the paralysis reigning in the upper echelons of the SED by 1989. The inclination to remain in the country was probably especially great among those in the intelligentsia whose disciplinary background was in the social sciences and humanities, where the party's "ideological penetration" was most pervasive. Because these fields often touched on central aspects of the SED's assertion of ideological primacy, the party was particularly concerned to staff positions in these areas with individuals committed to defending its rule. Such disciplines were better-fortified bastions of SED ideology and control than, say, the natural sciences, and their representatives were presumably less likely to leave the GDR in the fall of 1989.[22]

Thus were many in the intelligentsia inclined to remain in the GDR. Yet the motives of those among the intelligentsia who did leave also reveal important differences in outlook from those emigrants with less education. Political concerns — such as the lack of freedom of opinion and general political pressures — were most frequently named by all respondents as the decisive reason for emigrating from the GDR.[23] But the preoccupation with political and economic issues was not evenly distributed among the emigrants. One study of emigrants' motivations discerned a direct correlation between level of education and a desire for more political freedom. At the same time, the desire for an improved standard of living and a generally improved economic situation was found to be inversely related to educational background. As the emigrants' average level of education declined over time, economic concerns grew in significance vis-à-vis political concerns. Despite this divergence in motivations among different social groups, however, a resounding 83.9 percent of all emigrants from the GDR hoped for the accession of East Germany to the Federal Republic. Only 3.5 percent wished to see the continued existence of two German states; the other 12.6 percent favored some sort of confederation (see Voigt, Belitz-Demiriz, and Meck 1990, 737, and diagram 9, 744). Here was a clear harbinger of things to come.

The available evidence thus suggests that those groups among both the intelligentsia and the skilled labor force whose educational certificates and abilities promised relatively greater success in the West German labor market were overrepresented among those who left the GDR for the West. Yet bearers of advanced educational credentials demonstrated a relatively greater propensity than workers to depart the GDR during the period before 9 November, when such a move still involved considerable risk and the significant likelihood that one might never see one's family and friends again. To emigrate at this time required both courage and, particularly in the absence of relatives or contacts in the West, a good deal of self-confidence that one could make it in a relatively unfamiliar land from which there would be, one then assumed, no return. It was hardly a decision lightly taken. The emigration after the opening of the Berlin Wall, by contrast, had all the earmarks of a panic. That phase of the exodus was pushed by the fear that the SED would somehow retain its stranglehold on power, and pulled by the lure of the one hundred marks in "greeting money" that were handed out to each person upon arrival in the West.

The emigrant population from the GDR in the fall of 1989 thus shifted both in composition and in orientation as the break with SED rule gathered momentum. Those who left before the opening of the Berlin Wall in early November were disproportionately better educated, more motivated by political than by economic concerns, and more inclined to assume the daunting risks of flight than those who came later. Yet all of the emigrants seemed to be saying that the GDR was in deeper trouble than one might have concluded from press accounts of the efforts of the intellectual opposition to reform East German socialism. The voices of reform were by no means the only ones to be heard on East Germany's streets in 1989. But those voices, relatively familiar to the West German media, tended to receive greater media attention. The point of view of the dissident intelligentsia thus decisively but misleadingly shaped the "definition of the situation" in which the East German opposition to the SED found itself.[24]

Tongues Untied and Tied:
The Intelligentsia and the German Question

The mass emigration of 1989 had been made possible to a considerable degree by the Federal Republic's constitutional nurturance and financial subsidization of German national feeling during the years of the postwar German division, particularly after the building of the Berlin Wall in 1961. In its turn, the persistence of communal feeling — at least on the East German side — made possible the "intra-German" exodus and thus the very emergence of the "exit/voice" dynamic. As events quickly revealed, however, virtually no one on either side of the German-German border had thought seriously about or planned for the possibility of (re)unification. The emigration thus raised concretely an issue that the dissident intellectuals had not discussed in any programmatic detail because they tended to view even the preliminary step of eliminating SED rule as unachievable.[25] More interested in reconstructing the rights of citizens than in rebuilding a state embracing "all Germans," they were generally inclined to see only the negative features of the German question as popular forces were then thrusting it onto the historical agenda. Many of them believed that the extension of genuine citizenship rights could be carried out within a separate East German state that was reformed but still in some meaningful sense "socialist." This belief they shared with many in the SED,[26] whom the dissidents typically invited to participate in the envisioned rebuilding process.[27]

But some, particularly among the party intelligentsia, understood clearly that the ripening crisis of the East German regime could very quickly become a matter of the GDR's very survival. In mid-August, Otto Reinhold, rector of the party's Academy of Social Sciences, gave authoritative expression to the SED elite's awareness of the difficulties it confronted as a consequence of the mass exodus. In particular, Reinhold noted the peculiarly precarious existence of a "socialist fatherland" in a world organized, at least theoretically, according to the principle of national states:

> There is quite obviously a fundamental difference in this question between the GDR and other socialist countries. Before their socialist transformations, they all existed already as states with a capitalist or semifeudal order. Their statehood was thus not primarily dependent upon the social order. This is otherwise in the GDR. *The GDR is only imaginable as an antifascist, socialist state,*

as a socialist alternative to the FRG. What justification is there for a capitalist GDR next to a capitalist Federal Republic? There is none....There is therefore no room for playing around with...the socialist regime (Staatsmacht).[28]

With these remarks, Reinhold had gone to the heart of the matter being foisted on the historical agenda at that time. It is particularly notable that he speaks of the GDR as an *"antifascist,* socialist state," implying that *both* of these characteristics, building a sort of symbiotic unity, were central to the legitimation of the "other" German state.

Yet the antifascism identified by Reinhold as a crucial underpinning of the GDR's existence was fading as a popular source of ideological legitimacy for the regime. After a drawn-out process of obtaining permission from the Communist authorities for their research, a team of West German oral historians led by Lutz Niethammer set off in search of the "real" GDR in the second half of the 1980s. Of the quest for antifascist sensibilities among their many East German conversation partners, the investigators wrote that they had come up empty-handed: "It was not for want of trying that we can hardly report anything of a lived antifascist tradition in the industrial province of the GDR" (see Niethammer, Wierling, and von Plato 1991, 63). For his part, longtime dissident activist Ludwig Mehlhorn, a mathematician driven to work for the church as a result of his unorthodox political views, addressed the question of the persistence of the GDR's anti-Nazi legitimation in an interview in mid-October 1989. Mehlhorn argued that the antifascist consensus, which had held "for decades across wide segments of the East German population," had collapsed because the officially proclaimed antifascism — what the Jewish ex-Communist Ralph Giordano had called "antifascism by fiat" — had actually inhibited the process of an open discussion of the Nazi past in the GDR.[29] As the GDR began to fall hopelessly behind the Federal Republic in economic terms, most ordinary Germans no longer considered antifascism an important touchstone of their identity, even if they endorsed such a stance in principle. In other words, by the late 1980s, antifascist sentiment was, so to speak, a mile wide and an inch deep among the broader East German population.

Still, everyday life in the GDR was saturated with the residues of the antifascist struggle and of Nazism's defeat by the Allies, among whom the Soviet Union obviously occupied the position of first among equals. Despite the conclusions he drew about the lack of a lived antifascist tradition in the GDR's industrial hinterlands, Niethammer wrote in the heat of the dramatic events of 1989 that, in the GDR, "the Second World War is still very near" (Niethammer 1990a, 274). The struggle against fascism remained closer to people's experience in the socialist quarter of divided Germany than in the much-modernized Federal Republic, even if the result was a certain trivialization through overexposure. Yet, as the Nazi past receded in time and the threat of its resurgence lost credibility as a tool for mobilizing support for the party, the notion that the partition of Germany was appropriate punishment for Nazi crimes forfeited more and more of its persuasive power — to the extent that it had ever been accepted at all.

Commitment to the GDR as the embodiment of German anti-fascism had become principally, though by no means exclusively, the affair of older and more established East German intellectuals, even when they were critical of the paralysis and hypocrisy reigning at the top of the SED (see Erbe 1990). The persistence of these attitudes, a characteristically East German mixture of antifascism and anti-Stalinism, was reflected, for example, in a resolution issued by the presidium of the prestigious Academy of Arts on 4 October 1989, just three days before the official celebrations planned for the fortieth anniversary of the GDR's founding. In its ambiguity, the resolution pointed to the historical crossroads at which the GDR had arrived after four decades of existence. As if suspended at the threshold of a new era, the academy's leading figures both insisted on the need for "public-ness" *(Öffentlichkeit)* in dealings between the state and its citizens, and averred that "antifascism, love of peace, social justice, and the cultivation and increase of culture" are the "fundamental positions of our society."[30] There could hardly have been a better expression of the political enthusiasms and reticences of the more established East German intellectuals as they edged toward the precipice in the fall of 1989.

Yet the old formula linking the GDR, antifascism, and socialism no longer fired the imagination of younger East German intellectuals, even if they had by no means forgotten the crimes committed by Germans during the Third Reich. Discussing the emerging importance of the notion of "civil society" among politically attentive East Germans in a 1989 lecture in West Germany, exiled IFM cofounder

Wolfgang Templin described a new generation of East Germans that "no longer shared the doctrinaire claim to truth and the mentality of entrenched political camps typical of previous oppositions" (Templin 1989, 60). As Templin well knew, those camps had been defined in twentieth-century Germany principally as Communism and fascism. His discussion of the younger generation of East German intellectuals, sobered by more than half a century of dictatorship in Germany and increasingly concerned with "bourgeois" civil rights rather than with constructing a new utopia, is all the more remarkable in view of his own previous dogmatic Marxist orientation.

Still, most of the intellectual leaders of East Germany's burgeoning opposition groups traced their political heritage to left-of-center — and not infrequently Marxist — sources, as in the cases of Templin and Gerd Poppe, a protégé of Robert Havemann. The persistence of these attitudes caused considerable frustration among certain elements of the oppositionally inclined East German intelligentsia in the autumn of 1989. From his temporary residence in the United States, the émigré East German writer Uwe Kolbe chastised the "potential" opposition that emerged in the fall for its inability to escape from the older ways of seeing the world:

> The potential opposition in the GDR cannot assume clearer contours because it is bound to rules of language that derive directly from the existence of two German states. It desperately seeks a "Third Way" in order not to have to give up the demarcation *(Abgrenzung)* from the other Germany. It demands Western-style democracy — bourgeois democracy along the lines of the great human rights declarations — but one is not permitted to formulate this so directly. The division of Germany should be accepted — indeed, consolidated — as the result of the two wars initiated by Germany [in this century]. In any case, [that division] would be irrelevant in the future "European home" (it would in fact be terminated). Friends, it's hard to talk when your tongue is tied.[31]

Clearly, even the oppositional intelligentsia in the GDR was split internally on the eve of the Communist regime's final crisis; Kolbe's remarks constituted a direct challenge to the refusal of East Germany's dissident intellectuals to confront the political implications of the national question.

Soon enough, those figures would be swept aside by a massive upwelling of national sentiment among the East German citizenry. The dissidents' antipathy toward the national aspirations of their compatriots would help guarantee their marginality as popular enthusiasm for German unification grew during the final weeks of 1989. The national question represented a fundamental challenge to the project of civic reconstruction sought by the intellectuals who now called into being new citizens' movements as vehicles for wresting monopoly political power from the SED.

The Opposition Takes Form

Prodded into action by the emigration crisis, opposition groups at first consisting primarily (if not exclusively) of small groups of dissident intellectuals began to assume formal shape in the GDR in late summer 1989. While most of them sought to demonstrate their distance from the party-state with the symbolic trappings of newness and youthful enthusiasm, others tried to do so by asserting a claim to venerable older traditions in the German political heritage. The fledgling Social Democratic Party (SDP) led the way in making public its plans to build a new party,[32] but a group called New Forum was the first to gain wide publicity (via the Western media) with its manifesto "Awakening 89 — New Forum" on 10 September 1989. The group's founding meeting took place at the home of Katja Havemann, widow of the deceased regime critic Robert Havemann — a figure who was, according to West German press accounts, "still venerated" by New Forum's founding group, despite having passed away several years earlier. Its thirty initial signers were drawn almost exclusively from among the less established intelligentsia, and especially but not solely from the core groups of the intelligentsia — artists and scholars — as well as doctors, pastors, and others. Indeed, the founding group included some of the most prominent figures in the Berlin dissident scene.[33] New Forum quickly announced that it would seek official recognition as a constitutionally legitimate organization for the representation of social interests. The regime responded curtly that such an organization was simply unnecessary. On 18 October, the day Honecker was driven out of his post as SED general secretary in favor of his protégé Egon Krenz, the authorities insisted that the GDR already offered "all the necessary forms and forums"[34] for carrying out a dialogue on the future of socialism in the GDR.

Despite the party's initial refusal to bend to the dissidents' challenge, New Forum was soon followed by the formation of several other new organizations that sought to help resolve the crisis engendered by the mass emigration by building a more attractive social and political order in the GDR. In addition to New Forum and the Social Democratic Party, these included Democracy Now (Demokratie Jetzt), Democratic Awakening (Demokratischer Aufbruch), the Green Party (Grüne Partei), and the Independent Women's Association (Unabhängiger Frauenverband). An emphatically left-wing congeries promulgated the so-called "Böhlener Platform," from which a "United Left" (Vereinigte Linke) was supposed — but failed — to emerge, other than in the form of a small group of Marxists, Trotskyists, and other radical leftists.[35] Meanwhile, the IFM remained a small, elite group that did not make significant efforts to become a mass organization. Its tiny core of activists either remained in the IFM fold (Wolfgang Templin, Gerd Poppe) or — as in the cases of Bärbel Bohley (New Forum) and Ulrike Poppe (Democracy Now) — they branched off and helped form the nuclei of other groups. Thus despite a predictable process of elite differentiation, the emergent East German opposition groups revealed considerable continuity with their predecessors in the GDR's dissident landscape.

Recruitment of the Opposition Leadership

The early leaders of the groups that sprang up to challenge the SED's monopoly rule came primarily from among the narrow circles of activists involved in the grassroots groups in or on the fringes of the East German churches, principally in Berlin. They typically ranged in age from twenty-five to forty and tended to know each other, belong to the same cultural, political, and friendship circles, and share a sympathetically critical stance toward the GDR's socialist regime. Frequently, they had previously been involved together in other independent groups. Several of the founders of Democracy Now, for example, had earlier initiated the "Petition for a Renunciation of the Practice and Principle of Demarcation." Previous members of the coordinating committee for the (after 1984) annual gathering known as "Concretely for Peace" (Konkret für den Frieden), which had become a loose framework ensuring continuity in the work of the various grassroots groups, figured prominently among the leaders of the new groups.[36]

The available evidence indicates, moreover, that the founders and leaders of the mushrooming independent groups in East Germany that captured the world's attention in the wake of the emigration were drawn disproportionately from among the GDR's intelligentsia. Though many of these dissident activists had been the beneficiaries of higher education, it was not unusual to find among them people who had been unable to finish their degrees due to political persecution. Democracy Now cofounder Ulrike Poppe was a prominent example of this activist type.[37] Alternatively, having completed their academic training, they were driven out of work or into occupations inconsistent with their training or qualifications as a result of their political views or activities. The Ministry of State Security quite accurately believed that the leaders of the "hostile" groups with which it was preoccupied were drawn from among a sort of academic proletariat.[38]

Despite the predominance among the new groups of certain familiar figures from the dissident intellectual scene, however, the burgeoning revolutionary situation also created an opening for the recruitment of spokespeople and activists who had theretofore kept their discontents largely to themselves (or at least within bounds tolerated by the regime). One important recruiting ground for such new figures was the GDR's prestigious Academy of Sciences, which had been resurrected after the collapse of the Third Reich as the successor to the venerable Prussian Academy of Sciences. According to Wolfgang Thierse, a literary historian before his rapid climb from obscurity to the position of vice-chairman of the German Social Democratic Party:

> The Academy of Sciences was always a particular construction. It was distinguished from the university by virtue of the fact that there was no teaching going on there, so the ideological pressure was not as severe as it was in the university.... It was always an attempt to pursue a particular policy toward the intelligentsia, to get specialists to stay in the GDR and to let them work relatively undisturbed.... In political and ideological terms, the academy was an idyll by comparison to the university. That was an important difference. I myself was at the university long enough to be able to appreciate this difference. The academy was always viewed as a sort of bastion of the bourgeois intelligentsia. That explains in part why people suddenly came out of there that were totally unknown, but who had of course been doing serious scholarly work and who had, on the side, in small groups, in little circles, or otherwise developed their political convictions, their political utopias.[39]

The academy may have been in many ways idyllic compared to the rest of the GDR's scholarly landscape. Only later in the interview did

Thierse mention that, as a result of his steadfast refusal to join the SED, he would never have been able to rise above a certain level in the academy's hierarchy. A number of other important figures in the new political groups who came out of the Academy of Sciences shared similarly disrupted or derailed curricula vitae.[40]

Thierse's comparison of the situation of the Academy of Sciences with that of the universities suggests a more general principle concerning the political controls imposed upon intellectual life in the GDR: the more research-oriented the institution, the greater its relative freedom from ideological constraints. Because teachers at all levels bore the responsibility for inculcating in the GDR's youth the tenets of socialist virtue, the party generally subjected them to considerably more rigorous ideological vetting and supervision than it did mere researchers, the implications of whose work could be relatively easily contained within the relevant scholarly communities.

Further distinctions can be made regarding the degree to which different disciplines were subject to such controls, and hence regarding the extent of their respective contributions to the reform movement. Not surprisingly, those fields charged with the elaboration of the official Marxist-Leninist worldview were less likely to have been nests of reform sentiment, particularly (as Thierse's remarks suggest) if this activity was meant for student consumption. At the core of this category were the social sciences, history, law, and, to a somewhat lesser extent, psychology. During the heady last days of 1989, sociologist Manfred Lötsch of the party's Academy of Social Sciences himself celebrated a "farewell to the legitimating science" of sociology (Lötsch 1989). In an interview, Lötsch noted that his interest in undertaking sociological research on the intelligentsia was motivated in part by the desire to escape from the ritualized professions of ideological purity demanded in any writing about the working class.[41] The ideological demands placed on sociology were too great, and the selection processes used to recruit its practitioners too successful, however, for that discipline to develop into a significant source of reform thinking for the population at large (see Peter 1990).

The field of history was especially vulnerable to external ideological intervention as a result of its direct relevance to describing and interpreting the supposedly lawlike historical processes that had culminated in the advent of socialist society. Yet even here, the degree of historiographical partisanship depended on such factors as a subject's proximity to the present, its relevance to relations among the socialist allies (especially the Soviet Union), and the salience of the working class to the topic under discussion.[42]

In contrast to these academic fields, the law was not merely an ideological concern but a direct part of the state's functioning. Friedrich Wolf, vice-president of the Association of Jurists of the GDR, tried during late 1989 to draw up a balance sheet of "light and shadows" in answer to the question, "Is the GDR a state of laws *[Rechtsstaat]*?" Despite the identification of "grave shortcomings in the GDR's conformity to constitutionalism *[Rechtsstaatlichkeit]*," Wolf found that "light predominates" over the shadows in the East German legal system, primarily as a result of its achievement of certain kinds of "substantive justice" such as the right to work and to housing.[43]

Still, even in the highly sensitive area of jurisprudence, there were occasional exceptions to the generalization that none but the most politically reliable were to be found in the profession. Gregor Gysi, a young lawyer who would soon assume the chairmanship of a reformed SED, had defended dissidents such as Bärbel Bohley and represented New Forum in its bid to achieve legal recognition. Here again, however, the proximity of the Federal Republic helped pressure the regime into living up to its commitments under such international agreements as the Helsinki Final Acts or the Universal Declaration of Human Rights. Interestingly, Uwe-Jens Heuer, a professor of law who had been widely regarded before 1989 as one of the principal reformers within the SED, had been removed from a teaching post at the Humboldt University after his early writings on democracy and law in the socialist system; he ultimately landed in the Academy of Sciences as a section director in the Institute for Legal Sciences.[44]

This brief survey suggests that it is quite misleading to assert without qualification, as has Peter Marcuse, that "universities were hothouses of reform" (Marcuse 1991b, 846). At best, this approach tends to ignore the fact that most university departments and faculty went along with the ideological controls imposed upon them by the party and its organizations within the universities. The higher one rose in the academic and administrative hierarchy, moreover, the more true this was likely to have been.

At worst, this undifferentiated view of the GDR's universities slights the fact that very little reform activism came directly out of those institutions before late 1989, even if university students and faculty grew more politically active as the process of "wrapping up"

(Abwicklung) the universities gathered steam after unification, threatening the value of their degrees or their jobs (see Ammer 1991). Pastor Christian Führer of Leipzig's St. Nicholas Church, the meeting point from which the first dramatic Monday demonstrations departed in the fall of 1989, told me in an interview:

> As far as the intellectuals — the university and older high school students — are concerned, they played a very sad role in the "autumn revolution": namely, they weren't involved. They were all anxious about their careers, their hard-won privilege of studying, and they stood out primarily in terms of their conformism. So there was a certain irony to it when the students who didn't give a whit about us [the reformist activists before fall 1989], then in 1990, as the "wrapping up" was going on in the universities, they were all out on the street. Then there was no more police repression, they weren't risking anything. The role of the intellectuals [in the revolution] was an embarrassing chapter.[45]

Two aspects of Reverend Führer's remarks are especially noteworthy. Because he was a participant in and close observer of political developments in Leipzig throughout most of the 1980s, his description of the "very sad" role of the East German intellectuals in the fall of 1989 commands considerable credibility. Even more significant, perhaps, is Reverend Führer's tendency to equate the category of "intellectuals" with those educated people who supported the regime. The relative disinclination of East Germany's intelligentsia to challenge the state openly both distinguishes it from the traditionally obstreperous image of the East European intelligentsia *and* puts that behavior in the context of a longer, less salutary tradition regarding the political passivity of German intellectuals. While making allowance for some hyperbole, West German sociologist Karl Ulrich Mayer may have been closer to the mark than Marcuse when Mayer wrote, "This was probably the first revolution in which the universities — professors and students — stood on the side of the old regime" (K. U. Mayer 1991, 91).

In sum, the leaders of the independent political groups that emerged to challenge the SED's monopoly on political power in the fall of 1989 were not drawn from among the older, better-known intellectuals who had long been associated with the desire for a loosening of the party's control over ideas and information, but who had never crossed the line to "opposition." Rather, the groups were led primarily by younger, nonestablished intellectuals who were denied access to positions of power, income, and influence as a result of their lack of "political capital." They were East Germany's intellectual "blocked ascendants."

The intellectual character of the opposition elite was reflected both in the social bases of recruitment of their leaders and supporters and in the themes the groups emphasized. New Forum cofounder Jens Reich noted in an interview during October 1989 that, precisely due to the group's loose programmatic orientation toward dialogue, the organization appealed primarily to an "intellectual upper class that has made use of this [historic] opportunity and taken full advantage of glasnost and of speaking without fear."[46]

Naturally enough, the independent groups' relatively narrow recruitment base exposed the dissident intellectuals to attacks from a regime that still claimed to represent the working class. In mid-October, the SED elite indicated that it shared Reich's analysis of the social base and interests of the East German opposition. To the extent that they took any serious notice at all of the growing opposition,[47] in fact, the party's leaders appear to have viewed New Forum as something of an intellectuals' debating society. On 18 October 1989 (the day of Honecker's abdication as SED general secretary), the party hierarchy issued a circular designed to guide its functionaries' response to the burgeoning independent groups, particularly New Forum. That document quite accurately characterized the group's founding members as consisting of "intellectuals, students, and pastors," and went on to note that, "indicative of their goals, only one worker is to be found among them."[48] The party elite here clearly sought to rejuvenate the tactic, familiar from previous challenges to socialist rule in the GDR and elsewhere in the Soviet bloc, of discrediting the opposition as a mere conspiracy of self-serving intellectuals.

Indeed, at least in early October, this tactic was directly combined with the threat of violence. In a much-discussed and frequently reprinted statement, one of the "factory militias" *(Betriebskampfgruppen)* created by the SED early on to defend socialism in the GDR announced: "We are ready and willing to protect that which we have built with the work of our own hands in order to put an end to these counterrevolutionary actions — with weapon in hand, if necessary!"[49] Within a few days, however, the teeth had been taken out of this threat as the regime shrank from a threatened bloodbath during the next subsequent Monday demonstration in Leipzig, on 9 October. Contrary to Egon Krenz's later assertion that he had been responsible for averting a "Chinese solution" in Leipzig, the peace had been maintained by the efforts of the local citizens' movements and by the promulgation on radio of a joint declaration signed by the local party leadership and several prominent intellectuals (including the conductor Kurt Masur, now head of the New York Philharmonic Orchestra).[50] The much-feared possibility of a bloody defense of one-party rule failed to materialize as cooler heads prevailed far from the center of power in the East German capital. After the party elite's retreat from the precipice of violence on 9 October, its essential paralysis became manifest, and the path lay open for the dismantling of its power — even if this was by no means obvious to the participants at the time.

Programmatic Aspects of the Opposition

At least initially, all the groups that emerged in the fall of 1989 to challenge the wobbling Communist regime were more or less enthusiastic about some sort of "socialism," however defined. To be sure, support for socialism ranged from appeals to create a "true," democratic socialism to the East German SDP's more moderate endorsement of the "social market economy" that had proved so successful in the Federal Republic. Even if these groups were not opposed to the introduction of some market mechanisms, however, there were no paeans to the free market as could be found elsewhere among East Central European opposition movements by this time.[51] Indeed, there was considerable linguistic and programmatic overlap with the reformist visions of intellectuals in the ruling SED. Several philosophers and economists involved in the "Research Project on Socialist Theory" at Berlin's Humboldt University advanced the most serious and widely publicized reform proposals.[52] A number of these younger, reformist party intellectuals assumed the role of a sort of brain trust around lawyer Gregor Gysi when he was tapped to lead the SED's successor, the Party of Democratic Socialism (PDS), after interim general secretary Egon Krenz had been discredited and the party was forced to surrender its constitutionally guaranteed "leading role" on 1 December 1989.

Despite the broad enthusiasm among the leaders of the newly founded groups for a noncapitalist alternative to the GDR's deformed socialism, not all of them chose to refer directly to "socialism" in their public statements. They did not necessarily confuse their own reform-socialist political outlook with a widespread desire for a new "socialism"; many of the dissident intellectuals were well aware that the average East German did not hold in especially high regard the social order with which that term had come to be associated. On the one hand, the ill-fated independent group Democratic Awakening, which would soon be absorbed into the conservative, CDU-dominated "Alliance for Germany" after splitting into left- and right-wing factions, at first loudly proclaimed its enthusiasm for a "democratic socialism."[53] Democracy Now, on the other hand, spoke more circumspectly of building a "solidaristic society." Democracy Now cofounder Ulrike Poppe later claimed, however, that the use of this euphemism for "socialism" was a tactical move designed to avoid scaring off potential adherents.[54]

In contrast, the political initiative that most explicitly viewed itself as part of the tradition of European social democracy, the East German SDP, announced its allegiances straightforwardly and insisted on the binding character of that tradition. The fledgling party was officially founded at a meeting held near Berlin on 7 October 1989 — at the same time that Soviet leader Mikhail Gorbachev was embracing Erich Honecker at ceremonies commemorating the fortieth anniversary of the GDR's founding.[55] According to East German SDP cofounder Markus Meckel, the date of the meeting was chosen quite consciously as a way to challenge the regime's assertion of its "socialist" character and in order to insist on the SDP's more legitimate socialist paternity.[56] Meckel explicitly addressed the issue of the SED's deviations from social democratic tradition in his programmatic speech at the East German Social Democrats' first large-scale meeting in December 1989: "After the unification of SPD and KPD on the current territory of the GDR [in 1946], this [social democratic] tradition was quickly suppressed." In an effort to counter conservative electoral propaganda linking the East German Social Democrats (now abbreviated, after a rapprochement with the West German party, as the SPD) to the old "socialist" regime, the SPD distributed flyers analyzing the "forced unification" of the KPD and SPD in 1946 and asserting, "The SED was [subsequently] systematically Bolshevized by the Communists."[57] And indeed, as a consequence of social democracy's continued vitality in the Federal Republic, the SED had sought to eliminate the competitive influence of its venerable heritage ever since the early postwar campaigns against "social democratism."

The sudden proliferation of organizations had its origins at least as much in old personal rivalries among the dissident intellectuals as in substantive programmatic differences between the emerging independent groups. A number of persons insisted that their particular choice of organizational affiliation was largely accidental.[58] Given the groups' lack of programmatic concreteness and their general political similarities, this relative arbitrariness is hardly surprising; there was no obvious programmatic reason to prefer one group over another. Initially, at least, New Forum eschewed concrete demands and platform details in favor of what it vaguely insisted was the need for "democratic dialogue."[59] Jens Reich argued that this lack of concreteness was a matter of avoiding a new "paternalism" and a new monolithic stance in place of the old; Sebastian Pflugbeil averred that, were it not for the advantages of New Forum's programmatic openness, he would have joined the SDP.[60] Yet this reluctance among the new independent groups to articulate concrete strategies and positions is not likely to have bolstered their esteem in the eyes of the broader population, which clamored ever louder for firm steps to end one-party rule.

It was, indeed, the SDP founders' insistence on programmatic and organizational commitments that distinguished their approach from that of the other groups. The proposal for creating a Social Democratic Party in the GDR had been circulated by its authors in the late summer of 1989 and was at that time dismissed by a number of the later founders of other groups precisely for its insistence that it assume the organizational shape of a party rather than the looser "movement" form. In interviews, SDP cofounders Markus Meckel and Martin Gutzeit justified this approach with reference to Hegel's notion that "ethical life" *(Sittlichkeit)* — in contrast to Kant's abstract, general, but "categorical imperative" — had to be concrete and rooted in binding forms of social interaction.[61] In any case, just as the opportunity for mass support emerged, the inherited *querelles berlinoises* continued to help undermine the development of a coherent opposition force among East Germany's dissident intellectuals.

It is important to note in this connection that it was the weekly Monday demonstrations in Leipzig that initially sparked the mass popular movement for political reform, not the rallying cries of small groups of dissident intellectuals who had only just begun to form themselves into independent groups in late summer and early fall 1989. The Monday demonstrations were the more or less spontaneous outgrowth of the "peace prayers" in St. Nicholas Church that had been kept alive by Pastor Christian Führer and others over a seven-year period.[62] During these years, St. Nicholas hewed closely to its policy of being "open to all." This policy made it impossible for those grassroots groups who did not wish to cooperate with the would-be emigrants to exclude them from attendance or involvement, as occurred in Berlin. In the late 1980s, Pastor Führer had in fact created a support group focusing specifically on the needs and concerns of would-be emigrants and had undertaken (by his own reckoning) moderately successful efforts to achieve reconciliation between the two groups. In addition, one of the Leipzig grassroots groups, the Working Group on Justice (Arbeitskreis Gerechtigkeit), itself had a task force devoted to the subject of emigration. Indeed, Harald Wagner, a dissident activist from Leipzig, claimed that

> the history of the opposition in Leipzig [was] a very long and significantly different one than that in Berlin. In Berlin there were always more or less high profile people who . . . , as is often the case in leftist groups, battled each other in sectarian fashion and took shots at those who were closest to them. As long as I've been paying attention, since the late 1970s, that's been different in Leipzig. From the beginning, we've worked according to a more integrative concept. There were groups that integrated the entire spectrum, from the church to the SED.[63]

The Monday afternoon prayer sessions became the meeting point both for the grassroots groups and for would-be emigrants awaiting disposition of their applications.[64] Workers predominated among this latter group.[65] It was this mixture of large numbers primarily of non-intellectuals protesting for the right to leave the GDR and elements from the intellectually top-heavy independent grassroots groups participating in the Monday "peace prayers" that constituted the yeast that rose into the mass Monday demonstrations in the fall of 1989.

The Opposition Movement Spreads

Contrary to the widespread ascription of the outbreak of the revolutionary situation to the dissident intellectuals, the first demonstrators to take to the streets in 1989 were not the church-based opposition groups but the applicants for emigration who congregated at St. Nicholas Church. In what would prove to be a rehearsal for the fall, Minister of State Security Erich Mielke reported to his lieutenants that about half of the 650 participants in the "peace prayer" of 14 March 1989 took advantage of the presence of a substantial Western media contingent that was on hand for the semiannual Leipzig Trade Fair to mount a demonstration in the city's downtown. After some 850 [!] police and Stasi agents broke up the rally, the demonstrators shouted such slogans as "Stasi get out" and "Freedom — human rights." Security forces tore from the hands of one protester a poster with the inscription, "Travel freedom, not official arbitrariness."[66]

This scenario was repeated six months later when the Trade Fair returned, along with the Western media, in early September. Once again departing from the Monday "peace prayer" at St. Nicholas Church, applicants for emigration gathered to demonstrate in Leipzig's historic city center. And, once again, they raised their rallying cry, "We want out!" In contrast, the opposition groups comprised disproportionately of young intellectuals, church people, and representatives of the various alternative "scenes" threw down the gauntlet to the emigration applicants, defiantly proclaiming, "We're staying here!" Of course, they were simultaneously announcing to the East German regime their intention of staying and making life difficult for the dictatorship. According to a report in the West Berlin–based daily *Die Tageszeitung,* these two groups marched separately at the Monday demonstration in Leipzig on 4 September 1989, the great majority of whose participants demanded the freedom to emigrate.[67] Clearly, St. Nicholas Church has as strong a claim as anyplace to the title "cradle of the revolution," but the reform-oriented groups there were very much in the minority relative to the would-be emigrants. The antiregime energy and enthusiasm that "got the ball rolling" in East Germany, so to speak, had been that of the emigrants, though these protesters presumably had little interest in the reform of socialism in the GDR.

The demonstrations gathered strength and spread throughout the GDR in the subsequent weeks, but they were not necessarily organized by the intellectuals leading the citizens' movements. In fact, while support for New Forum had swelled to some thirty thousand by the end of October, this increase in adherents struck the group's founders quite by surprise. Predictably enough, as the number of signatories of New Forum's manifesto expanded, its following came more and more to represent the social structure of the GDR.[68] Already by mid-December, however, the activist core of that organization went through a shakeout that revealed New Forum to be heavily dominated by the intelligentsia and preoccupied with issues nearer to the heart of that stratum, such as ecology and education. The participation of working-class activists had already begun to recede considerably.[69] Similar developments were afoot in the other groups created by the "revolutionaries of the first hour," to the extent that they had ever reached beyond the intelligentsia in the first place.[70]

The attitudes and social background of the demonstrators in Leipzig, the city that author Christoph Hein called the "hero city of the revolution," are of special importance because of the signal effect of its Monday demonstrations on the rest of the GDR in the fall of 1989. First, in a study based on five thousand questionnaires distributed over a four-month period from mid-November to mid-February (with a response rate of 80–84 percent), Kurt Mühler and Steffen Wilsdorf discerned a tendency for workers to displace students and members of the intelligentsia among the population of demonstrators, as well as for men to supplant women. The demand for rapid reunification with the West increased in volume with the shift in the relative proportions of these groups present in the demonstrations. Over time, the respondents' evaluation of the concepts "GDR" and "FRG" also revealed significant differences, with students and members of the intelligentsia more positively oriented to the "GDR" without necessarily espousing its continued independence. In general, the divergence of opinion on the question of the speed with which the two countries should be (re)unified typically ran along age lines: the older the respondent, the more likely s/he was to support (re)unification (Mühler and Wilsdorf 1991, 40–42). Mühler and Wilsdorf thus point to a significant schism regarding the question of reform or (re)unification along lines of age and education. By January 1990, the workers had reasserted their control of the demonstrations and put the demand for (re)unification at the forefront. In the process, according to two other observers of the movement in Leipzig, "they had done nothing but reoccupy in the original sense the antisocialist public sphere initially created by those wishing to emigrate."[71]

Conclusion

Against the background of the pre-1989 history of the East German opposition and of the sociological characteristics and political attitudes of the emigration of 1989, it is clear that the dissident intelligentsia came to the fore primarily because of their ability, rooted in their greater stocks of cultural capital, to give voice to the discontent of the broader population, not because the citizenry backed their broader political goal of a reformed socialism. Still, of course, this "moral minority" briefly embodied and articulated the desire of the broader East German population to get rid of the SED's monopoly on political power. But beyond that, it was unclear how long the alliance would continue. Only with the opening of the Berlin Wall did the citizens of the GDR gain the opportunity to express clearly their attitudes toward the decisive historical and political question of German unification.

Five

The Prophets Outcast: The End of the GDR and the Coming of German Unification, 1989–90

After the crumbling of the Berlin Wall and the elimination of the constitutional clause guaranteeing the SED's monopoly on political power, the process of German unification was well under way. Sensing that they were powerless to halt the rising tide of prounification sentiment, the leftist intellectuals associated with both the SED and the citizens' movements reluctantly began to accept the shift in popular mood toward a project of *national* rather than *civic* reconstruction (embodied in the shift of slogans during November and December 1989 from "We are *the* people" to "We are *one* people"). Still, they raised various arguments against what was widely if problematically referred to as "reunification." Objections from the left to the melding of the two German states ranged from the fear of a resurgence of "Great German" temptations to the projected catastrophic consequences of an overhasty introduction of the market economy into East Germany. As the March elections to the parliament (Volkskammer) approached, however, survey data indicated that while the majority of the East German population had quite restrained expectations of the advantages associated with unification *in the short term,* they believed that it would bring improvements, especially of an economic nature, in the longer run. In short, the broader population tended to reject the talk of "colonization" that had attained great currency among the intelligentsia during this period (see D. Roth 1990, 383–85).

The first and last free elections in the GDR definitively confirmed the lack of popular support for a so-called third way between capitalism and Stalinism — the path so enthusiastically endorsed by many prominent East German intellectuals, both in and outside of the SED, as the break with Communism began. The March parliamentary elections demonstrated that the GDR's citizenry favored importing the already existing welfare-state democratic capitalism of the Federal Republic over the project of rebuilding a discredited socialism. For better or worse, the debate over *whether* the two German states should unify was thus finally put to rest; *how* unification should take place remained to be determined.

Yet the impending assimilation of the GDR and the Federal Republic left unclear the place of the East German intellectuals in the political landscape of a future united Germany. As unification increasingly took on the air of inevitability, those who objected to that outcome of the transformation process in the GDR were increasingly subjected to criticisms of a sort that recalled darker periods of anti-intellectualism in German history. Indeed, the GDR's disappearance from the world's stage was accompanied by an acrimonious controversy over the alleged role of the East German intellectuals in supporting the Communist dictatorship. For many of the dissident intellectuals who had been involved in the abortive process of promulgating a new constitution for the GDR, however, the achievement of constitutional reforms remained an important concern. As the two German states became officially united, a certain bifurcation occurred among the politically active elements of the former East German intelligentsia. Some of them found themselves marginalized by their attachment to concerns relating primarily to the GDR's dictatorial past, while others accommodated themselves to a greater or lesser extent to the new, "all-German" political situation.

Divided Loyalties:
The Dissident Intellectuals Defend the GDR

As a result of the SED's failure to undertake convincing changes in the political system during October and November, the emigration movement continued to swell in the final months of 1989. Under these circumstances, the leading figures of the recently formed movement for domestic political reforms recognized that this undertaking required appeal to the East Germans' loyalty — that force which, in

Albert Hirschman's scheme, helps moderate the propensity to choose the "exit" option.

It was to this concern for GDR-loyalty that reform-minded intellectuals quickly turned. In a massive demonstration at Berlin's monumental Alexanderplatz on 4 November, the reformist East German intellectuals acquired their most visible platform within the GDR until that time. This extraordinary show of support for political change, the largest protest rally in the GDR's history, had been organized chiefly by those associated with East Germany's theatrical stages. The speakers on that day personified some of the most important contradictions among the reform forces — contradictions that at that time still remained buried beneath the veneer of a popular movement united in opposition to the party's continued monopoly on power, information, and social rewards. In particular, the podium bore figures from among the younger, less prominent intellectuals who populated the ranks of the new civil rights movements; older, established intellectuals such as Christa Wolf and Stefan Heym; and, finally and most problematically, Politburo member Günter Schabowski and apostate former espionage boss Markus Wolf. One West German observer noted that the proximity of these intellectuals' generally anticapitalist views to those of the ruling party carried with it the risk that "the new opposition movements could become estranged from the population just as quickly as they became its mouthpiece" (Knabe 1989a, 19–20). As events would soon reveal, these were prescient words. Indeed, the most enduring message of the demonstration, which was variously estimated at five hundred thousand to one million, was embodied in Christa Wolf's words: "Imagine there was socialism and nobody went away."[1]

For any kind of socialism — whether reformed or of the one-party variety — the matter of stanching the outflow of East Germans to the Federal Republic had grown increasingly critical. Publicly, however, the party leadership continued to pretend that the mass exodus was a negligible — or at least manageable — problem. In contrast, the intellectual opposition voiced its distress over the mass emigration and its allegiance to the GDR in an appeal delivered over state radio on 8 November 1989 — the day before the opening of the Berlin Wall. Several prominent intellectuals and representatives of New Forum, Democratic Awakening, the Social Democratic Party, Democracy Now, and the Initiative for Peace and Human Rights had endorsed the appeal, which was read over the East German airwaves by Christa Wolf. Conceding the intellectuals' relative weakness in the face of the situation they confronted, the statement begins by noting, "We are aware of the powerlessness of words in the face of mass movements, but we have no other means than our words." The heart of the appeal, however, lay in an attempt to bind popular loyalties to the project of civic reconstruction. Aware of the sacrifices they were demanding from the East German population in choosing grassroots civic renewal over the consumerist quick-fix promised by the CDU, the appeal's signatories promised "not an easy, but a useful and interesting life[;] no quick prosperity, but participation in big changes."[2] The hardships associated with the institutional rebuilding process, the reform intellectuals suggested, would be repaid not in cash but in the inalienable coin of democratic self-esteem.

Coming immediately on the heels of the huge demonstration of 4 November, the statement was the expression of an intellectual opposition that still had little cause to believe that its leadership of the popular movement would be called into question. The reality, though not necessarily the illusion, of a continued alliance between the intellectuals and the broader citizenry was irrevocably destroyed, however, by the opening of the Berlin Wall. As only became apparent in retrospect, that momentous event signaled the de facto end of the GDR. But so soon after the mass outpouring of reform sentiment of 4 November, the vision of a rejuvenated socialism that had so dominated the rhetoric of that rally still danced in the heads of reformist intellectuals. Acutely aware of the potential diversion from the task of building an indigenous civil society that might result from the opening of the borders, New Forum issued a statement imploring the GDR's citizenry:

> Don't let yourselves be diverted from the demands for a political reconstruction of society! You were asked your opinion neither about the erection of the wall nor about its opening.... You are the heroes of a political revolution — don't let yourselves be pacified with travel possibilities and debt-driven injections of consumption![3]

As the East Germans turned increasingly toward the promise of Western prosperity, the gulf between the aims of the leaders of the intellectually top-heavy opposition and ordinary East Germans widened into a chasm.

The naive optimism characteristic of the dissidents' radio appeal of 8 November was perhaps understandable in the context of a bifurcated Germany whose dual statehood no one expected to change in the foreseeable future. Coming nearly three weeks after the opening of the Berlin Wall, however, the manifesto "For Our Country" raised numerous eyebrows among Germans East and West.[4] Dated 26 November 1989, the appeal amounted to a desperate plea for the defense of the rapidly failing GDR. Its authors argued that the East Germans should build a "solidaristic society" as a "socialist alternative to the Federal Republic." The statement starkly asserted that the alternatives confronting the GDR consisted exclusively in "the [continued] independence of the GDR" or "the sellout of our material and moral values." In particular, the manifesto appealed to the GDR's "antifascist and humanistic ideals" as a source of inspiration and legitimacy in defending the GDR's autonomy from the FRG. Given that these ideals had never been realized in the East Germany of the SED and that the party had long since "sold out" the country to the West as a result of its poor economic policies, however, this appeal to popular loyalty found little resonance among the broader population. Initial endorsement of this utopian vision of a democratized GDR came primarily from the more established East German intelligentsia. These supporters included a number of the country's most prominent intellectual figures, including writers Christa Wolf and Stefan Heym.

Somewhat inexplicably, however, longtime dissident activists Ulrike Poppe and Konrad Weiß, cofounders of the opposition group Democracy Now, and Pastor Friedrich Schorlemmer, a cofounder of Democratic Awakening, also signed the manifesto "For Our Country." In an interview, Poppe described her support for the appeal as follows:

> That came out of the fear that we would be rolled over by the Western system, and would thus lose our opportunity for self-determination. In addition, there was still a bit of a reform-socialist conception involved. We didn't just give up the critique of capitalism that we had held through all the years — we really didn't consider the Western system to be the alternative for us.[5]

"For Our Country" had, of course, been motivated more than "a bit" by a reform-socialist outlook; the document was, as Poppe's remarks suggest, strongly critical of the capitalist aspects of West German society.

The awkward overlap between this position and that of the collapsing SED emerged quickly and clearly after the East German media reported that recently installed party leader Egon Krenz and a number of other members of the SED's Politburo and Central Committee had also signed the appeal. The result was that an "unholy alliance" had come into being "that none of the initiators had sought or even considered possible" (see Streuel 1990, 92). Indeed, Ulrike Poppe admitted in the aforementioned interview that she and Konrad Weiß had received a good deal of flak for their endorsement of the manifesto.

By no means all of the GDR's reform-minded intellectuals accepted the view of sharply posed alternatives facing the East German population articulated in "For Our Country," however. Literary historian Wolfgang Thierse, who would soon rise to prominence in the Social Democratic Party, had refused to sign the statement because, he said,

> it was my impression that the intelligentsia wanted to use the population as the raw material for its next utopia, a population that was exhausted, spent from the realization and collapse of the last utopia. I can understand very well how one could come up with something like that in this situation, but I felt that it was too much to ask of people. The shift in slogans from "We are the people" to "We are *one* people" was precisely this reaction, that people said to themselves, "Why now build the next utopia, this time the real, the genuine, the wonderful socialism, and the real, beautiful GDR, where we had had only the shabby one up till then?" The majority said, "No, the achievable prosperity, the achievable freedom, the achievable democracy is so near, it's right next door, in the other part of Germany, that's what we have to achieve, all else is an illusion, we won't live to see that, we're supposed to be sacrificed again." I found that more intelligent than most.[6]

Thierse was surely correct to suggest with this last remark that those who refused to accept the popular embrace of the goal of German unification were less than optimistic about the political choices that would be made by a population that had paid them so little attention during their previous years of dissident activity.

More than any other document produced by the East German dissident intellectuals during the fall of 1989, "For Our Country" betrayed the peculiar situation in which the critics of SED rule found themselves in the GDR. They were caught on the horns of the dilemma that had already been noted by Academy of Social Sciences rector Otto Reinhold: the GDR and a noncapitalist alternative to the

Federal Republic were inextricably intertwined. One depended upon the other, and hence an endorsement of one entailed endorsement of the other. Even if one rejected the dictatorial model of Soviet-style socialism that was then unraveling in the GDR, any system beyond the Federal Republic's welfare-state democratic capitalism required for its realization the vehicle of a separate state. The GDR's anti-Stalinist opposition was thus trapped between its inherited critique of capitalism, itself powerfully rooted in antifascism, and its insistence on the achievement of "bourgeois" civil rights; between its desire to overcome the dangerous division of Europe and its lack of enthusiasm about Western institutions. As the sources of support for the manifesto "For Our Country" dramatically illustrated, this position made for strange and unexpected bedfellows, who soon enough realized their mutual desires were incompatible. When, only two days after the publication of "For Our Country," West German chancellor Helmut Kohl promulgated his "Ten-Point Program" calling for a gradual confederation of the two German states, the ironies of this situation were thrown into high relief. Still, even Chancellor Kohl's vision of the common German future clearly assumed that the GDR would continue to exist for some time to come.[7]

The younger generation of East German dissident intellectuals tended to view this desperate attempt to rescue the GDR's supposed "humanistic values" as the defense of a beachhead they had long since abandoned. They had experienced "socialism" as a system more of repressive paternalism and vegetative boredom than of working-class emancipation or a future-oriented antifascism (see Erbe 1990, 78–80). The thirty-seven-year-old Prenzlauer Berg poet Lutz Rathenow, for example, responded quite differently to the opening of the Berlin Wall than did his older colleagues who had initiated the appeal "For Our Country." Reflecting on the recent opening to the West, Rathenow wrote:

> Who could demand from one who had been imprisoned in his country for twenty-eight years that he not venture out through the suddenly flung-open door, but instead that he should undertake a thorough cleanup of his jail with the aim of transforming it into a normal apartment house? ... Not that I absolutely have to have *one* Germany, [however]. (Rathenow 1989, 285, 290)

With these remarks, Rathenow articulated clearly the attitudes of many among his generation of East German intellectuals. Born after the end of the Third Reich, their experience of Germany had been only of a postfascist nation divided against itself. Thus despite the collapse of socialism's utopian connotations for them, they have none of the enthusiasm for German unity that had characterized the older generations of intellectual dissidents. The attitude of these younger intellectuals is decidedly postnational; they do not identify in any affirmative way with Germanness, but at the same time they lack any nostalgia for the East German Communist *ancien regime*. "The history of our nation offers little occasion for celebration," Rathenow wrote as the German nation embarked on the process of reconstituting itself after a lengthy and generally hostile separation. "There's no reason to be a German, other than that one already is one" (Rathenow 1989, 290). As noted earlier, East Germany's younger intellectuals shared this outlook with their counterparts in the Federal Republic; both groups tended to identify less with German nationhood than their older compatriots.

The Collapse of the Old Regime and the End of Opposition Unity

It was against this background that the divergence in views between the heavily intellectual opposition and the broader East German population grew increasingly apparent. The popular movement of opposition to SED rule had succeeded with dizzying speed in bringing to its knees the Marxist-Leninist party that had ruled the GDR for some four decades. In the space of just three months after the return of the Monday demonstrations to Leipzig on 4 September, Erich Honecker was forced from office (17 October); the government of Willi Stoph resigned (6 November) and was replaced by that of the reform-oriented Hans Modrow (13 November); the party's constitutionally guaranteed "leading role" was stricken from the constitution (1 December); Honecker's successor as SED general secretary, Egon Krenz, came and went (6 December); representatives of the SED and the "bloc parties" began to meet with representatives of the citizens' movements at the "Round Table" negotiations (7 December); and the SED held an extraordinary party congress at which it renamed the party the PDS (Party of Democratic Socialism) and elected forty-year-old lawyer Gregor Gysi to its chairmanship (8–9 December).[8]

Around this same time, the intellectual leaders of the civil rights movements began to concede that their vision of a reconstructed civil society in an independent GDR was growing increasingly impracticable in view of the pressure of the street demonstrations in support of unification. On 12 December 1989, Democracy Now issued its "Three-Step Plan on Unification," which outlined an approach bearing significant traces of the older East German dissident intellectuals' aim of a unified Germany that was militarily neutral and politically reformed in both of its former constituent states. To the traditional goal of reforming West Germany in a "socialist" direction, however, the dissident intellectuals had added a concern for a process of constitution making that would make grassroots and plebiscitarian elements central to the process of state unification.[9]

Nevertheless, by the time the East German government agreed to introduce elements of political pluralism and the civil rights movements began (however reluctantly) to accept the coming of unification, a deep gulf had emerged between the intellectuals and the demonstrators in the East German streets. One worker gave vent to the popular alienation from the reform-oriented intellectuals in the unadorned accents of the Berlin proletariat: "When I hear that — by profession theater director, poet, painter — then I know: they don't know nothing about work. . . . They want us to build 'em a 'socialism with a human face.' For another ten years. Without me, I'll tell you that."[10] These remarks suggest that Wolfgang Thierse had accurately assessed the popular mood in late 1989.

In an interview, New Forum cofounder Jens Reich retrospectively described his own belated recognition of the distance that had separated the intellectuals leading the citizens' movements from the East German "man on the street," and the widespread perception among the latter that, despite their clamor for political change, the intellectuals were really just part of an untrustworthy elite. During a vacation in the countryside not long after the momentous events of 1989–90, Reich chanced upon a local farmer who recognized him from television. "What you do for a living anyway?" the farmer wanted to know. "Are you another one of these philosophy professors?" Reich comments on this:

> For him, there's no fundamental difference between me and Schabowski or Krenz. That was not clear to me [in the fall of 1989]. I always thought one could distance oneself from them, go to the people, and the moment you do that the whole system falls apart. But he just sees a "master of the word" in front of him, where

he himself is a "master of the deed." . . . They didn't see [SED party leader Erich] Honecker or [Minister for State Security Erich] Mielke as intellectuals *[Intelligenzler]*. For the worldview of these people, who didn't necessarily reflect any further, but who simply lived their normal lives, there was no fundamental difference, the boundary was simply between manual and mental labor. . . . That was more important than the difference between those who wanted a reformed . . . or true socialism or a third way and those who were against it.[11]

Reich's remarks suggest that many workers may have perceived the dissident intelligentsia as little different from the younger, more reform-minded SED leaders who undertook the abortive attempt to salvage one-party rule by replacing the aged Erich Honecker first with Egon Krenz and then, when that substitution failed to persuade the population of the party's seriousness about reform, with Dresden party secretary Hans Modrow. Both in terms of their intellectual habitus and their ideological commitments to a "reformed socialism," the workers seem to have viewed both groups as privileged and thus politically suspect. In the end, of course, Reich's comments tell us more about the self-perception of one of the GDR's leading dissident intellectuals than about the views of East Germany's less privileged strata. Still, they bespeak a sense, tempered by temporal distance, of the intellectuals' isolation in the insurgent days of late 1989 — an insight strengthened by hindsight that was also borne out by subsequent developments.

By December, the coincidence of the dissident intellectuals' attitudes with those of the street demonstrators was slackening fast, while the inclination grew among some representatives of the civil rights movements to ignore the sentiments being voiced in the streets. For his part, Uwe Kolbe took the opposition intellectuals to task for their tendency to dismiss those demands articulated by the protesters that departed from the goal of a reformed socialism:

When independent intellectuals, initiatives, and groups suddenly express discontent in the same tones as the powers that be, I see a disturbing sign. Under the banner of tolerance and the renewal of the politics of the popular front, something is brewing that I consider the narrow-mindedness of a stratum, no, of the intelligentsia that has become a class. (Kolbe 1990, 87)

Kolbe refers specifically in this passage to George Konrad and Ivan Szelenyi's theoretical approach to understanding the relationship between the party and the intelligentsia under socialism. According to them, socialist societies had increasingly come to be characterized by a rapprochement between the intelligentsia and the party, whose ranks were drawn increasingly from among the intelligentsia as time went on.[12]

Interestingly, Jens Reich indirectly confirmed Kolbe's argument regarding the awkward social and political position of the East German intelligentsia. Reich recounted in an interview that he, too, had come to recognize (after the fact) that the approach outlined by Konrad and Szelenyi was most appropriate for grasping the situation of the GDR's intelligentsia. Their analysis overcame what Reich called the "Djilas approach, which suggested that [the party and the intelligentsia] were enemies.... As a result of the structure of the system, we were so narrowed in our thinking that we were not creatively active. That was a contradiction between our political function and our creative ambitions."[13] To be sure, the complications arising from the apparent social and political proximity between the leadership of the party and the dissidents engendered considerable hostility among those who did not share the reformist intellectuals' views.

The gap between the worldview of at least parts of the socialist intelligentsia and the rest of the population became the subject of a sharp and high-profile exchange between Stefan Heym and émigré writer Monika Maron, the daughter of a prominent early SED functionary who had fled to Hamburg in 1988 after her first novel had been refused publication by the party's censors. In an indication of the fact that the events taking place in the GDR now had an undeniable "all-German" significance, the exchange took place in the pages of the West German newsweekly *Der Spiegel.* Heym had published an essay there in early December 1989 in which he reacted to the opening of the Berlin Wall and the East Germans' descent upon the consumer paradise that had thus become accessible to them. After noting that "the uplifting moments [of the revolution] are over," Heym continued:

> The population that, after years of subordination and escape, had summoned up its strength and taken its fate into its own hands, and that only yesterday appeared to strive nobly toward a radiant future, was transformed into a horde of the possessed who, pressed back-to-stomach, mobbed [the West Berlin department stores] Hertie and Bilka in pursuit of the golden trinket.[14]

Heym's response to the opening of the border bore striking similarities to the reaction of an earlier German literary figure to the revolutionary upheavals of his time. In the aftermath of the French Revolution, the important dramatist and aesthetic philosopher Friedrich Schiller had been similarly disappointed by the behavior of the masses. Though those epochal events had boldly opened up the possibility of enshrining Reason in human affairs, the great German thinker wrote, the "base desires" of the masses had stymied the realization of this tantalizing prospect.[15]

For her part, author Monika Maron caustically responded that Heym, who had published numerous works in the West over the years and thus led what was by East German standards a very privileged life, displayed in this piece "the arrogance of the well-fed man who is appalled by the table manners of the starving." Playing on Brecht's poem "The Solution," that ironic lampooning of the party's response to the workers' revolt of 1953, Maron claimed: "This time it's not the government that is disappointed by the people; this time, it's the poets [Dichter]. The heroic act of the revolution is hardly over, and they decide that the people went into the streets for the wrong goals — because they weren't those of the poets." In short, as the opposition intellectuals advocated a renewed, democratic socialism, "the chasm between the workers and the intellectuals," so frequently observable in German history, was surfacing yet again.[16]

Heym's negative reaction to the fall of the "intra-German" border was widespread among East German intellectuals.[17] Among older, socialist intellectuals such as Heym and Christa Wolf, this response derived from an anti-Western sensibility rooted fundamentally in their antifascist anticapitalism. For the younger intellectuals, however, the rejection of the West had more to do with an anticonsumerist mentality that was a feature of both the "antipolitical" politics that emerged throughout the East bloc and the "postmaterialist" outlook that had grown widespread among the younger, better-educated segments of Western democratic societies (see Knabe 1988). Still, in combination with the relatively narrow recruitment base from which the reformist opposition leaders were drawn, this attitude made the dissidents vulnerable to the charge that they were just spoiled intellectuals insensitive to the mundane, material interests of the general population. This charge is, indeed, a notable aspect of Maron's response to Heym.

In addition, Heym's articulation of the frustration felt by many intellectuals toward the behavior of ordinary East Germans suggests another important aspect of the gulf separating them from the popular majority. At least for some of them, their enthusiasm for popular movements extended only to those that supported the project of a reformed socialism, whatever exactly that might have meant. In effect, of course, it would mean what those who controlled the political transformation took it to mean. In *this* respect, at least, the intellectuals thrust to the fore of the popular movements in the GDR during late 1989 behaved like all revolutionary leaders before them: they used their superior ability to create images and to manipulate symbols to portray their own interests as those of the entire political community.

Yet in the face of a prosperous and democratic Federal Republic, popular support for this claim to leadership was extremely fragile. The existence of the other German state helped to sharpen and clarify the political differences among the East German citizenry as Communism collapsed. That other German state also posed a grave threat to the aspirations of those who sought to defend the notion of a post-national state-nation in Germany against those seeking to resurrect a nation-state of Germans defined in ethnic terms. As the latter approach to state building gathered momentum, the opportunity was lost to explore a "third way" beyond capitalism and Soviet-style socialism.

The Prophets Disarmed: The GDR's First Free Parliamentary Elections, March 1990

With the coming of the new year and the Round Table's promulgation of a date for elections, the GDR's path leading toward parliamentary democracy lay open. Yet the country's peculiar national situation created deep obstacles to the indigenous reconstruction of civic institutions. In particular, the dissident activists who called into life the various opposition groups in the fall of 1989 — the so-called revolutionaries of the first hour — complained with good reason that their chance to compete in the elections was robbed from them by interlopers from the Federal Republic. Ignoring a Round Table resolution barring them from making campaign appearances on GDR territory,[18] prominent West German politicians entered the fray in advance of the Volkskammer elections, muddying the clarity of sentiment among the East German populace toward its homegrown anti-Communist opposition. Still, data collected among a representative sample of 4,696 emigrants during the period 10 October through 14 March concerning their party preferences indicated that 44.2 percent would have voted for the CDU, while 21.4 percent said they would have voted SPD. Some 21 percent said they were undecided but would not have given their vote to the PDS (the reformed SED) (Voigt, Belitz-Demiriz, and Meck 1990, 738).

Yet public opinion polls carried out in the GDR itself continued to point to an SPD victory until shortly before the election. Even as late as early March, public opinion polls reported that the SPD would win 34 percent, the CDU just 22 percent if the election were to be held the following Sunday. Many observers expected a victory for the Social Democrats for three principal reasons. First, the East German population was generally thought to have been grateful to the Social Democrats for *Ostpolitik,* to which various improvements in everyday life in the GDR might have been attributed after the implementation of the Basic Agreement (Grundlagenvertrag) between the two German states in the early 1970s. Next, the territory of East Germany included relatively industrialized areas that were thought to have been Social Democratic bastions for reasons both of tradition and of social structure. This misconception was especially widespread with respect to so-called Red Saxony, which in fact had not been "red" since well before the coming of the Nazi dictatorship (see Walter 1991). Finally, the Social Democrats in the GDR were the only truly "clean" party in the March election campaign, having been formally founded only during the period of the break with Communism in the second half of 1989.

Those parties grouped in the so-called Democratic Bloc — the Christian Democratic Union (CDU), the Liberal Democratic Party of Germany (LDPD), the National Democratic Party of Germany (NDPD), and the Democratic Peasant Party of Germany (DBD) — had all functioned as "transmission belts" of SED rule under the old regime, their party statutes explicitly accepting its "leading role" in political affairs. Yet the West German CDU quickly adopted its East German counterpart, while the Federal Republic's FDP absorbed a reformed LDPD as the de facto unification of the political system proceeded in the run-up to the elections (see Weilemann et al. 1990).

In contrast, the SPD had been eliminated from the East German party system as a result of the 1946 merger with the Communists that gave birth to the SED, and the specter of "social democratism" had fuelled the ruling party's neuralgia about social democratic deviations ever since.[19] Moreover, at least initially, the East German SPD had had difficulty gaining the support of its West German namesake, in part as a result of disagreements over the party's *Ostpolitik*.[20]

As the election would soon reveal, however, the illusory expectation of a Social Democratic victory reflected Western observers' inclination to mechanically transfer assumptions derived from the electoral sociology of the Western democracies that were quite irrelevant to the political realities of the GDR. In the parliamentary (Volkskammer) election of 18 March 1990, the CDU-led Alliance for Germany in fact received 48 percent of the total vote, while the SPD won 21.9 percent. The remainder was distributed primarily among the PDS and various smaller parties and groupings, some old and some new. The electoral groupings representing the civil rights movements that had been the most visible indigenous advocates of a break with the SED monopoly on power together received less than 5 percent of the total vote.[21]

Though at the time it was assumed that the preelection polls were inaccurate because unrepresentative or otherwise unscientific, subsequent analysts have typically argued that last-minute changes in voter preferences explain the unexpected outcome.[22] Indeed, the period immediately preceding the election was marked by growing indications that the East German economy was in worse condition than anyone realized and by West German chancellor Helmut Kohl's fervent insistence during barnstorming junkets to the East that the fastest way to prosperity was through rapid unification.[23] The SPD had made no secret of its concern, shared with many of the representatives of the civil rights movements, that a sudden fusion of two radically different social and economic orders could cause severe economic hardship for the East German population. As antisocialist sentiment grew in the GDR, the CDU had not shrunk from using the SPD's moderate approach to unification to tar it with the brush of support for "socialism" — and this despite the East German CDU's own history as a "transmission belt" of SED rule. The East Germans' resounding endorsement of the former "bloc party" CDU suggested the degree to which the election was viewed in terms of unification and access to West German institutions rather than of the party system inherited from the old order.

The election thus revealed that the political preferences of the emigrants surveyed between October and March — excluding their rejection of the PDS — reflected much more accurately the political mood of their compatriots whom they left behind than did the media's attention to the Round Table and its negotiations with the lame-duck Communist government. Due to the lack of traditional electoral camps and the relative unfamiliarity of many of the candidates, the elections were a more or less purely issue-oriented affair, with the primary question being that of the speed with which unification would take place. Though by this time all the parties and the civil rights groups had made clear their commitment to unification, the CDU-dominated Alliance for Germany proclaimed most loudly its aim to push unification at top speed, whereas the left parties argued for a more gradual approach. In effect, the emigration had drained off a considerable element of East German prounification sentiment, leaving behind a vastly greater leftist voting potential among certain groups.

Closer analysis of the Volkskammer election indicates just how much this leftist electoral support was concentrated among the intelligentsia and students.[24] In the country as a whole, the SED's successor, the PDS, which advocated a go-slow approach to unification, achieved its best results among the intelligentsia. Thirty-one percent of that occupational stratum voted for the PDS — more than for any other single party. Some 20 percent of both students and "higher level managers" *(Leiter),* a small group drawn from more technical occupations in trade and industry, likewise voted for the PDS. Notably, however, support for the SED's heirs reached nearly 50 percent among the Berlin intelligentsia, where the party-bound intelligentsia was concentrated. At the same time, the two electoral coalitions of the civil rights movements, the Greens/Independent Women's Association (UFV) and Alliance '90, achieved above-average results among both the intelligentsia and students. Meanwhile, 55.4 percent of all workers voted for the CDU-led Alliance for Germany; in Saxony and Thuringia, indeed, the alliance received fully two-thirds of the working-class vote. By comparison, among workers the PDS won a mere 8 percent and the parties of the civil rights groups only 3.1 percent (D. Roth 1990, 377–78, tables 4 and 5).

The intelligentsia gave disproportionately great support to those candidates most strongly associated with the efforts to rescue or reform socialism. This fact, along with the underrepresentation of workers among supporters of those parties, ratified the trend toward a political schism between workers and intellectuals that had grown increasingly unmistakable since the opening of the Berlin Wall. The popular alliance between the intelligentsia and the rest of the East German population had been but a brief interlude that lasted only as long as a relatively unpolitical citizenry felt compelled to rely on the intellectuals for leadership in breaking with Communist rule. With the opening of the "intra-German" border, however, the East German population gained easy access to the already existing civil rights and prosperity of the Federal Republic. In that situation, the reform-socialist forces — from the PDS to the civil rights movements — lost their ability to persuade the populace of the need to rebuild an indigenous civil society from the ground up or, after forty years of SED misrule, that socialism was indeed reformable.

An examination of the social characteristics of the representatives voted into the first freely elected parliament in the GDR yields further evidence of the shift of support away from the "core" intellectuals who had so dominated the leadership of the various reformist groups that formed in the fall of 1989. To be sure, the East German parliament revealed the persistence of popular enthusiasm for academically trained intellectuals, a group that contributed some 85 percent of all representatives to the newly elected legislative chamber. But this finding must be qualified in several respects. Rather surprisingly, the SPD — which had been founded with the aim of contesting the SED's legitimacy as heir to the political traditions of the German working class — had the highest percentage of graduates of higher education *(Akademiker)* with 92.8 percent. Alliance '90 was close behind the SPD in terms of the number of *Akademiker* among its parliamentarians; seventeen of twenty had earned postsecondary degrees.[25]

In a reflection of the selection processes used by the SED to ensure its control over higher education, however, the parliamentary representatives of the PDS had by far the largest percentage of *doctoral* degrees (62 percent). The average percentage of Ph.D.'s among all parties and groups represented in the parliament was 40.1 percent; the corresponding percentages were, respectively, 36.4 percent for the SPD and 42.1 percent for Alliance '90. Virtually no workers were to be found among the parliamentarians of either the PDS or Alliance '90; approximately three-quarters of all such individuals in the parliament represented parties associated with the Alliance for Germany. In these respects, at least, the social structure of the parliamentary representatives also dimly mirrors that of their voter support.

Far from the mocking characterization of the GDR in the fall of 1989 as a "republic of priests,"[26] however, theologians were overshadowed in the first freely elected legislature in the GDR; the new parliament was, instead, "strongly dominated" by members of scientific, technical, and medical professions. Representatives of these occupations comprised slightly less than half of all *Akademiker* in the parliament. More than half of these, or 27.5 percent of all university-trained parliamentarians, were engineers of one kind or another. Possible explanations for this finding include the relative freedom of the sciences and engineering from ideological penetration and the perceived need for scientific and technical expertise in solving the economic problems whose urgency had grown so glaring since the demise of the SED's control over information.

Despite the voters' apparent preference for the practitioners of the more practical professions, clergy nonetheless played a significant role among the parliamentarians representing the genuinely new political forces in the GDR. Although theologians made up only 6.6 percent of the overall complement of representatives, they contributed 15.7 percent of the SPD delegation and 15 percent of the Alliance '90/ Greens contingent. Like the disparity in Ph.D.'s among the new parliamentary representatives, this result reflects an important feature of higher education under the old regime. The government generally denied access to higher education to those with strong religious attachments. Nonetheless, such institutions as the seminary at Naumburg or the so-called Sprachenkonvikt in Berlin, a church-run postsecondary institution where Alliance '90 representative Wolfgang Ullmann had taught church history, offered these students an opportunity for advanced training. At the same time, students who refused to acknowledge the leading role of the SED, or who had other disagreements with the regime, often found themselves forced to attend these church-related institutions whether or not they had strong religious convictions. Unlike the situation at the GDR's public universities, the educational experiences of these students tended to confirm or consolidate their oppositional attitudes toward the regime.

Given this evidence, there would seem to be little question that the decisive political dividing line in the GDR in these stages of the democratization process ran between the working class, on the one hand, and especially the nontechnical intelligentsia and its ultimate successors in the student population, on the other. When New Forum cofounder Jens Reich averred that he and his compatriots in the civil rights organizations had been unable to make a radical revolution in the GDR "because the producing classes were not with us,"[27] he spoke to a central feature of the East German transformation.

The Search for Civil Society:
Constitution Making after the Revolution

The elections had not done honor to the small group of dissident intellectuals who had often paid a great price for their political activities under the SED regime. Indeed, the conservatives had soundly thrashed the left-wing forces (SPD, Alliance '90, the Greens/UFV) created by the dissident intellectuals from the pre-1990 period. Yet the GDR now had a legitimate, democratically elected parliament. In this context, the attention of the dissident intellectuals turned toward a project to which they were very much attached, but whose prospects of realization seemed to grow dimmer with each passing day: namely, the promulgation of a new constitution for the GDR. For the representatives of the civil rights groups still participating in the discussions at the Central Round Table, that undertaking had a special significance as the fulfillment of their aspirations for more vigorously democratic political institutions.

The advance of unification increasingly pointed to the "all-German" dimensions of constitution making after the break with Communism in the GDR. In this context, Jürgen Habermas, the Frankfurt philosopher and social critic, lent his considerable authority to the voices of those East German civil rights activists who warned against the negative political and economic consequences of a premature unification. Central to Habermas's concerns was the threat to the democratic achievements of the East German break with Communism — as well as to those of the Federal Republic — from an overhasty unification process that had by now become unstoppable. So far, Habermas argued in the pages of the prestigious weekly journal of news and opinion *Die Zeit,* the Kohl government in West Germany had sought to channel national feelings toward a unification process on the terms of Article 23 of the Federal Republic's "Basic Law," the provisional constitution adopted in 1949. That article foresaw the possible future "accession" *(Beitritt)* of other areas to the jurisdiction of the Basic Law, a course once taken by the Saarland in the mid-1950s and viewed by conservatives as perfectly appropriate for the requirements of unification with the GDR.

Yet that approach to unification would, Habermas insisted, ride roughshod over Article 146 of the Basic Law. According to that clause, the temporary constitution was to surrender its validity after its replacement by a true constitution "adopted by a free decision of the German people *[dem deutschen Volke]*." Thus, unless unification of the two German states was approved by a West German plebiscite or followed by the promulgation of a genuine, permanent constitution covering the territory of those two states (and only that territory), the process would leave untouched the expressly provisional character of the Basic Law. Failure to attend to these elements of the temporary constitution, Habermas worried, might open the door to irredentist claims that the temporary constitution still did not cover the entire "German people." The question of one's "Germanness" would continue to be defined in terms of one's *ethnic identity* (i.e., as a nation-state) rather than in terms of one's membership in a political community (i.e., a state-nation). In short, this approach would consolidate the tragic German tendency to define citizenship in terms of the *ethnos* rather than the *demos*.[28]

Giving full vent to his misgivings about a process of unification lacking explicit popular ratification, Habermas invoked Auschwitz to remind Germans that, after the crimes committed by the Nazis on the basis of this criterion of political membership, *this* way of defining citizenship had henceforth been foreclosed to them. Only with the opportunity to say no to a draft constitution was it possible to make manifest the crucial fact that the "construction of a single nation of citizens *[Staatsbürgernation]* on the territory of the Federal Republic and the GDR is not *prejudged* by such prepolitical facts as linguistic commonality, culture, or history."[29] Habermas feared a retreat to a national self-understanding rooted in economic rather than democratic achievements. He thus articulated in the language of constitutional theory the reticence of many among the East German civil rights groups who viewed the GDR's "accession" to the Federal Republic as tantamount to surrendering their hopes of consolidating the institutions of a civil society that did better than the ritualized and episodic plebiscites of "party democracy."[30]

In many ways, the elections indeed recalled the post–World War II escape from memory (at least in West Germany) into a monomaniacal preoccupation with economic reconstruction. The

vote clearly pointed to the preeminent significance of economic concerns for the GDR's voters (D. Roth 1990, 384–85). Yet one of the
newly elected Volkskammer's first official acts attested the East German parliamentarians' concern that the past not be buried under
nationalist enthusiasm about the unification process. The division of
Germany that their election was to help eliminate had, after all, resulted from the Nazis' failed attempt to dominate all of Europe. In
a joint declaration sponsored by all parties represented in the chamber, the Volkskammer representatives solemnly proclaimed that the
guilt for these acts "must never be forgotten. We want to derive
from it our responsibility for the future."[31] This statement by the last
East German parliament demonstrated the continuing importance of
Germany's fascist past in the outlook of the GDR's emerging new
political elite, even as the "antifascist" GDR itself faded from the
historical map.

A parliamentary declaration of this nature in a CDU-dominated
chamber in West Germany would have been almost unthinkable at
this time, only a few short years after the so-called historians' debate. In that controversy, several prominent historians — including at
least one close to the Kohl government — had sought to relativize
the significance of Auschwitz by weighing it up against the Gulag.[32]
Now, despite the accelerating irreversibility of the German unification process, Chancellor Kohl continued for some time to exploit the
lack of a post–World War II peace treaty guaranteeing a secure Polish border as a means of mollifying the small but vocal revanchist
elements of his party in anticipation of the first "all-German" Federal elections in December 1990. This issue was not resolved until the
foreign ministers of the Allied powers and of the two German states
met in the "2 plus 4" talks of mid-July 1990. In those negotiations, it
was resolved that German unification should be permitted within the
borders of the then-existing Federal Republic and the GDR, in return
for a German guarantee of the current frontier with Poland and the
renunciation of any territorial claims.[33]

Only a week after the joint parliamentary declaration professing the East German representatives' desire to overcome the divisions
that had made the Nazi crimes possible, however, interim CDU prime
minister Lothar de Maiziere's inaugural statement once again cast
doubt on the prospect that Germany would join what Habermas
had described as the "classical state-nations of the West" by virtue
of their definition of citizenship in terms of civic rights and respon-

sibilities rather than ethnicity. To be sure, de Maiziere insisted that, after years of one-sided accusations regarding the *West* Germans' responsibility for National Socialism, the Germans in the GDR also had to confront their own implication in the crimes committed in the name of Germany. Yet the new East German premier failed to draw the constitutional consequences for the new Germany from this shared responsibility for Nazi crimes. "All Germans have a common history," de Maiziere proclaimed,

> *that was only apparently interrupted by the division of Europe after the Second World War.* Both German governments are agreed that the goal of the negotiations [on unification] is not a business partnership, but rather a genuine community *[Gemeinschaft]....* *Unification must develop out of the wishes of the people, not out of the interests of governments.*[34]

With these words, de Maiziere consecrated a primordial, transhistorical concept of "the nation" that places that entity utterly beyond the power of a state's citizens to alter. Contrary to the implication that unification had arisen from the wishes of "the people" in both East and West, however, the manipulation of national feeling for political ends had typified the discussion of unification since the promulgation of Chancellor Kohl's Ten-Point Program of November 1989.[35]

In the meanwhile, the East German intellectuals' grassroots democratic visions of constitution making had been shoved aside by the rapidly accelerating train of German unification. Fulfilling the charge issued by the first meeting of the Central Round Table,[36] that body's Working Group on a New Constitution submitted a draft constitution for the GDR to the newly elected parliament on 4 April 1990. The draft sought to improve upon traditional parliamentary democracy by incorporating elements of direct democracy and guarantees of social citizenship rights.[37]

The authors of the Round Table draft constitution were aware, however, that the political situation was not auspicious for their cause. The document explicitly included provisions for responding to a possible "accession" of the GDR to the Federal Republic according to Article 23 of the Basic Law rather than their preferred Article 146, which implied — but did not explicitly require — a plebiscite on a new constitution. Accordingly, the constitutional draft was oriented toward strengthening the GDR's position in negotiations on state unification. Should unification proceed on the basis of Article 23, any agreement regulating the conditions under which the Basic Law would be extended to the territory of the GDR would, according to the Round Table draft, require a two-thirds majority of the East German parliament and "confirmation" by a popular referendum. Such an agreement, moreover, should contain "regulations concerning the accelerated equilibration *[Angleichung]* of the . . . living conditions *[Lebensverhältnisse]* of the GDR's citizens with those of the residents of the Federal Republic." Finally, the draft mandated that the unification agreement would have to adopt for the entire expanded Federal Republic any rights accorded in the GDR (draft) constitution that were not guaranteed in the Basic Law.

Although the Round Table draft relied heavily on the Basic Law for its fundamental features, it went considerably beyond that model in certain respects. In particular, it included a lengthy catalog of social rights only vaguely addressed in the Basic Law, calling for constitutional guarantees of "adequate living space" and of "work or . . . assistance in finding work." In addition, by granting resident aliens the right to vote in local elections, the draft also challenged a notion that was much contested in the Federal Republic during this period. The constitutional draft would also have strengthened the rights of popular movements and included plebiscitarian elements absent from the Basic Law.[38] Clearly, the drafters intended their work in part as a means of protecting the East Germans from potentially unfavorable terms in the treaty of unification. Yet they also sought to institutionalize a broader, more grassroots conception of democracy, with plebiscitarian elements and guarantees for popular political movements complementing the provisions associated with the inherited parliamentary order.

By this time, however, the advancing prospect of unification was widely viewed as obviating the need for any new East German constitution. With economic, currency, and social union already in view, the new parliament essentially ignored the document given them by the Working Group on a New Constitution. The legislative representatives had adequate constitutional grounds for their failure to act on the draft document, for unlike the participants in the Round Table, they enjoyed the popular democratic legitimation of the East German citizenry. Even according to its own stated self-understanding, the Round Table could have no parliamentary or governmental function and was only to remain in existence until democratic elections had been held (see Herles and Rose 1990, 23). As those elections drew nearer, the Round Table increasingly became a lame duck, forfeiting both legitimacy and media attention (see Thaysen 1990c, 178, 185–86).

Nonetheless, at the last session of the Round Table on 12 March, that body resolved to recommend to the new parliament that a plebiscite be conducted on 17 June in which the East German citizenry would have the opportunity to accept or reject the draft constitution. In the discussion of the draft during that meeting, Gerd Poppe, an IFM representative to the Round Table and a member of the drafting group, asserted that the document amounted to the Round Table's opposition to any "accession" of the GDR to the Federal Republic according to Article 23 of the Basic Law. Any such procedure, Poppe insisted, would "injure... the self-esteem and the dignity of this [East German] people" (cited in Thaysen 1990c, 146). As one observer of the Round Table's deliberations commented, such arguments were in part an effort to develop the greatest possible independence of the GDR in order to achieve unification on the "best possible terms" for its population.[39] Still, when the draft constitution finally did become the object of a parliamentary debate in late April 1990, Poppe cited a recent poll conducted by a West German survey research institute that had found that 42 percent of East Germans desired a new constitution for the GDR, 38 percent wanted a new all-German constitution, and only 9 percent wanted to adopt the Basic Law in its current form (cited in Rein 1990, 400).

It is certainly true that as the most concentrated formal embodiment of East Germany's nonestablished dissident intelligentsia, the Round Table grew less and less representative of popular opinion in East Germany. Yet these figures indicate that the East Germans' enthusiasm for an abrupt, supine absorption into the Federal Republic may have been more the idyll of conservative politicians and voters than of the population as a whole. Indeed, polls taken in March 1990 indicated that a majority only of the supporters of the "Alliance for Germany" backed a very rapid process of unification. Among the voting population as a whole at that time, 55.6 percent preferred to take things slowly (see D. Roth 1990, 383, table 7). But with the landslide electoral victory of the Alliance for Germany, the voices of those advocating this more measured, cautious approach — the course so frequently advocated by most of the former dissident intellectuals — could hardly be heard any longer amid the general din of nationally minded enthusiasts.

The Prophets Outcast: The Debate about Christa Wolf

Indeed, in a dramatic fall from the dizzying heights to which they had risen just a few months before, Germany's leftist intellectuals became the objects of searching examination as state unification approached. With developments outrunning the arguments of those unenthusiastic about (if not necessarily opposed to) unification, many of these same figures came to be criticized as naively utopian or allegedly uncritical supporters of the SED dictatorship. For their insistence that a hasty process of unification would leave a nasty hangover, left-wing intellectuals in Germany drew the fire of newspaper columnists and ordinary people in terms drawn from an older, less fortunate German political vocabulary. The prominent West German author Günter Grass, for example, recounted in the pages of *Die Zeit* his own encounter with popular anti-intellectual sentiment. After Grass publicly voiced his skepticism concerning the goal of or the rapid approach to unification, a perfect stranger who met him at a train station accused him of being a "traitor to the fatherland" (see Grass 1990).

Now that the struggle for a democratically reformed, independent GDR had been lost, the battle was joined for the interpretation of the East German past. As occurs often in Germany, however, an essentially political debate took place in an apparently different discursive realm. Even before the ink was dry on the 1990 treaties on economic, currency, and social union and on state unification proper, the literary supporters of East German socialism — and, by association, the whole West German literary culture of the postwar era — came under intense bombardment in the literary-cultural *(Feuilleton)* pages of West Germany's leading newspapers in what came to be known as the "literature debate" *(Literaturstreit)*.[40]

The occasion for — if not the cause of — the controversy was the publication of Christa Wolf's novel *Was bleibt* (What remains).[41] The book is a novelistic account of her surveillance by the Stasi around the time of the protests against the exclusion of several members of the Writers' Union in 1979 (see chap. 3 above). Wolf originally wrote the work in the summer of 1979; she then revised the slim volume in the fall of 1989 in ways that she failed to explain. This omission became the basis for a charge of bad faith, given that Wolf had always been among the more privileged members of the East German cultural establishment and a member of the SED elite. Moreover, according to one critic, Wolf's failure to have made public her tailing by the Stasi *at the time* amounted to a refusal to risk her privileges by revealing the regime's intimidation of one of its best-known citizens, thus ensuring that that episode would have no wider political repercussions for the Communist government.[42]

The overarching issue in the controversy was precisely the intellectuals' role in supporting and stabilizing the GDR's socialist dictatorship. From the right (and, generally speaking, from a younger generation of critics) came a fusillade of attacks alleging that Wolf had been, in effect, a "court poet" *(Staatsdichterin)*. These attacks provoked edgy and aggressively defensive reactions from the left, which decried what was alleged to be an anti-Communist witch-hunt. Despite a counterattack by leftist intellectuals East and West who took issue with what East German dramatist Heiner Müller called the "Stalinism of the West" (cited in Huyssen 1991, 128), the debate also revealed a pronounced East-West cleavage. A number of East German participants responded to the attacks on Wolf by asserting that West Germans simply had very little idea what life had been like under the SED regime. Moreover, these critics claimed, the attacks on Wolf were part of a broader campaign to undermine the self-esteem of an East German population being rapidly and ruthlessly colonized by the West.[43]

In contrast to the thrust of these East-West *querelles,* the exiled political singer Wolf Biermann, who still identified strongly with the East despite his expulsion to the West years before, nonetheless insisted that this was "a controversy that was overdue." Biermann rejected the notion that there was anything inappropriate about examining the politics of anyone so politically influential as Christa Wolf (she had, after all, authored the preamble to the East German Round Table's draft constitution). In addition, he dismissed the talk of an anti-Communist witch-hunt with his characteristic bluntness: Western leftists were distressed, Biermann said, about the demise of the "animal experiment called the GDR," while "in the East it stinks of self-pity."[44] More recently, Biermann has claimed that, were his old friend Robert Havemann still alive, the latter would simply have had no time for all the "whining" from the East.[45]

In a constellation that would reappear in subsequent controversies among the German intellectuals, those such as Biermann who had suffered for their opposition to the old regime in the GDR were among the sharpest advocates of a close examination of those more established East German figures who were often celebrated as dissidents or heroes, but who had nonetheless "arranged themselves" with the party-state.[46] Biermann was, moreover, undoubtedly correct to observe that there was considerable disillusionment among the East German intellectuals who had been sympathetic to some sort of socialist project in the GDR. This feeling grew more pronounced as the GDR careened toward its official incorporation into the old Federal Republic on 3 October 1990 and as the first "all-German" elections of early December reaffirmed the conservative hegemony in both parts of the new, united Germany.

The First "All-German" Elections of December 1990

As had been widely expected, the CDU/CSU/FDP coalition was confirmed in government in the first nationwide parliamentary elections in united Germany on 2 December 1990.[47] In the elections to the legislatures of the newly reconstituted states *(Länder)* in the territory of the former GDR on 14 October, all the non-Communist parties had gained in strength at the expense of the SED's successor, the PDS.[48] The December elections bore witness to another trend in the direction of the Federal Republic's party system: compared to the October voting results, all the parties in the election other than tiny fringe groupings forfeited electoral support except the centrist FDP. These results suggested that the FDP, traditionally the political home of entrepreneurs and higher civil servants in the Federal Republic, had consolidated its role as the party of the middle in the changing party system.

With the parliamentary (Bundestag) elections of 2 December 1990, the governing CDU was able to increase slightly — from 40.8 percent to 41.8 percent — its share of votes among citizens of the former East Germany in comparison to its showing in March. However, one of the CDU's former partners in the Alliance for Germany, the Deutsche Soziale Union (German Social Union, or DSU), sank into insignificance with just 1.0 percent of the East German vote, while its other electoral ally, the civil rights group Democratic Awakening, had been absorbed into the larger party and had thus gone out of existence.

While the PDS lost a considerable number of voters from its March 1990 peak of 16.4 percent, it nonetheless managed to hold on to more than 11 percent of the old GDR's electorate. This outcome is particularly noteworthy in view of the fact that the PDS's membership had shrunk to some 10 to 15 percent of its pre-1990 strength of 2.3 million. As in March, the PDS achieved its best results by far in East Berlin, where the party garnered nearly one-quarter of the total vote. Meanwhile, the SPD was able to increase its share of the East German vote, from 21.9 percent in March to 24.3 percent in December.

The electoral coalition of Alliance '90 and the Greens, representing those East German civil rights groups who (along with the SPD) had shown the greatest reluctance about rapid unification, also managed to expand their voter base in the East relative to the March elections. They, too, lost some of their supporters from the time of the October state elections, however. Despite the tiny proportion of the vote garnered by these "children of the revolution" in Germany as a whole, they succeeded in acquiring parliamentary seats because the Federal Constitutional Court had mandated that the rule requiring a minimum 5 percent of the total vote for legislative representation be applied *separately* in East and West Germany in this one, extraordinary situation.[49] While the grassroots movement of the East thus gained Bundestag representation, however, the most striking outcome of the December 1990 elections was the more established West German Greens' failure to surmount that same 5 percent barrier. The Greens, the most visible remaining political manifestation of the West German New Left, were thus excluded from parliament for the first time since 1983.

In view of the East Germans' lack of recourse to relevant voting traditions in the Volkskammer elections of March 1990, a comparison of the social structural aspects of that vote with those of the Bundestag election may help reveal the emergence of at least preliminary trends in the future relationship between social structure and voting behavior in the former GDR. Whereas support for the CDU in eastern Germany correlated more or less directly with age — support rose with age — the propensity to vote for the parties of the civil rights movements was inversely related to that demographic characteristic. The movements comprising Alliance '90 and the Greens in the East clearly appealed more to younger voters.

Continuing its remarkable success in eastern Germany among groups that have traditionally supported the Social Democrats, the CDU once again did very well among the workers in that part of the newly united country. That social stratum that had, under the old regime, been jokingly referred to as the "ruling class" actually increased its support for the CDU — from 48.1 percent in the March Volks-kammer election to 49.8 percent in the December vote. Yet the SPD was also able to improve its showing among workers, from 22.2 per-cent to 24.8 percent. Both parties gained among working-class voters primarily at the expense of the PDS, which continued to experience a "shakeout" of its voter base.[50]

With regard to the intelligentsia, it is not easy to say what sorts of continuities might have emerged from the elections of December 1990. Previous analyses of the electoral behavior of the East German intelligentsia may have been unsatisfactory as a result of definitional difficulties. But with the coming of unification, it is simply no longer possible to compare the behavior of that group in the March parlia-mentary elections with that in the Bundestag elections of December 1990: the "intelligentsia" no longer exists as a category of electoral sociology among (West) German voting analysts.

One can scarcely avoid the conclusion that the demise of this clas-sificatory category owes to some ironic cunning of history: despite the intelligentsia's prominent role in the break with Communist rule, the process of unification has led to the elimination of the "intelligentsia" from German electoral sociology. The sociological category of the "intelligentsia," itself an artifact of Stalinist rule, is disappearing as the formerly eastward-oriented parts of Germany are brought into a Federal Republic that has been substantially Westernized during the postwar period. This does not, of course, mean that "intellectuals" no longer exist, only that the order into which the East Germans have been incorporated does not recognize that group as relevant to the sociology of voting behavior.

Conclusion

During an interview in late 1991, New Forum cofounder Sebastian Pflugbeil gave poignant expression to the sense of marginalization among some of the former East German dissidents as a result of unification. Pflugbeil noted that the dissident intellectuals had been much more concerned with the replacement of the SED's monop-oly on power by a democratic system than they had been with the reconstruction of capitalism. Indeed, he continued,

> it was clear to all of us ... that if our goal was West German cap-italism, then the participatory control [*Mitbestimmung*] over the country would once again come to naught. In that respect, we are

especially disappointed about the course of events, *because we now have even fewer opportunities to influence in any way that which takes place here.*[51]

These comments attest the persistence of a strikingly anticapitalist orientation among East Germany's civil rights activists. Yet the target of that attitude is crucially important for understanding their politics: rather than deriving from a class-based analysis of the ways in which capitalism exploits nonowners of property, the East German dissident intellectuals opposed "capitalism" because it deprived them (and, presumably, others) of access to democratic participation. They were, in short, democrats who were both anticapitalist *and* anti-Communist. Their "third way," though recalling the notion of an alternative road to socialism that had had a long heritage in German left-wing politics, emphasized rights of civic codetermination over those of property arrangements.

In view of the GDR's acquisition of a relatively stable constitutional democracy in the process of its assimilation into the Federal Republic, Pflugbeil's comments reveal a remarkable disillusionment regarding the outcome of the GDR's break with Communism. Yet these comments reflected a sentiment that was widespread among leftist intellectuals in the aftermath of the civil rights activists' poor showing in the electoral battles of 1990. The disenchantment conveyed by Pflugbeil suggests a dissatisfaction with "mere" parliamentary democracy that had its roots in the structural conditions of opposition in the old GDR. With *that* kind of democracy right across the border in the other Germany, the effort to recruit sympathizers and to sustain commitments to democratic activism in the old GDR necessitated the invocation of more utopian prospects than the Federal Republic's "really existing capitalism." Thus the notion of "grassroots democracy" — truer, more democratic than the parliamentary version — dominated at least the more romantic vision of East Germany's possible future. This preoccupation with a form of political organization that was considered more genuine than existing parliamentary models had hardly contributed, however, to an acceptance of the more mundane, mass-mediated, "party democracy" that the East Germans inherited as their state collapsed around them.[52]

Yet the sort of disappointed resignation expressed by Pflugbeil was by no means the only response among dissident intellectual activists in the civil rights groups as German unification was completed.

In a late 1990 speech, Democracy Now cofounder Ulrike Poppe directly challenged the pessimistic assessment offered by such figures as Pflugbeil, an outlook that had become especially characteristic of certain elements of New Forum. In contrast to these views, Poppe insisted: "Despite the disappointed voices that can sometimes be heard from our ranks, we undoubtedly have much better chances now than compared with the situation before October 1989. The way forward is open." This view of the situation confronting the civil rights activists after the absorption of the GDR into the Federal Republic will be vital to avoiding the political pitfall of remaining obsessively engrossed with the concerns and debates of the past. Figures such as Ulrike Poppe (and her husband Gerd Poppe, who became an Alliance '90 member of the Bundestag) understand that their contribution to the political culture of the new Germany lies in the effort to expand the conception of "civil society" to include initiatives toward the "self-organization of society" beyond the party system. In particular, this undertaking entails a challenge to received definitions of the nature of citizenship in the political community: "Herein lies a new opportunity for us to take leave of 'unpolitical politics' (Havel)."[53] This is precisely the challenge facing those nonestablished intellectuals whose political role was so prominent — despite its weak popular echo — in the process of toppling one-party rule in the East German break with Communism.

Six

The Abortive Revolution Continues:
East German Civil Rights Activists
after Unification

Analyzing the political significance of the East Central European upheavals of 1989, Jürgen Habermas characterized them collectively as
a "catching-up revolution" *(nachholende Revolution),* the most noteworthy feature of which was its "almost complete lack of innovative
ideas" (Habermas 1990b, 181). Similarly, Ralf Dahrendorf has described the process of casting off Communist rule in East Central
Europe as a fundamentally liberal transformation, consisting in the
achievement of "an open society, *the* open society to be exact, for
while there can be many systems, there is only one open society"
(Dahrendorf 1990, 36). Reflecting specifically on the political impact of the East German civil rights activists who briefly headed the
GDR's transformation process, the well-known sociologist Wolf Lepenies, rector of Berlin's Institute of Advanced Studies, has written that
"the only thing they brought into the unification process was their
suffering" (see Lepenies 1992). According to these views, in short,
the dramatic developments in East Central Europe in 1989 amounted
more to a *restoration* than a *revolution,* and their chief protagonists
in East Germany had relatively little to contribute to the politics of
the transformation.

In contrast to these views, Sigrid Meuschel has insisted that the
East German civil rights activists' concern with reconstructing civil
society offered evidence of the forward-looking quality of their ideas
(Meuschel 1990b, 18). While it is difficult to see how the attention

to the project of widening opportunities for democratic participation makes them *innovative,* Meuschel is correct to suggest that the East German civil rights activists' legacy may help shape politics in the new Germany, even despite their relative powerlessness in the contemporary German parliamentary order.

When discussing the East German opposition activists associated with the 1989–90 period, there is a widespread tendency to use terms that mislead us into thinking they are essentially indistinguishable from the "new social movements" in Western societies. It has often been said, for instance, that the figures associated with Alliance '90 — the parliamentary expression of the core of what remains of East German civil rights activism — were the leaders of a "citizens' movement" *(Bürgerbewegung).* This usage, however, inappropriately applies to them a concept derived from the study of new social movements in Western liberal democracies. As one influential volume on the subject recently put it, such movements combine "the coexistence of radical critique of the existing order, on the one hand, and *de facto* integration into the existing society and into the political arena, on the other" (Kuechler and Dalton 1990, 281). This, of course, could hardly have been said about the East bloc dissidents before 1989.

In German discussions, at least, some of the confusion between citizens' movement *(Bürgerbewegung)* and civil *rights* movements *(Bürgerrechtrechtsbewegung)* is surely linguistic in origin; it derives from the fact that the terms are so close to one another etymologically. Much of the scholarly confusion, however, is traceable to certain similarities in political themes and social recruitment bases among social movements that emerged in the Soviet bloc during the 1980s and the "new social movements" in the Western democracies.[1] The relevant political concerns were those of peace, environmentalism, feminism, anti-imperialism, and third-world development. To be sure, these ideological overlaps between the "citizens' movements" descended from the West German New Left and the civil rights activism of the GDR are real enough. Indeed, these programmatic commonalities comprised the basis upon which a fusion of the West German Greens with Alliance '90, the party of the East German civil rights groups, emerged as a political possibility.

Thus while it is perfectly accurate in *ideological* terms to describe the activists from the former GDR as a conglomeration of "red-green intellectuals" (Pollack 1990b, 1222), this should not mislead us into thinking that they are mere carbon copies of their would-be Western counterparts. Especially by comparison to the Greens, the East German civil rights activists are a different breed of political intellectual with origins in a Communist system that denied them most of the rights that left-wing intellectuals in the Federal Republic took for granted — freedoms that constituted the very condition of possibility of their political activism, in fact. The East German dissident intellectuals, in contrast, had first to *achieve* these political preconditions: that is, civil rights such as freedom of speech, freedom of assembly, freely contested democratic elections, and so on.[2] They are thus particularly sensitive to any intimations of sympathy for the system they have left behind. Moreover, they have spent substantial political effort in exhuming and exorcising the spirits of that past.

Since the collapse of the Communist regime and the disappearance of the GDR, the East German civil rights activists have, of course, been able to enjoy these civil rights as a result of the importation of the Federal Republic's constitutional order. Yet this outcome was by no means necessarily their aim as the demise of Communist rule got underway in East Germany in 1989. The dissident intellectuals responded to the political opportunity following on the emigration wave of 1989 by seeking a reconstruction of *civil society,* not of the *nation-state.* Popular pressure, both in the streets and at the ballot box, aborted that project. Enthusiasm for a rejuvenated civil society in the GDR, developments revealed, was restricted to that small group of "grassroots" democratic intellectuals that had created the opposition groups that briefly rose to prominence in the fall of 1989 — New Forum, Democracy Now, the Initiative for Peace and Human Rights, and others. Since unification, activists from these groups both in and out of parliament have put the consolidation of democracy, the broadening of democratic rights, and the extension of those rights to wider categories of German residents at the center of their political activity. They have pursued these aims in two principal ways — one looking backward, with the aim of appropriating the legacy of the East German dictatorship for purposes of democratic renewal, and another looking forward to the constitutional shape of the new, united Germany. On both fronts, their political efforts have been strongly marked by a concern with interpretation and symbolism, the classical domain of intellectuals — especially relatively powerless ones making a bid for more power.

Appropriating the Past for a More Democratic Future

On 15 January 1990, a decisive turning point had been reached in the dismantling of Communist power in the German Democratic Republic. While the Socialist Unity (Communist) Party's legally guaranteed "leading role" in the state had been struck from the constitution on 1 December 1989, the GDR's internal security forces — the Stasi and its successor, the Office of National Security — had not yet been dissolved. As a result, East Germans had grown increasingly critical of the foot-dragging of Prime Minister Hans Modrow's supposedly reformist government on this count. New Forum called for a peaceful demonstration at the Stasi headquarters in East Berlin's Normannenstrasse to protest the government's inaction and apparent dissembling about the secret police issue. The demonstration spun out of control, however, as protesters stormed the building, threatening to disrupt the relative orderliness with which the East German transformation had progressed up till that point. GDR citizens widely perceived the event as the definitive beginning of the elimination of the most crucial and fearsome instrument of Communist rule in the GDR (Thaysen 1990c, 64–70). In the immediate aftermath of these dramatic developments, "citizens' committees" sprang up around the country to take over where the government appeared to be failing in the task of dismantling the Stasi's various regional outposts. The citizens' committees saw the rescue and preservation of secret police files as one of their chief tasks.[3]

At its meeting one week later, the Central Round Table moved to transform the legacy of the GDR's police-state Communism into a symbolic admonition that such tyranny should never again be permitted on German soil. Although the Round Table brought together representatives of both the old regime and the opposition, the body adopted a resolution of the East German Green Party calling for the creation of a "Memorial and Research Center on Stalinism" in the GDR. To enhance the proposal's symbolic punch, its supporters argued that it would be most appropriate to locate the memorial in the building that had housed the offices of Minister of State Security Erich Mielke. The resolution suggested that the ministry's archival materials could thus be made available to researchers and went on to propose that such a center might offer an opportunity for those citizens who had fallen victim to the Stasi's harassment to examine the contents of the files collected about them. The archives could be useful, moreover, in preparing possible criminal charges against Stasi collaborators. Finally, the resolution made explicit its concern to protect individuals' rights to privacy and against misuse of data gathered about them. Along with the more strictly commemorative component of the Green Party's proposal, the four aims outlined in this resolution — accepted while the Stasi was still regarded as a powerful social force — have been central to the East German civil rights activists' efforts to appropriate the GDR's dictatorial past in the service of a more democratic future.[4]

The birth pangs of the Normannenstrasse Research and Memorial Center were mild, however, in comparison to the legal arrangements for preserving and making publicly available the files of the Ministry of State Security. Contravening the demands of the citizens' committees that had overseen the dismantling of the Stasi offices throughout the GDR, the Council of Ministers of the GDR's first freely elected government, dominated by the CDU, adopted a resolution in May 1990 that ordered a 110-year gag rule on all Stasi data referring specifically to persons. There ensued a period of considerable controversy over the new government's apparent stonewalling about the Stasi legacy. In response to pressures from those advocating the opening of the files, the East German parliament created a special nonpartisan committee to oversee the storage and administration of the Stasi files under the direction of Rostock pastor Joachim Gauck. Shortly after this development, the parliament passed by a substantial majority a law mandating that the Stasi files should remain on the territory of the GDR, to be housed in the Stasi headquarters in the Normannenstrasse and in archives scattered around the country under the control of the *Länder* (state) governments.

In this respect, the Volkskammer law of 24 August 1990 explicitly contradicted the stipulations of the draft Unification Treaty, which foresaw the transfer of the files to the West German federal archives in Koblenz. Though the final version of the Unification Treaty included a provision that the Stasi files would remain on the GDR's territory, dissatisfaction among East German activists with the course of events concerning the Stasi files led in September 1990 to a renewed occupation of the Stasi headquarters and countrywide protests, including hunger strikes by prominent figures such as Wolf Biermann and others. The protesters' principal objections to the Unification Treaty's provisions concerned the lack of adequate guarantees that Stasi victims would have access to their files and the failure to prohibit use of the files by the Federal Republic's secret services (i.e., the Federal Office for the Protection of the Constitution, the Bundesnachrichtendienst, etc.). This chapter in the struggle over the disposition of the Stasi files was brought to a close in an addendum to the final Unification Treaty that called upon the first "all-German" parliament (to be elected on 2 December 1990) to "take full account" of the principles outlined in the East German parliament's law of late August.[5]

As a consequence of the citizens' committees' distress concerning the legal disposition of the Stasi files, the remnants of the GDR's intellectual opposition who had made the leap into the new parliament began to take independent initiative to shape the law being considered by the Bundestag. In cooperation with the parliamentary group Alliance '90/The Greens and the West German Heinrich Böll Foundation, representatives of the East German citizens' committees developed a legislative proposal whose basic principles had been outlined in the original Round Table proposal for a Memorial and Research Center on Stalinism in East Germany: access for the Stasi's victims to information gathered about them, the notion of a comprehensive political "reckoning" *(Aufarbeitung)* with the past, decentralized storage of the files, and a bar on all uses of the files by secret services. The citizens' committees submitted this draft legislation for public discussion in February 1991, thus initiating the second postunification round of struggle over the disposition of the Stasi files. As a result of conservative (CDU/CSU) domination of the Bundestag, however, the proposal met with little resonance in parliament.[6]

Picking up on the citizens' committees' barren initiative, the parliamentary representatives from Alliance '90/The Greens then proposed their own draft law. Alliance '90 thus kicked off a debate in the new "all-German" parliament that lasted much of the remainder of 1991. Largely ignoring the proposals of the remnants of the East German civil rights groups, the main parties represented in the Bundestag, the CDU/CSU, the FDP, and the SPD, introduced their own draft laws. The citizens' committees and Alliance '90/The Greens quickly criticized the three largest parties' proposed law for abrogating the citizens' committees' bedrock principal that victims of Stasi harassment should be guaranteed uncomplicated access to the data gathered about them by the secret police. An open breach between the older parties and the new forces from the East came in mid-June

1991 as the likelihood of a centralized approach to storage of the files grew increasingly strong.

From the point of view of the civil rights activists, the concentration of Stasi files in one enormous bureaucracy affording only very limited rights of access to the secret police's victims defeated the purpose of opening the files in the first place. From their point of view, that purpose, reiterated in the version of the law finally passed by the Bundestag, had always been the "historical, political, and judicial process of coming to terms" with the Stasi's nefarious legacy.[7] Yet, in the view of the East German civil rights activists, that process was to have taken place in a more decentralized, less bureaucratic, and less legalistic fashion. In the meanwhile, the process of "coming to terms with the past," one facet of which had been the publication of a number of books documenting the workings of the Stasi, had been short-circuited in favor of the distribution or denial of *Persilscheine* (seals of approval) concerning individuals suspected of collaboration. Accordingly, the activists saw in the law as finally adopted by the German parliament the "vision of a mammoth agency for an officially sanctioned process of coming to terms with the past," not the realization of their less bureaucratic plans for "working through" that past.[8]

These developments reflected a pattern that would repeat itself in other political controversies in the new Germany: after the former East German dissident intellectuals had taken the initiative and mobilized popular opinion through various public forums to discuss their proposals, the issue would be taken over by the federal parliament and watered down in such a way that it no longer conformed to the aims of those who had initiated the process. Given the small minorities that elected these activists into parliamentary office, of course, one could hardly expect any other outcome. Still, in view of this pattern, it is not difficult to understand why many intellectuals in the East regarded the process of unification as a form of "colonization."

In the aftermath of the lost battle over the law regulating the disposition of the Stasi files, the sense of frustration among these forces rose notably. In accordance with the law, the files were opened on 2 January 1992 to much media fanfare, stimulating a spate of sensational revelations and volleys of charges and countercharges. Despite the intentions of the East German civil rights activists, the hysteria associated with the revelations in the Stasi files distracted attention from the alleged crimes of those to whom the Stasi reported, namely, the SED leadership. Meanwhile, the trials of these leading SED officials lagged or could not be initiated for lack of adequate charges — or, in the prominent case of party chairman Erich Honecker, for lack of a defendant. It was in this context that New Forum cofounder Bärbel Bohley made the widely reported quip, "We wanted justice and got the constitutional state *[Rechtsstaat]*."[9]

The slow turning of the wheels of jurisprudence led, however, to calls for more productive ways to satisfy the yearning for at least a certain moral justice. In one of the most noted examples of these efforts, several prominent East German civil rights activists appealed in January 1992 for the creation of an unofficial but public "tribunal" in which to "come to terms" with the injustices of the East German regime. Responding to criticisms of earlier proposals for such an entity, the initiators noted that their undertaking could have no *legal* competence. In view of the constitutional constraints on the prosecution of injustices sponsored by the old regime, however, the tribunal's proponents insisted that "the moral right of those who may justifiably consider themselves victims of the GDR system requires that they at least receive public satisfaction."[10] By giving victims an opportunity to confront their tormenters, the tribunal was thus intended to come to terms with some of those moral aspects of the dictatorship that cry out for avenging but are beyond the reach of legal remedies. More broadly, the initiators intended the tribunal to enhance the political culture of postunification Germany by helping to clarify the distinction between what they regarded as "perpetrators" and "victims."

In the eyes of some of the civil rights activists, at least, the matter of distinguishing between these two groups has grown increasingly central to the whole discussion since the opening of the Stasi files. As the extent of the spying apparatus became more well known, the perception spread in the West that the entire East German population were informants or collaborators. Indeed, a spate of allegations of Stasi collaboration among those associated with the dissident scene threatened to destroy the credibility of even those who actively opposed the regime, many of whom were involved in the unofficial cultural and political milieu in East Berlin's Prenzlauer Berg district. As a result of revelations regarding Stasi infiltration of dissident activities, the intellectual opposition often appeared to have been an operation almost entirely conceived and run by the Stasi. These revelations have helped further blur the boundaries between the victims and the perpetrators under the socialist regime.[11]

The debate over the distinction between perpetrators and victims heated up considerably after Brandenburg prime minister Manfred Stolpe made public his conspiratorial contacts with the Stasi over more than two decades as an official in the Berlin-Brandenburg Evangelical Church.[12] These contacts certainly put his earlier actions as a church official in a dubious light. Yet Stolpe also at times drew the negative attention of the Stasi for his support of the grassroots groups organized under the protective aegis of the Lutheran Church.[13] Nor can it be said that the criticisms of Stolpe are merely another attack by West Germans on the East, as has often been argued. While the campaign to force his ouster from office was initially promoted by a West German television reporter,[14] some of Stolpe's most vigorous critics have been figures from the old East German dissident scene.[15] Prominent West German politicians, especially from Stolpe's own SPD, quickly issued declarations of solidarity when he came under fire for his revelations. Some of his defenders have recalled from previous German history the unsavory compromises thrust upon anyone who seeks to ameliorate conditions under a dictatorship.[16] Yet these statements of support and CDU pressure for Stolpe to resign only fed charges that the Stasi files were being instrumentalized for party/political ends.

Moreover, the statements of support for Stolpe also exacerbated the sense among earlier East German regime critics that the capacity for differentiation between perpetrators and their victims is a scarce resource among West Germans. Gerd Poppe, an Alliance '90 member of the Bundestag whose troubles with the SED government went back to his involvement in protests against Wolf Biermann's expatriation in 1976, remarked in this regard that the sympathetic understanding for the hard choices forced upon people by the dictatorship has sometimes gone too far. In these cases, the result is "greater sympathy for the small and middle-level perpetrators than for the victims."[17] This is an important point, for it speaks to the tendency in the West to "forgive and forget" — to forgive those who made bad or unsavory choices under adverse circumstances, while forgetting those marginal individuals who acted more honorably under those same conditions. The result of this attitude may be to ignore the legacy of those who resisted the temptations and comforts of conformity under a regime that demanded little else.

The East German civil rights activists' insistence on dividing per-petrators from victims should be distinguished from the approach to the old system advocated by such figures as Václav Havel, with whom they otherwise shared so much during the pre-1989 period. In his important essay "The Power of the Powerless," Havel argued that no such neat division was possible; all were both victims and sup-porters of an all-pervasive system that above all required that people get along by going along.[18] Many of the intellectual dissidents from the former GDR, however, feel compelled to emphasize the differ-ences between these two groups. Otherwise, since they have been largely banished from a role in the politics of postunification Ger-many, we might well draw the conclusion that *their sacrifices were for naught and that they have, accordingly, no particular claim to our attention.* This conclusion would, of course, have devastating conse-quences for the perceived political relevance of these groups in the new Germany. At least initially, Havel and those Czechoslovak dissi-dents who suffered at the hands of the old regime had no competitors in the matter of leading the post-Communist order. By contrast, the East German civil rights activists have had to actively fight their mar-ginalization by established political forces as a result of unification. Contemporary German politics is thus marked at once by a debate over the *nature* of the Communist past and a debate over whether that past is at all *relevant* to an understanding of politics and of the kind of Germany that will eventually emerge from the unification process.

Despite the support for the "tribunal" concept among prominent East German civil rights activists, the idea fell flat, attracting little public interest. As in the case of the law regarding the Stasi files, how-ever, the impulse from extraparliamentary sources to push for a pub-lic process of "coming to terms" with the East German Communist system was picked up by the Bundestag in the form of the so-called Commission of Inquiry into the History and Consequences of the SED Dictatorship in Germany (Enquete-Kommission "Aufarbeitung von Geschichte und Folgen der SED-Diktatur in Deutschland").[19] The commission has neither power nor wish to punish; its intention is to illuminate the structures of power, the lines of responsibility, the sources of corruption — and those of mere conformity. Markus Meckel, vice-chairman of the commission and a cofounder of the East German SDP/SPD in 1989, succinctly described the commission's task as that of seeking answers to such questions as these:

When did we simply make mistakes? Where and when did we allow ourselves to get caught up in the system? When were we cowardly and opportunistic? Still, it is clear, cowardice and opportunism are not punishable. But when did they put us in a position in which we incurred guilt? How great was the pressure really, in everyday life? Who really believed that what s/he was doing was right? And when must one speak instead of betrayal?[20]

It is noteworthy that Meckel formulates these questions in the first person plural. For they are questions best addressed from the perspective of a participant who shared, however indirectly, in the commission of the acts under consideration. Such a perspective helps to reduce the ever-present danger of self-righteousness in such discussions, though it may not satisfy those who insist that, contrary to Václav Havel's assertions, not everyone shares the same burden of guilt for sustaining the Communist order. In view of the fact that the commission seeks to illuminate rather than prosecute, Meckel's remarks also recall Habermas's dictum that "in processes of enlightenment, there can only be participants" (Habermas 1973, 40).

The history of the commission of inquiry is noteworthy for the various legislative proposals advanced by different parliamentary parties and groups. Led by such figures as Markus Meckel and other veterans of the East German dissident experience, the Social Democratic faction of the Bundestag was the first to submit a draft law designed to install the commission of inquiry. Their draft spoke of a body that would undertake the "political reckoning [Aufarbeitung] with repression in the Soviet Zone of Occupation and the GDR." Apart from calling attention to the incontrovertible fact of tyrannical rule in East Germany, this wording recalled the fact that the SPD had been absorbed with the German Communist Party in 1946 into the Socialist Unity Party (SED), a fact to which the re-created SPD called considerable attention during the first free elections in the GDR in March 1990. In the context of the media sensationalism occasioned by the opening of the Stasi files as well as of loud calls for "drawing a thick line" under the GDR's unsavory history, the SPD parliamentary faction sought a middle way between foreclosing discussion of that past and the tendency to reduce the Communist system solely to the problem of the secret police.[21]

In contrast to the SPD's proposal, the SED successor party, the PDS, advocated a body that would undertake merely the "political *Aufarbeitung* of *the history of the GDR*" (emphasis added). The absence of references to the SED or of such terms as "dictatorship" pointed up the PDS faction's belief that such a commission could only constitute a further example of what it regarded as the West's "victor's justice."[22] At the other end of the spectrum, the Alliance '90/The Greens parliamentary faction proposed to create a commission whose task would be the "*Aufarbeitung* of the history and consequences of the SED dictatorship" *and* the "promotion of extraparliamentary initiatives on the same subject." While the SPD's proposal had noted that there could be "no monopoly" on the political process of coming to terms with the past, the Alliance '90 draft law emphasized that "parliamentary initiatives concerning the *Aufarbeitung* of injustice in the German Democratic Republic can only complement and promote, not replace that of those affected and those who participate in the process." The group further proposed a panoply of extraparliamentary activities, such as exhibitions, round tables, conversations between perpetrators and victims, regional history workshops, and "tribunals" designed to stimulate broader citizen involvement in this process of historical appropriation. The Alliance '90 legislation also would have mandated an annual subsidy of 20 million marks to support such projects.[23]

After the CDU/CSU, the FDP, and the SPD introduced a joint legislative proposal in early March 1992, the Bundestag adopted their plan to constitute a commission of inquiry devoted to the "*Aufarbeitung* of the history and consequences of the SED dictatorship in Germany." The inclusion of the words "in Germany" may have signaled a concession to the persistent criticism that the process of "coming to terms" with the Communist past tended to ignore the Federal Republic's complicity in sustaining the GDR and thus constituted another aspect of the West's so-called colonization of the East.

While there may be good reason to consider how the Federal Republic helped prop up the GDR, however, it cannot be said that the examination of the Communist order's crimes and shortcomings was exclusively the product of a conservative and Western-driven campaign to discredit the left, to demoralize the citizens of the East, and thus to smooth the process of the takeover of the East by the West. Around this time, a group including several of the most prominent East German civil rights activists published ten "theses on the illumination *(Aufklärung)* of the past" in which they asserted unambiguously: "The discrediting of the *Aufarbeitung* as the product of a sort of flippant 'victor's mood' of the West that is being forced onto the East...is an attempt to cover over the past."[24] The appeal was signed by such figures from the East German dissident scene as Bärbel Bohley, Katja Havemann, Jürgen Fuchs, and Gerd Poppe, none of whom could be described as overly sympathetic to the West or to the prevailing politics of the unification process.

Despite the commission's origins in the activism of the GDR's civil rights campaigners, the law as passed reflected the power constellation obtaining in the federal parliament at the time: the CDU/CSU would have seven representatives to the commission, the SPD five, the FDP two, and the groups Alliance '90/The Greens and the PDS one each. The commission would be chaired by CDU representative Rainer Eppelmann, an East Berlin pastor long associated with the GDR's dissident scene, especially the peace movement.[25] According to the law, the commission of inquiry was to contribute to "political-historical analysis and political-moral evaluation." Specifically, the parliament mandated that the commission take up the following themes:

1. the structures, strategies, and instruments of the SED dictatorship;

2. the significance of ideology, integrative factors, and disciplinary practices;

3. the violation of international conventions and norms of human rights as well as possibilities for material and moral compensation;

4. possibilities and forms of deviant and oppositional behavior and oppositional action;

5. the role and self-understanding of the church;

6. the impact of international conditions, especially Soviet influence;

7. the impact of the relationship between the Federal Republic and the GDR; and, last but hardly least,

8. the question of the continuities of thinking, of behavior, and of the structures in twentieth-century German history, particularly from the time of the National Socialist dictatorship.

The commission was charged with examining these issues in their variation over time, taking special account of some of the major turning points in the history of the GDR and the Soviet bloc such as the workers' rebellion of 17 June 1953, the invasion of Czechoslovakia in 1968, the transfer of power from Ulbricht to Honecker, and the "peaceful revolution" of 1989. Consistent with the origins of the enthusiasm for "coming to terms" with the history of the GDR in the experience of the East German civil rights activists, the commission's mandate specifically included organizing public hearings with affected individuals, scholars, and citizens' initiatives concerned with these subjects.[26]

The first public hearing of the commission, a two-day affair held in the Reichstag building, addressed the experiences of those who had been subjected to various kinds of repression by the SED government.[27] The next, held in Leipzig in early December, dealt with the difficulties associated with prosecuting government criminality under the Communist regime. The discussion turned on the division between the proponents of the legal positivist view, which privileges the principle *nulla poena, nullum crimen sine lege* (no punishment, no crime without a law) enshrined in Article 103 of the Federal Republic's Basic Law, and those who argued for the natural law notion that prosecution could proceed on the basis of a "higher law." In a situation with certain analogies to the post-1945 period, this conflict of interpretations was rejuvenated in the wake of the GDR's collapse as a result of the problematic legal basis for prosecuting East German political leaders and border guards. The discussion yielded one possible "third way" in resolving this dilemma. Indictments could be based, commission member Dorothee Wilms asserted, on the paragraph in the GDR's criminal code precluding any recourse to claiming that one had simply followed orders in criminal cases where fundamental and human rights had been violated. The principles adumbrated in the Nuremberg trials of Nazi "crimes against humanity" might thus serve, in a later context, as the basis for punishing the injustices carried out against victims of the East German dictatorship.[28]

In another indication of the possible benefits to be had from the commission's public forums, the body met again in early December 1992 to discuss the role of the so-called "block parties" in the GDR. These parties, all of which had assented to the SED's "leading role" in the GDR's political life, were generally known — in standard Leninist parlance — as "transmission belts" of the Communists. Yet the hearing revealed a remarkable difference between West and East German perceptions of the "block flutes," as they were popularly characterized. A West German scholar of these matters, Peter Joachim Lapp, argued that the members of the "block parties" had been neither resisters nor opportunists, but somewhere in between these two. Commission member Gerd Poppe, a cofounder of the GDR's first dissident group devoted explicitly to human rights, the Initiative for Peace and Human Rights, vigorously contradicted this view, however, insisting that the block parties were simply a way for those with careerist ambitions to avoid joining the SED.

This clash of opinions suggests the extent to which West German analysts, far from seeking to dispense with the GDR and its socialist experiment, had come under the sway of the more tolerant, "immanent" approach to the GDR and to socialist regimes generally that is associated with the work of political sociologist Peter Christian Ludz (see Ludz 1972). Fundamentally, critics of this approach have insisted since 1989, practitioners of this type of analysis had come to accept the durability of — and, by implication, to relax their political guard against — Soviet-style Communism. Social scientists, among others, in effect were accused of having coddled the old regime by relaxing the hostility toward it that had been typical of the period when totalitarian theories had reigned supreme among academic analysts (and, of course, many politicians and others). The exchange reported above also offers striking evidence that the impulse for "coming to terms" with the Communist past emanates from the East and especially from the former dissident community. The judgments of Gerd Poppe, the commission member from the East who had lived under the old system until the end, are considerably harsher than those of the West German "expert."[29]

True to the larger attempt to reappropriate history in the interest of a more democratic future, the commission chose the dates for its meetings with an eye to their symbolic significance. For example, on 15 January 1993 — the third anniversary of that fateful day in 1990 when outraged masses "stormed" the secret police headquarters in Berlin and initiated the beginning of the Stasi's end — a hearing took place concerning the role and nature of the Stasi. The principal witness that day, longtime GDR analyst Karl-Wilhelm Fricke, hammered home the point that the Stasi was not a "state-within-the-state," as was often asserted, but rather precisely what it had claimed to be: the "sword and shield of the party."[30]

The commission of inquiry also scheduled a public event for 17 June 1993. The commission chose this date, of course, because it coincided with the fortieth anniversary of the East German workers' rebellion. The commemoration of those events, too, played a role in the East German civil rights activists' politically oriented efforts to appropriate the past since unification. Until 1990, the 17th of June was celebrated in the Federal Republic as the legal "day of German unity"; the events of that bygone day, when East German workers had demanded freedom and reunification, fit neatly into the commemorative narrative[31] of anti-Communism and national unity that was the rhetorical stock-in-trade of West German political elites during the Cold War era. With the Berlin Wall's crumbling, however, the cultivation of that particular enemy would no longer be of much use in binding Germans to the new nation-building project that now confronted them. The treaty of union between the two German states took advantage of the not-yet-faded glow of national feeling to announce that, henceforth, the German national holiday would be held on 3 October — the official date of German unification.[32]

The unification treaty's provisions thus undercut much of the debate over the question of which events would be chosen as the touchstone of national mythmaking. Not surprisingly, the choice of a national holiday commemorating the results of the contractual labors of political and bureaucratic elites in West and East, and that constituted a paean to national rather than democratic habits of mind, could hardly generate much enthusiasm among the grassroots democrats of the East German civil rights groups. Accordingly, in parliamentary debates on 17 June 1992, Alliance '90/The Greens representatives took the opportunity to highlight the potential but missed significance of the 17th of June for the political culture of united Germany. In a Bundestag debate over the execrably named SED-Unrechtsbereinigungsgesetz (more or less literally, the Law for the Cleansing of SED-Sponsored Injustice), Alliance '90 parliamentarian Werner Schulz invoked the anniversary of the East German workers' rebellion in support of Germany's still unachieved "inner unity, the humane, the civil, the democratic society." During another debate the same day over the future of the European Community in the immediate shadow of the Danish vote rejecting the Maastricht Treaty, Alliance '90 representative Gerd Poppe took the occasion to decry the Maastricht Treaty's "democratic deficit" and to plead for a referendum on the issue in Germany.[33]

The heirs of East Germany's civil rights activism thus sought on several fronts to appropriate the history of the Communist dictatorship in the service of their vision of a more democratic society. As in their electoral efforts during the waning days of the old GDR, their efforts have not generally been rewarded by notable popular support for their political goals. The same must be said for the other important area in which they strove to realize that democratic vision, namely, the more direct route of constitutional reform.

Constitution Making after the Revolution

As noted earlier, the Central Round Table had resolved at its very first meeting in early December 1989 — long before it had become clear that the upheaval in the GDR would culminate in German unification — to draft a new constitution for the German Democratic Republic. This move reflected the East German civil rights activists' special devotion to *constitution making* as the supreme act consecrating the overthrow of a tyrannical regime and the foundation of a new order.[34] Thus was created the Round Table's Working Group on a New Constitution, which included representatives of numerous groups from the East as well as West German constitutional law experts such as Ulrich K. Preuss of the University of Bremen. At the Round Table's last session less than one week before the elections of 18 March 1990, the group presented its draft document and — again indicating its attentiveness to historical symbolism — proposed that a referendum on the draft should be held on 17 June. As we now know, of course, that referendum never took place; the outcome of the parliamentary elections of 18 March 1990, in which the civil rights campaigners fared miserably, helped ensure that such projects would receive only scant further attention.

The former dissident intellectuals' constitutional aims rapidly faded in significance as the newly elected East German parliament moved quickly to effect unification with the Federal Republic according to Article 23 of the Basic Law in early 1990. Unification according to Article 23 certainly short-circuited much of the debate over a permanent constitution for the newly enlarged Federal Republic. Still, Article 5 of the unification treaty charged the Federal Republic's legislative bodies with the task of considering possible changes or additions to the Basic Law in connection with unification. For all the opposition to Article 146 among the more conservative parties who largely controlled the treaty-making process, in fact, the treaty specifically raised the question of the possible relevance of Article 146, as well as that of a popular referendum on the constitution. In response to this provision of the unification treaty, the federal parliament instituted a constitutional commission to consider changes in the fundamental law governing the new Germany. The commission held its first session in mid-January 1992 and was originally charged with completing its deliberations and making proposals to parliament for amendments and revisions of the Basic Law by the end of March 1993.[35] Given the constellation of political forces in the Bundestag and their general hostility toward constitutional changes, however, the federal parliament's co-optation of the constitutional initiative signaled the final phase of the East German civil rights activists' "abortive revolution." Within the commission, the East German civil rights activists pushed for such constitutional changes as the adoption of the initiative and referendum and of a general right to vote for resident aliens (above and beyond the right to vote in *local* elections).

Contrary to the wishes of the East German activists, the parliamentary co-optation of the process of constitutional reform substantially removed that process from the public eye. Even before unification had been officially effected, however, the dissident intellectuals had begun to marshal their own forces, as well as those of sympathetic West Germans, for the aim of drawing up a new constitution for united Germany. Once again seeking to draw symbolic capital from the heritage of popular mobilization in the GDR, a number of leading figures from the intellectual left in East and West gathered in Berlin's Reichstag building on the evening of 16 June 1990 to announce the formation of what they called the Curatorium for a Democratically Organized Federation of German States (Kuratorium für einen demokratisch verfaßten Bund deutscher Länder).

The group's wordy self-characterization indirectly indicates the nature of its purposes. Its name recalls the federations of German states that preceded the unified German empire of 1871 — adding the modification that, unlike those states, the states comprising post-unification Germany should be "democratically organized." Created to a substantial degree by veterans of the East German experience of hypertrophic centralism, the organization sought by way of constitutional reform to decentralize political decision making and generate civic participation outside the party system. At a time when, according to a public opinion poll, nine out of ten (adult) Germans had little or no confidence in the major parties,[36] the stimulation of popular political initiative presented itself to democratic activists as a corrective to the aimless irresolution that characterized the German political class following unification.

The curatorium's founding statement reiterated the activists' previously expressed desire for a new "all-German" constitution taking the best from both the Basic Law and the Round Table's draft constitution. According to the curatorium, the document should be promulgated by a constitutional convention and ratified by popular vote.[37] Describing itself as the "first all-German citizens' initiative,"[38] the organization seeks to correct what it regards as the "democratic deficits" in the Basic Law and to achieve these ends through a broad process of public discussion and involvement. The curatorium held its first larger public event, a conference entitled "Constitution with Referendum," in September 1990 in the symbolically significant (eastern German) city of Weimar, cradle of Germany's first attempt at constitutional democracy. At a second conference in Potsdam toward the end of 1990, the group explicitly rejected the Bundestag's recently announced plans to create the aforementioned constitutional commission. They argued that such a path to the new constitution "gives the population no chance to bring themselves into the constitutional process." The Potsdam Declaration repeats the catalog of rights the curatorium's members would like to see codified in the new German constitution, many of which are derived from the Round Table draft. In wording that would grow in significance during subsequent years, the signatories also insisted that any new constitution would have to "express not only the fundamental rights of all *Germans,* but those of all *persons.*" This passage signaled clearly the curatorium's preoccupation with the problem of the rights of foreigners in Germany and indeed of what they regard as the inadequacies of German citizenship law more generally.[39]

Again drawing on the German past in an effort to lend legitimacy to their activities, the curatorium held a major public event at St. Paul's Church (the Paulskirche) in Frankfurt on 16 and 17 June 1991. On that occasion, several hundred participants discussed the curatorium's draft constitution in the place where the bourgeois revolutionaries of 1848 had deliberated upon and promulgated a liberal constitution for Germany. Unlike the symbolism of the East German workers' rebellion of 17 June 1953, however, that of the Paulskirche was notably ambiguous: the labors of the German liberals of 1848 came to nought, after all, when the Prussian king Frederick Wilhelm IV refused to accept the crown they offered him to rule over a constitutional monarchy. Moreover, the revolution of 1848 was as much a *national* as it was a *liberal* revolution, and the political concerns of the East German civil rights activists and their West German allies are anything but national in orientation.

Indeed, the protagonists of the abortive revolution in the GDR have been in the forefront of efforts to transform the German concept of nationhood.[40] In the curatorium's draft constitution, the authors took direct aim at the definition of citizenship based on blood relations that is enshrined in the Basic Law. Where that document speaks of "Germans," the curatorium's draft referred to "citizens" and defines "the people" *(das Volk)* from whom sovereignty issues as "the totality of all citizens," without any reference to "Germans." In its revised Article 116, which regulates citizenship and naturalization, the draft constitution would guarantee the opportunity to become naturalized to German citizenship to all foreigners who have lived on German territory for at least five years, halving the then current requirement of ten years — one of the most restrictive in Europe.[41] In a speech in the Bundestag, Konrad Weiß, one of the curatorium's principal supporters from the East, spoke explicitly of the need to replace citizenship based on *jus sanguinis* (the law of the blood) with that based on *jus soli* (i.e., a definition rooted in territorial residence).[42] The civil rights activists' push for the constitutional acceptance of dual citizenship subsequently spread well into the mainstream of the German party system, finding support among such major CDU figures as Berlin mayor Eberhard Diepgen and President of the Parliament Rita Süssmuth, as well as from the then chief justice of Germany's highest court and now federal president, Roman Herzog.[43]

More broadly, the advocates of constitutional reform from the old GDR sought to institute a conception of constitutionally guaranteed human rights rooted in the concept of *personhood* rather than in that of *national belonging*. This impulse has clear roots in their experience under the Communist regime. For example, several of the curatorium's supporters are veterans of two particular groups from the old East German dissident scene: the Initiative for Peace and Human Rights and the awkwardly named group "For the Renunciation of the Practice and Principle of Demarcation." As noted above, the Initiative for Peace and Human Rights was the first group in the GDR's dissident circles to campaign explicitly for human rights (other than the right to emigrate). The other group, it will be recalled, was composed largely of religiously motivated activists who sought to overcome the Communist regime's ban on freedom of travel and

association; one of its aims had been to ensure that Germans' stereotypes and prejudices toward foreigners would not be aided by state
policies hindering international contacts, especially with Poles.[44] In
the debate over changes in Germany's asylum law in the aftermath of
unification, the curatorium argued that it is "essential to take leave
of the dependence of fundamental rights on nationalities, to take the
step from the democracy of the nation-state to that of citizens male
and female, from the society of mutually exclusive peoples to the civil
society of equal peoples."[45]

In keeping with this effort, Alliance '90's parliamentary representatives have proposed laws on settlement, refugees, and citizenship
that seek to ease the integration of foreigners into the German
polity.[46] Members of Alliance '90 as well as East German civil rights
activist Markus Meckel of the SPD were among the most vigorous
critics of the so-called compromise on asylum policy reached by the
major parties, joining advocacy groups for foreigners and asylum-
seekers in roundly condemning the agreement for what they described
as its massive de facto limitations on access to asylum in Germany.[47]
Finally, while the right to asylum in Germany has been substantially
curtailed, there is also evidence that the civil rights activists' pressure for the adoption of new policies regarding the acquisition of
citizenship may have had some impact.[48]

It is by no means the case that the intellectual left's enthusiasm
for a new constitution has been shared across the political spectrum,
however. Much of the debate over a new constitution since 1990 has
reduced the matter to the virtues and vices of the plebiscitary elements it would add to the existing constitution.[49] Critics of enhanced
popular initiative frequently point to the Weimar Constitution as evidence that such proposals are less desirable than they might appear.
Yet those who make this objection tend to interpret history rather
tendentiously. After all, the Weimar order fell apart not as a result of
popular legislative initiatives, but because of parliamentary elections,
the system's lack of defenders, and, finally, the *Ermächtigungsgesetz*
(Enabling Law) that handed power to Hitler. Those who object that
such procedures as initiative and referendum are not provided for in
the Basic Law neglect to add that they are codified in the constitutions
of the individual states, including the five newly reconstituted states
in the territory of the former GDR. In view of the Basic Law's clause
requiring conformity of state laws with those of the federal constitution (Article 28), it is unpersuasive to argue that such provisions

would be unconstitutional at the federal level.[50] Finally, some oppose the adoption of more plebiscitarian elements because they believe the proponents of these reforms desire to install an unworkable "direct democracy." Yet the advocates of these changes have repeatedly stated that they view them as a *complements to*, not *replacements for*, the institutions of representative democracy. This suggests that opponents of these measures simply fear greater political participation, on the grounds that this would lead to less desirable political outcomes. Opposition to such "direct democratic" institutions would thus appear to fall under what Albert Hirschman has dubbed the "perversity" category of the "rhetoric of reaction": critics oppose it because they claim it will bring about the opposite of its intended aims (see Hirschman 1991).

In addition to the controversy over plebiscitarian elements *in* a revised constitution, conflict swirled around the issue of a referendum *on* the newly drafted constitution itself. Opponents of this procedure have expressed concern that the new constitution could fail to be ratified or that popular participation in the vote could be so poor that the legitimating consequences of the ratification process would be vitiated.[51] Those on this side of the constitutional debate also frequently argue that the Basic Law has proven itself a perfectly serviceable or, indeed, praiseworthy foundation upon which four decades of reasonably stable German democracy have been built. Proponents of a constitutional referendum, in contrast, insist that popular ratification — even if only one to make the Basic Law a permanent constitution — is the only way for the German citizenry to exercise its sovereign power to give itself the laws under which it is to be ruled. Here the advocates of a new constitution seek to rectify what they regard as the "birth defect" of the Basic Law. In keeping with the founders' view that they were creating nothing more than a stop-gap, the provisional constitution was promulgated in 1949 by a "parliamentary council" rather than the more formal "constitutional assembly" called for by the curatorium. The Basic Law was, moreover, never submitted to a popular vote but was instead ratified by the West German state parliaments. This course of events had less to do with the founders' reservations about popular ratification of the Basic Law per se, however, than with concerns that the Communists in the East would exploit a constitutional referendum for their own purposes, as well as with a variety of practical considerations.[52]

Today, in the absence of these extenuating circumstances, there is no compelling reason why a constitutional referendum *could not* be held. The Curatorium for a Democratically Organized Federation of German States pressed precisely this demand. But the various initiatives of the heirs of the East German dissident intellectuals in the constitutional commission — guarantees of social rights, introduction of plebiscitarian elements, as well as the adoption of gender equality and environmental goals as constitutional principles — have failed for lack of support by the parties in control of the government, the CDU/CSU and the FDP. Though the constellation of political forces never boded well for the advocates of a public process of ratification of a revised constitution, neither was that possibility excluded altogether. Yet by mid-1993, it was clear that any constitutional changes to be suggested to the federal parliament would be of marginal import at best.[53] In view of this outcome, one must conclude that the civic "revolution" sought by the East German intellectuals associated with the movements that played a prominent role in wresting power from the SED during 1989–90 had finally come to an end. Some, indeed, have rejuvenated the term "conservative revolution" from Weimar days to characterize the results of the abortive constitutional process set in motion by the opposition to and collapse of Communism in the GDR.[54]

The Greens/Alliance '90 Merger and the Legacy of East German Civil Rights Activism

Rather than being completely marginalized in the new "all-German" political order, the East German civil rights activists have in fact played a leading part in stimulating two of the most significant political discussions of the postunification period. Yet it would be foolhardy to assert that these forces are destined to challenge the major parties in importance. Is their activity anything more than a tale of sound and fury, ultimately signifying nothing, as the fate of constitutional reform might suggest?

The decision of Alliance '90/The Greens, the chief organized political expression of the heirs of East German civil rights activism under the old Communist regime, to fuse with the West German Greens in an effort to save them both from the dustbin of electoral history suggests that the ideas of the GDR's dissident intellectuals may play a continued if never dominant role in the political life of the new Germany. Yet one of the striking features of this East-West political marriage was the considerable controversy it provoked on both sides of the former "intra-German" border.[55] These prenuptial disagreements were anything but a replay of the long-running split between "fundamentalists" and "realists" within the West German Greens, as one might have expected. Rather, the difficulties attending the union of the parliamentary embodiment of the West German new social movements with that of the East German civil rights activists derive from their profoundly different historical and social origins.

What separates the two groups is their background in strikingly contrasting political systems as well as their social trajectories. The West German Greens are the political avatars of postwar Germany's affluent new middle class. In particular, their members and supporters are drawn overwhelmingly from among the younger, well-educated segments of West German society — in other words, from the ranks of university students and graduates located occupationally in the tertiary sector of the economy. Ideologically, the party and its supporters are preoccupied principally with so-called postmaterialist concerns such as participatory democracy, environmentalism, and feminism. They tend to be antinationalistic, and hence, like their counterparts in East Germany, the younger, better-educated segments of the population of the Federal Republic were relatively unenthusiastic, or at least apathetic, about unification (see Brämer and Heublein 1990). As noted earlier, one of the more spectacular results of the first national elections in postunification Germany in December 1990 had been the Greens' failure to scale the 5 percent minimum required for parliamentary representation. Voting analysts suggested that the reason for the Greens' remarkable failure lay in the party's adherents' relative lack of interest in the election's main issues — namely, the tasks associated with unification. These commentators were nonetheless not prepared to predict that the Greens would disappear from the German political scene, however, pointing to the stability of the party's voter base in the "postmaterialist" new middle class (Gibowski and Kaase 1991, 20).

The East German civil rights activists, by contrast, far from being the political expression of a broader social stratum, were drawn primarily from among a narrow group of marginal intellectuals. The disproportion between their *cultural* and their *political* capital gave rise to tensions that could only be resolved by the party's surrender of its would-be monopolistic control over state and society. Those tensions did not, however, lead to ties between these marginal intellectuals and broader groups of East Germans dissatisfied with the regime. As Robert Brym has argued, popular mobilization and the political opportunities it creates tend to be an essential prop of radicalism among intellectuals (Brym 1980, 25). Of such popular mobilization there was very little in the GDR between the time of the workers' rebellion of 1953 and the mass exodus and subsequent demonstrations of 1989. Unable to act as spokespersons and ideologists for larger social groups, whose inclination to oppose the regime was always undermined by a number of factors discussed earlier,[56] the marginal intellectuals in the GDR cultivated an isolated and, to most of their compatriots, quixotic existence. As a result, they tended their own gardens, struggling to realize their particular interests — in freedom of association, of opinion, of expression (leaving aside for the moment the question whether those might actually be said to have been *universal* interests). In sum, the social trajectory of this group led to (or consolidated) its alienation from the social and political order in the course of the 1980s. But this alienation could not by itself forge intergroup alliances against the state as had occurred in Poland, for instance, with the intellectually dominated group KOR (Workers' Defense Committee) and the working-class-based Solidarity trade union in the early 1980s.

Rather, the East German dissident intellectuals' situation was much more like that of the Czechoslovak dissidents, who were drawn principally from among narrow intellectual circles and who were similarly isolated from other social groups. Limiting their appeal to wider elements of the population even further, however, was the GDR dissidents' relative lack of interest in the national question — a reticence conditioned in part by the horrific legacy of German nationalism, in part by the dissidents' desire to win supporters for change *in* an East German state that virtually everyone expected to persist for at least the remainder of their own lifetimes. As a result, the dissidents in the GDR developed the mentality of a virtuous but ever-embattled sect, a sort of "moral minority" with few ties beyond their own (admittedly growing) milieu. As one of the most prominent leaders of the East German civil rights groups, Ulrike Poppe, once put it: "In the opposition role, we cultivated for too long a disturbed relation to power, regarded a revolution as unlikely, and sought our identity entirely in the ethics of resistance" (see Poppe 1990b). Those who had suffered for their activism under the old regime were thus ill-prepared to organize larger groups when the possibilities of pluralism presented themselves in the fall of 1989 and after. They were unable to transform their virtuous actions into a fund of moral capital that would help them lead and sustain a larger movement.

It is thus not surprising that the civil rights activists have a tendency to reduce politics to the activities of discussion, interpretation, and symbolism. They are hardly the first to do this; politicized intellectuals often define politics as *talk* and thus privilege their own role. Students for a Democratic Society's emphasis on participatory democracy in its programmatic Port Huron statement, for example, gave certain advantages to those — such as students — who had the time and enthusiasm for extensive meetings. At a more theoretical level, Jürgen Habermas has apotheosized talk, apparently almost limitless talk, as undistorted communication and the model of democratic equality. From Gracchus Babeuf to Mao Zedong to Alvin Gouldner and Pierre Bourdieu, a long line of critics has taken issue with the universalistic claims of the intelligentsia rooted in their superior control of "cultural capital." This tradition of analysis grew increasingly critical in the aftermath of Karl Mannheim's lofty but abstract characterization of the intelligentsia as "free-floating" in *Ideology and Utopia.*

To criticize the politics of intellectuals on these grounds is perfectly well taken; Marx, for instance, was surely right to note that all would-be ruling classes shroud their particular interests in the cloak of the more broadly appealing universal variety. But saying this does not necessarily mean that the universalistic claims of intellectuals are merely cloaks for self-interest. While such claims may germinate in, and speak chiefly to the concerns of, specific social groups, that does not necessarily mean that they are simply specious. While only workers may obviously benefit from a reduction of tax-levies on the laboring classes, all groups presumably have an interest in the civil rights guarantees that constitute the occupational sine qua nons of intellectual work: rights to freedom of expression, to freedom of assembly, to protection from the state's interference. The reason is that nonintellectuals may, at least at the margin, also benefit from these rights and freedoms. Trade-union organizing, for example, would be unthinkable without them. That is also the reason that, historically, the nineteenth-century labor movement was so closely bound up with the achievement of democratic *political* rights, such as the right to vote. In burgeoning electoral democracies, the action repertoire of the workers' movement would have remained quite restricted without the ability to elect their party representatives into parliament. The achievement of such rights may have been precisely what took the wind out of the sails of the socialist movement in the twentieth century. But, as the debate over asylum law in Germany reminds us, rights are never given in perpetuity; they must be renewed, affirmed, and, at times, recovered in order to remain effective. It seems likely that this area will comprise the principal realm of political activity for the former East German dissident intellectuals during the coming years.

Conclusion

Clearly, the voter base of Alliance '90 and the Greens remains strongly confined to the new middle classes in postunification German society. Electoral results indicate that their activities are regarded with relatively little enthusiasm by the less educated, who presumably do not find their concerns reflected in the civil rights activists' efforts. Still, their quest for a more democratic political order, as yet unborn, can be expected to persist. At least for the time being, this may remain a matter for the margins — despite the likely growth of the new middle-class groups that provide their social base. In the East, this peripheral brushfire may be joined to the tinder collecting among the growing number of intellectuals trained under the old system who have found no foothold in the new. Widespread unemployment has, after all, led to political unrest among intellectuals in Germany (and elsewhere) before. But this is not the only possible response to occupational dislocation. Malaise and demoralization may be as likely to follow as outrage and mobilization. The ultimate fate of the inheritance of East German civil rights activism will lie in the ways larger groups respond to the current crisis: whether they succeed in developing a coherent response to the problems of the new Germany and whether the mass parties manage to recover from their current aimlessness and succeed once again in providing political orientation for substantial strata of the population.

The principal domestic problem facing Germany today is not the integration of two halves of a preexisting nation but rather the (re-)creation of a nation. This fact has been papered over so far by the pronouncements of political elites who pretend that some primordially defined "Germany" has for the last forty years been rent asunder and that the task now is simply to sew that entity back

together. To be sure, the constitutional guarantees of automatic citizenship to those in the East and such policies as the earlier Hallstein
Doctrine (the notion that the Federal Republic alone represented the
German nation and that any formal recognition of the GDR by other
states would lead to a loss of diplomatic ties with West Germany)
helped sustain the feeling among many Germans that they belong together in one state. Yet there is much to be said for Eric Hobsbawm's
dictum that "states make nations, not the other way around,"[57]
even if this can hardly account entirely for the complex relationship between nations and states, especially in the nineteenth century.
The Germans lived long enough in two states to make necessary a
renewed effort to "make Germans" by the new "all-German" state.

The lack of enthusiasm for unification among the East German
civil rights activists, disproportionately recruited from among their
country's under-forty-five generation, was thus not simply evidence of
their political naïveté. Instead, it expressed, at least to some degree,
the fate of national consciousness among those who grew up knowing
nothing but a "Germany" that existed in two separate states. Only
since official unification on 3 October 1990 have we become fully
aware of the degree to which their weak interest in unification was
shared by wide segments of the West German population that is now
being asked to pay the costs of that undertaking. Likewise, the eastern Germans' initial euphoria over unification has subsided in large
measure because so many of them view themselves as having been
cheated by the powers-that-be, who promised so much and delivered
so little. The East German civil rights activists warned them in the
period of the *Wende* that reliance on the West to solve the problems
of the East could have disastrous consequences. They had hoped to
encourage a process of civic rather than national reconstruction. Although that appeal went unheeded, the civil rights activists' project
of "nation building from below" remains a critical task in the new
Germany. Only if *this* task is achieved will the sacrifices being asked
of Germans as a result of unification bring anything but further discontent. There is, after all, no *intrinsic* reason that the citizens of one
German state should pay to "bail out," as they see it, the victims of
another. The East German civil rights activists' efforts to appropriate
the past and to make constitutional reforms in the service of a common future may still have some chance of helping bring together that
which — Willy Brandt to the contrary notwithstanding — does not
necessarily belong together.

The spate of candlelight demonstrations against xenophobic violence that emerged in late 1992 suggests one way in which popular movements might achieve this aim. The protest movement joins a particular interpretation of the past with the demand that, in the new Germany, that past not be allowed to be repeated. And this was the product of popular initiative: impatient with the dithering of the German political leadership, these protesters refused to wait for parliament to act. Instead, they took responsibility themselves for protesting against the wave of antiforeigner attacks in Germany.[58] Clearly, the former East German dissident intellectuals are not wrong to believe that there are traditions of humane, democratic citizenship that can be drawn upon to build a more tolerant German nation in the newly unified state. And if they are to leave any legacy at all to the new Germany that their efforts helped make possible, it is this.

Appendix 1

List of Interviewees

Jürgen Fuchs, dissident writer exiled in 1977, Berlin, 12 November 1990.

Manfred Lötsch, sociologist at SED's Academy of Social Sciences, Berlin, 27 February 1991; 28 January 1992.

Siegfried Grundmann, sociologist at SED's Academy of Social Sciences, Berlin, 27 February 1991; 26 March 1991; and 9 April 1991.

Erhart Neubert, cofounder of citizens' initiative Democratic Awakening, pastor, sociologist employed by the East German Lutheran Church, Berlin, 27 March 1991.

Wolfgang Kühnel, sociologist at East Berlin's Humboldt University, Berlin, 4 April 1991.

Katrin Deyda, teacher of handicapped children, Dresden, 21 May 1991.

Henry Hocke, invalided worker, Leipzig, 25 May 1991.

Tom Güldermann, student of African culture at Karl Marx University, Leipzig, 25 May 1991.

Heidi Stuhler, near-Ph.D. in sociology, journalist, Berlin, 11 June 1991.

Ulrike Poppe, activist on peace and human rights issues, Conway, N.H., 23 June 1991.

Christof Cordt, ecological and New Forum activist, Leipzig, 8 July 1991.

Jochen Lässig, activist in Leipzig "Work Circle on Justice" and New Forum activist, Leipzig, 9 July 1991.

Maria Jacobi, assistant to Dresden Catholic bishop Christof Ziemer, Dresden, 10 July 1991.

Gustav Just, former general secretary of the Writers' Union, imprisoned for his involvement in the "Harich Group" in 1956, Prenden bei Berlin, 14 July 1991; 1 February 1992.

Helmut Warmbier, New Forum activist and former professor of Marxism-Leninism at Karl Marx University, Leipzig, 29 July 1991.

Günter Lehmann, student of Ernst Bloch, professor of cultural studies at Karl Marx University, Leipzig, 29 July 1991.

Roland Wötzel, lawyer and first secretary of the Leipzig SED, Leipzig, 29 July 1991.

Dr. Heidrun Pretzschner, local SED official, Dresden, 30 July 1991.

Jürgen Bönninger, engineer and dissident activist, Dresden, 30 July 1991.

Uwe Haeseler, engineer, Berlin, 6 August 1991.

Lutz Rathenow, poet and author, Berlin, 7 August 1991.

Dr. Dietmar Lucht, engineer and Round Table representative of the Green League, Berlin, 20 August 1991.

Dr. Ingrid Brandenburg, economic adviser to New Forum in Round Table negotiations; and *Dr. Klaus Brandenburg,* historian and New Forum representative/adviser at Round Table, Berlin, 21 August 1991 (joint interview).

Wolfgang Thierse, literary historian at the Academy of Sciences, Berlin, 23 August 1991.

Fred Ebeling, engineer and cofounder of Democratic Awakening, Berlin, 23 August 1991; 28 January 1992.

Dr. Wolfgang Ullmann, Church historian and cofounder of Democracy Now, Berlin, 25 August 1991.

Jens Reich, doctor/biologist at the Academy of Sciences, Berlin, 26 August 1991.

Martin Gutzeit, pastor and cofounder of the East German SPD, Berlin, 28 August 1991.

Wolfgang Templin, cofounder of Initiative for Peace and Human Rights, in West German exile until 9 November 1989, Berlin, 29 August 1991; 3 February 1992.

Lotte Templin, activist in Initiative for Peace and Human Rights, 3 February 1992.

Matthias Platzeck, engineer and cofounder of the Green League, Potsdam, 29 August 1991.

Christian Führer, pastor of St. Nicholas Church, Leipzig, 4 September 1991.

Sebastian Pflugbeil, physicist at Academy of Sciences, Berlin, 5 September 1991.

Günter Jeschonnek, cofounder in 1987 of the "Working Group on GDR Citizenship Rights," emigrated to West Berlin in late 1987, Berlin, 12 September 1991.

Konrad Weiss, film director and cofounder of Democracy Now, Berlin, 13 September 1991.

Markus Meckel, pastor and cofounder of the East German SPD, Berlin, 14 September 1991.

Wolfgang Herger, Director of the SED Central Committee's Section on Security Affairs, Berlin, 16 September 1991; 30 January 1992.

Carlo Jordan, longtime ecological activist and cofounder of the East German Green Party, Berlin, 16 September 1991.

Günter Schabowski, member of the SED Politburo, Berlin, 19 September 1991.

Werner Eberlein, member of the SED Politburo, Berlin, 2 February 1992.

Bärbel Bohley, cofounder of New Forum, Cambridge, Mass., 2 April 1993.

Joachim Gauck, pastor and head of the agency administering the files of the former Ministry of State Security (Stasi), Boston, Mass., 25 April 1993.

Appendix 2

List of New Political Groupings Emerging in 1989–90

Bund Freier Demokraten (BFD): Alliance of liberal parties, including the Liberal-Demokratische Partei, the Deutsche Forumpartei, and the Freie Demokratische Partei

Bündnis '90 (Alliance '90): Electoral alliance of Democracy Now, New Forum, and Initiative for Peace and Human Rights

Demokratie Jetzt (DJ): Democracy Now

Demokratischer Aufbruch (DA): Democratic Awakening

Deutsche Soziale Union (DSU): German Social Union

Grüne Partei: Green Party

Neues Forum (NF): New Forum

Sozialdemokratische Partei (SDP/SPD): Social Democratic Party of East Germany

Unabhängiger Frauenverband (UFV): Independent Women's Association

Appendix 3

Glossary of Names

Names of those for whom biographies may be found in this glossary are indicated by italics.

Ackermann, Anton: Born 1905, prominent early advocate of a "specifically German road to socialism." Joined the KPD in 1926, then trained at the Lenin School in Moscow. Antifascist activities in Berlin in 1933; 1936–37 in Spain; then to the Soviet Union. After 1943 active in the Moscow-based National Committee for a Free Germany, director of its radio station "Free Germany." In 1945, leader of the Ackermann Group in Saxony that, parallel to the Ulbricht Group near Berlin, helped build the new political administration in the Soviet Occupation Zone. Joined the KPD and then the SED; author of the "party line" advocating an autonomous German road to socialism. In the wake of the Stalin-Tito dispute, forced to recant this position; then demoted to a position as state secretary in the Ministry of Foreign Affairs from October 1949 to October 1953. From October 1950 to January 1954, member of the SED's Central Committee, October 1950 to July 1953 a candidate member of the Politburo. Gradually driven from his party offices in the aftermath of the workers' rebellion of June 1953 for his support of the opposition to *Walter Ulbricht* grouped around *Rudolf Herrnstadt* and *Wilhelm Zaisser.*

Becher, Johannes R.: Born 1891, prominent early GDR cultural figure. Member of the KPD in 1919. Secretary of the League of Proletarian-Revolutionary Writers, 1928–33. Emigration in Czechoslovakia, France, and the Soviet Union, 1933–1945. Return to Germany, 1945. President of the Kulturbund, 1945–58, and of the Academy of Arts, 1952–56. Member of the SED Central Committee, 1950–58. Minister of Culture, 1954–58. Died 1958.

Biermann, Wolf: Born 1936, prominent GDR dissident socialist singer-songwriter and poet who became a cause célèbre of the dissident East German intelligentsia when the authorities refused to let him back into the country after a concert tour in West Germany in 1976. The son of a Jewish Communist father who was killed in Auschwitz and a Communist mother, Biermann left his native Hamburg at the age of seventeen and settled in the young GDR. For years a Communist critic of both East and West Germany, Biermann long insisted the GDR was the "better German state." In 1989–90, however, he was sharply critical of SED rule and did not share in the enthusiasm among many intellectuals for saving the GDR.

Bohley, Bärbel: Born 1945, cofounder of New Forum. Studied fine arts at the University of the Arts (Kunsthochschule) in East Berlin, thereafter independent artist and graphic designer. Cofounder (with *Ulrike Poppe*) of the independent peace initiative Women for Peace. Imprisoned from December 1983 to January 1984 for contacts with a peace activist of the West German Greens. Cofounder of the Initiative for Peace and Human Rights. Arrested in the aftermath of the 1988 Rosa Luxemburg demonstration. To escape a possible lengthy jail sentence, she temporarily left the country for the Federal Republic and England. Her unenthusiastic response to the opening of the Berlin Wall and her opposition to unification were among the most widely reported reactions of the East Germany intellectual dissidents to developments in the fall of 1989. Frequently described as the "mother of the revolution."

Brandt, Heinz: Born 1909, SED functionary in the Berlin party organization. As a Communist and Jew, Brandt was incarcerated in Auschwitz and Buchenwald during the Nazi period. Thereafter secretary for Agitation and Propaganda until his demotion in the aftermath of the 1953 East German workers' rebellion. Emigration to the Federal Republic in 1958, editor of the journal of the West German metalworkers' union, *IG Metall.* Kidnapped from West Berlin by the Stasi in 1961 and sentenced to thirteen years of forced labor for alleged spying activities. Freed in 1964 after worldwide protests. Friend of Robert Havemann and author of memoirs of his experience in the SED apparatus, *Ein Traum, der nicht entführbar ist* (A dream that can't be kidnapped, 1967).

Eberlein, Werner: Born 1919, member of the SED Politburo, 1986–89. Son of KPD and Comintern cofounder Hugo Eberlein, he fled with his family to the Soviet Union in 1934. His father, Hugo Eberlein, later fell victim to the purges of the Stalin years. Eberlein himself spent eight years at hard labor in Siberia in the wake of the Hitler-Stalin pact. Upon his return to Berlin in 1948, however, he immediately presented himself to the SED's Central Committee to ask for his duties to the party. Journalistic activity for the SED organ *Neues Deutschland;* for a time, editor of the paper's economic section. Russian translator for General Secretary Walter Ulbricht and later for his successor, Erich Honecker. Beginning in 1959, worked in various functions in the party apparatus. Elevated into SED Central Committee at tenth party congress in 1981. From 1983–89, first secretary of the SED in Magdeburg. November 1985 to June 1986 candidate member, then full member of the SED Politburo. Long a sympathizer of Gorbachev's reforms in the Soviet Union, Eberlein, after the upheaval of the fall of 1989, was charged by the SED with the task of dissolving the Stalinist structures in the party and calling to account those who had been guilty of corruption.

Eppelmann, Rainer: Born 1943, cofounder of the citizens' initiative Democratic Awakening in fall 1989. Refused to carry out his military service and "substitute service" *(Ersatzdienst)* as a "construction soldier" *(Bausoldat).* Apprenticeship as bricklayer, then study of theology; from 1974–89 pastor of the East Berlin Protestant Church of the Good Samaritan. In early 1982, coauthor (with *Robert Havemann*) of the "Berlin Appeal — Make Peace without Weapons." Representative of Democratic Awakening at the Central Round Table in Berlin. Minister of defense and disarmament after the parliamentary elections of 18 March. After the first "all-German" Bundestag elections of 2 December, CDU member of the parliament.

Fuchs, Jürgen: Born 1950, prominent exiled writer and critic. Studied psychology in Jena, 1971–75; literary publications beginning 1974. Forced out of the university and thrown out of the SED in 1975. Jailed in the aftermath of the *Biermann* affair, November 1976 to August 1977; accepted exile in West Berlin instead of further incarceration.

Führer, Christian: Pastor at St. Nicholas Church in Leipzig. Led the weekly "peace prayers" that became the basis for the Monday demonstrations against the SED in the fall of 1989.

Grotewohl, Otto: Born 1894, first prime minister of the GDR. Grotewohl had been a member of the SPD since 1912 and one of its representatives in the German parliament (Reichstag) prior to the Nazi seizure of power. Jailed for seven months under the Nazis for violating the law against rebuilding banned parties. Chairman of the Berlin SPD after the collapse of the Third Reich in 1945; vigorous advocate of the fusion of the KPD and the SPD into the Socialist Unity Party in 1946. Thereafter, member of the Central Secretariat and later Politburo. Prime minister of the GDR from 1949 until his death in 1964 (succeeded by Willi Stoph, who held this position from 1964 to 1973 and 1976 to 1989).

Gysi, Gregor: Born 1948, after December 1989 chairman of the SED, then the PDS. Son of former minister of culture and state secretary for church affairs Klaus Gysi and of Irene Lessing Gysi, daughter of a prosperous Jewish merchant in St. Petersburg and for many years section director in the Ministry of Culture. Apprenticeship in livestock cultivation, then study of law at the Humboldt University in East Berlin; beginning 1971, legal practice. Along with *Lothar de Maiziere* and Wolfgang Schnur, one of the few lawyers who represented regime critics. Chairman of the bar association *(Rechtsanwaltskollegium)* in East Berlin and of the bar association of the GDR, 1988–89. Elected chairman of the SED at the SED's extraordinary congress on 8 December 1989. Elected to East German parliament on 18 March 1990, and then into the Bundestag on 2 December 1990.

Hager, Kurt: Born 1912, member of SED Politburo from 1963 to 1989. Member of the KPD, 1930. Antifascist resistance activities. From 1950 to 1954, candidate member, thereafter full member of the SED Central Committee. From 1955 to 1989, central committee secretary for culture and science. From 1958 to 1963, candidate member, thereafter full member of SED Politburo. Critic of the reform policies of Mikhail Gorbachev. Forced out of the Politburo on 3 November 1989.

Harich, Wolfgang: Born 1923, principal figure in the East German "revisionism" controversy of 1956–57. Studied philosophy in Berlin. After 1945 journalistic work for the Soviet-controlled *Tägliche Rundschau.* Joined the SED in 1946. Taught Marxist-Leninist philosophy at the Humboldt University starting 1948; named full professor 1949. Cofounder and editor-in-chief of the liberal-minded *Deutsche Zeitschrift für Philosophie* (German journal of philosophy), 1949–56. Arrested in November 1956 and sentenced in March 1957 to ten years imprisonment for his alleged involvement in a "conspiratorial treasonous group" that advocated liberalization, a "German road to socialism," and reunification with the Federal Republic. Released before the end of his term in 1964. Thereafter editor in the Akademie-Verlag publishing house in East Berlin and author of ecologically oriented books on the future of Communism, but without political influence. From 1979 to 1981, in West Germany and Austria; returned to the GDR in 1981.

Havemann, Robert: Born 1910, prominent regime critic. Studied chemistry 1929–33 in Munich and Berlin. Joined KPD in 1932, antifascist resistance activities during the Nazi period. Sentenced to death by the Nazi courts in 1943; sentence commuted due to his involvement in "research important to the war effort." Liberated from the prison in Brandenburg-Görden by the Red Army in spring 1945. Professor of physical chemistry at Humboldt University in East Berlin, 1946–64; director of various important research institutes. Cofounder and member of the board of the Cultural Federation for the Democratic Renewal of Germany (the Kulturbund), 1945–48; 1950–63 representative in the East German parliament. Purged from the SED and forced out of the university in March 1964 after his lecture course "Dialectics without Dogma" during the previous semester. Director of the research section on photochemistry; dismissed from that post December 1965. Forced out of the Academy of Sciences in April 1966. Thereafter supported by his pension as a "victim of fascism." Until his death in April 1982, constant surveillance and frequent house arrest at his house in Grünheide near Berlin, which was the locus of much dissident activity. Coauthor with *Rainer Eppelmann* of the "Berlin Appeal" for disarmament.

Herrnstadt, Rudolf: Born 1903, rival of SED leader *Walter Ulbricht* around the time of the 1953 workers' rebellion. The son of a successful Silesian lawyer who was killed in Auschwitz, Herrnstadt joined the KPD in 1924. Journalistic work for a Berlin newspaper in Warsaw and Moscow. Beginning 1933, expert on German affairs in the secret information services of the Red Army; adopted Soviet citizenship. Cofounder of the National Committee for a Free Germany in 1943 and editor-in-chief of the newspaper *Freies Deutschland.* Return to Berlin in 1945, editor-in-chief of the relatively independent *Berliner Zeitung.* Editor-in-chief of the official party daily *Neues Deutschland,* 1949–53. Member of the Central Committee and candidate member of the Politburo, 1950–53. Driven from these positions on 26 July 1953 for building a "faction" together with Minister for State Security *Wilhelm Zaisser;* excluded from the SED January 1954. Thereafter employed in a provincial archive; writings on Marxist theory and the workers' movement. Died 1966.

Heym, Stefan: Born 1913 (as Hellmuth Fliegel) in Chemnitz, prominent East German writer. Studied philosophy, German literature, and journalism in Berlin. Fled Germany in 1933, first to Czechoslovakia and then to the United States. Resumed university studies at the University of Chicago, from which he received a Ph.D. Editor of a German-language antifascist newspaper in New York, 1937–39. Soldier in the U.S. army, then officer in a psychological warfare company 1943–45. Cofounder of the newspaper *Neue Zeitung* in Munich in 1945; disagreements with U.S. military over its alleged anti-Communism. Released from military service and returned to the United States. Chief of the American delegation to the World Peace Congress in Warsaw, 1950. Return to Germany, 1952. Thereafter, independent author in East Berlin. Recipient of various national prizes for his literary works. Member of the board of the East German Writers' Union. Purged from the Writers' Union in June 1979 after publishing his novel *Collin* without proper permission from the East German authorities. In fall 1989, one of the initial signatories of the appeal "For Our Country," pleading for the maintenance of an independent GDR.

Honecker, Erich: Born 1912, general secretary of the SED. Son of a miner, apprenticeship as a roofer. Member of the KPD beginning 1929; attended the Lenin School in Moscow; after 1930, full-time KPD functionary. Antifascist resistance activities beginning 1933; arrested in 1935 and sentenced to ten years in prison in 1937; incarcerated in the same jail as *Robert Havemann.* Liberated by the Red Army 1945. From 1946 to 1955, first chairman of the Free German Youth, the SED's youth organization. Beginning 1946, member of the Central Committee; 1950–58, candidate member of the Politburo, then full member. From 1958 to 1971, Central Committee secretary for security affairs. Successor to *Walter Ulbricht,* 1971–76, as first secretary, 1976–89, as general secretary of the SED. Driven from his various offices in the party and state offices on 18 October 1989. Fled to Chile to avoid prosecution for crimes committed under his regime. Died 1993.

Jeschonnek, Günther: Born 1950, founder of the Working Group on GDR Citizenship Rights. Apprenticeship in and university study of agricultural science; studies interrupted for one year due to his refusal to participate in paramilitary training. Until 1978, agricultural engineer involved in research. Then study of theater directing in East Berlin; theater director in various places in the GDR. Applied for permission to emigrate 1986; thereafter unemployed. Peace-related activities in church-based peace movement during the mid-1980s. Founded the working group in September 1987; emigration on 10 December 1987, the UN Day of Human Rights and the day he was to have given a speech in East Berlin's Gethsemane Church introducing the working group's activities to the dissident and alternative "scene."

Jordan, Carlo: Born 1951, longtime activist in the East German environmental movement. Building engineer and philosophy student. Cofounder of the Umweltbibliothek in East Berlin's Church of Zion, then of the Green Network "Arc." Cofounder in 1989 of the East German Green Party and one of its representatives at the Central Round Table. Elected into East German parliament on 18 March 1990, but not into the "all-German" Bundestag. Involved in the "Memorial to the Victims of Stalinism" in East Berlin.

Just, Gustav: Born 1921, member of the "Harich Group" during 1956. Son of a worker and cofounder of the Czech Communist Party;

soldier of the Wehrmacht during the Third Reich. Moved to the SBZ from his native northern Bohemia after the war, graduate of a "new teachers" course *(Neulehrerkurs)*. Teacher until 1948, then active in political functions for the SED in Thuringia and in the Central Committee's Section of Fine Arts in Berlin. General secretary of the East German Writers' Union, 1954–56; then assistant editor of the respected weekly newspaper *Sonntag*. Sentenced to four years in prison in connection with the activities of the Harich Group in mid-1957. Thereafter worked as translator; no further political activities until fall 1989. Elected SPD member of the parliament of the state of Brandenburg in October 1990. Resigned as senior member *(Alterspräsident)* of the Brandenburg parliament after revelations about his involvement in a Wehrmacht commando unit that executed six partisans in the Ukraine during World War II.

Kant, Hermann: Born 1926, writer and general secretary of the East German Writers' Union. Military service in the Nazi Wehrmacht. In Polish POW camps, 1945–49; founder of the Committee on Anti-Fascism in the camp in Warsaw. Joined the SED in 1949. Attendance at the Worker-and-Peasant Faculty in Greifswald, 1949–51; studied at Humboldt University, 1952–56; student of *Alfred Kantorowicz*. Thereafter engaged in research in German literature at the Humboldt University. Editor of the prominent literary journal *Neue deutsche Literatur,* 1957–62. Cultural-political commentator in party organ *Neues Deutschland*. From May 1969 to May 1978, vice-president, from May 1978 to 1989, president of the East German Writers' Union (successor of Anna Seghers). Active in a variety of party functions beginning in the late 1970s; elevated into SED Central Committee in April 1986.

Kantorowicz, Alfred: Born 1899, prominent "old Communist" and critic of the SED regime. Active participation in the International Brigades during the Spanish Civil War. After exile during the Third Reich, returned to East Berlin after 1945, in part to make preparations for the return of prominent novelist Heinrich Mann. Thereafter professor of German literature at the Humboldt University and editor of the journal *Ost und West* from mid-1947 until it was banned by the government in 1949. Constant frictions with the regime until his emigration to the West in the late 1950s.

Kolbe, Uwe: Born 1957, poet, writer, and editor of the independent literary journal *Mikado,* 1983–87. Active in East Berlin's Prenzlauer Berg cultural scene until his emigration in 1987 with a visa allowing for his return. During the fall of 1989, a guest professor at the University of Texas, Austin.

Krenz, Egon: Born 1937, during 1989 briefly Erich Honecker's successor as general secretary of the SED. Beginning 1953, a functionary in the Free German Youth (FDJ), the party's youth organization. Studied at the party school in Moscow, 1964–67. Secretary of the Central Council of the FDJ, 1961–64 and 1967–74; 1974–83, first secretary of the FDJ. Candidate member, 1971–83, of the SED's Central Committee. Thereafter, Central Committee secretary for security affairs, youth, and sport and full member of the Politburo until 1989. Elected by the Central Committee to replace Erich Honecker on 18 October 1989, but unable to develop trust among either the general population or the party. Resigned his party offices on 3 December 1989, his state posts on 6 December. Replaced as party chairman by *Gregor Gysi.*

Läßig, Jochen: Born 1961, leader of New Forum in Leipzig. Student of theology at church institution in Leipzig, activist in the Working Circle on Justice there. Discontinuation of studies because of political disagreements with church hierarchy. Forced to work odd jobs to survive. Organizer of a "street music festival" in Leipzig during the summer of 1989. Cofounder of New Forum, Leipzig; after 1989 elected one of its representatives to the city council.

Lötsch, Manfred: Born 1936, sociologist at the Academy of Social Sciences of the SED Central Committee. Reform-oriented sociological analyst and theorist, with special interest in the intelligentsia beginning in the early 1980s.

de Maiziere, Lothar: Born 1940, transitional prime minister of the GDR. Scion of a prominent Huguenot family, de Maiziere was a musician and lawyer who, after working as a musician for many years, was forced to give up that career for health reasons. Practice of law in East Berlin beginning 1976; after 1982 member of the board of the Berlin Bar Association, after 1987 vice-chairman of the bar under *Gregor Gysi.* A professing Christian who had had difficulties in school as a result, de Maiziere defended primarily young conscientious objectors. A rank-and-file member of the East German CDU since 1956, he became its chairman after the resignation of its longtime chairman Gerald Götting on 11 November 1989. Confirmed in office at an extraordinary congress of the CDU on 15–16 December 1989. Elected prime minister after elections of 18 March 1990.

Mayer, Hans: Born 1907, prominent literary critic and professor of German literature in Leipzig until his emigration to the Federal Republic in 1963.

Meckel, Markus: Born 1952, cofounder of East German SDP. Born the son of a pastor near the Polish border, thrown out of school at age seventeen; studied theology at seminaries in Naumburg and Berlin. Pastor in rural Mecklenburg, then near Magdeburg. Active in the peace and human rights movement throughout the 1980s. Drafted plan for creation of an East German Social Democratic Party in mid-1989 with Martin Gutzeit. Elected to the East German parliament on 18 March 1990, then foreign minister in the transitional government of Prime Minister Lothar de Maiziere. Member of the SPD delegation in the "all-German" Bundestag.

Mehlhorn, Ludwig: Born 1950, cofounder of the citizens' movement Democracy Now. Mathematician, driven from his position at the Computing Center of the University of Economics (Hochschule für Ökonomie) in 1985 for political reasons. Thereafter worked in church-supported jobs. Active in initiating the "Petition for the Renunciation of the Practice and Principle of Demarcation" in 1987.

Mielke, Erich: Born 1907, minister of state security 1957–89. Member of Communist youth organization and KPD by 1926; active in party apparatuses. Involved in KPD's security and self-defense organizations in early 1930s. After being accused of two 1931 murders by Nazi courts, Mielke fled to the Soviet Union, where he attended a party school. In Spain, 1936–39, as an agent of the Comintern; then returned to the Soviet Union. After 1945, played a leading role in the creation of the East German secret police forces. Replaced Ernst Wollweber as minister for state security in the wake of Walter Ulbricht's efforts to strengthen his position in the intraparty struggles following the twentieth party congress of the CPSU; remained in this function until *Erich Honecker*'s overthrow in October 1989. By 1950 member of SED Central Committee; 1971–76, candidate member, after 1976, full member of the SED Politburo.

Modrow, Hans: Born 1928, prime minister of the GDR from November 1989 to March 1990. Joined the SED in 1949; 1953–61, head of the FDJ in East Berlin; 1961–67, secretary of the SED in Berlin-Köpenick; thereafter member of the SED Central Committee and secretary for agitation and propaganda in Berlin. Graduate of the SED party school, Ph.D. in economics at Humboldt University. After Honecker's accession to power in 1971, director of the Central Committee's Department of Agitation. From 1973–79, first secretary of the SED for the Dresden region. Thereafter a controversial figure in the party who, unlike other regional party secretaries, was never called to be a candidate or full member of the Politburo. Widely considered a party reformer and supporter of Gorbachev, he enjoyed sympathy well beyond the SED membership. Elected prime minister by the East German Volkskammer after the fall of *Erich Honecker.* Elected as PDS representative to new Volkskammer on 18 March 1990, and into the "all-German" Bundestag on 2 December 1990.

Pflugbeil, Sebastian: Born 1947, cofounder of New Forum. The son of practicing Christian parents, Pflugbeil was active in the FDJ during his days as a student of physics at the University of Greifswald. Beginning 1971, physicist at the Institute for Heart and Circulatory Research of the Academy of Sciences in Berlin, where he continued his activities in the FDJ. Increasing conflict with the party after he began to hold lectures on the dangers of atomic weapons testing; adviser to the group Doctors for Peace. Practicing Christian. Cofounder of New Forum and one of its representatives at the Central Round Table. Briefly minister without portfolio in the "Government of National Responsibility" during early 1990. Elected to the East Berlin city council *(Stadtverordnetenversammlung)* in the local elections of 6 May 1990.

Poppe, Gerd: Born 1941, cofounder of the Initiative for Peace and Human Rights. Physicist in an electrical works near Berlin, 1965–76. As a result of his signature on a letter of protest against the expatriation of his friend *Wolf Biermann* in 1976, he was unable to take up a position at the Academy of Sciences. Thereafter worked in various manual jobs. Acquainted with such figures as *Robert Havemann,* Rudolf Bahro, and the West German student leader Rudi Dutschke. In late 1985 and early 1986, participation in the founding of the Initiative for Peace and Human Rights (IFM). IFM representative at the Central Round Table; minister without portfolio in the "Government of National Responsibility" under *Hans Modrow* during February–March 1990. Elected as IFM representative to the Volkskammer on 18 March 1990, and as representative of Alliance '90 in the "all-German" Bundestag election of 2 December 1990.

Poppe, Ulrike: Born 1953, cofounder of citizens' initiative Democracy Now. Daughter of a historian at the Academy of Sciences, studied history until she was thrown out of the university for political reasons. Created an independent day-care center in East Berlin's Prenzlauer Berg district; ran this center until it was shut down by the authorities in 1983. Cofounder with *Bärbel Bohley* of Women for Peace; jailed for six weeks during December 1983–January 1984 for her peace-related activities. Thereafter, participated in the activities of the Initiative for Peace and Human Rights and, along with her husband *Gerd Poppe,* organized readings by dissident writers. Cofounder of Democracy Now and one of its representatives at the Central Round Table. Recipient of the 1990 Martini Prize for her political work in the GDR.

Rathenow, Lutz: Born 1952, well-known writer of the younger generation in East Berlin's Prenzlauer Berg cultural scene. Originally from Jena, where he organized independent literary circles. Imprisoned for several months in 1980.

Reich, Jens: Born 1940, cofounder of New Forum. Son of a doctor, Reich studied medicine and then became a molecular biologist employed at the Academy of Sciences, but hindered in his professional activities for political reasons. Initial signatory of New Forum's first appeal. Representative of New Forum at the Central Round Table, then elected as one of its representatives to the Volkskammer on 18 March 1990.

Rüddenklau, Wolfgang: Born 1953, cofounder (with *Carlo Jordan*) of the Umweltbibliothek in East Berlin. Active in church-based peace

and environmental circles beginning 1983. After 1986 in the Umweltbibliothek; editor of its journal, *Umweltblätter.* Arrested during the
Stasi raid on the Umweltbibliothek in November 1987. Since 1989,
editor of *Telegraph,* the successor to *Umweltblätter.*

Schirdewan, Karl: Born 1907, rival to SED leader *Walter Ulbricht*
in the intraparty struggles following the twentieth party congress of
the CPSU. Joined KPD in 1925 and active in its youth organizations. Illegal activities after 1933; jailed and interned in concentration
camps under the Nazis. Member of the KPD in 1945, of the SED
thereafter; involved in various party functions, particularly in cadre
matters. Member of the Politburo, July 1953–February 1958. Along
with *Ernst Wollweber,* relieved of all party and state offices in early
1958 because of their alleged factional activities. Thereafter director
of a state archive in Potsdam. Practiced self-criticism and recanted
all "deviations" in 1959. Then chairman of the local Committee of
Anti-Fascist Resistance Fighters.

Schorlemmer, Friedrich: Born 1944, cofounder of the citizens' initia-
tive Democratic Awakening. Pastor and theologian in Wittenberg, the
town where Luther had been pastor and where he nailed his "Ninety-
Five Theses" to the door of the *Schloßkirche.* Long active in the East
German peace movement. Speaker at the demonstration in Berlin's
Alexanderplatz on 4 November 1989; initial signer of the appeal "For
Our Country." Recipient of the 1989 Carl-von-Ossietzky Prize of the
International League for Human Rights. After conservative elements
gained control of Democratic Awakening at its founding meeting,
transferred to the SPD.

Templin, Regina ("Lotte"): Born 1953, activist in the Initiative for
Peace and Human Rights (IFM). Married to *Wolfgang Templin.* Af-
ter her early involvement in the IFM, she worked with the Working
Group on GDR Citizenship Rights (see *Günther Jeschonnek*), a group
whose activities were extremely controversial among dissident ac-
tivists. Arrested in late January 1988 in the aftermath of the Rosa
Luxemburg demonstration; released from prison into the Federal
Republic with a temporary visa. Returned to the GDR after the open-
ing of the border in 1989; representative of the IFM at the Berlin
Round Table.

Templin, Wolfgang: Born 1948, cofounder of the Initiative for Peace and Human Rights (IFM). Married to *Lotte Templin.* Studied library science, then philosophy at Humboldt University in late 1960s/early 1970s. Joined SED in 1970. Participated in a Trotskyist discussion group in the early 1970s; at the same time acted as a spy for the Stasi. Ended this activity on his own initiative. Exchange student in Poland 1976–77, where he made contacts with the Polish opposition and with critical churchpersons. Active in peace circles of the Berlin Evangelical Church and in Naumburg starting 1981. Increasing career-related difficulties around this time because of his political views. Resigned his party membership and left his position at the Academy of Sciences in 1983, then unable to find work. Cofounder of the IFM in 1985–86; along with Peter Grimm and Ralf Hirsch one of its first spokespersons. Active in the Working Group on GDR Citizenship Rights in 1987. Arrested in late January 1988 in the aftermath of the Rosa Luxemburg demonstration; released from prison into the Federal Republic with a temporary visa. Returned to the GDR after the opening of the border in 1989; representative of the IFM at the Central Round Table.

Ulbricht, Walter: Born 1893, general (or first) secretary of the SED, 1950–71. Apprentice as a furniture-maker. Joined the SPD in 1912, the KPD in 1919. Member of the KPD's Central Committee (later Politburo) in 1923. Emigrated to various countries after 1933. Cofounder of the Moscow-based National Committee for a Free Germany, 1943. As leader of the so-called Ulbricht Group, played a decisive role in rebuilding governmental administration in the SBZ after the collapse of the Third Reich. After the founding of the SED, uninterrupted membership in the Central Committee and Politburo. Replaced by Erich Honecker under pressure from the Soviet Union in May 1971.

Warmbier, Helmut: Born 1930, professor of Marxism-Leninism in Leipzig who was dismissed from his position in the early 1970s for his liberal views. Son of a Communist and participant in the sailors' rebellion in Kiel in 1919. Joined the KPD/SED in March 1946. Imprisoned 1977–79, forced to learn a trade in order to survive. Continued contacts to SED and other dissident circles; New Forum member of city council after 1989.

Weiß, Konrad: Born 1942, cofounder of citizens' initiative Democracy Now. Refused admission to study for the *Abitur* (high school diploma normally entitling its bearer to university admission) as son of a civil servant and as practicing Christian; apprenticeship as electrician. Later earned the *Abitur,* worked for a time as an electrician; then, after attendance at a Catholic seminary, worked for the Catholic Church in Magdeburg. Studied documentary filmmaking at the University for Film Arts in Potsdam-Babelsberg, graduating with a major in directing. Director of films for children and young people at the famous DEFA studios. Long active in the Aktion Sühnezeichen and elected to its board in 1988. Spoke out on neo-Nazi and right-wing extremist activities in the GDR in 1988. Representative of Democracy Now at Central Round Table; then elected as one of its representatives to the Volkskammer on 18 March 1990. Elected into "all-German" Bundestag as representative of Alliance '90 on 2 December 1990.

Wötzel, Roland: Born 1938, first secretary of the SED in Leipzig. Joined SED in 1959. Lawyer and economist. One of the six figures in Leipzig responsible for averting bloodshed at the Monday demonstration of 9 October 1989.

Wolf, Christa: Born 1929, prominent East German author. She and her family were driven out of their home after the war, coming to Mecklenburg in the northern part of the SBZ. Joined the SED in 1949. Studied German literature in Leipzig and Jena, 1949–53. Editorial, literary, and research work; for a time, SED party secretary in the Halle chapter of the Writers' Union. Candidate member of the SED Central Committee, 1963–67; defended the Warsaw Pact invasion of Czechoslovakia in August 1968. Member of the presidium of East German PEN Center and of the Academy of Arts. One of the first signatories of the letter opposing the involuntary expatriation of *Wolf Biermann* in November 1976; protested against the exclusion from the Writers' Union of *Stefan Heym* and eight other writers in June 1979. Recipient of numerous prizes for her literary efforts, both in the GDR and abroad. Left the SED in mid-1989. Prominent advocate of a reformed socialism and signatory of the appeal "For Our Country" for an independent GDR in November 1989. Wrote preamble of the draft constitution written by the Round Table's Working Group on a New Constitution.

Wollweber, Ernst: Born 1898, associated with the rivalry between *Karl Schirdewan* and *Walter Ulbricht.* Joined the KPD in 1919. Active in KPD party apparatuses. Antifascist activities in Nazi Germany, then in exile; arrested and sentenced to three years in prison in Sweden in 1940; released to the Soviet Union at its request. Functions in the state apparatus of the SBZ, particularly in Ministry of Transport. Successor of *Wilhelm Zaisser,* first as state secretary for state security, July 1953–November 1955, then as minister of state security until 1957. Member of the SED Central Committee, 1954–58. Together with *Schirdewan,* driven out of his positions in February 1958 in connection with their alleged "factional activity."

Zaisser, Wilhelm: Born 1893, purged from the SED after the 1953 workers' rebellion in connection with the rivalry between *Walter Ulbricht* and *Rudolf Herrnstadt.* Joined the KPD in 1919. Active in various functions, many of them military (e.g., as a co-organizer of the Communist rebellion in Canton), in the international Communist movement. Under the code name "General Gomez," leader of all International Brigades during the Spanish Civil War; then in party-related activities in the Soviet Union, 1938–45. Police chief of Saxony-Anhalt, 1947; home minister of Saxony and chief instructor of the People's Police (Volkspolizei), 1948–50. First minister of state security in the GDR, 1950–53. Member of the SED Central Committee and of the Politburo, 1950–53. Driven out of his various positions in July 1953 along with *Herrnstadt.*

Notes

Preface and Acknowledgments

1. Enthusiasm for a "third way" also existed in Hungary as Communism collapsed. But this approach was associated with a conservative populist tradition reaching back to the 1930s. Its political lineage was thus quite different from the sort of "third way" advocated by East Germany's dissident intellectuals, who understood it as a decidedly left-wing undertaking. Moreover, the Hungarian advocates of a "third way," typically from outside the nation's capital, were not generally identified over the years with the dissident opposition, which was carried mostly by a small group of Budapest intellectuals.

2. As Václav Havel later put it in an essay called "Second Wind" (1991, 9), "The fun was definitely over."

Introduction: Intellectuals and Politics

1. Verdery 1991, 15–16. In making this critique of intellectual hubris, Verdery is drawing on the work of Bauman 1987.

2. See Mosse 1990. Albert Einstein makes a similar point in his exchange of letters with Sigmund Freud titled *Why War?* (Einstein and Freud 1939, 6–7). The war in former Yugoslavia, instigated to a considerable degree by intellectuals, should leave no doubt that that group has often been at the forefront of those fanning the flames of war.

3. For a valuable critique of Gouldner, see Walzer 1980.

4. *Der Irrweg einer Nation* (1946) was the title of Alexander Abusch's early postwar analysis of the sources in German tradition of the Nazi catastrophe. Abusch's book is one of the central contributions to the so-called misery theory of German history, an early and persistent feature of the Communist response to German fascism. Yet this negative view of German history, suggesting as it did the deep inadequacies of German political culture, would complicate the task of developing

a postfascist, socialist order among the Germans by making that order seem puni-
tive and alien. Particularly under the pressure to "demarcate" *(abgrenzen)* the GDR
from the Federal Republic in response to the Social Democrat–initiated *Ostpolitik*
of the 1970s and 1980s, SED intellectuals sought to identify positive touchstones in
German tradition and to appropriate them as comprising the origins of the GDR's
socialist national history. On these points, see Meuschel 1992, 65–66 and 283–91.

5. Almost a year after the "forced merger" *(Zwangsvereinigung)* of the KPD
and the SPD in the Soviet Occupation Zone, the newly formed Christian Democratic Union in the British Zone began its "Ahlen Program" of February 1947 with
the unambiguous declaration that "capitalist striving for power and profit cannot
be the content and aim of the new political order in Germany" (cited in Helmut
Schmidt et al., "Weil das Land sich ändern muß," *Die Zeit* [overseas edition], 20
November 1992, p. 3). Still, the historian Helga Grebing (1989, 84) has written that
the Ahlen Program "has accurately been called both the zenith and the end of the
influence of... Christian socialism in the CDU." By contrast to this anticapitalist enthusiasm, the German Communists, initially intent on continuing a "popular front"
strategy, averred in their founding statement of June 1945 that the times called for
an "antifascist, democratic regime," but one that nonetheless ensured the "completely
unhindered development of free trade and of private entrepreneurial initiative." It is
also worth noting that the Communist statement also opposed the introduction of
the Soviet system into Germany because this approach was "inappropriate" to the
conditions in the country at that time. See H. Weber 1985, 71–72.

6. Interview with Carlo Jordan of the Umweltbibliothek, the Green Network
"Ark," and later the East German Green Party, August 1991.

7. See Habermas 1990b, 181. Habermas's critics have argued that he failed to
understand the centrality of the "round tables" and "forums" that characterized the
period of transition in many of these countries. But as anyone familiar with Hannah
Arendt's *On Revolution* (1984) is aware, this approach to democracy has a venerable
history in the twentieth century. Moreover, this institution for handling public affairs
generally arose in the heat of the moment rather than as an elaborated vision of a
future society.

1: *The Making of an East German Intelligentsia*

1. Ulbricht's remark is reported in Leonhard 1990, 440. Leonhard, himself a
young Communist functionary in the Moscow-based National Committee for a Free
Germany (Nationalkomitee Freies Deutschland) who returned to Germany with the
Ulbricht Group, fled the SBZ in early 1949. His book is the best available eyewitness
account of the German Communists' experience in Soviet emigration and of the years
leading up to the founding of the GDR in 1949.

2. Christa Wolf, "Überlegungen zum 1. September 1939: Rede in der Akademie
der Künste, Berlin," in Wolf 1990a, 73–74.

3. Interview, Cambridge, Mass., 2 April 1993.

4. An important case in point was the scientist, inventor, and member of the
East German parliament (Volkskammer) Manfred von Ardenne. See Ardenne 1990.

5. For an excellent discussion, see Epstein 1991.

6. See Pike 1982. Among the most prominent representatives of this group were
Johannes R. Becher, Willi Bredel, Alfred Kurella, and Friedrich Wolf.

7. On this group, see Heilbut 1984.

8. Wary especially of Walter Ulbricht, however, Thomas Mann's brother Heinrich delayed his return and died before he was able to make the planned trip. See
Jäger 1982, 13.

9. See "Der Kampf gegen den Formalismus in Kunst und Literatur, für eine fortschrittliche deutsche Kultur," in Schubbe 1972, 178–86. This resolution, passed at the fifth plenum of the SED's Central Committee, had been preceded on 20–21 January 1951 by a lengthy, pseudonymously authored article in the Soviet-controlled newspaper *Tägliche Rundschau* attacking formalism in the arts (see N. Orlow, "Wege und Irrwege der modernen Kunst," in Schubbe 1972, 158–70.

10. Interview, Prenden bei Berlin, 1 February 1992.

11. Kantorowicz 1959, 39–40. Still, Kantorowicz was one of the few prominent East German intellectuals who opted — with profound regrets about the sullying of the socialist cause he believed was occurring in the GDR — for this "open rejection": he published these words after departing East Germany for the Federal Republic.

12. See the table in Wendt 1991, 390.

13. For an in-depth discussion of the causes of emigration that seeks to distinguish between those who "fled" the SBZ/GDR and those who simply moved West for reasons that were not directly political, see Storbeck 1963.

14. Erbe 1982, 88. Erbe notes that party leader Walter Ulbricht found it prudent to address these complaints in his speech to the third party congress in 1950. See Walter Ulbricht, "Referat auf dem III. Parteitag der SED," in Ulbricht 1960, 342.

15. See Erbe 1982, 88, and Staritz 1985, 44. Average monthly income was DM 256 in 1950, rising to DM 354 in 1955.

16. See "Über die Notwendigkeit der Forderungen der Intelligenz," 27 May 1951, in *Dokumente der SED,* vol. 3, quoted in Lange, Richert, and Stammer 1953, 197.

17. Party conferences, the most important party assemblies beside party congresses, are numbered consecutively in between the latter. The last previous party congress was the third, held in 1950. That congress passed the first Five-Year Plan, which went into effect in 1951.

18. "Beschluß der II. Parteikonferenz der SED (1952): Zur Gegenwärtigen Lage und zu den Aufgaben im Kampf für Frieden, Einheit, Demokratie und Sozialismus," excerpted in H. Weber 1963, 448.

19. See Staritz 1985, 77–79. The quotation is from "Beschluß der II. Parteikonferenz," in *Protokoll der Verhandlungen der Sozialistischen Einheitspartei Deutschlands. 9, bis 12. Juli 1952 in der Werner-Seelenbinder-Halle zu Berlin* (Berlin: Dietz, 1952), 493.

20. See Storbeck 1963, 161. Despite the perception that the children of the intelligentsia suffered from "reverse discrimination" under the Communists, Gustav-Wilhelm Bathke has found that at no time did the intelligentsia contribute less than its own share of the overall population to its own reproduction. To put it differently, the proportion of the children of the intelligentsia who subsequently advanced into that stratum never fell below the intelligentsia's share of the total population. See Bathke 1990b, 121.

21. Belitz-Demiriz and Voigt 1990, 93. We should be careful not to impute any great precision to these numbers; given the changes taking place in statistical practices at this time, they reflect orders of magnitude rather than exact figures.

22. These quotations are from Lange, Richert, and Stammer 1953, 198–99.

23. Interview with Manfred Lötsch, Berlin, 27 February 1991. Describing the support Alfred Kantorowicz received from the Soviet authorities for his journal *Ost und West,* Manfred Jäger has written (1982, 19) that "an outsider like Kantorowicz was probably more inclined to listen to the arguments of Soviet friends of Germany, whereas he did not get along at all with the stereotypical German Communist Party functionary." Given that Kantorowicz had been a member of the KPD since 1931, the only things that could lead Jäger to refer to him as an "outsider" are the fact that, unlike the SED apparatchiks whom he criticized so vigorously, he had not spent

the years of exile in the Soviet Union or that, as a prominent intellectual, he was a rare and somewhat undesirable species in the KPD/SED.

24. *Dokumente der SED,* vol. 4, pp. 428ff.; quoted in H. Weber 1985, 235.

25. Tocqueville 1955, 177. Indeed, Heinz Brandt, who in June 1953 was secretary for agitation and propaganda in the Berlin SED leadership but later defected to West Germany, made this point about the New Course and its consequences almost verbatim in his memoirs: "Like every reactionary, obsolescent regime, [the SED government] failed at precisely the point when it attempted — suddenly and without public participation — to carry out *half-measures* in order to *survive*" (see Brandt 1967, 213). Brandt's book is one of the best insider accounts of the struggles within the SED leadership around the time of the East German workers' rebellion and during the 1950s generally.

26. For a discussion of the causes of the strikes — or of their absence — in various industries and regions of the GDR, see Baring 1966, 70–78.

27. Baring 1966, 86–92; Staritz 1985, 85; H. Weber 1985, 239–42; and Jänicke 1964, 53.

28. "Beschluß der 14. Tagung des ZK der SED, 21. Juni 1953," in *Dokumente der SED,* vol. 4 (Berlin: Dietz, 1954), 436ff., reproduced as "Erste Stellungnahme des ZK der SED zum 17. Juni: Falsche Politik und faschistischer Putsch," in Spittmann and Fricke 1988, 210–14.

29. Baring 1966, 68–69. Baring bases his conclusion here on the findings in H. Köhler 1952.

30. Hermann Weber (1985, 229) has noted that at this point "the GDR was far ahead of the Federal Republic in the dissemination of antifascist literature; such literature was 'discovered' only much later by wider circles in the West." Likewise, Gustav Just, who was general secretary of the East German Writers' Union in 1954–55, insisted in an interview (Prenden bei Berlin, 14 July 1991) that certain leftist authors, such as Anna Seghers, found publishers for their work much more readily in the GDR than in the West and were thus more inclined to stay in and to support the East German order.

31. Stefan Heym, "Memorandum zum Juni-Aufstand," in Spittmann and Fricke 1988, 150. For an official account of the June uprising written some years after the events in question, see *Geschichte der SED: Abriß* 1978, 288–98, esp. 294, which includes both the "Western secret services" charge and the admission that the population harbored "dissatisfaction."

32. Heym, "Memorandum zum Juni-Aufstand," 151.

33. Kuba, "Wie ich mich schäme," *Neues Deutschland,* 20 June 1953, reprinted in Spittmann and Fricke 1988, 3. Kuba uses the word "forgotten" *(vergessen)* rather than "forgiven" *(vergeben),* but the effect is clearly the same.

34. This translation of Bertolt Brecht's poem is quoted from Willett and Manheim 1976, 440. In his discussion (1990b, 14), Garton Ash notes that, at least initially, Brecht kept unpublished the reaction to the uprising to which this poem gives expression.

35. On this point, see Rühle 1960, 262.

36. *Neues Deutschland,* 23 June 1953, quoted in Mohr 1988, 88. The German texts of both "The Solution" and the telegram to Ulbricht are reproduced there (pp. 88 and 90, respectively).

37. Jänicke 1964, 33. Mohr 1988, 111 n. 7, concurs in this assessment of Brecht's position.

38. Deutscher 1966, 619. Deutscher notes that it is unclear whether Zhdanov died or was murdered.

39. The text of the resolution is reprinted as "Vorschläge des Kulturbundes vom

3. Juli," in Spittmann and Fricke 1988, 228–29. This is the source of all quotations from the document in the next few paragraphs.

40. Kantorowicz 1961, 363. The words "publicity agent" are in English in the original.

41. Johannes R. Becher, *Auf andere Art so große Hoffnung: Tagebuch 1950,* entry of 30 March, quoted in H. Weber 1985, 228.

42. Johannes R. Becher, "Poetische Konfessionen," *Sinn und Form* 3/4 (1953), quoted in Jänicke 1964, 56–57.

43. Quoted in Rühle 1988, 185–86. The English translation is from Willett and Manheim 1976, 436–47.

44. Wolfgang Harich, "Es geht um den Realismus," *Berliner Zeitung,* 14 July 1953, reprinted in Spittmann and Fricke 1988, 229–31. The *Deutsche Zeitschrift für Philosophie* (German journal of philosophy), founded in 1953 and edited by Harich and the well-known Marxist philosopher Ernst Bloch, quickly became a forum for dissident views, including those of Georg Lukács.

45. Walter Ulbricht at the fifteenth plenum of the Central Committee, 24–26 July 1953, excerpted in Spittmann and Fricke 1988, 232–33.

2: Intellectuals, the State, and Opposition, 1956–80

1. The article, which originally appeared in *Neues Deutschland* on 4 March 1956, is excerpted as "Ulbricht über den XX. Parteitag der KPdSU (1956)," in H. Weber 1963, 496–500. The quotation here is taken from p. 500.

2. For a discussion of Stalin's offer, see Wettig 1982.

3. Interview with Gustav Just, Prenden bei Berlin, 2 February 1992.

4. Ulbricht's speech at the congress, which emphasized "the contest in Germany between two systems," is reprinted as "Fragen der deutschen Nationalliteratur," in Schubbe 1972, 421–26.

5. The excerpts of Becher's speech to the Writers' Union that appeared in *Neues Deutschland* are reproduced as "Von der Größe unserer Literatur," in Schubbe 1972, 395–408. Just made his remarks on Becher's speech in an interview, Prenden bei Berlin, 2 February 1992.

6. Robert Havemann (1978, 79) notes in his autobiography that Ulbricht himself had asked him to write an article advocating such a "conflict of opinions" *(Meinungsstreit).* The article, largely an attack on the philosophical views of Wolfgang Harich, originally appeared as "Für den wissenschaftlichen Meinungsstreit — gegen den Dogmatismus," *Neues Deutschland,* 8 July 1956. It is reprinted in Havemann 1990, 17–27.

7. These quotations are taken from a report on the congress by Georg Piltz, "Die Fenster sind aufgestoßen," *Sonntag,* 17 June 1956, quoted in H. Mayer 1977, 447. Mayer here offers a useful account of the context of this controversy.

8. Excerpts from the lecture, the text of which originally appeared in *Sonntag* on 2 December 1956, are reprinted in Schubbe 1972, 449–50.

9. Their speeches are reproduced in Schubbe 1972, 473–84.

10. See the table in Wendt 1991, 388.

11. Wollweber 1990, 364. Wollweber originally dictated these reflections (to his wife) in 1964.

12. Hertwig 1977, 480. In his recently published memoirs, Gustav Just (1990, 149) also refers to the search for a "German Gomulka."

13. On the higher-status social origins of medical students compared with those of university students in other disciplines, see Bathke 1985, 30.

14. Wollweber 1990, 365; see also Jänicke 1964, 150–52.

15. "Erklärung zum Sieg der ungarischen Werktätigen über die Konterrevolution," in *Dokumente der SED,* vol. 6 (Berlin: Dietz, 1958), 153–55, excerpted as "Erklärung der SED nach der ungarischen Revolution," in H. Weber 1963, 501–2.

16. A number of accounts of these events have been written by the participants themselves. In addition to those of Hertwig and Just cited above, see Zöger 1960; and Janka 1989. For an account in English, see Croan 1962.

17. Interview with Professor Günter Lehmann, Leipzig, 29 July 1992. Lehmann's assessment of Bloch's politics is seconded by Jürgen Teller, another former student of Bloch's. See " 'Dreck, Lumpen und Traum': Der Leipziger Philosophie-Historiker Jürgen Teller über die Utopie Blochs nach dem Niedergang des Sozialismus," *Der Spiegel,* 20 January 1992.

18. On this issue, see the insightful discussion by Woods 1986, 18–19.

19. Hertwig 1977, 477. Kolakowski's essay "The Intellectuals and the Communist Movement," an expression of the revisionist ferment among Polish intellectuals during the "Polish October," was published in the theoretical journal of the Polish United Workers' (Communist) Party in September 1956. See Kolakowski 1968.

20. "Anschlag gegen den Frieden und den Bestand des Staates," *Neues Deutschland,* 26 July 1957, reprinted in Eichhorn and Reinhardt 1990, 185–87.

21. Interview with Gustav Just, Prenden bei Berlin, 2 February 1992.

22. "Entschließung des Präsidialrates des Kulturbundes zur demokratischen Erneuerung Deutschlands [24. Februar 1957, Auszug]," in Schubbe 1972, 460.

23. Kersten 1957, 164. The text of the resolution of the composers' and musicologists' union (Verband Deutscher Komponisten und Musikwissenschaftler) is reproduced as "Zeitgenössischer Realismus — sozialistische Ideologie," in Schubbe 1972, 460–64. This statement, too, appeared originally in the newly purged *Sonntag.*

24. Interview, Prenden bei Berlin, 2 February 1992.

25. See "Die politische Plattform Harichs und seiner Freunde," originally published in *SBZ-Archiv* 5/6 (25 March 1957): 72–74, excerpted in H. Weber 1963, 598–603.

26. "Nachgefragt: Walter Janka — Ein Interview," in Eichhorn and Reinhardt 1990, 174.

27. In his recent account of these events, Janka (1989, 91) writes that, for him, "The greatest disappointment of the entire trial was the fact that not a single one of Lukács's friends who were present in the courtroom managed to stand up and protest against these baseless accusations." It might be noted that Anna Seghers, at least, had especially close Hungarian connections: she was married to the Hungarian sociologist and writer Laszlo Radvanyi.

28. Interview, Prenden bei Berlin, 2 February 1992.

29. Schirdewan 1990, 503. In an interview with the present author (Berlin, 2 February 1992), former Politburo member Werner Eberlein described Schirdewan as having had differences with Ulbricht concerning the implications for the GDR of the twentieth party congress of the CPSU, but as having lacked the "reputation and the intellectual stature" of an Anton Ackermann or Fred Oelssner, the latter being an important party propagandist during the 1950s.

30. Interview with Helmut Warmbier, Leipzig, 29 July 1991.

31. The declaration was published in the organ of the Initiative for Peace and Human Rights, the samizdat publication *Grenzfall* (see no. 3 [1986]), under the title "Gemeinsame Erklärung aus Osteuropa zum 30. Jahrestag der ungarischen Revolution," reprinted in Hirsch and Kopelew 1989, 14. One of Havemann's political protégés, the physicist Gerd Poppe, responded to the characterization of himself and the other signers as "fascists" by formally accusing the author of these articles of slander. His letter to the state's attorney responding to these charges can be found in

Hirsch and Kopelew 1989, 36–38. The complaint brought by the signatories against the editor of the *Weißenseer Blätter,* and an exchange of letters between them and the state's attorney, can be found in Kroh 1988a, 227–29.

32. Interview with Professor Günter Lehmann, Leipzig, 29 July 1991.

33. For succinct accounts of the Hungarian revolution of 1956 and the Czechoslovak reform movement, see Rothschild 1989, 157–60 and 169–73, respectively.

34. "Bericht des Politbüros an das 35. Plenum des ZK der SED, vorgetragen von Erich Honecker," in Schubbe 1972, 517.

35. Walter Ulbricht, "Fragen der Entwicklung der sozialistischen Literatur und Kultur," in Schubbe 1972, 552.

36. "Die aktive gesellschaftliche Funktion der sozialistischen Kultur voll wirksam machen," in Schubbe 1972, 1409.

37. For a discussion of East Germany's loss of highly educated persons as a result of emigration in the latter half of the 1950s, see Staritz 1985, 145; see also Prokop 1984. For the numbers of emigrants, see Wendt 1991, 388.

38. Christa Wolf related this information during a telephone interview with Todd Gitlin on 1 March 1993 for which I served as interpreter.

39. Interview with Bärbel Bohley, Cambridge, Mass., 2 April 1993.

40. Interview with Manfred Lötsch, Berlin, 28 January 1992.

41. See Jäger, "Weggegangen, dageblieben, ausgestiegen, mitgelaufen: Verdrängte Konflikte unter Schriftstellern aus der ehemaligen DDR," *Frankfurter Rundschau,* 30 September 1992, 20.

42. H. Weber 1985, 350–52. For a brief discussion of "revisionist" economic ideas in the East bloc during the post-1956 period, see Kornai 1989, 86ff.

43. Burens 1981, 63. For an account of the ideas of the East German revisionist economists, see Jänicke 1964, 104–10 and passim.

44. See "Zu einigen Problemen des geistigen Lebens [Bericht des Politbüros an das 5. Plenum des ZK der SED, vorgetragen von Horst Sindermann, 3. bis 7. Februar, 1964, Auszug]," in Schubbe 1972, 916–17.

45. "[Bericht des Politbüros an das 11. Plenum des ZK der SED, vorgetragen von Erich Honecker]," in Schubbe 1972, 1076–78.

46. Robert Havemann, "Sozialismus und Demokratie: Der 'Prager Frühling' — Ein Versuch, den Teufelskreis des Stalinismus zu durchbrechen," in Havemann 1990, 150.

47. "Gemeinsamer Brief an das Zentralkomitee der Kommunistischen Partei der Tschechoslowakei," *Neues Deutschland,* 18 July 1968, 1, cited in Burens 1981, 36.

48. See Wolf Biermann, "In Prag ist Pariser Kommune," in Biermann 1968, 70; and Havemann 1972, 215.

49. Interview with Jürgen Fuchs, Berlin, 12 November 1990. As fate would have it, when Fuchs was arrested later for his oppositional views and activities, he was accused of having subscribed to the views articulated in the famous "2000 Words" statement in the CSSR from 1968 — a document that, he insisted, he had "never even seen." On this point, see Fuchs 1990a, 11.

50. "An alle Bürgerinnen und Bürger der DDR," *Neues Deutschland,* 21 August 1968, excerpted in H. Weber 1986, 303–4.

51. Interviews with Werner Eberlein, Berlin, 2 February 1992, and with Wolfgang Herger, Berlin, 30 January 1992. Former president of the East German parliament Horst Sindermann has also denied that troops of the Nationale Volksarmee participated in the invasion (see interview in *Der Spiegel,* 7 May 1990, 62). Of course, these statements may have been motivated by a desire to avoid possible legal consequences associated with East Germany's participation in the invasion or out of a simple lack of familiarity with the facts, though the latter seems unlikely. Moreover, the claim has recently received independent confirmation in Wenzke 1990a, 31. I am

indebted to Professor A. James McAdams of the University of Notre Dame for this reference.

52. Interview with Professor Günter Lehmann, Leipzig, 29 July 1991.

53. Interview with Helmut Warmbier, Leipzig, 29 July 1991; see also Jordan n.d., 2. For an account of the demolition of the University Church in Leipzig, see Rosner 1992.

54. The history was offered as a series in the issues of *Grenzfall* dated July 1987 to October 1987. See Hirsch and Kopelew 1989, 86, 96–97, 110–11, and 124–25.

55. "Zahlreiche Sympathie-Bekundungen für die CSSR auch in Ost-Berlin," *Der Tagesspiegel* (West Berlin), 24 August 1968, quoted in Fricke 1984, 148–49.

56. Interview with Carlo Jordan, Berlin, 16 September 1991.

57. On the Polish case, see Pravda 1982, 168–69.

58. "Hauptaufgabe umfaßt auch weitere Erhöhung des kulturellen Niveaus," excerpted in Rüß 1976, 287.

59. Plenzdorf 1976. See the debate provoked by the novel and carried out in the pages of the Academy of Arts journal *Sinn und Form,* in Rüß 1976, 676–95.

60. After the collapse of the socialist experiment in the East, he sardonically described the situation upon his arrival from Hamburg as follows: "When I came to the GDR in 1953 — to a little village in Mecklenburg called Gadebusch — I found Communism in the best of health and, indeed, already almost fully realized. Our beloved Stalin had just died, and I didn't catch much of the 17th of June in this little hole. I felt tremendous because I had no idea what was going on" (see Wolf Biermann, "Das wars. Klappe zu, Affe lebt," *Die Zeit,* 2 March 1990, reprinted as "Duftmarke setzen," in Biermann 1990, 315–31).

61. See Biermann, "Tapferfeige Intellektuelle: Über Stefan Heyms Roman *Collin,*" in Biermann 1990, 142.

62. "Biermann das Recht auf weiteren Aufenthalt in der DDR entzogen," *Neues Deutschland,* 17 November 1976, reprinted in Lübbe 1984, 309.

63. See Carla Boulboulle, "Solidaritätsbewegung mit Wolf Biermann in Ost- und West-Deutschland," in Roos 1977, 81–146. In contrast to this interpretation, Wolfgang Templin told me (interview, Berlin, 3 February 1992) that he was disappointed by the weakness of the protests against Biermann's involuntary expatriation.

64. Interview with Professor Günter Lehmann, Leipzig, 29 July 1991.

65. The statement, which appeared in the West German press as early as 23 November 1976, can be found along with the list of signers under the heading "DDR-Künstler gegen Biermann-Ausbürgerung," in Jäger 1982, 162; emphasis added.

66. Havemann's letter, which appeared originally in *Der Spiegel,* 22 November 1976, is excerpted in Roos 1977, 113–16. The quoted passage from Heinz Brandt's article can be found in Roos 1977, 102.

67. The power of anticapitalist ideology among intellectuals in East Germany was brought home to me in an off-the-cuff remark by Heidi Stuhler, a journalist after 1989 who had been refused her Ph.D. in sociology from East Berlin's Humboldt University for political reasons. Discussing her reaction to the events of 1989–90, she told me that, despite her lack of nostalgia for the old order, she was having an extremely difficult time not viewing the reintroduction of capitalism into the old GDR as "a historically retrograde development," because capitalism is, after all, a "lower stage" of historical development than socialism. Ms. Stuhler's remarks were a striking indication of the enduring power of ideology to shape our understanding of the social world. Interview with Heidi Stuhler, Berlin, 11 June 1991.

68. A partial list is offered by Jäger 1982, 163. See also Childs 1988, 224.

69. See Joachim Walther, "Die Amputation: Zur Vor- und Nachgeschichte der Ausschlüsse," in Walther et al. 1991, 9–11.

70. See "Entschließung der Parteiorganisation der Berliner Schriftsteller," in Lübbe 1984, 340. Those reprimanded for their "unpartisan behavior" (*unparteimäßiges Verhalten*) were Jurek Becker, Volker Braun, Stephan Hermlin, Sarah Kirsch, Günter Künert, Christa Wolf, Gerhard Wolf, Reimar Gilsenbach, and Karl-Heinz Jakobs. Only the latter two were not among the initial signatories of the statement protesting the punishment of Heym.

71. See Lübbe 1984, 339. After initially signing the protest statement, the well-known sculptor Fritz Cremer declared that his name had been misused after his son-in-law was arrested for his involvement in a public rally in opposition to the Biermann expatriation. The son-in-law was soon released. It seems altogether possible that the party "got to" Volker Braun, a National Prize–winning author, in similar fashion.

72. Robert Havemann, "Schreiben für die DDR," in Havemann 1976, 26.

73. See Fricke 1976. The original German version of the "Petition to Secure Full Human Rights" can be found there. An English translation is available in Woods 1986, 177–78.

74. These events are discussed in Fricke 1984, 169–74.

75. Interview with Wolfgang Templin, Berlin, 29 August 1991.

76. See Fuchs's exchange of letters with judicial authorities after the fall of the East German regime in Fuchs 1990b, 108ff.

77. See Faust 1980, 166ff. The quotation, which literally says that Havemann and Biermann regarded him as "having died," can be found on p. 172.

78. Childs 1988, 90–92. See also Werner Volkmer's interesting discussion of the centrality of the "national question" in East German opposition politics in Volkmer 1979.

79. Yet the charge that the emigrants were not devoted to the life of politics was rather subjectively applied. Carlo Jordan, a representative of the Green Party at the 1989–90 Round Table negotiations, excused the retreat from political activity of his fellow representative Dr. Marianne Dörfler, saying that she saw herself principally as a writer rather than a political activist. Ultimately, he said, "politics just wasn't her thing" (interview, Berlin, 16 September 1991).

80. Interview with Helmut Warmbier, Leipzig, 29 July 1991. Warmbier is referring to Wollenberger's acceptance of an offer by the Anglican Church to study in England rather than to serve a potentially lengthy jail term in the aftermath of the Rosa Luxemburg demonstration of January 1988.

81. Rudolf Bahro, "Selbstinterview," in Bahro 1977, 71.

82. For the international reaction to Bahro's arrest, see Liselotte Julius, "Nachwort," in Bahro 1977, 113–28.

83. Bahro 1978, 346. See also Reyman 1979, 167–70.

84. The "manifesto," first published in *Der Spiegel* in two parts in early January 1988, is reprinted with related documents in Johannes and Schwarz 1978. For expert analyses, see pp. 161–98. An English translation of the "manifesto" is available in Silnitsky, Silnitsky, and Reyman 1978, 233–42.

85. Kleßmann 1991, 60. Kleßmann notes (60, n. 56) Stefan Heym's belief that the "manifesto" was a Stasi fabrication. However, see Niemann 1991. Niemann insists the "manifesto" was genuine and claims (p. 538) that a dissertation at the secret police training school in Eiche also treated the document as authentic.

86. See the interview with Ilse Spittmann, editor-in-chief of the West German journal *Deutschland-Archiv* and herself an early victim of the SED's purges, in Johannes and Schwarz 1978, 162.

3: The Intelligentsia and the Development of Opposition in the GDR during the 1980s

1. Indeed, Robert Havemann once wrote (1978, 23): "Until the famous declaration protesting Biermann's expatriation, not a single one of the GDR's bourgeois intellectuals [sic] had expressed openly and publicly their support for Biermann or for our position, or, indeed, for an unambiguous critique of SED policies. All these people, many of them very likable, intelligent, and with great artistic talents, would not risk sticking their necks out like Wolf, or appearing next to him, because they feared being denied the freedom to do their work [Berufsverbot], which had been imposed on him for all to see." After his expatriation, Biermann recounted that Heym had called Havemann in the aftermath of the eleventh plenum of the SED's Central Committee in December 1965 and informed him that he no longer wished to have contact of any kind with him. Mustn't Heym have known, Biermann wondered, that it was no longer a matter of risking "his life, but at most the good life"? See Biermann 1990, 135.

2. After his departure, Jurek Becker was quoted as saying, "If it's a question of keeping my mouth shut, then I would rather keep it shut in the Bahamas" (cited in Childs 1988, 224).

3. Ingrid Pawlowitz, "Kein Duft von wilder Minze," *Weimarer Beiträge* 9 (September 1982), excerpted in Woods 1986, 219–21. The quotation here is taken from p. 220; emphasis added. On the generational shifts in the self-understanding of East Germany's writers, see Erbe 1987.

4. A vigorous debate over the relationship between workers and intellectuals in Solidarność has developed since the publication of Lawrence Goodwyn's study, *Breaking the Barrier* (Goodwyn 1991). For an earlier account, which is also the target of much of Goodwyn's critical ire, see Garton Ash 1983.

5. Wolf Biermann, "Gott in Poln," in Biermann 1990, 28.

6. Interview with Professor Günter Lehmann, Leipzig, 29 July 1991.

7. See "Polenwitze: Zwei Anträge des Pfarrers Friedrich Schorlemmer aus Wittenberg an die Synode in Halle (5.11.81)," in Büscher et al. 1982, 202–3.

8. *Neues Deutschland,* 8 September 1981, quoted in Winters 1981a, 1010. Winters's article is a scathing attack on the "unpolitical" response of the Germans in the GDR to the Polish workers' efforts to achieve greater freedoms.

9. See Winters 1980, 1016; and Winters 1981c, 5. The Bundesnachrichtendienst is similar to the American FBI, a domestic police and spying organization. The Springer publishing house, producers of the mass circulation daily newspaper *Bild,* was a favorite target of German leftists East and West for its conservative political stance, particularly with respect to the GDR. Indeed, only around this time did the editors knuckle under to political realities and drop the policy of placing the abbreviation DDR in quotation marks.

10. *Neues Deutschland,* 5 December 1980; on this point, see Winters 1981c, 7.

11. See Krüger 1982, 20. Here the "Peace Appeal of European Writers" is said to have been initiated by the Verband Deutscher Schriftsteller (the West German Writers' Union) under Engelmann's chairmanship. The assertion that the appeal was jointly initiated by Engelmann and Kant may be found on the back cover of the volume *Zweite Berliner Begegnung* 1983.

12. *Berliner Begegnung zur Friedensförderung* 1982, 48–49, 56–59. In one statement (p. 32), Kant specifically endorsed the Soviet proposal for a moratorium on nuclear weapons, noting that "I'm more inclined to listen to my friends than I am to listen to those who are not my friends." It should perhaps be noted that, despite the book title's reference to a "meeting of writers," the participants in the 1981 meeting

included representatives of a much broader swath of the intellectual and scientific elite in the GDR. In contrast, the follow-up Zweite Berliner Begegnung, held in April 1983 in West Berlin, could more accurately be described as a convocation of writers. See *Zweite Berliner Begegnung* 1983.

13. *Berliner Begegnung zur Friedensförderung* 1982, 136, 142.

14. See Pittman 1982, 91–94; and Sodaro 1990, 296–97. The apparent successes arising from the Schmidt-Honecker meeting at Lake Werbellin soon gave way to heightened tensions as the Cold War intensified, in part under pressure from the newly elected administration of Ronald Reagan in the United States.

15. Quoted in *Berliner Begegnung zur Friedensförderung* 1982, 65.

16. Heym's statement, dated 14 January 1982, is reprinted as "Was ist das für ein Sozialismus?" in Büscher et al. 1982, 235–37. An English translation can be found in Woods 1986, 138–39.

17. See the exchange between Grass and Abusch in *Berliner Begegnung zur Friedensförderung* 1982, 134–35. Grass's literary rendering of the 1953 workers' rebellion can be found in Grass 1989.

18. Interview, Berlin, 3 February 1992.

19. "Jens Reich: Am wichtigsten ist die Befreiung von der Angst" (interview with Gerhard Rein, Berlin, late October 1989), in Rein 1989, 32. For a classic criticism — from a German — of the German proclivity for the abstractions of theory and the attendant disinclination toward concrete politics, see Heine 1983, 31: "Franzosen und Russen gehört das Land / Das Meer gehört den Briten / Wir aber besitzen im Luftreich des Traums / die Herrschaft unbestritten" (The land belongs to the French and the Russians / The seas belong to the British / But we own in the airy empire of dreams / A sovereignty that is uncontested).

20. Interview, Berlin, 26 August 1991; emphasis added.

21. One indication of this influence is the sustained attention to developments in Poland in the pages of the IFM's samizdat publication, *Grenzfall* (see below).

22. See the "Letter to the Congregations" of the Conference of Protestant Church Leaderships of the GDR, the highest body of the East German Lutheran Church, reprinted under the heading "Glaubwürdigkeit der DDR-Friedenspolitik fraglich," in Büscher et al. 1982, 69–77. An English translation is available in Woods 1986, 185–92.

23. The formula "church in socialism" *(Kirche im Sozialismus),* which was formalized in talks between the leadership of the SED and that of the League of Evangelical Churches in the GDR under Albrecht Schönherr on 6 March 1978, went back to an official church statement of 1971. See Albrecht Schönherr, "Weder Opportunismus noch Opposition: Kirche im Sozialismus — Der beschwerliche Weg der Protestanten in der DDR," *Die Zeit* (overseas edition), 14 February 1992. The compromise with the regime implicit in this arrangement has been a matter of intense controversy since the collapse of the East German order. For a critical view by an East German theologian, who urged use of the more neutral "church in the GDR," see "Nochmals: Kirche im Sozialismus — Wie der Ostberliner Theologe Richard Schröder vor dem Fall der Mauer mit Marxisten diskutierte," *Die Zeit* (overseas edition), 28 February 1992.

24. Havemann's "Open Letter to Leonid Brezhnev" can be found along with a listing of the initial signatories in Büscher et al. 1982, 181–84. The "Berlin Appeal" can be also found there on pp. 242–44. An English translation of the latter is available in Woods 1986, 195–97.

25. The interview is reprinted as "Perspektive Entmilitarisierung und Wiedervereinigung?" in Büscher et al. 1986, 193.

26. For a sampling of representative early views of East German ecological and anti-industrial activists, see Wensierski and Büscher 1981.

27. Knabe 1988, 555. Given that the model of "new social movements" analysis was originally developed to describe nonparty reform movements in Western democratic welfare states, however, there is good reason to doubt the applicability of the model of "new social movements" to Soviet-type socialist societies such as the GDR. Still, the "slavishness to Western models" (Jens Reich) of the East German alternative and dissident groups frequently gave their activities the appearance of imitations of the Greens and their attendant subcultures. I am indebted to Professor Christian Joppke of the European University Institute in Florence for discussion of this point.

28. See Gerhard Rein's report on the first meeting of the assembly in Dresden in early 1988 in Rein 1990, 72–73.

29. Edgar Dusdal, interview with Christian Joppke, 26 July 1991. Professor Joppke has kindly made the transcript of this interview available to me.

30. See Ronge 1985. For the numbers of emigrants, see the table in Wendt 1991, 388.

31. Interview with Wolfgang Templin, Berlin, 3 February 1992.

32. These two quotations are taken from Templin and Weißhuhn 1991, 149–150. Weißhuhn later joined the personal staff of Gerd Poppe, who became an Alliance '90 member of the Bundestag and was himself an early IFM activist.

33. Interview with Ulrike Poppe, Conway, N.H., 23 June 1991.

34. The statement is reprinted in Hirsch 1988, 211–12.

35. Interviews with Günter Jeschonnek, Berlin, 12 September 1991, and with Pastor Christian Führer, Leipzig, 4 September 1991. This criticism — essentially a charge of hubris and ingratitude on the part of dissident activists — constituted one element of the controversy surrounding the early 1992 revelations by Manfred Stolpe, formerly a prominent lawyer for the Berlin-Brandenburg Church who was elected prime minister of the state of Brandenburg in 1990, concerning his contacts with the Stasi in his capacity as a high-level church functionary. On this controversy, see *Der Spiegel*, 20 January 1992 and 27 January 1992.

36. Interview with New Forum activist Jochen Läßig, Leipzig, 9 July 1991. For more on the controversy over the relationship between the church and the opposition in the GDR, see Robert Leicht, "Hochmut kommt nach dem Fall: Wie an Manfred Stolpe ein Exempel später Selbstgerechtigkeit statuiert werden sollte," *Die Zeit*, 14 February 1992; and Albrecht Schönherr, "Weder Opportunismus noch Opposition" (see n. 23 above).

37. Interview with Ulrike Poppe, Conway, N.H., 23 June 1991. The term *querelles berlinoises* was used by Südwestfunk radio reporter Gerhard Rein in a broadcast on 4 December 1987, reprinted in Rein 1990, 48. Confirming Rein's view, Leipzig New Forum activist Jochen Läßig spoke critically about the factionalism among the Berlin dissident groups in an interview, Leipzig, 9 July 1991. More generally, Roger Woods has noted that, in East Germany, "dissident intellectuals [could] expend much energy arguing among themselves" (Woods 1986, 46).

38. Interview with Regina (Lotte) Templin, Berlin, 3 February 1992.

39. Ulrike Poppe, remarks at a conference on social movements in East Germany at the Wissenschaftszentrum Berlin, June 1991.

40. The document is reproduced in Hirsch 1988, 213–14.

41. All issues of the publication from the first, dated June 29, 1986, through that of November–December 1987, are reprinted in Hirsch and Kopelew 1989. The quotation and the figures regarding the print run are taken from Hirsch's remarks on the back cover of this collection. The figure is confirmed by Heller 1988, 1189.

42. Interestingly, the East German intellectual dissidents had an important prece-

dent within the Soviet sphere for using Western media to communicate views unpalatable to the powers-that-be: this was, of course, precisely the approach taken by Khrushchev to convey the contents of his "secret speech" at the twentieth CPSU congress to the East European population.

43. For a discussion of the concept of civil society and its significance in East European dissident discourse, see Garton Ash 1989b. Discussion of the concept in East German dissident circles arrived very late on the scene. On this point, see Tismaneanu 1989 and Templin 1989. Templin had been in the West for about a year by the time he gave the lecture upon which this article is based.

44. See "Vorstellung der Initiative 'Frieden und Menschenrechte' zum Tag der Menschenrechte am 10. 12. 1987 in der Gethsemanekirche," in Hirsch and Kopelew 1989, viii.

45. Hirsch and Kopelew 1989, 29. Havel's programmatic statement about the importance of taking open action against Soviet-style totalitarianism is "The Power of the Powerless," reprinted in Havel 1986, 36–122.

46. See the statement in the publication's first issue in Hirsch and Kopelew 1989, 1.

47. See the remarks of Ulrike Poppe, an early IFM activist and later a cofounder of the citizens' movement Democracy Now: "My hopes are with the cross-bloc peace movement, which should not dissolve into sectarian groups and which should take account of political realities. To be concrete: I want to work within the framework of the laws of the GDR and not against the state. But the willingness to engage in dialogue must be present on both sides" (cited in Fricke 1984, 189).

48. "Vorstellung der 'Initiative Frieden und Menschenrechte,'" in Hirsch and Kopelew 1989, viii.

49. Interview with Carlo Jordan, Berlin, 16 September 1991.

50. A complete collection of the Umweltblätter has recently been published under the auspices of the *Umweltbibliothek* in Berlin. Many of the most important texts have been reprinted with extensive commentary in Rüddenklau 1992.

51. For an insider's overview of East Berlin's "parallel culture," see Rosenthal 1988. For a survey of samizdat publications through late 1988, see Heller 1988.

52. "Der Streit der Ideologien und die gemeinsame Sicherheit: Gemeinsame Erklärung der Grundwertekommission der SPD and der Akademie für Gesellschaftswissenschaften beim ZK der SED vom 27. August 1987," in *Kultur des Streits* 1988, 11, 16.

53. Heino Falcke, "Antrag und Begründung," in Bickhardt 1988, 118. See also the remarks of Pastor Friedrich Schorlemmer, who speaks similarly of "a new style, a new openness, a commonality that admits of differences," in Rein 1990, 22.

54. Quoted in Helmut Löhlöffel, "Ein Papier, das zur Entängstigung beitrug," *Frankfurter Rundschau,* 16 October 1992, 4.

55. See Stephan Michalke, "Kommentiert," in Hirsch and Kopelew 1989, 102.

56. Ulrike Poppe, "Neue Wege?" in Hirsch and Kopelew 1989, 144–45.

57. Quoted in Löhlöffel, "Ein Papier, das zur Entängstigung beitrug."

58. Quoted in Bahrmann and Links 1990, 23. Hager's remark provoked one of the many witty posters that appeared later at the huge demonstration in East Berlin on 4 November 1989: "We need architects, not wallpaper-hangers." For this and a number of others, see Schüddekopf 1990, 205–6.

59. Numerous interview partners told me that it was around this time that people began to sense that "things just can't go on like this much longer." No one ever persuasively explained to me, however, what would have happened if "things" had so continued, so that this often struck me as an ex post facto judgment from the vantage point of those who knew that, in fact, "things" *had not* "gone on like this."

60. Interview with Manfred Lötsch, Berlin, 28 January 1992. See also "Der Streit der Ideologien und die gemeinsame Sicherheit," in *Kultur des Streits* 1988, 21.

61. For an indication of Lötsch's sociological approach, see Lötsch 1988. Lötsch was most concerned with the disastrous lack of economic efficiency in Soviet-style socialist societies, and his work was thus primarily oriented toward analysis of the situation of the technical intelligentsia. For an assessment of the social and political significance of Lötsch's work for the GDR in the 1980s, see Belwe 1990. I would like to thank Dr. Belwe for making available to me this valuable analysis.

62. Interview with Manfred Lötsch, Berlin, 28 January 1992.

63. See "Solidarität hier und jetzt: Erklärung von Uwe Kolbe in der Gethsemanekirche Ost-Berlin am 4. Februar 1988," in Rein 1990, 66–67.

64. Interview with Carlo Jordan, Berlin, 16 September 1991.

65. According to Gerhard Rein, the authorities justified their action at the Umweltbibliothek with reference to the forthcoming issue of *Grenzfall*. See Rein 1990, 39.

66. Interview with Lotte Templin, Berlin, 3 February 1992.

67. Hirsch 1988, 232–33. While most of those involved remained in the Federal Republic, Bärbel Bohley followed recent expellee Vera Wollenberger to England, where the latter was studying philosophy and theology on a fellowship from the Anglican Church.

68. Reinhard Schult wrote these lines in the organ of the peace group Friedenskreis Friedrichsfelde, the *Friedrichsfelder Extrablatt* (April 1988); quoted in Kroh 1988b, 54. Schult goes on to quote "the laconic remark of a Chilean friend" who said simply, "They were bad revolutionaries."

69. Jeschonnek is especially interesting as a representative of that peculiar and rare GDR hybrid, making use of "voice" to gain "exit." His parents were prominent party members, and Jeschonnek was forced to keep his application secret from them for fear that they might apply pressure on him to change his mind. Jeschonnek's difficulties with the East German order went back to the early 1970s, when his refusal to participate in military training led to a year-long interruption of his studies. He later attempted unsuccessfully to escape from the country. While this curriculum vitae was not atypical of many would-be emigrants, Jeschonnek had been more involved in political activities than most. He and his wife were members of the Gethsemane Church in Prenzlauer Berg. Jeschonnek had participated as the church's representative in the planning of the independent "East Berlin Pilgrimage" of September 1987, an attempt by the dissident forces to wrest the peace issue from the regime on the occasion of the international Olaf Palme Peace March.

70. Interview with Günter Jeschonnek, Berlin, 12 September 1991.

71. Interview with Günter Jeschonnek, Berlin, 12 September 1991.

72. Interview with Pastor Christian Führer, Leipzig, 4 September 1991.

73. Ulrike Poppe estimated in 1988 that, in the GDR as a whole, there were approximately 325 church-based groups working on one political theme or another, but bound together in the countrywide network "Frieden konkret." No mention is made of groups organizing around the issue of emigration. See Poppe 1990a, 68–69.

74. Interview with Carlo Jordan, Berlin, 16 September 1991.

75. Interview with Carlo Jordan, Berlin, 16 September 1991.

76. See Bilke 1980, 12. At least one respondent to a randomly distributed questionnaire told of her reluctance to apply for emigration out of fear that her parents would suffer for her action.

77. Interview with Günter Jeschonnek, Berlin, 12 September 1991.

78. Interview with Carlo Jordan, Berlin, 16 September 1991. Many dissidents thus unwittingly shared the bureaucratic language of a Stasi report noting tensions

between the grassroots groups and the emigrants; the report spoke of the emigrants' "misuse" of underground political activity "for their egotistical purposes," namely, to effect a positive disposition of their applications for emigration. See Mitter and Wolle 1990, 62.

79. Interview with Lotte Templin, Berlin, 3 February 1992. In a separate interview, Wolfgang Templin went to the heart of the issue that so poisoned relations between dissidents and emigrants: "As a political oppositionist, I can choose to support a program, or a vision, namely to change this state. But I can't form a human rights group and, over the long term, insist, 'These kinds of human rights, namely the domestic political changes, those are the legitimate ones.' Because then somebody comes along and says, 'But there's a little problem here: I have decided differently about the matter of freedom of movement' " (interview, Berlin, 29 August 1991).

80. Jeschonnek 1988a, 256. Wolfgang Templin confirmed Jeschonnek's account of his and his wife's support for the Working Group on GDR Citizenship Rights, adding that the matter had been the source of much soul-searching and debate within the IFM.

81. Interview with Carlo Jordan, Berlin, 16 September 1991; see also Jeschonnek 1988b, 849.

82. Heinz Kamnitzer, "Die Toten mahnen," *Neues Deutschland,* 28 January 1988, reprinted in Rein 1990, 61. Kamnitzer had also participated in the campaign to defame Wolf Biermann after his expulsion from the GDR in 1976. For his comments during that affair, see Lübbe 1984, 319–20.

83. Ludwig Drees, "Aus der Isolation zu Wegen der Identifikation," in Bickhardt 1988, 45–46.

84. See Hirsch and Kopelew 1989, 57–58. *Grenzfall*'s reprinting of the petition can be found there as well.

85. "Absage an Praxis und Prinzip der Abgrenzung," in Bickhardt 1988, 16–17. The signatories to the appeal calling on parishioners to support the petition who were also cosigners of Democracy Now's initial statement in 1989, "Aufruf zur Einmischung in eigener Sache," included Dr. Hans-Jürgen Fischbeck, a physicist; Ludwig Mehlhorn, a trained mathematician who had been unable to work in his profession for political reasons for some time; Stephan Bickhardt, a pastor; Martin König; and Reinhard Lampe. See Bickhardt 1988, 25, and "Aufruf zur Einmischung," in Rein 1989, 59–61.

86. See Ludwig Mehlhorn, "Wir brauchen ein dialogförderndes Klima: Europa und der Dialog zwischen Deutschen und Polen," in Bickhardt 1988, 87–92.

87. "Absage an Praxis und Prinzip der Abgrenzung," in Bickhardt 1988, 16–17.

88. Hubertus Knabe made this point at a symposium on social movements in the GDR held at the Wissenschaftszentrum Berlin in June 1991.

4: The Intelligentsia in the Socialist Denouement

1. See Tocqueville 1955, 177, for his famous remarks about the dangers of a bad regime attempting to reform itself.

2. Interview with Werner Eberlein, Berlin, 2 February 1992.

3. See Stefan Scheytt and Oliver Schröm, "Lebenslänglich Bundesbürger," *Die Zeit,* 26 June 1992.

4. This account is based on Rüddenklau 1992, 195–98. Robert Darnton (1991, 100) reports incorrectly that the ban of *Sputnik* occurred in May 1989.

5. " 'Sputnik' in der DDR verboten. Kommentar," *Umweltblätter,* December 1988, 8, reprinted in Rüddenklau 1992, 249–50.

6. See "DDR-weite Proteste gegen Verbot des 'Sputnik'," *Umweltblätter,* December 1988, 4, reprinted in Rüddenklau 1992, 248–49.

7. Interview with Sebastian Pflugbeil, Berlin, 5 September 1991.

8. See "Information über beachtenswerte Aspekte des aktuellen Wirksamwerdens innerer feindlicher, oppositioneller und anderer negativer Kräfte in personellen Zusammenschlüssen," in Mitter and Wolle 1990, 49.

9. Interview with former Politburo member Günter Schabowski, Berlin, 19 September 1991.

10. *Neues Deutschland,* 5 June 1989, quoted in *DDR Journal zur Novemberrevolution* n.d. [1990], 6.

11. Interview with Günter Schabowski, Berlin, 19 September 1991.

12. Matthias Geis, "Als Reaktion auf die Ausreisewelle...: Bisher sind die vielfältigen Gruppen der DDR-Opposition keine ernstzunehmende Gegenmacht," *Die Tageszeitung,* 15 August 1989, reprinted in *DDR Journal zur Novemberrevolution* n.d. [1990], 6.

13. For example, Bernhard Prosch and Martin Abraham write that "the demonstrations...were the cause of the transformation in the GDR" (see Prosch and Abraham 1991, 293).

14. The enormous costs associated with this kind of assistance led Bonn to cut off such aid after the elections of March 1990 in an effort to stem the continuing tide of refugees. See Serge Schmemann, "Bonn Will Cut Aid to East Germans Who Move West," *New York Times,* 21 March 1990, A1, A8.

15. See the useful discussion in Walser Smith 1991, 241–42.

16. For monthly figures, see the table in Wendt 1991, 393. See also "Zuzug aus Osten weiter stark," *Frankfurter Rundschau,* 6 June 1991, 1, which reports that the exodus in 1990 was 330,000, a mere 10,000 fewer than in 1989, and that some 10,000 to 20,000 East Germans continued to leave for the West each month during 1991.

17. See "Neues Deutschland über die Ausreisewelle vom 2. Oktober 1989," in Gransow and Jarausch 1991, 68–69.

18. Hilmer and Köhler 1989a, 1385. It should be noted that these figures are not mutually exclusive; it was by no means uncommon for young people in East Germany to complete an apprenticeship before embarking upon academic studies.

19. Schmidt n.d. [1990], 25. The figure used for the percentage of the intelligentsia among employees in industry is that for the entire GDR; the relevant figures for Berlin are unavailable.

20. For points 1–4, see Schmidt n.d. [1990], 24–25. I add point 5 to indicate that, beyond these "material" considerations, there was at least some degree of ideological commitment to the system.

21. Meyer 1985, 523. Meyer notes that holders of degrees in the *Gesellschaftswissenschaften* are graduates of either the Academy of Social Sciences of the Central Committee of the SED or of the Karl Marx Party School of the Central Committee; as we shall see below, the two were very different institutions.

22. For an insightful discussion, drawing on Bourdieu, of the logic of the relations between the East German state and different scholarly fields, see Engler 1991.

23. Hilmer and Köhler (1989a, 1385) and Voigt, Belitz-Demiriz, and Meck (1990, 736) agree on this point.

24. Robert Darnton's (1991) account of events in East Germany offers an excellent sense of the mood of the period, primarily from the viewpoint of the intelligentsia. So compelling was the (illusory) sense of the possibility of a reformed GDR at that time that even Darnton found himself swept up in the enthusiasm about an East German "third way" between capitalism and Soviet-style Commu-

nism. I hope to indicate below why this was a misreading of the situation, to which most of us (I explicitly include myself here) were susceptible.

25. Several prominent East German dissident intellectuals had offered their views on the "German question" in a "hearing" on this subject at the annual meeting of the German Evangelical Church in West Berlin on 8 June 1989. See "Deutsche Einsichten," in Rein 1990, 150–61. As my interviews with Wolfgang Templin and Sebastian Pflugbeil confirmed, the opposition regarded as quite poor the prospects of their overthrowing the SED in the fall of 1989.

26. For a fascinating look at the vehement debate among the party rank and file over the character and achievements of socialism at this time, see Gruner 1990. The book is a collection of letters responding to Christa Wolf's article, "Das haben wir nicht gelernt" (We never learned that), which had appeared in the weekly newspaper *Wochenpost* on 21 October 1989. In the article, Wolf had sharply criticized the teachers of the GDR for cultivating "immature citizens" *(unmündige Bürger)*. The debate documented in the volume revolved around the intriguing question whether an educational system as ossified as that described by Wolf could have brought forth the outpouring of social and political activism gripping the country at the time the article first appeared.

27. See the interview with Sebastian Pflugbeil, "Wir müssen die Reform mit den Genossen machen," in Rein 1989, 23.

28. "Otto Reinhold zur DDR-Identität am 19. August 1989," in Gransow and Jarausch 1991, 57; emphasis added.

29. See "Ludwig Mehlhorn: Wir brauchen eine vom Staat unabhängige Gesellschaft," in Rein 1989, 74. Giordano's term, *der verordnete Antifaschismus,* is not easily translated into English, but the point is made, I hope, with the notion of an "antifascism by fiat." See Giordano 1987.

30. "Erklärung des Präsidiums der Akademie der Künste der DDR vom 4. Oktober 1989," in Schüddekopf 1990, 62–63. Meanwhile, the presidium of the Kulturbund issued a communiqué on 10 October condemning the "hate-filled psychological war being carried out in the media by nationalist forces in the FRG against the GDR," but wondering nonetheless "why we have not succeeded in winning especially the younger people among the emigrants for the difficult but promising life here in our country." The statement held up as the Kulturbund's goals "the GDR as antifascist alternative, social security, and real humanism." The similarities with the language and outlook embodied in the manifesto "For Our Country" (see below) are striking. See "Kommunique der Sitzung des Präsidiums des Kulturbundes der DDR," in Mitteldeutscher Verlag Transparent 1990, 59–60.

31. Uwe Kolbe, "Gebundene Zungen. Ein offener Brief," in Naumann 1990, 88. This piece is an "open letter" addressed to New Forum cofounder Bärbel Bohley.

32. See "Aufruf zur Bildung einer Initiativgruppe, mit dem Ziel eine sozialdemokratische Partei in der DDR ins Leben zu rufen," in Rein 1989, 87. This "appeal," jointly authored by Protestant pastors Markus Meckel and Martin Gutzeit, is dated 24 July 1989; Rein notes that it was first presented publicly on 26 August 1989 and was released to the public on 3 September. In an interview (4 September 1991), Markus Meckel characterized this delay in making their intentions public as a substantial political blunder that undermined the prospects of the East German Social Democrats.

33. For the document and a list of the first signers along with their occupations, see "Aufbruch 89 — NEUES FORUM," in *Die ersten Texte des neuen Forum* n.d. [1990?], 1–2. See also "Druck im Kessel," *Der Spiegel,* 18 September 1989, 17, which describes the founding of New Forum in remarkably subdued tones, given the dramatic developments that soon ensued.

34. "SED: Wir verfügen über alle erforderlichen Formen und Foren," in Rein 1989, 236.

35. See "Böhlener Plattform," in Rein 1989, 105–11.

36. See "Information über beachtenswerte Aspekte des aktuellen Wirksamwerdens, etc." in Mitter and Wolle 1990, 48.

37. Ulrike Poppe spoke of her career difficulties in our interview in Conway, N.H., 23 June 1991.

38. See Findeis 1990, 95; and "Information über beachtenswerte Aspekte des aktuellen Wirksamwerdens," in Mitter and Wolle 1990, 48.

39. Interview with Wolfgang Thierse, Berlin, 23 August 1991. Though he never clarified what he meant by the term "bourgeois intelligentsia," Thierse was presumably referring to those who refused to endorse the socialism of the SED, especially if they held strong religious convictions. Thierse's analysis of the reasons for the comparatively liberal atmosphere of the Academy of Sciences is corroborated by Eckert 1992, 29–30.

40. See my interviews with Jens Reich, Sebastian Pflugbeil, and Klaus Brandenburg, a New Forum representative at the Round Table negotiations with the government who had been thrown out of his job as a historian at the Academy of Sciences for political reasons during the early 1980s.

41. Interview with Manfred Lötsch, Berlin, 27 February 1991.

42. For discussions of partisanship in East German historiography, see H. Weber 1990; Küttler 1992; Blaschke 1992; and Mommsen 1992.

43. F. Wolf 1989. Wolf had defended Walter Janka during his trial in 1957. For contrasting views on the nature of the GDR's constitutionalism and on the degree to which laws were bent in the service of party aims, see Uwe-Jens Heuer and Michael Schumann, "Wo verläuft die Grenze zwischen DDR-Recht und -Unrecht? Zur juristischen Bewertung des Realsozialismus taugen nur die früher dort gültigen Gesetze," Frankfurter Rundschau, 26 October 1992, 12, and Karl-Wilhelm Fricke, "Aus 'erzieherischen Gründen' wurde die Todesstrafe verhängt: Die Strafjustiz in der DDR war dem SED-Parteiapparat untergeordnet," Frankfurter Rundschau, 29 October 1992, 24.

44. See Amtliches Handbuch des Deutschen Bundestages 1990, 46. Heuer was elected to the Bundestag as a representative of the PDS in the elections of March 1990.

45. Interview with Pastor Christian Führer, Leipzig, 4 September 1991.

46. Jens Reich, "Am wichtigsten ist die Befreiung von der Angst," in Rein 1989, 29.

47. In my interview with him, former Politburo member Günter Schabowski (Berlin, 19 September 1992) insisted that the Politburo did not take seriously the challenge of the independent groups until it was too late.

48. "SED: Wir verfügen über alle erforderlichen Formen und Foren," in Rein 1989, 236.

49. See "Werktätige des Bezirkes fordern: Staatsfeindlichkeit nicht länger dulden," Leipziger Volkszeitung, 6 October 1989, 2, reprinted in Neues Forum Leipzig 1989, 63.

50. For the text of the declaration, sometimes referred to as the "Appeal of the Six," see Neues Forum Leipzig 1989, 82–83. For the background to the appeal, see my interview with Roland Wötzel, one of the party secretaries and a signatory of the appeal (Leipzig, 19 July 1991). Katrin Deyda, a teacher from Dresden whose father was a member of one of the "factory militias," told me in an interview (Berlin, 21 May 1991) that, according to him, no one in his militia was prepared to shoot

demonstrators and that his commander had refused to carry out orders to distribute live ammunition in any case.

51. Hans-Jürgen Fischbeck, a cofounder of Democracy Now and earlier a member of the group opposed to the "practice and principle of demarcation," offers one (generally negative) assessment of the future role of the market in Fischbeck 1989.

52. For an example of the approach of this group, see the article by Rainer Land, Rosi Will, and Dieter Segert in Schüddekopf 1990, 146–56.

53. See "Vorläufige Grundsatzerklärung," in Rein 1989, 43.

54. For Democracy Now's first statement, which is dated 12 September 1989 and uses the phrase "solidaristic society," see "Aufruf zur Einmischung in eigener Sache," in Rein 1989, 59–61. Ulrike Poppe made this point in remarks at a symposium on the citizens' movements in the former GDR at the Wissenschaftszentrum Berlin in June 1991.

55. For the party's founding statement, see "Gründungsurkunde vom 7. 10. 89," in Rein 1989, 89.

56. Interview with Markus Meckel, Berlin, 14 September 1991.

57. See the mimeograph " 'Das Anknüpfen an die deutsche sozialdemokratische Tradition': Programmatischer Vortrag von Markus Meckel anläßlich der Gründung der Sozialdemokratischen Partei in der DDR am 7. Oktober 1989 in Schwante (Kreis Oranienburg)," and the flyer "Thema: 1946 — Zur erzwungenen Vereinigung von SPD und KPD," dated February 1990, both in the author's personal collection. Despite its founders' efforts to ensure a clear, untainted political image for the party, the SPD — the only truly new party (as opposed to citizens' movement) running in the parliamentary elections of March 1990 — ultimately was unable to avoid being tarred with what proved to be the fatal brush of "socialist sympathies."

58. See, for instance, "Sebastian Pflugbeil: Wir müssen die Reform mit den Genossen machen," in Rein 1989, 20.

59. See "Aufbruch 89 — NEUES FORUM," in Die ersten Texte des neuen Forum n.d. [1990?], 1.

60. See "Jens Reich: Am wichtigsten ist die Befreing von der Angst," in Rein 1989, 28, 30; and "Sebastian Pflugbeil: Wir müssen die Reform mit den Genossen machen," in Rein 1989, 21.

61. My understanding of the background to the founding of the SDP comes largely from my interviews with cofounders Martin Gutzeit (Berlin, 28 August 1991) and Markus Meckel (Berlin, 14 September 1991). Interestingly, both Meckel and Gutzeit had received their theological training at the seminary in Naumburg, which played a notable role in sustaining political engagement among the Protestant clergy under the old regime. The seminary is described in Judith Saitz, "Ein Schutzraum wird geschlossen," Die Zeit, 5 June 1992.

62. Using a rational choice approach, Karl-Dieter Opp has similarly argued that East Germans' participation in the wave of mass demonstrations that developed across the country in late 1989 was the product not of organization but of what he calls "spontaneous cooperation." See Opp 1991, 314.

63. "Harald Wagner: Die Leute hatten Angst um ihre Kinder," in Rein 1989, 175. Although Elvers and Findeis (1990b, 9) quote this passage approvingly, Findeis writes elsewhere that Wagner's claim "cannot stand up to close scrutiny" (see Findeis 1990, 92). However, Leipzig activist Jochen Läßig confirmed, in conversations with me, the notion that "things were different" in Leipzig.

64. Interview with Pastor Christian Führer, Leipzig, 4 September 1991.

65. See Michael Hofmann and Dieter Rink, "Der Leipziger Aufbruch: Zur Genesis einer Heldenstadt," in Grabner et al. 1990, 114–22.

66. See "Information über eine provokatorisch-demonstrative Aktion von Antrag-stellern auf ständige Ausreise in Leipzig," in Mitter and Wolle 1990, 28.

67. Petra Bornhöft, "Ausreiser und Bleiber marschieren getrennt," *Die Tages-zeitung*, 9 September 1989, reprinted in *DDR Journal zur Novemberrevolution* n.d. [1990], 8–9. Johannes Richter, a pastor at nearby St. Thomas Church in Leipzig, confirmed this account in a November 1989 interview documented in Rein 1989, 183. Pastor Christian Führer, one of those chanting "We're staying here" from the balcony of his apartment across from St. Nicholas, also confirmed this account in my interview with him, Leipzig, 4 September 1991.

68. Marianne Schulz, "Neues Forum: Von der illegalen Opposition zur legalen Marginalität," in Müller-Enbergs, Schulz, and Wielgohs 1991, 14.

69. See Schulz, "Neues Forum," in Müller-Enbergs, Schulz, and Wielgohs 1991, 20–21.

70. See Jan Wielgohs and Helmut Müller-Enbergs, "Die Bürgerbewegung Demo-kratie Jetzt," and Wolfgang Templin and Reinhard Weißhuhn, "Initiative Frieden und Menschenrechte," both in Müller-Enbergs, Schulz, and Wielgohs 1991, 105–47, 148–65, respectively.

71. Michael Hofmann and Dieter Rink, "Der Leipziger Aufbruch: Zur Genesis einer Heldenstadt," in Grabner et al. 1990, 121.

5: The Prophets Outcast

1. For transcripts of the speeches made that day by Stefan Heym, Christa Wolf, Friedrich Schorlemmer, Günter Schabowski, Markus Wolf, and many others, as well as many of the posters and placards carried that day, see Initiativgruppe 4. 11. 89, 1990. The quotation here is from p. 39.

2. The appeal is reprinted in Wolf 1990a, 169–70.

3. "Die Mauer ist gefallen," in *Die ersten Texte des Neuen Forum* n.d. [1990?], 20. The statement was signed by Jens Reich, Sebastian Pflugbeil, Bärbel Bohley, Reinhard Schult, Eberhard Seidel, and Jutta Seidel.

4. For a copy of the document and a list of the initial signatories, see Streuel 1990, 91. Gransow and Jarausch (1991, 100) note in their introduction to this doc-ument that on 2 December 1989 a number of West German leftists issued their own appeal, entitled "For Your Country, for Our Country," in support of the East German reformists' aims.

5. Interview with Ulrike Poppe, Conway, N.H., 23 June 1991. Unfortunately, Pastor Schorlemmer declined my request for an interview, citing a lack of time.

6. Interview with Wolfgang Thierse, Berlin, 23 August 1991.

7. See "Kohls Zehn-Punkte-Programm zur Deutschlandpolitik vom 28. Novem-ber 1990 [sic]," in Gransow and Jarausch 1991, 101–4.

8. For an account of this period focusing particularly on developments within the SED, see Glaeßner 1990, 3–20.

9. See "Drei-Stufen-Plan zur Einigung von Demokratie Jetzt vom 14. Dezember 1989," in Gransow and Jarausch 1991, 110–11. On 3 December, the SDP had issued a "statement on the German question" that, while clearly expressing the party's support for the "unity of the German nation," also warned of the poten-tially disastrous consequences of an overhasty process of unification. See "Erklärung der SDP zur deutschen Frage," signed in the party's name by Markus Meckel (in the present author's private collection). For the evolution of Meckel's views on the German question, see Meckel and Gutzeit 1992.

10. See " 'Hier ist nischt mehr zu retten': DDR-Arbeiter über Pfarrer, Sozialismus und die Wiedervereinigung," *Der Spiegel*, 18 December 1989. These remarks strongly

recall the proud proletarian attitudes documented among workers in the United States that emphasize the muscular dignity that derives from "knowing the meaning of a day's work." On this point, see Halle 1984.

11. Interview with Jens Reich, Berlin, 26 August 1991.

12. For patterns of recruitment to the SED leadership during the last years of the GDR, see Meyer 1991.

13. Interview with Jens Reich, Berlin, 26 August 1991.

14. Stefan Heym, "Aschermittwoch in der DDR," *Der Spiegel,* 2 December 1989; reprinted in Naumann 1990; the quotation here is on pp. 71–72 in Naumann.

15. See Schiller 1965, 35. See also the discussion of Schiller's views on the French Revolution in Bendix 1978, 401–4.

16. Monika Maron, "Die Schriftsteller und das Volk," *Der Spiegel,* 12 February 1990.

17. For one example, see my interview with Leipzig university student Tom Guldermann, Leipzig, 25 May 1991.

18. See the resolution "Zum Wahlgesetz" of 5 February 1990, in Herles and Rose 1990, 107.

19. For a brief discussion of the nature and functions of the so-called bloc parties in the East German party system, see Siegfried Suckut, "Persönlicher oder politischer Eigensinn im demokratischen Block?" *Das Parlament,* 8 May 1992. A more extended treatment is available in Lapp 1988.

20. Interview with Markus Meckel, Berlin, 14 September 1991.

21. See D. Roth 1990, 372; for a breakdown of the election results by state, see the table in Jung 1990, 7. Alliance '90 consisted of the civil rights movements New Forum, Democracy Now, and the Initiative for Peace and Human Rights. In the March 1990 elections they ran separately from another electoral slate that arose from among the forces that emerged during the fall 1989 period, the Greens and the Independent Women's Association.

22. Walser Smith 1991, 243. For an overview of public opinion polls during this period and a discussion of the reasons underlying the trend toward the CDU and away from the SPD, see Förster and Roski 1990, 127–58.

23. See the Alliance for Germany election pamphlet *Zeitung zur Wahl* from March 1990, reprinted as "Kohl im Wahlkampf: Wohlstand durch Einheit," in Gransow and Jarausch 1991, 140–43.

24. Despite the fact that both Matthias Jung and Dieter Roth are using data from the Forschungsgruppe Wahlen in Mannheim, they define the category of the *Intelligenz* somewhat differently. According to Jung (1990, 9), and consistent with East German statistical practice, the intelligentsia consists of "employees with post-secondary degrees and artistic producers." In contrast, Roth (1990, 379) defines the intelligentsia as "the occupants of higher positions in the administration, the justice system, the party apparatus, the social groups [presumably this refers to quasi-party organizations such as the Free German Youth], the media, academia, and teachers."

25. The analysis in this and the next two paragraphs is based on Kloth 1991 (see especially the table on p. 468) and on Thomas Ammer, "Abgeordnete der Volkskammer nach der Wahl im März," *Das Parlament,* 15 June 1990.

26. The prominent role of theologians among the dissident leadership during the autumn upheaval had given rise to the description of the GDR as a "republic of priests." See Neubert 1991a, 21. While this description may have had an element of truth in the fall, it no longer accurately characterized the parliament elected on 18 March.

27. Reich, in a speech at the opening ceremonies of the twelfth annual Volksuniversität at the Humboldt University in (East) Berlin, 17 May 1991, which I attended.

28. On this distinction, see Lepsius 1986.

29. Habermas 1990a. The quotation is from the version in Gransow and Jarausch 1991, 151. An expanded version of this essay appears as "Nochmals: Zur Identität der Deutschen. Ein einig Volk von aufgebrachten Wirtschaftsbürgern?" (Habermas 1990c). An English translation of the expanded version is available in Habermas 1991.

30. See Preuß 1990. In addition to the excerpted version that appears in Gransow and Jarausch 1991, this article is reprinted in full in Kuratorium für einen demokratisch verfaßten Bund deutscher Länder in Zusammenarbeit mit der Heinrich-Böll-Stiftung 1990, 46–52. Preuß, a professor at the University of Bremen in West Germany, was an adviser to the Round Table's Working Group on a New Constitution.

31. The declaration is reprinted as "Volkskammer-Erklärung zur deutschen Geschichte," in Gransow and Jarausch 1991, 155–56.

32. For a masterful account, see Maier 1988.

33. See " 'Zwei plus Vier' zur deutschen Grenze," in Gransow and Jarausch 1991, 197–98.

34. "Regierungserklärung des Ministerpräsidenten der Deutschen Demokratischen Republik, 19. April 1990," in Herles and Rose 1990, 471; emphasis added.

35. For a discussion of the political manipulation of national feeling during the unification process, see Offe 1990.

36. For the Round Table resolution calling for the drafting of a new constitution, see Herles and Rose 1990, 24.

37. See Arbeitsgruppe Neue Verfassung der DDR des Runden Tisches 1990.

38. See Arbeitsgruppe Neue Verfassung der DDR des Runden Tisches 1990, paragraph 132. For a good discussion of the differences between the Federal Republic's Basic Law and the Round Table's draft constitution, see Quint 1991, 494–97.

39. Thaysen 1990c, 146. The passage is also quoted approvingly by Süß 1991a, 607.

40. In a striking indication of the degree of political influence accorded to and believed to be exercised by the *Intellektuellen* in Germany, two (in some respects overlapping) volumes have appeared to document this debate. Anz (1991) is more in the manner of a documentary collection with commentary; Deiritz and Krauss (1991) includes some of the original contributions to the debate, but commentaries predominate.

41. Wolf 1990b. Without a question mark, the title is ambiguous. Literally, the phrase suggests "that which remains." Because of the possible meaning of the German *was* as the abbreviation of the word *etwas* (something), however, the title could also mean, more affirmatively, "something remains."

42. Frank Schirrmacher, " 'Dem Druck des härteren, strengen Lebens standhalten,' Auch eine Studie über den autoritären Charakter: Christa Wolfs Aufsätze, Reden und ihre jüngste Erzählung 'Was bleibt,' " *Frankfurter Allgemeine Zeitung,* 2 June 1990, reprinted in Anz 1991, 88.

43. For a version of this argument by a German-American observer, see Schoefer 1990.

44. Biermann, "Nur wer sich ändert, bleibt sich treu," *Die Zeit* (overseas edition, 31 August 1990). East German writer Rolf Schneider adopted a similar position justifying the examination of the political role of the East German intellectuals in Rolf Schneider, "Volk ohne Trauer: Der Schriftsteller Rolf Schneider über seine Erfahrungen als DDR-Intellektueller," *Der Spiegel,* 29 October 1990.

45. Biermann made this point in remarks during a concert at Tufts University, Boston, October 1992. Biermann's metamorphosis, it should be mentioned, has been

quite profound; he was one of those German leftists who came out prominently in support of the Gulf War of early 1991, primarily due to concern for Israel. In general, Biermann's rhetoric has shifted away from class and toward a stronger identification with his Jewish background.

46. I refer here in particular to the case of Manfred Stolpe, who has admitted to having had extensive contacts with the Stasi before 1989, but became the highest elected official in the resurrected state of Brandenburg. See my analysis, "German Intellectuals and Politics after Unification: Some Aspects of 'Working Through' the East German Past," unpublished MS, 1992.

47. The following discussion is based on Gibowski and Kaase 1991; for a breakdown of election results by state, see the table on pp. 5–6.

48. For a comparison of the results of the GDR Volkskammer elections of 18 March, the state parliament elections of 14 October, and the Bundestag elections of 2 December, see the table in Gibowski and Kaase 1991, 5.

49. For an excellent discussion of the controversies associated with the first all-German elections of 2 December 1990, see Quint 1991, 581–87.

50. See the figures presented in Gibowski and Kaase 1991, 5 and 19.

51. Interview with Sebastian Pflugbeil, Berlin, 5 September 1991; emphasis added.

52. In an interview with Erhart Neubert — a sociologist and cofounder of "Democratic Awakening" — in Berlin on 27 March 1991, I was rather surprised to learn that he had never heard the German equivalent of the term "civil society." This lacuna seemed especially indicative of the peculiarities of the East German situation given the model significance of the notion of civil society elsewhere among East European dissident intellectuals.

53. These two quotations are taken from Poppe 1990b.

6: The Abortive Revolution Continues

1. For one example, see Knabe 1988.

2. On this point, I am indebted to the discussion in Joppke 1991.

3. Die Arbeitsgruppe des Bürgerkomitees, "Ohne Aufarbeitung des Stasi-Systems kein gesellschaftlicher Neuanfang," in Heinrich-Böll-Stiftung 1991, 13.

4. Herles and Rose 1990, 86. According to a brochure from the center, renamed the Forschungs- und Gedenkstätte Normannenstrasse (Normannenstrasse Research and Memorial Center), it was given legislative backing by resolution of the East German Council of Ministers on 16 May 1990 and opened its doors on 7 November 1990.

5. The foregoing account is based on Günter Saathoff, "Chronologie der Auflösung des Ministeriums für Staatssicherheit der ehemaligen DDR (MfS) und des Umgangs mit den Stasi-Unterlagen," in Heinrich-Böll-Stiftung 1991, 68–71.

6. For the foregoing, see Die Arbeitsgruppe der Bürgerkomittees, "Ohne Aufarbeitung des Stasi-Systems kein gesellschaftlicher Neuanfang," 14–15.

7. Para. 1, sec. 3, Gesetz über die Unterlagen des Staatssicherheitsdienstes der ehemaligen Deutschen Demokratischen Republik (Stasi-Unterlagen-Gesetz — StUG), 20 December 1991, Bundesgesetzblatt, Jahrgang 1991, pt. 1, p. 2273.

8. Knabe 1991, 1014. A longtime object of Stasi attentions himself, Knabe, a West German, has worked in the so-called Gauck agency as a scholarly assistant.

9. Reported in Joachim Jahn, "Warum ist die Verfolgung der DDR-Regierungskriminalität so schwer?" Das Parlament, 10 April 1992, 17.

10. For the text of the appeal, see "Ohne Aufklärung bleibt der Makel des Versagens haften." The appeal's initial signers were Joachim Gauck, Friedrich Schorlemmer, Wolfgang Thierse, Wolfgang Ullmann, Gerd and Ulrike Poppe, Hans

Misselwitz, Marianne Birthler, Reinhard Höppner, Christoph Ziemer, and Burghard Brinksmeier.

11. For a discussion of the Stasi *Schlammschlacht* (mud-slinging battle) among the old Prenzlauer Berg "scene," see Iris Radisch, "Die Krankheit Lüge," *Die Zeit,* 24 January 1992. In an interview, Bärbel Bohley told me that the dissident milieu was so thoroughly penetrated by secret police informants that it was "a miracle that we accomplished anything." She also claimed that, contrary to the IFM's policy of openness and "living in truth," she had selectively and secretively asked certain acquaintances about forming New Forum because she feared early discovery by the secret police (interview, Cambridge, Mass., 2 April 1993).

12. See *Der Spiegel,* 20 January 1992.

13. For one example, see "Information über die Unterbindung einer von feindlichen, oppositionellen Kräften am 7. Juni 1989 in der Hauptstadt der DDR, Berlin, geplanten Provokation," in Mitter and Wolle 1990, 72–74.

14. I refer here to Klaus Mertes of *Bayerischer Rundfunk.*

15. Chief among these has been Bärbel Bohley. She has criticized Stolpe for acting *in the name* but without the *consent* of a number of dissidents arrested in connection with the 1988 Rosa Luxemburg demonstration (see above). Stolpe helped cut a deal with the regime allowing several prominent dissident figures, of whom Bohley was one, to escape jail terms by accepting temporary or permanent exile in the West.

16. For a prominent example, see Klaus von Dohnanyi, "Pakt mit dem Teufel," *Der Spiegel,* 27 January 1992, 36–38.

17. See his Bundestag speech, excerpted as "Weiße Flecken der Geschichte sichtbar machen," *Das Parlament,* 20 March 1992, 4.

18. "In the post-totalitarian [Communist] system...," Havel wrote, "everyone in his or her own way is both a victim and a supporter of the system" (see "The Power of the Powerless," in Havel 1986, 53).

19. For a report on and the various contributions to the debate, see *Das Parlament,* 20 March 1992, 1–6.

20. "Eine Aufgabe ohne Vergleich," *Das Parlament,* 20 March 1992, 5.

21. See *Bundestagsdrucksache* 12/2152, Deutscher Bundestag, 12. Wahlperiode, 21 February 1992.

22. See *Bundestagsdrucksache* 12/2226, Deutscher Bundestag, 12. Wahlperiode (undated).

23. See *Bundestagsdrucksache* 12/2220 (neu), Deutscher Bundestag, 12. Wahlperiode, 9 March 1992.

24. "Thesen zur Aufklärung der Vergangenheit" 1992, 446.

25. See Dirk Klose, "Deutsche Vergangenheiten fair und offen aufarbeiten," *Das Parlament,* 20 March 1992, 1.

26. *Bundestagsdrucksache* 12/2597, Deutscher Bundestag, 12. Wahlperiode, 14 May 1992. See also Enquete-Kommission Aufarbeitung von Geschichte und Folgen der SED-Diktatur in Deutschland, "Gliederung der künftigen Kommissionsarbeit im Hinblick auf den zu erstellenden Bericht," Bonn, 30 June 1992, in the author's possession.

27. See Stefanie Hoffmeister, "Enquete-Kommission hört Zeitzeugen: 'Ich geriet in die Brutalität der Machtmechanismen,'" *Das Parlament,* 11 December 1992, 13.

28. For an account of this hearing, see Eckhard Wiemers, "Hat der Rechtsstaat keine Mittel gegen 'gesetzlose Gesetze' der DDR?" *Das Parlament,* 4 December 1992, 11.

29. Dirk Klose, "Referiertes und Selbsterlebtes: Enquete-Kommission zum SED-Unrecht," *Das Parlament,* 18/25 December 1992, 13.

30. See Jürgen Faulenbach, "Herrschaftsinstrument der Partei, nicht Staat im Staate," *Das Parlament,* 29 January 1993, 7.

31. I am indebted to Sarah Farmer, Center for European Studies, Harvard University, for this felicitous phrase.

32. See *Der Vertrag zur deutschen Einheit: Ausgewählte Texte* 1990, Article 2, 45.

33. For excerpts from Schulz's and Poppe's speeches, as well as of other speakers in these two debates, see *Das Parlament,* 26 June 1992.

34. On this count, at least, the East German civil rights activists behaved as good Arendtian revolutionaries, seeing in a new constitution the central act completing the break with the old order. See Arendt 1984, 125.

35. See Eckart Busch, "Der neue Artikel 23 soll Bund und Länder nach Europa führen," *Das Parlament,* 28 August 1992, 19.

36. "Erst vereint, nun entzweit: Spiegel-Umfrage über die Einstellung der West- und Ostdeutschen zueinander," *Der Spiegel,* 18 January 1993, 60. It might be noted in this regard that a recent demonstration against xenophobia in Munich that drew more than four hundred thousand people had its quite extraparliamentary origins in the distress of a circle of four friends over the late 1992 wave of antiforeigner violence in Germany. See Norbert Kostede, "Erleuchtung für die Politik: Der Umschwung kam von den Bürgern: Die Lichterketten gegen Ausländerhaß und Gewalt verändern die Republik," *Die Zeit 5* (overseas edition), 5 February 1993, 3.

37. See Kuratorium für einen demokratisch verfaßten Bund deutscher Länder in Zusammenarbeit mit der Heinrich-Böll-Stiftung 1990, 22–23.

38. Tine Stein, "Arbeiten für eine gesamtdeutsche Bürgerinitiative — west-östlicher Geschäftsbericht," in Kuratorium für einen demokratisch verfaßten Bund deutscher Länder in Zusammenarbeit mit der Heinrich-Böll-Stiftung 1991, 47.

39. See the "Potsdamer Erklärung" signed by the Curatorium's Working Committee in Kuratorium für einen demokratisch verfaßten Bund deutscher Länder in Zusammenarbeit mit der Heinrich-Böll-Stiftung 1991, 49; emphasis added.

40. For a discussion, see Brubaker 1992.

41. Kuratorium für einen demokratisch verfaßten Bund deutscher Länder in Zusammenarbeit mit der Heinrich-Böll-Stiftung 1991, Article 116, 182. Recent changes in German law make it possible for those aged sixteen to twenty-three to acquire citizenship if they have lived in the country legally for eight years and are willing to renounce their previous citizenship. It is the refusal to grant dual citizenship, however, that seems to play a larger role in holding down the relative numbers of foreigners naturalizing to German citizenship. For a discussion of these issues, see Brubaker 1992, 77–79.

42. See Konrad Weiß, "Rede im Deutschen Bundestag," in Bündnis '90/Die Grünen im Bundestag n.d. [1992], 90.

43. See Rolf Clement, "Konzentration auf Asylfrage: Ausländerpolitik der Parteien," *Das Parlament,* 8–15 January 1993, 5; see also Stephen Kinzer, "Germans Plan to Make It Easier for Some to Obtain Citizenship," *New York Times,* 25 January 1993, A8; "Roman Herzog für neues Staatsbürgerrecht," *Das Parlament,* 2 April 1993, 1.

44. See Templin and Weißhuhn 1991; and Bickhardt 1988.

45. Kuratorium für einen demokratisch verfaßten Bund deutscher Länder, "Erklärung des Kuratoriums für einen demokratisch verfaßten Bund deutscher Länder zur Frage des Asylrechts und der Rechtslage von Flüchtlingen in der Bundesrepublik Deutschland," flyer, 10 November 1992, Berlin, in the author's possession.

46. The draft laws, submitted to parliament in early 1992, are reproduced in Bündnis '90/Die Grünen im Bundestag n.d. [1992], 92–108.

47. See the statements by Konrad Weiß in the Bundestag on 10 December 1992;

Wolfgang Ullmann, "Asylrecht in Flammen," *Freitag,* 4 September 1992; Markus Meckel, "Presseerklärung zur Vereinbarung zur Asylrechtsregelung vom 11. 12. 1992," *Deutscher Bundestag,* 14 December 1992; and Pro Asyl, "Asylkompromiß: Niederlage des Rechtsstaates," 7 December 1992, flyer in the author's possession.

48. See Kinzer, "Germans Plan to Make It Easier," A8.

49. For an account of a recent conference on these matters held by the Section on Law of the Society for Research on Germany (Gesellschaft für Deutschlandforschung), see Peter Juling, "Bei der Frage des Plebiszits scheiden sich die Geister: Verfassungsänderung oder Verfassungsgebung?" *Das Parlament,* 23 October 1992, 13.

50. See Evers 1991, 5–7. For analyses of the constitutions of four of the *Länder* that have been reincarnated on the territory of the old GDR, see Peter Juling, "Verfassung mit bemerkenswerten Neuerungen: Brandenburgs Bürger entscheiden am 14. Juni," *Das Parlament,* 12–19 June 1992, 14; Michael Groth, "Werte und Haltungen, die die Mitbürger erträumt haben: Die sächsische Verfassung — ein solider Kompromiß," *Das Parlament,* 26 June 1992, 15; Peter Juling, "Verfassung der moderaten Töne: 101 Artikel für Sachsen-Anhalt," *Das Parlament,* 18–25 September 1992, 14; and Sven Hölscheidt, "Öffentliche Diskussion findet wenig Resonanz: Mecklenburg-Vorpommern legt Verfassungsentwurf vor," *Das Parlament,* 16 October 1992, 13.

51. See Jörg Kürschner, "Grundgesetz-Legitimation durch Volksabstimmung?" *Das Parlament,* 10 April 1992, 17.

52. For a discussion of these issues, see Niclauß 1992, 5–8.

53. For an extremely critical view of the constitutional commission, see Tilman Evers, "Das Scheitern war vorhersehbar, ja gewollt: Ein Lehrstück der besonderen Art: Warum die Verfassungskommission sich verläßlich blockierte," *Frankfurter Rundschau,* 25 March 1993, 16; for a more evenhanded discussion that ultimately agrees that the commission has done little, see Hartmut Klatt, "Das Ringen um die Änderungen und Ergänzungen des Grundgesetzes: Zwischenbilanz der Gemeinsamen Verfassungskommission von Bundestag und Bundesrat — Teil 1," *Das Parlament,* 2 April 1993, 11.

54. See Gunter Hofmann, "Eine Chance wird vertan: Die Verfassungskommission spielt bei der Grundgesetz-Reform nur eine Nebenrolle — das hat der Eklat um den Umweltschutz sichtbar gemacht," *Die Zeit* (overseas edition), 26 February 1993, 5.

55. See Stephen Kinzer, "Green Party Merges with an East German Group," *New York Times,* 20 January 1993, A7, and Norbert Kostede, "Fusion und Konfusion," *Die Zeit* (overseas edition), 22 January 1993, 5. For an excellent indication of the foundation of the differences between (some of) the western and eastern partners, see " 'Du fällst auf die Schnauze': Joschka Fischer und Günter Nooke über die Vereinigung von Grünen und Bündnis '90," *Der Spiegel,* 11 January 1993, 27–30.

56. For a valuable discussion of the obstacles to the mobilization of popular opposition in the GDR, see Hirschman 1993, 182–83.

57. Or at least this dictum is half right. For, as the Czechoslovak, Yugoslav, Soviet, and perhaps even the Italian cases suggest, states may also *fail* to make nations — collectivities that share communal feelings. See Hobsbawm 1990, 10.

58. See Norbert Kostede, "Erleuchtung für die Politik — Der Umschwung kam von den Bürgern: Die Lichterketten gegen Ausländerhaß und Gewalt verändern die Republik," *Die Zeit* (overseas edition), 5 February 1993, 3.

Bibliography

Not all of the works listed below have been cited in the text, but I include them because they have been valuable in one way or another in carrying out this research. In addition to the publications listed below, I have consulted a number of newspapers and magazines, especially *Die Zeit, Der Spiegel,* and *Das Parlament.* Where pertinent, these are cited in full in the notes.

Abbreviations used:

APZ   *Aus Politik und Zeitgeschichte*

DA   *Deutschland Archiv*

KZfSS   *Kölner Zeitschrift für Soziologie und Sozialpsychologie*

NYR   *New York Review of Books*

ZParl   *Zeitschrift für Parlamentsfragen*

Abendroth, Wolfgang. 1973 [1965]. *A Short History of the European Working Class.* Translated by Nicholas Jacobs and Brian Trench. New York: Monthly Review Press.

Abusch, Alexander. 1946. *Der Irrweg einer Nation: Ein Beitrag zum Verständnis der deutschen Geschichte.* Berlin: Aufbau.

Allen, Bruce. 1991. *Germany East: Dissent and Opposition.* Rev. ed. Montreal and New York: Black Rose Books.

Ammer, Thomas. 1991. "Der Konflikt um die 'Abwicklung' an den Hochschulen in der ehemaligen DDR." *DA* 24/2 (February): 118–20.

Amtliches Handbuch des Deutschen Bundestages, 1990. 11. Wahlperiode, Teil 2, 1. Ergänzungslieferung, 20 December.

Anz, Thomas, ed. 1991. *"Es geht nicht um Christa Wolf"*: *Der Literaturstreit im vereinten Deutschland*. Munich: Edition Spangenberg.

Arbeitsgruppe Neue Verfassung der DDR des Runden Tisches, ed. 1990. *Entwurf: Verfassung der Deutschen Demokratischen Republik*. Berlin: BasisDruck.

Ardenne, Manfred von. 1990. *Die Erinnerungen*. Rev. ed. Munich: F. A. Herbig.

Arendt, Hannah. 1984 [1963]. *On Revolution*. New York: Penguin.

Ascherson, Neal. 1982. *The Polish August: The Self-Limiting Revolution*. New York: Penguin.

Bahrmann, Hannes, and Christoph Links. 1990. *Wir sind das Volk: Die DDR zwischen 7. Oktober und 17. Dezember 1989 — Eine Chronik*. Berlin and Weimar: Aufbau.

Bahro, Rudolf. 1977. *"Ich werde meinen Weg fortsetzen"*: *Eine Dokumentation*. Cologne and Frankfurt: Europäische Verlagsanstalt.

————. 1978 [1977]. *The Alternative in Eastern Europe*. Translated by David Fernbach. London: New Left Books.

Baring, Arnulf. 1966 [1957]. *Der 17. Juni 1953*. 3rd rev. ed. Cologne and Berlin: Kiepenheuer & Witsch.

Bathke, Gustav-Wilhelm. 1985. "Sozialstrukturelle Herkunftsbedingungen und Persönlichkeitsentwicklung von Hochschulstudenten." Ph.D. diss. (B), Akademie für Gesellschaftswissenschaften beim Zentralkomitee der SED, Institut für Marxistisch-Leninistische Soziologie, Berlin.

————. 1990a. "Soziale Reproduktion und Persönlichkeitsentwicklung von Hochschulstudenten in der DDR." Paper presented to conference entitled "The Intelligentsia and Social Change" of the German Political Science Association, Section on Socialist Societies, Marburg, 13–17 February.

————. 1990b. "Soziale Reproduktion und Sozialisation von Hochschulstudenten in der DDR." *Zeitschrift für Sozialisationsforschung und Bildungssoziologie* (1 Beiheft): 114–28.

Bauman, Zygmunt. 1987. *Legislators and Interpreters: On Modernity, Postmodernity, and Intellectuals*. Ithaca, N.Y.: Cornell University Press.

Baylis, Thomas A. 1974. *The Technical Intelligentsia and the East German Elite*. Berkeley: University of California Press.

Belitz-Demiriz, Hannelore, and Dieter Voigt. 1990. *Die Sozialstruktur der promovierten Intelligenz in der DDR und in der Bundesrepublik Deutschland, 1950–1982: Der Einfluß der politischen Systeme auf die unterschiedliche Entwicklung in den beiden deutschen Staaten*. Bochum: Universitätsverlag Dr. N. Brockmeyer.

Belwe, Katharina. 1984. "Annäherung von Arbeiterklasse und Intelligenz: Eine 'Nivellierung nach unten.'" *DA* 17/2 (February): 161–67.

————. 1989. "Sozialstruktur und gesellschaftlicher Wandel in der DDR." In *Deutschland-Handbuch: Eine doppelte Bilanz, 1949–1989*, edited by Werner Weidenfeld und Hartmut Zimmermann. Munich and Vienna: Carl Hanser.

————. 1990. "Entwicklung der Intelligenz innerhalb der Sozialstruktur der DDR in den Jahren 1978 bis 1989: Eine Literaturanalyse." MS, Gesamtdeutsches Institut, Bundesanstalt für gesamtdeutsche Aufgaben, Analysen und Berichte no. 1/1990 (8 January).

Bendix, Reinhard. 1978. *Kings or People: Power and the Mandate to Rule*. Berkeley and Los Angeles: University of California Press.

Bergsdorf, Wolfgang. 1991. "Von der Vorhut zur Nachhut." *DA* 24/2 (February): 113–15.

Berliner Begegnung zur Friedensförderung: Protokolle des Schriftstellertreffens am 13./14. Dezember 1981. 1982. Darmstadt and Neuwied: Luchterhand.

Best, Heinrich. 1990. "Nationale Verbundenheit und Entfremdung im zweistaatlichen Deutschland: Theoretische Überlegungen und empirische Befunde." *KZfSS* 42/1 (March): 1–19.

Bickhardt, Stephan, ed. 1988. *Recht ströme wie Wasser: Christen in der DDR für Absage an Praxis und Prinzip der Abgrenzung. Ein Arbeitsbuch aus der DDR.* Berlin: Wichern.

Biermann, Wolf. 1968. *Mit Marx- und Engelszungen: Gedichte, Balladen, Lieder.* Berlin: Klaus Wagenbach.

———. 1990. *Klartexte im Getümmel: 13 Jahre im Westen — Von der Ausbürgerung bis zur November-Revolution.* Cologne: Kiepenheuer & Witsch.

———. 1991. *Über das Geld und andere Herzensdinge: Prosaische Versuche über Deutschland.* Cologne: Kiepenheuer & Witsch.

Bilke, Jörg Bernhard. 1980. "Menschenrechte im SED-Staat." *APZ* B46/80 (15 November): 3–19.

Blaschke, Karlheinz. 1992. "Geschichtswissenschaft im SED-Staat: Erfahrungen eines 'bürgerlichen' Historikers in der DDR." *APZ* B17–18/92 (17 April): 14–27.

Bloch, Ernst. 1977 [1955]. "Über die Bedeutung des XX. Parteitags." In *Entstalinisierung: Der XX. Parteitag der KPdSU und seine Folgen,* edited by Reinhard Crusius and Manfred Wilke. Frankfurt: Suhrkamp.

Bortfeldt, Heinrich. 1991. "Die SED ihr eigener Totengräber?" *DA* 24/7 (July): 733–36.

Bourdieu, Pierre. 1991. "Politisches Kapital als Differenzierungsprinzip im Staatssozialismus." In Bourdieu, *Die Intellektuellen und die Macht.* Edited by Irene Dölling. Hamburg: VSA.

Brämer, Rainer, and Ulrich Heublein. 1990. "Studenten in der Wende? Versuch einer deutsch-deutschen Typologie vor der Vereinigung." *APZ* B44/90 (26 October): 3–16.

Bramhoff, Michael, and Bernd Woidtke. 1974. "Die Problematik der Chancenungleichheit in sozialistischen Ländern am Beispiel der DDR." *KZfSS* 26/3 (November): 588–629.

Brandt, Heinz. 1967. *Ein Traum, der nicht entführbar ist: Mein Weg zwischen Ost und West.* Munich: Paul List.

Brant, Stefan [Klaus Harpprecht]. 1957 [1954]. *Der Aufstand: Vorgeschichte, Geschichte, und Deutung des 17. Juni 1953,* 2nd ed. Stuttgart: Steingrüben.

Brenske, Peter. 1991. *Bauarbeiter aus der DDR: Eine empirische Untersuchung über gruppenspezifische Merkmale bei Flüchtlingen und Übersiedlern der Jahre 1989 und 1990.* Ph.D. diss., Fakultät für Sozialwissenschaften, Sektion Soziologie, Ruhr-Universität-Bochum.

Breslauer, George, ed. 1991. *Dilemmas of Transition in the Soviet Union and Eastern Europe.* Berkeley, Calif.: Berkeley-Stanford Program in Slavic and East European Studies.

Brubaker, Rogers. 1992. *Citizenship and Nationhood in France and Germany.* Cambridge, Mass.: Harvard University Press.

Brym, Robert J. 1980. *Intellectuals and Politics.* Boston: George Allen & Unwin.

Buch, Günther. 1987. *Namen und Daten wichtiger Personen der DDR.* 4th rev. ed. Berlin and Bonn: J. H. W. Dietz Nachf.

B[und] D[emokratischer] K[ommunisten] D[eutschlands]. 1979. "Manifesto." In Silnitsky, Silnitsky, and Reyman 1978. (Originally published in *Der Spiegel,* 2–9 January 1978.)

Bündnis '90/Die Grünen im Bundestag, eds. n.d. [1992]. *Für eine offene Bundesrepublik.* Bonn.

Burens, Peter Claus. 1981. *Die DDR und der Prager Frühling: Bedeutung und Auswirkungen der tschechoslowakischen Erneuerungsbewegung für die Innenpolitik der DDR im Jahre 1968*. Berlin: Duncker & Humblot.

Büscher, Wolfgang, et al., eds. 1982. *Friedensbewegung in der DDR: Texte, 1978–1982*. Hattingen: Edition Transit.

Childs, David, 1988. *The GDR: Moscow's German Ally*. 2nd rev. ed. London: George Allen & Unwin.

Chirot, Daniel. 1991a. *The Crisis of Leninism and the Decline of the Left: The Revolutions of 1989*. Seattle and London: University of Washington Press.

———. 1991b. "What Happened in Eastern Europe in 1989?" In Chirot 1991a.

Craig, Gordon. 1978. *Germany, 1866–1945*. New York: Oxford University Press.

Cramer, Dettmar. 1991. "Freikauf: Ein Beispiel für stilles Dienen." Review of *Freikauf: Die Geschäfte der DDR mit politisch Verfolgten 1963–1989*, by Ludwig A. Rehlinger. DA 24/6 (June): 652–54.

Croan, Melvin. 1962. "East German Revisionism: The Spectre and the Reality." In *Revisionism: Essays on the History of Marxist Ideas*, edited by Leopold Labedz. New York: Praeger.

Crusius, Reinhard, and Manfred Wilke, eds. 1977. *Entstalinisierung: Der XX. Parteitag der KPdSU und seine Folgen*. Frankfurt: Suhrkamp.

Dahrendorf, Ralf. 1967. *Society and Democracy in Germany*. New York: W. W. Norton.

———. 1990. *Reflections on the Revolution in Europe*. London: Chatto & Windus.

Darnton, Robert. 1991. *Berlin Journal, 1989–1990*. New York: Norton.

DDR Journal zur Novemberrevolution: August bis Dezember 1989. Vom Ausreisen bis zum Einreißen der Mauer. n.d. [1990]. n.p.: Die Taz.

DDR Journal nr. 2: Die Wende der Wende. Januar bis März 1990: Von der Öffnung des Brandenburger Tores zur Öffnung der Wahlurnen. n.d. [1990]. Frankfurt: Die Taz.

Deiritz, Karl, and Hannes Krauss, eds. 1991. *Der deutsche-deutsche Literaturstreit: oder, "Freunde, es spricht sich schlecht mit gebundener Zunge."* Hamburg and Zurich: Luchterhand Literaturverlag.

Deppe, Rainer, Helmut Dubiel, and Ulrich Röchl, eds. 1991. *Demokratischer Umbruch in Osteuropa*. Frankfurt: Suhrkamp.

Deutscher, Isaac. 1966 [1949]. *Stalin: A Political Biography*. 2nd ed. New York: Oxford University Press.

Deutsches Institut für Wirtschaftsforschung. 1985. *Handbuch DDR-Wirtschaft*. 4th exp. ed. Reinbek: Rowohlt.

Diederich, Torsten. 1991. *Der 17. Juni in der DDR*. Berlin: Dietz.

Djilas, Milovan. 1957. *The New Class: An Analysis of the Communist System*. New York: Harcourt Brace Jovanovich.

Draper, Theodore. 1992. "Who Killed Soviet Communism?" NYR, 11 June.

Eckert, Rainer. 1992. "Entwicklungschancen und -barrieren für den geschichtswissenschaftlichen Nachwuchs in der DDR." APZ B17–18/92 (17 April): 28–34.

Eichhorn, Alfred, and Andreas Reinhardt, eds. 1990. *Nach langem Schweigen endlich sprechen: Briefe an Walter Janka*. Berlin and Weimar: Aufbau.

Einstein, Albert, and Sigmund Freud. 1939 [1933]. *Why War?* London: Peace Pledge Union.

Elias, Norbert. n.d. [1939]. *The Civilizing Process*. Vol. 1: *The History of Manners*. Translated by Edmund Jephcott. New York: Pantheon.

Elvers, Wolfgang, and Hagen Findeis. 1990a. "Die politisch alternativen Gruppen im gesellschaftlichen Wandel: Eine empirische Studie zu ihrem Selbstverständnis." In Wolf-Jürgen Grabner et al. 1990.

———. 1990b. "Was ist aus den politisch alternativen Gruppen geworden? Eine soziologische Auswertung von Interviews mit ehemals führenden Vertretern in Leipzig und Berlin." MS, Religionssoziologisches Institut Emil Fuchs, Universität Leipzig.

Engler, Wolfgang. 1991. "Stellungen, Stellungnahmen, Legenden: Ein ostdeutscher Erinnerungsversuch." In Deppe, Dubiel, and Röchl 1991.

Epstein, Catherine. 1991. " 'Some Sat in Prison...Others Spoke on the Radio': Communist Political Pasts and the Consolidation of the East German Regime 1945–1953." MS, Department of History, Harvard University.

Erbe, Günter. 1982. *Arbeiterklasse und Intelligenz in der DDR: Soziale Annäherung von Produktionsarbeiterschaft und wissenschaftlich-technischer Intelligenz im Industriebetrieb?* Opladen: Westdeutscher Verlag.

———. 1984. "Produktionsarbeiterschaft und wissenschaftlich-technische Intelligenz in der DDR." In *Das Ende der Arbeiterbewegung? Ein Diskussionsband für Theo Pirker,* edited by Rolf Ebbighausen and Friederich Tiemann. Opladen: Westdeutscher Verlag.

———. 1987. "Schriftsteller in der DDR: Eine soziologische Untersuchung der Herkunft, der Karrierewege und der Selbsteinschätzung der literarischen Intelligenz im Generationenvergleich." DA 20/11 (November): 1162–79.

———. 1990. "Die Schriftsteller und der politische Umbruch in der DDR." *Prokla* 20/3 (September): 71–83.

Die ersten Texte des Neuen Forum. n.d. [1990?]. Berlin.

Evers, Tilman. 1991. "Volkssouveränität im Verfahren: Zur Verfassungsdiskussion über direkte Demokratie." APZ B23/91 (31 May 1991): 3–15.

Ewers, Klaus, and Thorsten Quest. 1988. "Die Kämpfe der Arbeiterschaft in den volkseigenen Betrieben während und nach dem 17. Juni." In Spittmann and Fricke 1988.

Faust, Siegmar. 1980. *In welchem Lande lebt Mephisto?* Munich and Vienna: Günter Olzog.

Findeis, Hagen. 1990. "Überblick über die sozialethisch engagierten Gruppen in Leipzig Anfang 1989." In Wolf-Jürgen Grabner et al. 1990.

Fink, Hans Jürgen. 1990. "Bündnis 90: Die Revolutionäre der ersten Stunde verloren die Wahl." DA 23/4 (April): 515–17.

Finn, Gerhard, and Liselotte Julius, eds. 1983. *Von Deutschland nach Deutschland: Zur Erfahrung der inneren Übersiedlung.* Bonn: Bundeszentrale für politische Bildung.

Fischbeck, Hans-Jürgen. 1989. "Marktwirtschaft im Sozialismus." In Knabe 1989.

Fitzpatrick, Sheila. 1979a. *Education and Social Mobility in the Soviet Union, 1921–1934.* New York: Cambridge University Press.

———. 1979b. "Stalin and the Making of a New Elite, 1928–1939." *Slavic Review* 38/3 (September): 377–402.

———. 1982. *The Russian Revolution, 1917–1932.* New York: Oxford University Press.

Fogt, Helmut and Pavel Uttitz. 1984. "Die Wähler der Grünen 1980–1983: Systemkritischer neuer Mittelstand." ZParl 15/2: 210–26.

Förster, Peter, and Günter Roski. 1990. *DDR zwischen Wende und Wahl: Meinungsforscher analysieren den Umbruch.* Berlin: LinksDruck.

Frentzel-Zagorska, Janina, and Krzysztof Zagorski. 1989. "East European Intellectuals on the Road of Dissent: The Old Prophecy of a New Class Re-examined."
Politics & Society 17/1 (March): 89–113.

Fricke, Karl Wilhelm. 1971. *Warten auf Gerechtigkeit: Kommunistische Säuberungen
und Rehabilitierungen.* Cologne: Verlag Wissenschaft und Politik.

———. 1976. "Zwischen Resignation und Selbstbehauptung: DDR-Bürger fordern
Recht auf Freizügigkeit." *DA* 9/11 (November): 1135–39.

———. 1979. *Politik und Justiz in der DDR: Zur Geschichte der politischen Verfolgung 1945–1968. Bericht und Dokumentation.* Cologne: Verlag Wissenschaft und
Politik.

———. 1982. *Die DDR-Staatssicherheit: Entwicklung, Strukturen, Aktionsfelder.*
Cologne: Verlag Wissenschaft und Politik.

———. 1984. *Opposition und Widerstand in der DDR: Ein politischer Report.*
Cologne: Verlag Wissenschaft und Politik.

———. 1991. "Honeckers Sturz mit Mielkes Hilfe." *DA* 24/1 (January): 5–7.

———. 1992. "'Schild und Schwert der Partei': Das Ministerium für Staatssicherheit—Herrschaftsinstrument der SED." *APZ* B21/92 (15 May): 3–10.

Friedrich, Carl J., and Zbigniew Brzezinski. 1965 [1956]. *Totalitarian Dictatorship
and Autocracy,* 2nd rev. ed. Cambridge, Mass.: Harvard University Press.

Friedrich, Walter. 1990. "Mentalitätswandlungen der Jugend in der DDR." *APZ*
B16–17/90 (13 April): 25–37.

Fritze, Lothar. 1990. "Ausreisemotive—Hypothesen über die Massenflucht aus der
DDR." *Leviathan* 18/1: 39–54.

Fuchs, Jürgen. 1984. *Einmischung in eigene Angelegenheiten: Gegen Krieg und
verlogenen Frieden.* Reinbek: Rowohlt.

———. 1990a [1977, 1978]. *Gedächtnisprotokolle; Vernehmungsprotokolle.* Reinbek: Rowohlt.

———. 1990b. *"...und wann kommt der Hammer?:" Psychologie, Opposition und
Staatssicherheit.* Berlin: BasisDruck.

Galtung, Johann. 1991. "Deutschland in Europa." *Constructiv* 2/7 (July): 13–15.

Gaus, Günter. 1986 [1983]. *Wo Deutschland liegt: Eine Ortsbestimmung.* Munich: DTV.

Garton Ash, Timothy. 1983. *The Polish Revolution: Solidarity.* New York: Vintage.

———. 1989a. "The German Revolution." *NYR,* 21 December.

———. 1989b. *The Uses of Adversity: Essays on the Fate of Central Europe.* New
York: Random House.

———. 1990a. "Eastern Europe: The Year of Truth." *NYR,* 15 February.

———. 1990b. "East Germany: The Solution." *NYR,* 26 April.

———. 1990c. "The Revolution of the Magic Lantern." *NYR,* 18 January.

Geißler, Rainer. 1983. "Bildungschancen und Statusvererbung in der DDR." *KZfSS*
35/4 (December): 755–70.

———. 1987. "Soziale Schichtung und Bildungschancen." In *Soziale Schichtung
und Lebenschancen in der Bundesrepublik,* edited by Rainer Geißler. Stuttgart:
Ferdinand Enke.

———. 1990a. "Entwicklung der Sozialstruktur und Bildungswesen." In *Vergleich von Bildung und Erziehung in der Bundesrepublik Deutschland und
in der Deutschen Demokratischen Republik,* edited by Bundesministerium für
innerdeutsche Beziehungen. Cologne: Verlag Wissenschaft und Politik.

———. 1990b. "Die soziale Schließung der Hochschulen in der DDR und ihre Ursachen." Paper delivered at the conference of the German Association of Political

Science's Section on Socialist Societies entitled "Intelligenz und gesellschaftlicher Wandel" (The intelligentsia and social change), Marburg, 13–17 February.

———. 1991. "Soziale Ungleichheit zwischen Frauen und Männern im geteilten und im vereinten Deutschland." *APZ* B14–15/91 (29 March): 13–24.

Gella, Aleksander, ed. 1976. *The Intelligentsia and the Intellectuals.* Beverly Hills, Calif.: Sage.

Lucas, Michael. 1989–90. "Germany after the Wall." Interviews by with Bärbel Bohley, Harald Lange, Karsten Voigt, and Yuri Davidov. *World Policy Journal* 7/1 (Winter): 189–214.

Geschichte der SED: Abriß. 1978. Berlin: Dietz.

Gibowski, Wolfgang. 1990. "Demokratischer (Neu)Beginn in der DDR: Dokumentation und Analyse der Wahl vom 18. März 1990." *ZParl* 21/1 (May): 5–22.

Gibowski, Wolfgang, and Max Kaase. 1991. "Auf dem Weg zum politischen Alltag: Eine Analyse der ersten gesamtdeutschen Bundestagswahl vom 2. Dezember 1990." *APZ* B11–12/91 (8 March): 3–20.

Giddens, Anthony. 1987. *The Nation-State and Violence.* Berkeley and Los Angeles: University of California Press.

Giesen, Bernd, and Claus Leggewie, eds. 1991. *Experiment Vereinigung: Ein sozialer Großversuch.* Berlin: Rotbuch.

Giordano, Ralph. 1987. *Die zweite Schuld — oder, Von der Last, ein Deutscher zu sein.* Hamburg: Knaur.

Glaeßner, Gert-Joachim. 1990. "Vom 'realen Sozialismus' zur Selbstbestimmung: Ursachen und Konsequenzen der Systemkrise in der DDR." *APZ* B1–2/90 (5 January): 3–20.

Goodwyn, Lawrence. 1991. *Breaking the Barrier: The Rise of Solidarity in Poland.* New York: Oxford University Press.

Gorholt, Martin, and Norbert Kunz, eds. 1991. *Deutsche Einheit — Deutsche Linke: Reflexionen der politischen und gesellschaftlichen Entwicklung.* Cologne: Bund.

Görlich, J. Wolfgang. 1968. *Geist und Macht in der DDR: Die Integration der kommunistischen Ideologie.* Olten and Freiburg im Breisgau: Olten.

Gouldner, Alvin. 1979. *The Future of Intellectuals and the Rise of the New Class.* New York: Continuum.

———. 1985. *Against Fragmentation: The Origins of Marxism and the Sociology of Intellectuals.* New York: Oxford University Press.

Grabner, Wolf-Jürgen, et al., eds. 1990. *Leipzig im Oktober: Kirchen und alternative Gruppen im Umbruch der DDR. Analysen zur Wende.* Berlin: Wichern.

Gramsci, Antonio. 1971. *Selections from the Prison Notebooks.* Edited and translated by Quintin Hoare and Geoffrey Nowell Smith. New York: International Publishers.

Gransow, Volker. 1975. *Kulturpolitik in der DDR.* Berlin: Volker Spiess.

Gransow, Volker, and Konrad H. Jarausch, eds. 1991. *Die deutsche Vereinigung: Dokumente zu Bürgerbewegung, Annäherung und Beitritt.* Cologne: Verlag Wissenschaft und Politik.

Grass, Günther. 1989 [1966]. *Die Plebejer proben den Aufstand: Ein deutsches Trauerspiel.* Frankfurt: Luchterhand.

———. 1990. "Kurze Rede eine vaterlandslosen Gesellen." *Die Zeit* 16 February. (Reprinted in *"Nichts wird mehr so sein, wie es war": Zur Zukunft der beiden deutschen Republiken,* edited by Frank Blohm and Wolfgang Herzberg. Stuttgart: Luchterhand, 1990.)

Grebing, Helga. 1977. "Die intellektuelle Opposition in der DDR seit 1956: Ernst Bloch—Wolfgang Harich—Robert Havemann." *APZ* B45/77 (12 November): 3–14.

———. 1989. "Die Parteien." In *Die Geschichte der Bundesrepublik Deutschland*, edited by Wolfgang Benz. Vol. 1. Frankfurt: Fischer.

Grundmann, Siegfried. 1990. "Die sozialräumlichen Konsequenzen des politischen Umbruchs in der DDR und der deutschen Einigung für Ostdeutschland." Paper presented to the conference of the Berliner Institut für Sozialwissenschaftliche Studien entitled "Social Change in the GDR and Eastern Germany in the Process of Transformation of 'Really Existing Socialist' Systems in Eastern Europe," 6–7 December.

———. n.d. [1990]. "Zum Einfluß der Binnenwanderung und Außenwanderung auf die Regional- und Stadtentwicklung in der DDR." In Siegfried Grundmann and Ines Schmidt, *Wanderungsbewegungen in der DDR 1989*. Berliner Arbeitshefte und Berichte zur Sozialwissenschaftlichen Forschung, no. 30. Zentralinstitut für sozialwissenschaftliche Forschung, Freie Universität Berlin.

Gruner, Petra, ed. 1990. *Angepaßt oder mündig? Briefe an Christa Wolf im Herbst 1989*. Frankfurt: Luchterhand.

Günther, Thomas. 1992. "Die subkulturellen Zeitschriften in der DDR und ihre kulturgeschichtliche Bedeutung." *APZ* B20/92 (8 May): 27–36.

Habermas, Jürgen. 1970. *Toward a Rational Society: Student Protest, Science, and Politics*. Translated by Jeremy J. Shapiro. Boston: Beacon Press.

———. 1973. *Theory and Practice*. Boston: Beacon Press.

———. 1987. "Geschichtsbewußtsein und posttraditionale Identität: Die Westorientierung der Bundesrepublik." In *Eine Art Schadensabwicklung: Kleine politische Schriften VI*. Frankfurt: Suhrkamp.

———. 1990a. "Der DM-Nationalismus." *Die Zeit*, 30 March. (Excerpted in Gransow and Jarausch 1991, 148–52.)

———. 1990b. "Nachholende Revolution und linker Revisionsbedarf: Was heißt Sozialismus heute?" In Habermas, *Die nachholende Revolution: Kleine politische Schriften VII*. Frankfurt: Suhrkamp.

———. 1990c. "Nochmals: Zur Identität der Deutschen. Ein einig Volk von aufgebrachten Wirtschaftsbürgern?" In Habermas, *Die nachholende Revolution: Kleine politische Schriften VII*. Frankfurt: Suhrkamp.

———. 1991. "Yet Again: German Identity—A Unified Nation of Angry DM-Burghers?" *New German Critique* 52 (Winter 1991): 84–101.

Hager, Kurt. 1988. "Friedenssicherung und ideologischer Streit." *DA* 21/1 (January): 92–98.

Halle, David. 1984. *America's Working Man*. Chicago: University of Chicago Press.

Hamerow, Theodore. 1958. *Restoration, Revolution, Reaction: Economics and Politics in Germany, 1815–1871*. Princeton, N.J.: Princeton University Press.

———. 1969. *The Social Foundations of German Unification, 1858–1871: Ideas and Institutions*. Princeton: Princeton University Press.

———. 1972. *The Social Foundations of German Unification, 1858–1871: Struggles and Accomplishments*. Princeton: Princeton University Press.

Hanke, Helmut. 1990. "Identität in der Krise." *DA* 23/8 (August): 1223–31.

Hanke, Irma. 1987. *Alltag und Politik: Zur politischen Kultur einer unpolitischen Gesellschaft*. Opladen: Westdeutscher Verlag.

Haraszti, Miklos. 1987 [1983]. *The Velvet Prison: Artists under State Socialism*. Translated by Katalin and Stephen Landesmann with Steve Wasserman. New York: Noonday Press.

Hartung, Klaus. 1990. "Der große Radwechsel oder Die Revolution ohne Utopie." In *"Nichts wird mehr so sein, wie es war": Zur Zukunft der beiden deutschen Republiken,* edited by Frank Blohm and Wolfgang Herzberg. Stuttgart: Luchterhand.

Haufe, Gerda, ed. 1992. *Die Bürgerbewegungen in der DDR und in den ostdeutschen Bundesländern.* Opladen: Westdeutscher Verlag.

Havel, Václav. 1986. *Living in Truth.* Edited by Jan Vladislav. London and Boston: Faber and Faber.

———. 1991. *Open Letters: Selected Writings, 1965–1990.* Translated and edited by Paul Wilson. New York: Knopf.

Havemann, Robert. 1972 [1970]. *Fragen — Antworten — Fragen: Aus der Biographie eines deutschen Marxisten.* Reinbek: Rowohlt.

———. 1976. *Berliner Schriften.* Edited by Andreas W. Mytze. Berlin: Verlag europäische Ideen.

———. 1978. *Ein deutscher Kommunist: Rückblicke und Perspektiven aus der Isolation.* Edited by Manfred Wilke. Reinbek: Rowohlt.

———. 1979. "The Socialism of Tomorrow." In Silnitsky, Silnitsky, and Reyman 1978.

———. 1990. *Die Stimme des Gewissens: Texte eines deutschen Antistalinisten.* Edited by Rüdiger Rosenthal. Reinbek: Rowohlt.

Heilbut, Anthony. 1984. *Exiled in Paradise: German Refugee Artists and Intellectuals in America from the 1930's to the Present.* Boston: Beacon Press.

Heine, Heinrich. 1983. *Deutschland: Ein Wintermärchen.* Frankfurt: Insel.

Heinrich-Böll-Stiftung, ed. 1991. *Die Kontinuität des Wegsehens und Mitmachens: Stasi-Akten oder die schwierige Bewältigung der DDR-Vergangenheit.* Cologne: Heinrich-Böll-Stiftung.

Heller, Frithjof. 1988. "Unbotmäßiges von 'Grenzfall' bis 'Wendezeit': Inoffizielle Publizistik in der DDR." *DA* 21/11 (November): 1188–96.

Henrich, Rolf. 1989. *Der vormundschaftliche Staat: Vom Versagen des real existierenden Sozialismus.* Reinbek: Rowohlt.

Herles, Helmut, and Ewald Rose, eds. 1990. *Vom Runden Tisch zum Parlament.* Bonn: Bouvier.

Hertwig, Manfred. 1977. "Deformationen: Die Rebellion der Intellektuellen in der DDR." In Crusius and Wilke 1977.

Heublein, Ulrich, and Rainer Brämer. 1990. "Studenten im Abseits der Vereinigung: Erste Befunde zur politischen Identität von Studierenden im deutsch-deutschen Umbruch." *DA* 22/9 (September): 1397–1410.

Heym, Stefan. 1974. *Fünf Tage im Juni.* Munich: Bertelsmann.

———. 1982–83. "Gespräch mit Stefan Heym." *GDR Monitor* 8 (Winter): 1–14.

———. 1989. "Aschermittwoch in der DDR." *Der Spiegel,* 4 December. (Reprinted in Naumann 1990.)

———. 1991. "Ash Wednesday in the GDR." (Translation of Heym 1989.) *New German Critique* 52 (Winter): 31–35.

Hilmer, Richard, and Anne Köhler. 1989a. "Der DDR läuft die Zukunft davon: Die Übersiedler-/Flüchtlingswelle im Sommer 1989." *DA* 22/12 (December): 1383–88.

———. 1989b. "Die DDR im Aufbruch: Was halten die Bundesdeutschen Ende Oktober 1989 von Flüchtlingswelle und Reformen?" *DA* 22/12 (December): 1389–93.

Hirsch, Ralf. 1988. "Die Initiative Frieden und Menschenrechte." In Kroh 1988a.

Hirsch, Ralf, and Lew Kopelew, eds. 1989. *Initiative Frieden & Menschenrechte. Grenzfall. Vollständiger Nachdruck aller in der DDR erschienenen Ausgaben.* Berlin.

Hirschman, Albert O. 1970. *Exit, Voice, and Loyalty: Responses to Decline in Firms, Organizations, and States.* Cambridge, Mass.: Harvard University Press.

———. 1991. *The Rhetoric of Reaction: Perversity, Futility, Jeopardy.* Cambridge, Mass.: Harvard University Press.

———. 1993. "Exit, Voice, and the Fate of the German Democratic Republic: An Essay in Conceptual History." *World Politics* 45/2 (January): 175–98.

Hobsbawm, E. J. 1990. *Nations and Nationalism since 1780.* New York: Cambridge University Press.

Hofmann, Michael, Ricarda Merkwitz, and Dieter Rink. n.d. [1990]. "Soziale Bewegungen in Leipzig: Zur Genesis einer Heldenstadt." MS, Universität Leipzig.

Huyssen, Andreas. 1991. "After the Wall: The Failure of German Intellectuals." *New German Critique* 52 (Winter).

Initiativgruppe 4. 11. 89, ed. 1990. *40 Jahre DDR — TschüSSED, 4. 11. 89.* Bonn: Stiftung Haus der Geschichte der Bundesrepublik.

Jäger, Manfred. 1982. *Kultur und Politik in der DDR: Ein historischer Abriß.* Cologne: Edition Deutschland Archiv.

Jänicke, Martin. 1964. *Der Dritte Weg: Die antistalinistische Opposition gegen Ulbricht seit 1953.* Cologne: Neuer Deutscher Verlag.

Janka, Walter. 1989. *Schwierigkeiten mit der Wahrheit.* Reinbek: Rowohlt.

Jarausch, K. H. 1974. "The Sources of German Student Unrest, 1815–1848." In *The University in Society.* Vol. 2: *Europe, Scotland, and the United States from the 16th to the 20th Century,* edited by Lawrence Stone. Princeton, N.J.: Princeton University Press.

Jeschonnek, Günter. 1988a. "Ausreise — Das Dilemma des ersten deutschen Arbeiter- und Bauernstaates?" In Kroh 1988a.

———. 1988b. "Der 17. Januar — und kein Ende?" *DA* 21/8 (August): 849–54.

———. 1989. "Ideologischer Sinneswandel in der SED-Führung? Ein kritischer Kommentar zum Stichwort: Reiseregelungen in DA 1/1989." *DA* 22/3 (March): 278–83.

Jesse, Eckhard. 1990. "Oppositionelle in der DDR — gestern Widerstand, heute Opposition." *ZParl* 21/1 (May): 137–46.

Johannes, Günter, and Ulrich Schwarz, eds. 1978. *DDR: Das Manifest der Opposition. Eine Dokumentation.* Munich: Wilhelm Goldmann.

Joppke, Christian. 1991. "Some Characteristics of Social Movements in Leninist Regimes." MS, Department of Sociology, University of Southern California.

Jordan, Carlo. n.d. [1991]. "Rückblick/Ausblick: Vom anti-stalinistischen Aufbruch zur grün-bürgerbewegten Wende." MS, Berlin.

Jung, Matthias. 1990. "Parteiensystem und Wahlen in der DDR: Eine Analyse der Volkskammerwahlen vom 18. März und der Kommunalwahlen." *APZ* B27/90 (29 June): 3–15.

Jung, Matthias, and Dieter Roth. 1992. "Politische Einstellungen in Ost- und Westdeutschland seit der Bundestagswahl 1990." *APZ* B19/92 (1 May): 3–16.

Just, Gustav. 1990. *Zeuge in eigener Sache.* Frankfurt: Luchterhand.

Kaminski, Bartlomiej. 1991. *The Collapse of State Socialism: The Case of Poland.* Princeton, N.J.: Princeton University Press.

Kantorowicz, Alfred. 1959. *Deutsches Tagebuch.* Pt. 1. Munich: Kindler.

———. 1961. *Deutsches Tagebuch.* Pt. 2. Munich: Kindler.

Kennedy, Michael. 1992. "The Intelligentsia in the Constitution of Civil Societies and Post Communist Regimes in Hungary and Poland." *Theory and Society* 21:29–76.

Kersten, Heinz. 1957. *Aufstand der Intellektuellen: Wandlungen in der kommunistischen Welt. Ein dokumentarischer Bericht.* Stuttgart: Seewald.

Kleßmann, Christoph. 1991. "Opposition und Dissidenz in der Geschichte der DDR." *APZ* B5/91 (25 January): 52–62.

Kloth, Hans Michael. 1991. "Einige Zahlen zur 10. Volkskammer." *ZParl* 22/3 (September): 467–73.

Knabe, Hubertus. 1987. "Neue soziale Bewegungen als Problem der sozialistischen Gesellschaft: Zur Entstehung und Bedeutung neuartiger Bewußtseinslagen in der DDR und Ungarn." In *Das Profil der DDR in der sozialistischen Staatengemeinschaft: 20. Tagung zum Stand der DDR-Forschung in der Bundesrepublik Deutschland,* edited by Ilse Spittmann-Rühle and Gisela Helwig. Cologne: Edition Deutschland Archiv.

———. 1988. "Neue soziale Bewegungen im Sozialismus: Zur Genesis alternativer politischer Orientierungen in der DDR." *KZfSS* 40:527–50.

———. 1989a. "Die deutsche Oktoberrevolution." In Knabe 1989.

———. 1989b. "Die wichtigsten Gruppen der Opposition." In Knabe 1989.

———. 1990a. "Making Haste Quickly." *East European Reporter* 4/2 (Spring/Summer): 44–46.

———. 1990b. "Politische Opposition in der DDR: Ursprünge, Programmatik, Perspektiven." *APZ* B1–2/90 (5 January): 21–32.

———. 1991. "Vergangenheitsbewältigung per Gesetz?" *DA* 24/10 (October): 1012–14.

———, ed. 1989. *Aufbruch in eine andere DDR: Reformer und Oppositionelle über die Zukunft ihres Landes.* Reinbek: Rowohlt.

Köhler, Anne. 1990. "Ist die Übersiedlerwelle noch zu stoppen? Ursachen — Erfahrungen — Perspektiven." *DA* 23/3 (March): 425–31.

Köhler, Hans. 1952. *Zur geistigen und seelischen Situation der Menschen in der Sowjetzone.* Bonn.

Kolakowski, Leszek. 1968 [1956]. "The Intellectuals and the Communist Movement." In *Towards a Marxist Humanism: Essays on the Left Today.* Translated by Jane Zielonko Peel. New York: Grove Press.

Kolbe, Uwe. 1990. "Gebundene Zungen: Ein offener Brief." In Naumann 1990.

Königsdorf, Helga. 1990a. *Adieu DDR: Protokolle eines Abschieds.* Reinbek: Rowohlt.

———. 1990b. *1989: Oder Ein Moment Schönheit.* Berlin and Weimar: Aufbau.

———. 1991. "Die Phasen der Revolution." *Politik und Kultur* 17/5:46–48.

Konrad, George, and Ivan Szelenyi. 1979. *The Intellectuals on the Road to Class Power: A Sociological Study of the Role of the Intelligentsia in Socialism.* Translated by Andrew Arato and Richard E. Allen. New York: Harcourt Brace Jovanovich.

———. 1989. "Intellectuals and Domination in Post-Communist Societies." MS, Budapest (August).

Kornai, Janos. 1989. "The Hungarian Reform Process: Visions, Hopes, and Reality." In Nee and Stark 1989.

Kozakiewicz, Mikolaj. 1984. "Bildung und Beschäftigung: Ein wachsendes Problem zentralgeplanter Gesellschaften." *Zeitschrift für Pädagogik* 30/4 (August): 457–69.

Krieger, Leonard. 1957. *The German Idea of Freedom: History of a Political Tradition.* Boston: Beacon Press.

Kroh, Ferdinand, ed. 1988a. *"Freiheit ist immer Freiheit . . .": Die Andersdenkenden in der DDR.* Frankfurt and Berlin: Ullstein.

———. 1988b. "Havemanns Erben — 1953 bis 1988." In Kroh 1988a.

Krüger, Ingrid, ed. 1982. *Mut zur Angst: Schriftsteller für den Frieden.* Darmstadt and Neuwied: Luchterhand.

Kuechler, Manfred, and Russell J. Dalton. 1990. "New Social Movements and the Political Order: Inducing Change for Long-term Stability?" In *Challenging the Political Order: New Social and Political Movements in Western Democracies,* edited by Dalton and Kuechler. New York: Oxford University Press.

Kühnel, Wolfgang, Jan Wielgohs, and Marianne Schulz. 1990. "Die neuen politischen Gruppierungen auf dem Wege vom politischen Protest zur parlamentarischen Interessenvertretung: Soziale Bewegungen im Umbruch der DDR-Gesellschaft." *ZParl* 21/1 (May): 22–37.

Kuhnert, Jan. 1983. "Überqualifikation oder Bildungsvorlauf? Aktuelle Legitimationsprobleme der DDR angesichts des Widerspruchs von Bildungsabschluß und Arbeitsanforderung." *DA* 16/5 (May): 497–519.

Kultur des Streits: Die gemeinsame Erklärung von SPD und SED. Stellungnahmen und Dokumenten. 1988. Cologne: Pahl-Rugenstein.

Kuratorium für einen demokratisch verfaßten Bund deutscher Länder in Zusammenarbeit mit der Heinrich-Böll-Stiftung, eds. 1990. *In freier Selbstbestimmung: Für eine gesamtdeutsche Verfassung mit Volksentscheid.* Berlin, Cologne, and Leipzig.

———. 1991. *Vom Grundgesetz zur deutschen Verfassung.* Berlin, Cologne, and Leipzig.

Kuron, Jacek, and Karol Modzelewski. 1968. "Open Letter to Members of the University of Warsaw Sections of the United Polish Workers' Party and the Union of Young Socialists." In *Revolutionary Marxist Students in Poland Speak Out, 1964–1968,* edited by George Lavan Weissman. New York: Merit.

Küttler, Wolfgang. 1992. "Neubeginn in der ostdeutschen Geschichtswissenschaft." *APZ* B17–18/92 (17 April): 3–13.

Labedz, Leopold. 1962. *Revisionism: Essays in the History of Marxist Ideas.* New York: Praeger.

Ladd, Everett Carll, Jr., and Seymour Martin Lipset. 1972. "Politics of Academic Natural Scientists and Engineers." *Science* 176 (9 June): 1091–1110.

Land, Rainer, and Ralf Possekel. 1992. "Intellektuelle aus der DDR — Kulturelle Identität und Umbruch: Hypothesen für ein Forschungsprojekt." *Berliner Debatte — INITIAL* 1:86–95.

Lange, Max Gustav, Ernst Richert, and Otto Stammer. 1953. "Das Problem der 'Neuen Intelligenz' in der sowjetischen Besatzungszone: Ein Beitrag zur politischen Soziologie der kommunistischen Herrschaftsordnung." In *Veritas Iustitia Libertas: Festschrift zur 200–Jahrfeier der Columbia University New York.* New York and Berlin: Colloquium.

Lapp, Peter Joachim. 1988. *Die "befreundeten Parteien" der SED: DDR-Blockparteien heute.* Cologne: Verlag Wissenschaft und Politik.

Leonhard, Wolfgang. 1990 [1955]. *Die Revolution entläßt ihre Kinder.* Cologne: Kiepenheuer & Witsch.

Lepenies, Wolf. 1992. *Folgen einer unerhörten Begebenheit.* Munich: Corso bei Siedler.

Lepsius, M. Rainer. 1986. " 'Ethnos' und 'Demos': Zur Anwendung zweier Kategorien von Emerich Francis auf das nationale Selbstverständnis der Bundesrepublik und auf die europäische Einigung." *KZfSS* 38/4 (December): 751–59.

Lindner, Bernd. 1990. "Die politische Kultur der Straße als Medium der Veränderung." *APZ* B27/90 (29 June): 16–28.

Lipset, Seymour Martin. 1981 [1959]. *Political Man.* Expanded ed. Baltimore: Johns Hopkins University Press.

Lipset, Seymour Martin, and Richard B. Dobson. 1972. "The Intellectual as Critic and Rebel: With Special Reference to the United States and the Soviet Union." *Daedalus* 101/3 (Summer): 137–98.

Loest, Erich. 1991. *Die Stasi war mein Eckermann, oder: mein Leben mit der Wanze.* Göttingen: Steidl.

Lötsch, Ingrid, and Manfred Lötsch. 1985. "Soziale Strukturen und Triebkräfte: Versuch einer Zwischenbilanz und Weiterführung der Diskussion." In *Jahrbuch für Soziologie und Sozialpolitik 1985.* Berlin.

Lötsch, Manfred. 1980. "Zur Entwicklung der Intelligenz in der Deutschen Demokratischen Republik." In Autorenkollektiv, *Die Intelligenz in der sozialistischen Gesellschaft.* Berlin: Dietz.

———. 1985. "Arbeiterklasse und Intelligenz in der Dialektik von wissenschaftlich-technischem, ökonomischem und sozialem Fortschritt." *Deutsche Zeitschrift für Philosophie* 33/1 (January): 31–41.

———. 1988. "Sozialstruktur der DDR: Kontinuität und Wandel." In *Sozialstruktur und sozialer Wandel in der DDR,* edited by Heiner Timmermann. Saarbrücken: Rita Dadder.

———. 1989. "Abschied von der Legitimationswissenschaft." In Knabe 1989.

Lötsch, Manfred, and Joachim Freitag. 1981. "Sozialstruktur und soziale Mobilität." In *Jahrbuch für Soziologie und Sozialpolitik 1981.* Berlin.

Lötsch, Manfred, and Michael Thomas. 1987. "Soziologische Kontroversen um die Intelligenz heute." *Deutsche Zeitschrift für Philosophie* 35/8 (August): 692–702.

Lowenthal, Richard. 1970. "Development vs. Utopia in Communist Policy." In *Change in Communist Systems,* edited by Chalmers Johnson. Stanford, Calif.: Stanford University Press.

Lübbe, Peter, ed. 1984. *Dokumente zur Kunst-, Literatur- und Kulturpolitik der SED, 1975–1980.* Stuttgart: Seewald.

Ludz, Peter Christian. 1972. *The Changing Party Elite in East Germany.* Cambridge, Mass.: MIT Press.

———. 1973. "Experts and Critical Intellectuals in East Germany." In *Upheaval and Continuity: A Century of German History,* edited by E. J. Feuchtwanger. London: Oswald Wolff.

Maier, Charles. 1988. *The Unmasterable Past: History, Holocaust, and German National Identity.* Cambridge, Mass.: Harvard University Press.

Mann, Thomas. 1977. *Essays.* Vol. 2. Edited by Hermann Kurzke. Frankfurt: Fischer.

Mannheim, Karl. 1936 [1929]. *Ideology and Utopia.* Translated by Louis Wirth and Edward Shils. New York: Harcourt, Brace and World.

———. 1952. "The Problem of Generations." In Mannheim, *Essays on the Sociology of Knowledge.* Edited by Paul Kecskemeti. New York: Oxford University Press.

———. 1956. "The Problem of the Intelligentsia: An Enquiry into Its Past and Present Role." In Mannheim, *Essays on the Sociology of Culture.* Edited by Paul Kecskemeti. London: Routledge and Kegan Paul.

Marcuse, Peter. 1991a. *Missing Marx: A Personal and Political Journal of a Year in East Germany, 1989–1990.* New York: Monthly Review Press.

————. 1991b. " 'Wrapping Up' East Germany." *The Nation,* 30 December.

Marz, Lutz. 1991. "Der prämoderne Übergangsmanager: Die Ohnmacht des 'real sozialistischen' Wirtschaftskaders." In Deppe, Dubiel, and Röchl 1991.

Mayer, Hans. 1977. "Ein Tauwetter, das keines war: Rückblick auf die DDR im Jahre 1956." In Crusius and Wilke 1977.

Mayer, Karl Ulrich. 1991. "Soziale Ungleichheit und Lebensverläufe: Notizen zur Inkorporation der DDR in die Bundesrepublik und ihre Folgen." In Giesen and Leggewie 1991.

McAdams, A. James. 1991. "The German Question Revisited." In Breslauer 1991.

McCauley, Martin, ed. 1977. *Communist Power in Europe, 1944–1949.* New York: Barnes and Noble Books.

Meckel, Markus, and Martin Gutzeit, eds. 1992. *Texte aus 10 Jahren politischer Arbeit in der DDR.* MS, Berlin.

Meier, Artur. 1974. *Soziologie des Bildungswesens: Eine Einführung.* Berlin.

————. 1990. "Abschied von der sozialistischen Ständegesellschaft." *APZ* B16–17/90 (13 April): 3–14.

Meier, Artur, and Achim Reimann. 1977. "Überblick über Ergebnisse bildungssoziologischer Forschung in der DDR." *Informationen zur soziologischen Forschung in der Deutschen Demokratischen Republik* 13/3:1–57.

Menge, Marlies. 1990. *"Ohne uns läuft nichts mehr": Die Revolution in der DDR.* Stuttgart: Deutsche Verlags-Anstalt.

Merson, Allan. 1985. *Communist Resistance in Nazi Germany.* London: Laurence and Wishart.

Meuschel, Sigrid. 1990a. "Revolution in der DDR." In *Die DDR auf dem Weg zur deutschen Einheit: Probleme, Perspektiven, Fragen. Dreiundzwanzigste Tagung zum Stand der DDR-Forschung in der Bundesrepublik Deutschland 5. bis 8. Juni 1990,* edited by Ilse Spittmann and Gisela Helwig. Cologne: Edition Deutschland Archiv.

————. 1990b. "Revolution in the German Democratic Republic." (Translation of 1990a.) *Critical Sociology* 17/3 (Fall): 17–34.

————. 1991. "Wandel durch Auflehnung: Thesen zum Verfall bürokratischer Herrschaft in der DDR." *Berliner Journal für Soziologie* 1 (special issue): 15–27.

————. 1992. *Legitimation und Parteiherrschaft: Zum Paradox von Stabilität und Revolution in der DDR 1945–1989.* Frankfurt: Suhrkamp.

Meyer, Gerd. 1985. "Zur Soziologie der DDR-Machtelite: Qualifikationsstruktur, Karrierewege und 'politische Generationen.'" *DA* 18/5 (May): 506–28.

————. 1991. *Die DDR-Machtelite in der Ära Honecker.* Tübingen: Francke.

Der Ministerrat der Deutschen Demokratischen Republik. 1990. Rheinbreitenbach: Neue Darmstädter Verlagsanstalt.

Minnerup, Günter. 1989. "Politische Opposition in der DDR vor dem Hintergrund der Reformdiskussion in Osteuropa." In *Die DDR im vierzigsten Jahr: Geschichte, Situation, Perspektiven. Zweiundzwanzigste Tagung zum Stand der DDR-Forschung in der Bundesrepublik Deutschland, 16.-19. Mai 1989,* edited by Ilse Spittmann and Gisela Helwig. Cologne: Edition Deutschland Archiv.

Mitteldeutscher Verlag Transparent, ed. 1990. *Wir sind das Volk: Aufbruch '89.* Pt. 1: Die Bewegung — September/October 1989. Leipzig: Mitteldeutscher Verlag.

Mitter, Armin. 1991. "Die Ereignisse im Juni und Juli 1953 in der DDR: Aus den Akten des Ministeriums für Staatssicherheit." *APZ* B5/91 (25 January): 31–41.

Mitter, Armin, and Stefan Wolle, eds. 1990. *"Ich liebe euch doch alle!": Befehle und Lageberichte des MfS, Januar-November 1989.* Berlin: BasisDruck.

Mohr, Heinrich. 1988. "Der 17. Juni als Thema der Literatur in der DDR." In Spittmann and Fricke 1988.

Mommsen, Wolfgang J. 1992. "Die Geschichtswissenschaft in der DDR: Kritische Reflexionen." *APZ* B17–18 (17 April): 35–43.

Mosse, George. 1990. *Fallen Soldiers.* New York: Oxford University Press.

Mühler, Kurt, and Steffen H. Wilsdorf. 1991. "Die Leipziger Montagsdemonstration — Aufstieg und Wandel einer basisdemokratischen Institution des friedlichen Umbruchs im Spiegel empirischer Meinungsforschung." *Berliner Journal für Soziologie* 1 (special issue): 37–45.

Müller, Emil-Peter. 1988. "Der Bundestag ist gebildeter geworden: Zur Entwicklung des Bildungsstandes der Bundestagsabgeordneten seit 1949." *ZParl* 19/2 (June): 200–219.

Müller, Marianne, and Egon Erwin Müller. 1953. *". . . stürmt die Festung Wissenschaft!" Die Sowjetisierung der mitteldeutschen Universität seit 1945.* Berlin: Colloquium.

Müller-Enbergs, Helmut. 1991. "Welchen Charakter hatte die Volkskammer nach den Wahlen am 18. März 1990?" *ZParl* 22/3 (September): 450–67.

Müller-Enbergs, Helmut, Marianne Schulz, and Jan Wielgohs, eds. 1991. *Von der Illegalität ins Parlament: Werdegang und Konzept der neuen Bürgerbewegungen.* Berlin: LinksDruck.

Naumann, Michael, ed. 1990. *"Die Geschichte ist offen": DDR 1990 — Hoffnung auf eine andere Republik: Schriftsteller aus der DDR über die Zukunftschancen ihres Landes.* Reinbek: Rowohlt.

Nee, Victor, and David Stark, eds. 1989. *Remaking the Economic Institutions of Socialism.* Stanford, Calif.: Stanford University Press.

Neubert, Erhart. 1989. "Motive des Aufbruchs." In Knabe 1989.

———. 1990. *Eine protestantische Revolution.* n.p.: Edition KONTEXT.

———. 1991a. "Protestantische Kultur und DDR-Revolution." *APZ* B19/91 (3 May): 21–29.

———. 1991b. "Revolutionen sind der Griff nach der Notbremse." *Berliner Journal für Soziologie* 1 (special issue): 29–36.

Neues Forum Leipzig. 1989. *Jetzt oder nie — Demokratie!* Leipzig: Forum Verlag.

Niclauß, Karlheinz. 1992. "Der Parlamentarische Rat und die plebiszitären Elemente." *APZ* B45/92 (30 October 1992): 3–14.

Niemann, Heinz. 1991. "Leserforum: Der sogenannte 'Bund Demokratischer Kommunisten Deutschlands' in der Opposition und Dissidenz der DDR: Zu einem Artikel von Christoph Kleßmann in 'Aus Politik und Zeitgeschichte.' " *DA* 24/5 (May): 533–38.

Niethammer, Lutz. 1990a. "Das Volk der DDR und die Revolution: Versuch einer historischen Wahrnehmung der laufenden Ereignisse." In Schüddekopf 1990.

———. 1990b. "Volkspartei neuen Typs? Sozialbiografische Voraussetzungen der SED in der Industrieprovinz." *Prokla* 20/3 (September): 40–70.

Niethammer, Lutz, Dorothee Wierling, and Alexander von Plato. 1991. *Die volkseigene Erfahrung: Eine Archäologie des Lebens in der Industrieprovinz der DDR.* Berlin: Rowohlt.

Offe, Claus. 1990. "On the Tactical Use Value of National Sentiments." *Critical Sociology* 17/3 (Fall): 9–15.

Opp, Karl-Dieter. 1991. "DDR '89: Zu den Ursachen einer spontanen Revolution." *KZfSS* 43/2 (July): 302–21.

Ost, David. 1990. "The Transformation of Solidarity and the Future of Central Europe." *Telos* 79 (Spring): 69–94.

Parkin, Frank. 1969. "Class Stratification in Socialist Societies." *British Journal of Sociology* 20/4 (December): 355–74.

———. 1971. *Class Inequality and Political Order: Social Stratification in Capitalist and Communist Societies.* London: MacGibbon and Kee.

———. 1982 [1972]. "System Contradiction and Political Transformation." In *Classes, Power, and Conflict: Classic and Contemporary Debates,* edited by Anthony Giddens and David Held. Berkeley and Los Angeles: University of California Press.

Pelikan, Jiri, and Manfred Wilke. 1977. *Menschenrechte: Ein Jahrbuch zu Osteuropa.* Reinbek: Rowohlt.

Peter, Lothar. 1990. "Legitimationsbeschaffung oder 'machtkritische Subkultur'? Marxistisch-leninistische Soziologie und Systemzerfall in der DDR." *KZfSS* 42/4 (December): 611–41.

Pike, David. 1982. *German Writers in Soviet Exile, 1933–1945.* Chapel Hill: University of North Carolina Press.

Pittman, Avril. 1992. *From Ostpolitik to Reunification: West German-Soviet Political Relations since 1974.* Cambridge: Cambridge University Press.

Plenzdorf, Ulrich. 1976 [1973]. *Die neuen Leiden des jungen W.* Frankfurt: Suhrkamp.

Pollack, Detlef. 1990a. "Außenseiter oder Repräsentanten? Zur Rolle der politisch alternativen Gruppen im gesellschaftlichen Umbruchsprozeß der DDR." *DA* 23/8 (August): 1216–23.

———. 1990b. "Das Ende einer Organisationsgesellschaft: Systemtheoretische Überlegungen zum gesellschaftlichen Umbruch in der DDR." *Zeitschrift für Soziologie* 19/4 (August): 292–307.

———. 1990c. "Sozialethisch engagierte Gruppen in der DDR: Eine religionssoziologische Untersuchung." In *Die Legitimität der Freiheit: Zur Rolle der politisch alternativen Gruppen in der DDR unter dem Dach der Kirche,* edited by Pollack. Frankfurt: Peter Lang.

———. 1990d. "Ursachen des gesellschaftlichen Umbruchs in der DDR aus systemtheoretischer Perspektive." In Wolf-Jürgen Grabner et al. 1990.

———. 1991. "Selbstverlust durch Engagement: Das Gift wirkt weiter — Später Triumph der Stasi." *Lutherische Monatshefte* 5/91 (May): 213–15.

Poppe, Ulrike. 1990a [1988]. "Das kritische Potential der Gruppen in Kirche und Gesellschaft." In *Die Legitimität der Freiheit: Zur Rolle der politisch alternativen Gruppen in der DDR unter dem Dach der Kirche,* edited by Detlef Pollack. Frankfurt: Peter Lang.

———. 1990b. "Warum haben wir die Macht nicht aufgehoben...: Rede von Ulrike Poppe zur Verleihung des Martini-Preises '90." *Bündnis 2000: Forum für Demokratie, Ökologie und Menschenrechte* 1/1 (14 December): 3.

Prahl, Hans-Werner. 1970. "Intelligenz- und Elitegruppen in der DDR-Gesellschaft." *DA* 3/2 (February): 128–34.

Pravda, Alex. 1982. "Poland 1980: From 'Premature Consumerism' to Labour Solidarity." *Soviet Studies* 34/2 (April): 167–99.

Preuß, Ulrich K. 1990. "Auf der Suche nach der Zivilgesellschaft." *Frankfurter Allgemeine Zeitung,* 28 April. (Excerpted in Gransow and Jarausch 1991.)

Probst, Lothar. 1991a. "Bürgerbewegungen, politische Kultur und Zivilgesellschaft." *APZ* B19/91 (3 May): 30–35.

———. 1991b. "Bürgerbewegungen und politische Kultur: Zwischenbilanz einer Regionalstudie über das Neue Forum Rostock." Materialien und Ergebnisse aus

Forschungsprojekten des Instituts für kulturwissenschaftliche Deutschlandstudien an der Universität Bremen, no. 1.

Prokop, Siegfried. 1984. "Zur politischen und sozialen Entwicklung der Intelligenz der DDR (1955 bis 1961)." *Jahrbuch für Geschichte* 31:153–86.

———. n.d. [1990]. "Probleme der Periodisierung der Geschichte der Intelligenz der DDR." Paper delivered at the conference of the German Association of Political Science's Section on Socialist Societies entitled "Intelligenz und gesellschaftlicher Wandel" (The intelligentsia and social change), Marburg, 13–17 February.

Prosch, Bernhard, and Martin Abraham. 1991. "Die Revolution in der DDR: Eine strukturell-individualistische Erklärungsskizze." *KZfSS* 43/2 (June): 291–301.

Quint, Peter. 1991. "The Constitutional Law of German Unification." *Maryland Law Review* 50/3: 475–631.

Rakovski, Marc. 1978. *Towards an East European Marxism.* London: Allison and Busby.

Rathenow, Lutz. 1989. "Nachdenken über Deutschland." In Knabe 1989.

Redaktion des Fischer Weltalmanach, ed. 1990. *Der Fischer Weltalmanach: Sonderband DDR.* Frankfurt: Fischer.

Rehlinger, Ludwig A. 1991. *Freikauf: Die Geschäfte der DDR mit politisch Verfolgten 1963–1989.* Berlin: Ullstein.

Rein, Gerhard, ed. 1989. *Die Opposition in der DDR: Entwürfe für einen anderen Sozialismus.* Berlin: Wichern.

———. 1990. *Die protestantische Revolution, 1987–1990: Ein deutsches Lesebuch.* Berlin: Wichern.

Reyman, Karl. 1978. "Preface: The Special Case of East Germany." In Silnitsky, Silnitsky, and Reyman 1978.

Ringer, Fritz K. 1969. *The Decline of the German Mandarins: The German Academic Community, 1890–1933.* Cambridge, Mass.: Harvard University Press.

———. 1977. "Cultural Transmission in German Higher Education in the Nineteenth Century." In *Power and Ideology in Education,* edited by Jerome Karabel and A. H. Halsey. New York: Oxford University Press.

Rink, Dieter. n.d. [1991]. "Bürgerbewegungen im Übergang: Von der Einforderung der Bürgerrechte zur Vertretung (neuer) sozialer Interessen." MS, Universität Leipzig.

Rink, Dieter, and Michael Hofmann. n.d. [1991]. "Oppositionelle Gruppen und alternative Milieus in Leipzig im Prozeß der Umgestaltung in Ostdeutschland." MS, Universität Leipzig.

Ronge, Volker. 1985. *Von drüben nach hüben: DDR-Bürger im Westen.* Wuppertal: Leske and Budrich.

Roos, Peter, ed. 1977. *Exil: Die Ausbürgerung Wolf Biermanns aus der DDR. Eine Dokumentation.* Cologne: Kiepenheuer & Witsch.

Rosenthal, Rüdiger. 1988. "Hintergrund und Widerstand — Die Parallelkultur in Berlin-Ost." In Kroh 1988.

Rosner, Clemens. 1992. *Die Universitätskirche zu Leipzig: Dokumente einer Zerstörung.* Leipzig: Forum Verlag.

Roth, Dieter. 1990. "Die Wahlen zur Volkskammer in der DDR: Der Versuch einer Erklärung." *Politische Vierteljahresschrift* 31/3 (September): 369–93.

Roth, Heidi. 1991. "Der 17. Juni 1953 im damaligen Bezirk Leipzig: Aus den Akten des PDS-Archivs Leipzig." *DA* 24/6 (June): 573–84.

Rothschild, Joseph. 1989. *Return to Diversity: A Political History of East Central Europe since World War II.* New York: Oxford University Press.

Rüddenklau, Wolfgang. 1992. *Störenfried: DDR-Opposition 1986–1989. Mit Texten aus den "Umweltblättern."* Berlin: BasisDruck.

Rühle, Jürgen. 1960. *Literatur und Revolution: Die Schriftsteller und der Kommunismus.* Cologne and Berlin: Kiepenheuer & Witsch.

——. 1988. "Der 17. Juni und die Intellektuellen." In Spittmann and Fricke 1988.

Rüß, Gisela. 1976. *Dokumente zur Kunst-, Literatur- und Kulturpolitik der SED, 1971–1974.* Stuttgart: Seewald.

Sander, Hans-Dietrich. 1972. *Geschichte der schönen Literatur in der DDR: Ein Grundriß.* Freiburg: Rombach.

Schiller, Friedrich. 1965 [1801]. *On the Aesthetic Education of Man.* Translated with introduction by Reginald Snell. New York: Frederick Ungar.

Schirdewan, Karl. 1990. "Fraktionsmacherei oder gegen Ulbrichts Diktat? Eine Stellungnahme vom 1. Januar 1958." *Beiträge zur Geschichte der Arbeiterbewegung* 32/4: 498–512.

Schmidt, Ines. n.d. [1990]. "Zur Übersiedlung aus Berlin, Hauptstadt der DDR: Strukturen, Motive, Konsequenzen." In Siegfried Grundmann and Ines Schmidt, *Wanderungsbewegungen in der DDR 1989.* Berliner Arbeitshefte und Berichte zur Sozialwissenschaftlichen Forschung, 30. Zentralinstitut für sozialwissenschaftliche Forschung, Freie Universität Berlin.

Schneider, Michael. 1990. *Die abgetriebene Revolution: Von der Staatsfirma in die DM-Kolonie.* Berlin: Elefanten Press.

Schneider, Rolf. 1989. "Die Einheit wird kommen." *Der Spiegel,* 27 November.

Schoefer, Christine. 1990. "The Attack on Christa Wolf." *The Nation,* 22 October.

Schubbe, Elimar, ed. 1972. *Dokumente zur Kunst-, Literatur- und Kulturpolitik der SED.* Stuttgart: Seewald.

Schüddekopf, Charles, ed. 1990. *"Wir sind das Volk": Flugschriften, Aufrufe, und Texte einer deutschen Revolution.* Reinbek: Rowohlt.

Schumpeter, Joseph. 1942. *Capitalism, Socialism, and Democracy.* New York: Harper and Brothers.

Schützsack, Axel. 1990. *Exodus in die Einheit: Die Massenflucht aus der DDR 1989 (Deutschland-Report No. 12).* Melle: Ernst Knoth.

Silnitsky, Frantisek, Larisa Silnitsky, and Karl Reyman, eds. 1978. *Communism and Eastern Europe: A Collection of Essays.* New York: Karz.

Sodaro, Michael J. 1983. "Limits to Dissent in the GDR: Fragmentation, Cooptation, and Repression." In *Dissent in Eastern Europe,* edited by Jane Leftwich Curry. New York: Praeger.

——. 1990. *Moscow, Germany, and the West: From Khrushchev to Gorbachev.* Ithaca, N.Y.: Cornell University Press.

Spittmann, Ilse. 1988. "Der 17. Juni im Wandel der Legenden." In Spittmann and Fricke 1988.

Spittmann, Ilse, and Karl-Wilhelm Fricke, eds. 1988 [1982]. *17. Juni 1953: Arbeiteraufstand in der DDR.* 2nd expanded ed. Cologne: Edition Deutschland Archiv.

Spittmann, Ilse, and Gisela Helwig, eds. 1990. *Chronik der Ereignisse in der DDR.* Cologne: Edition Deutschland Archiv.

Stallmann, Herbert. 1980. *Hochschulzugang in der SBZ/DDR, 1945–1959.* Sankt Augustin: Richarz.

Staritz, Dietrich. 1976. *Sozialismus in einem halben Land.* Berlin: Klaus Wagenbach.

——. 1984. *Die Gründung der DDR: Von der sowjetischen Besatzungsherrschaft zum sozialistischen Staat.* Munich: DTV.

——. 1985. *Geschichte der DDR 1949–1985.* Frankfurt: Suhrkamp.

Stark, David, and Victor Nee. 1989. "Toward an Institutional Analysis of State Socialism." In Nee and Stark 1989.

Starke, Uta. 1990. "Studenten im politischen Umbruch der DDR." Paper delivered at the conference of the German Association of Political Science's Section on Socialist Societies entitled "Intelligenz und gesellschaftlicher Wandel" (The intelligentsia and social change), Marburg, 13–17 February.

Stern, Fritz. 1960. "The Political Consequences of the Unpolitical German." *History: A Meridian Periodical* 3 (September): 104–34.

Storbeck, Dietrich. 1963. "Flucht oder Wanderung? Eine Rückschau auf Motiven, Folgen und Beurteilung der Bevölkerungsabwanderung aus Mitteldeutschland seit dem Kriege." *Soziale Welt* 14/2: 153–71.

Streuel, Irene Charlotte. 1990. "Umschwung in der Kulturpolitik und neue Initiativen der Künstler." *DA* 23/1 (January): 85–92.

Süß, Walter. 1991a. "Bilanz einer Gratwanderung — Die kurze Amtszeit des Hans Modrow." *DA* 24/6 (June): 596–608.

———. 1991b. "Mit Unwillen zur Macht: Der Runde Tisch in der DDR der Übergangszeit." *DA* 24/5 (May): 470–78.

Szelenyi, Ivan. 1982. "The Intelligentsia in the Class Structure of State-Socialist Societies." In *Marxist Inquiries: Studies of Labor, Class, and States,* edited by Michael Burawoy and Theda Skocpol. Chicago: University of Chicago Press.

———. 1986–87. "The Prospects and Limits of the East European New Class Project: An Auto-critical Reflection on 'The Intellectuals on the Road to Class Power.'" *Politics and Society* 15/2:103–44.

———. 1989. "Eastern Europe in an Epoch of Transition: Toward a Socialist Mixed Economy?" In Nee and Stark 1989.

Szelenyi, Ivan, et al. 1988. *Socialist Entrepreneurs: Embourgeoisement in Rural Hungary.* Madison: University of Wisconsin Press.

Teckenberg, Wolfgang. 1989. "Die relative Stabilität von Berufs- und Mobilitätsstrukturen: Die UdSSR als Ständegesellschaft im Vergleich." *KZfSS* 41:298–326.

Templin, Wolfgang. 1989. "Zivile Gesellschaft — Osteuropäische Emanzipationsbewegung und unabhängiges Denken in der DDR seit Beginn der 80er Jahre." In *Die DDR im vierzigsten Jahr: Geschichte, Situation, Perspektiven. Zweiundzwanzigste Tagung zum Stand der DDR-Forschung in der Bundesrepublik Deutschland,* edited by Ilse Spittmann and Gisela Helwig. Cologne: Edition Deutschland Archiv.

Templin, Wolfgang, and Reinhard Weißhuhn. 1991. "Initiative Frieden und Menschenrechte." In Müller-Enbergs, Schulz, and Wielgohs 1991.

Thaa, Winfried. 1991. "Mehr als Adaption und Regression: Über die Auswirkungen der Herbstrevolution von 1989 auf die Entwicklung der Demokratie in Deutschland." *DA* 24/4 (August): 831–40.

Thaysen, Uwe. 1990a. "Der Runde Tisch. Oder: Wer war das Volk? Teil I." *ZParl* 21/1 (May): 71–100.

———. 1990b. "Der Runde Tisch. Oder: Wer war das Volk? Teil II." *ZParl* 21/2 (June): 257–308.

———. 1990c. *Der Runde Tisch, oder: Wo Blieb das Volk? Der Weg der DDR in die Demokratie.* Opladen: Westdeutscher Verlag.

———. 1991. "The GDR on Its Way into Democracy." Lecture delivered at St. Antony's College, Oxford, 1 February.

"Thesen zur Aufklärung der Vergangenheit." 1992. *DA* 25/4 (April): 445–47.

Tismaneanu, Vladimir. 1989. "Nascent Civil Society in the German Democratic Republic." *Problems of Communism* 38/3 (March-June): 90–111.

————. 1992. *Reinventing Politics: Eastern Europe from Stalin to Havel*. New York: Free Press.

Tocqueville, Alexis de. 1955 [1856]. *The Old Regime and the French Revolution*. Translated by Stuart Gilbert. Garden City, N.Y.: Doubleday Anchor Books.

Tökes, Rudolph L., ed. 1979. *Opposition in Eastern Europe*. London: Macmillan.

————. 1990. "Vom Post-Kommunismus zur Demokratie: Politik, Parteien, und Wahlen in Ungarn." *APZ* B45/90 (2 November): 16–33.

Torpey, John. 1988. "Introduction: Habermas and the Historians." *New German Critique* 44 (Spring/Summer): 5–24.

————. 1992. "German Intellectuals and Politics after Unification: Some Aspects of 'Working Through' the East German Past." MS.

Trotsky, Leon. 1972 [1937]. *The Revolution Betrayed: What Is the Soviet Union and Where Is It Going?* New York: Pathfinder.

Ulbricht, Walter. 1960. *Zur sozialistischen Entwicklung der Volkswirtschaft seit 1945*. Berlin.

Ulrich, Ralf. 1989. "DDR ohne Mauer? Einige Überlegungen zur Übersiedlerbewegung DDR-BRD." MS, Hochschule für Ökonomie "Bruno Leuschner," Institut Ökonomik der Entwicklungsländer, Berlin.

Verdery, Katherine. 1991. *National Ideology under Socialism: Identity and Cultural Politics in Ceausescu's Romania*. Berkeley: University of California Press.

Der Vertrag zur deutschen Einheit: Ausgewählte Texte. 1990. Frankfurt and Leipzig: Insel.

Voigt, Dieter, and Hannelore Belitz-Demiriz. 1987. "Zum Bildungsniveau der Eltern von Promovierten im deutsch-deutschen Vergleich: Eine empirische Untersuchung über den Einfluß von Herkunftsfamilie und Gesellschaftsystem auf die akademische Elitebildung in den Jahren 1950 bis 1982." In *Elite in Wissenschaft und Politik: Empirische Untersuchungen und theoretische Ansätze*, edited by Dieter Voigt. Schriftenreihe der Gesellschaft für Deutschlandforschung, 21. Berlin: Duncker & Humblot.

Voigt, Dieter, Hannelore Belitz-Demiriz, and Sabine Meck. 1990. "Die innerdeutschen Wanderungen und der Vereinigungsprozeß: Soziodemographische Struktur und Einstellungen von Flüchtlingen/Übersiedlern aus der DDR vor und nach der Grenzöffnung." *DA* 23/5 (May): 732–46.

Volkmer, Werner. 1979. "East Germany: Dissenting Views during the Last Decade." In Tökes 1979.

Vollnhals, Clemens, ed. 1991. *Entnazifizierung: Politische Säuberung und Rehabilitierung in den vier Besatzungszonen, 1945–1949*. Munich: DTV.

Walser Smith, Helmut. 1991. "Socialism and Nationalism in the East German Revolution, 1989–90." *East European Politics and Society* 5/2 (Spring): 234–46.

Walter, Franz. 1991. "Sachsen — ein Stammland der Sozialdemokratie?" *Politische Vierteljahresschrift* 32/2 (June): 207–31.

Walther, Joachim, et al., eds. 1991. *Protokoll eines Tribunals: Die Ausschlüsse aus dem DDR-Schriftstellerverband 1979*. Reinbek: Rowohlt.

Walzer, Michael. 1965. *The Revolution of the Saints: A Study in the Origins of Radical Politics*. Cambridge, Mass.: Harvard University Press.

————. 1980. "Intellectuals to Power?" In Walzer, *Radical Principles: Reflections of an Unreconstructed Democrat*. New York: Basic Books.

Weber, Hermann. 1978. "Der Dritte Weg: Bahro in der Traditionslinie der antistalinistischen Opposition." In *Antworten auf Bahros Herausforderung des "realen Sozialismus*," edited by Ulf Wolter. Berlin: Olle & Wolter.

————. 1985. *Geschichte der DDR*. Munich: DTV.

————. 1990. " 'Weiße Flecken' in der DDR-Geschichtsschreibung." *APZ* B11/90 (9 March): 3–15.

————, ed. 1963. *Der deutsche Kommunismus: Dokumente.* Cologne and Berlin: Kiepenheuer & Witsch.

————. 1986. *DDR: Dokumente zur Geschichte der Deutschen Demokratischen Republik 1945–1985.* Munich: DTV.

Weber, Max. 1978. *Economy and Society.* Edited by Günther Roth and Claus Wittich. 2 vols. Berkeley: University of California Press.

Weidenfeld, Werner. 1981. *Die Frage nach der Einheit der deutschen Nation.* Munich and Vienna: Olzog.

Weidenfeld, Werner, and Hartmut Zimmermann, eds. 1989. *Deutschland-Handbuch: Eine doppelte Bilanz, 1949–1989.* Munich and Vienna: Carl Hanser.

Weilemann, Peter R., et al. 1990. *Parteien im Aufbruch: Nichtkommunistische Parteien und politische Vereinigungen in der DDR vor der Volkskammerwahl am 18. März 1990 (Deutschland-Report No. 8).* Melle: Ernst Knoth.

Wendt, Hartmut. 1991. "Die deutsch-deutschen Wanderungen — Bilanz einer 40-jährigen Geschichte von Flucht und Ausreise." *DA* 24/4 (April): 386–95.

Wensierski, Peter, and Wolfgang Büscher, eds. 1981. *Beton ist Beton: Zivilisationskritik aus der DDR.* Hattingen: Edition Transit.

Wenzke, Rüdiger. 1990a. *Prager Frühling, Prager Herbst: Zur Intervention der Warschauer-Pakt-Streitkräfte in der CSSR 1968.* Berlin.

————. 1990b. "Zur Beteiligung der NVA an der militärischen Operation von Warschauer-Pakt-Streitkräften gegen die CSSR 1968: Einige Ergänzungen zu einem Beitrag von Walter Rehm." *DA* 24/11 (November): 1179–86.

Wettig, Gerhard. 1982. "Die sowjetische Deutschland-Note vom 10. März 1952: Wiedervereinigungsangebot oder Propagandaaktion?" *DA* 15/2 (February): 130–48.

————. 1988. "Die sowjetische Deutschland-Politik am Vorabend des 17. Juni." In Spittmann and Fricke 1988.

Wielgohs, Jan, and Marianne Schulz. 1990. "Reformbewegung und Volksbewegung: Politische und soziale Aspekte im Umbruch der DDR-Gesellschaft." *APZ* B16–17/90 (13 April): 15–24.

Wienke, Peter. 1989. *Die promovierte naturwissenschaftlich-technische Intelligenz in der DDR: Eine empirische Untersuchung ihrer Karrieremuster mit denen von promovierten Naturwissenschaftlern und Ingenieuren aus der Bundesrepublik Deutschland.* Bochum: Studienverlag Dr. N. Brockmeyer.

Willett, John, and Ralph Manheim, eds. 1976. *Bertolt Brecht Poems 1913–1956.* London: Eyre Methuen.

Winters, Peter Jochen. 1980. "Zur Reaktion der DDR auf die Ereignisse in Polen." *DA* 13/10 (October): 1013–18.

————. 1981a. "Angst vor dem polnischen Bazillus." *DA* 14/10 (October): 1009–12.

————. 1981b. "Polnische Parteiführung im Schußfeld: Zur Reaktion der DDR auf die Ereignisse in Polen (III)." *DA* 14/7 (July): 686–89.

————. 1981c. "Zur Reaktion der DDR auf die Ereignisse in Polen (II)." *DA* 14/1 (January): 4–8.

————. 1983. "Honeckers Polen-Reise." *DA* 16/10 (October): 1012–17.

Wolf, Christa. 1990a. *Reden im Herbst.* Berlin and Weimar: Aufbau.

————. 1990b. *Was bleibt.* Frankfurt: Luchterhand.

Wolf, Friedrich. 1989. "Ist die DDR ein Rechtsstaat?" In Knabe 1989.

Wolle, Stefan. 1991. "Das MfS und die Arbeiterproteste im Herbst 1956 in der DDR." *APZ* B5/91 (25 January): 42–51.

Wollweber, Ernst. 1990. "Aus Erinnerungen: Ein Porträt Walter Ulbrichts." *Beiträge zur Geschichte der Arbeiterbewegung* 32/3: 350–78.

Wolter, Ulf, ed., *Antworten auf Bahros Herausforderung des "realen Sozialismus."* Berlin: Olle & Wolter.

Woods, Roger. 1984. "East German Intellectuals in Opposition." *Survey* 28/3 (Autumn): 111–23.

———. 1986. *Opposition in the GDR under Honecker, 1971–1985.* London: Macmillan.

———. 1987–88. "Opposition or Alternative Political Culture in the GDR?" *East Central Europe* 14–15:151–78.

Zöger, Heinz. 1960. "Die politischen Hintergründe der Harich-Prozesse." *SBZ-Archiv* 12:198–200.

Zweite Berliner Begegnung: Den Frieden erklären. 1983. Darmstadt and Neuwied: Luchterhand.

Zwerenz, Gerhard. 1958. "Junge Intelligenz unter Ulbricht." *Die neue Gesellschaft* (July-August): 311–14.

Index

John Torpey is currently a Jean Monnet Fellow at the European University Institute in Florence, Italy. He received a Ph.D. in sociology at the University of California, Berkeley, and then spent a year as a postdoctoral fellow at the Center for European Studies, Harvard University. He has taught at Mount Holyoke and Smith Colleges and worked for a time as program officer at the United States Institute of Peace in Washington, D.C. He has published widely on European politics and society in journals such as *Theory and Society, Dissent, German Politics, German Politics and Society,* and *New German Critique.* He is currently working on a study of the history of the passport.

DATE DUE

MAY 20 1996	
MAR 0 2 1997	
APR 0 8 1997	APR 0 9 1999
MAY 1 7 1997	JUL 0 2 1999
APR 0 8 1997	
	JUN 0 7 2000
OCT 2 3 1998	
DEC 0 4 1998	
1999	

Printed
in USA